MW00636009

Who's the Bigot?

Who's the Bigot?

Learning from Conflicts over Marriage and Civil Rights Law

LINDA C. McCLAIN

OXFORD
UNIVERSITY PRESS

OXFORD
UNIVERSITY PRESS

Oxford University Press is a department of the University of Oxford. It furthers
the University's objective of excellence in research, scholarship, and education
by publishing worldwide. Oxford is a registered trade mark of Oxford University
Press in the UK and certain other countries.

Published in the United States of America by Oxford University Press
198 Madison Avenue, New York, NY 10016, United States of America.

Library of Congress Cataloging-in-Publication Data
Names: McClain, Linda C., author
Title: Who's the bigot? : learning from conflicts over marriage and civil rights law /
Linda C. McClain.
Description: New York : Oxford University Press, 2020. | Includes index. |
Identifiers: LCCN 2019037421 (print) | LCCN 2019037422 (ebook) |
ISBN 9780190877200 (hardback) | ISBN 9780190877217 (updf) |
ISBN 9780190877224 (epub) | ISBN 9780190063726 (Online)
Subjects: LCSH: Discrimination—Law and legislation—United States. |
Equality before the law—United States. | Civil rights—United States. |
Interfaith marriage—Law and legislation—United States. |
Interracial marriage—Law and legislation—United States. |
Same-sex marriage—Law and legislation—United States. |
Sexual minorities—Civil rights—United States. | Racism—United States. |
Toleration—United States.
Classification: LCC KF4755 .S76 2020 (print) | LCC KF4755 (ebook) |
DDC 342.7308/7—dc23
LC record available at https://lccn.loc.gov/2019037421
LC ebook record available at https://lccn.loc.gov/2019037422

1 3 5 7 9 8 6 4 2

Printed by Integrated Books International, United States of America

For my mother, Marilyn McClain-West, who has modeled a life of respecting and valuing diversity and rejecting bigotry

CONTENTS

ACKNOWLEDGMENTS

In writing this book, I have benefited from the advice and thoughts of family and many friends and colleagues as well as from institutional support. Boston University School of Law provided generous research leave during a sabbatical as well as summer research funding. I thank former Dean Maureen O'Rourke and Dean Angela Onwuachi-Willig. I also am grateful for the support of the Paul M. Siskind Research Scholar fund and the Robert Kent Professorship Fund. At BU Law, organizing a conference on the 50th anniversary of the Civil Rights Act of 1964 helped me to dive into some of the history presented in this book. My colleagues at BU Law also provided many constructive comments when I presented draft chapters in faculty workshops.

A sabbatical year, in 2016–2017, spent at Princeton University's wonderful University Center for Human Values as a Laurance S. Rockefeller Visiting Faculty Fellow, provided a crucial opportunity for the ideas in this book to grow and develop. I am grateful to UCHV for financial and institutional support and to director Melissa Lane and her capable staff. While there, I benefited from the camaraderie of other fellows and graduate fellows, as well as from their constructive comments on a chapter of this book that I presented in the weekly Laurance S. Rockefeller Seminar. My assigned commentator, Joshua Cherniss, generously provided a careful and incisive evaluation of the chapter. While at Princeton I also benefited from discussing the book in the Crossroads in Religion and Politics Series, sponsored by the Center for the Study of Religion and Woodrow Wilson School of Public and International Affairs; the Human Values Forum; the Law and Public Affairs Works-in-Progress Workshop Series; Professor Stephen Macedo's Religion and Politics Seminar and his Ethics and Public Policy class; and a debate with Ryan Anderson, sponsored by the *Princeton Tory*. Conversations with Dean Sarah-Jane Leslie and Professors Susan Fiske, Liz Harman, Dirk Hartog, Desmond Jagmohan, Alan Patten, and Robert Wuthnow helped point me in fruitful directions. In addition, the regular encouragement, companionship, and constructive help provided by my writing support group, Kathy Abrams, Susan Brison, and Karen Jones, were crucial. Thanks also to former UCHV Fellow Amy Sepinwall for inviting me back to Princeton in May 2018 to share a chapter in the conference "Law, Religion, and Complicity," cosponsored by UCHV and the Program in Law and Public Affairs.

As this book took shape, many colleagues at different schools and at conferences and workshops offered thoughtful feedback. In October 2018, Professor Imer Flores, at the Instituto de Investigaciones Juridicas at Universidad Nacional Autónoma de México, generously hosted a conference on my book manuscript. At that event, Imer, John Corvino, Jim Fleming, Steve Macedo, Itzel Mayans, Melissa Murray, and Douglas NeJaime provided varied and constructive commentary. I am grateful to Professor Justin Dyer, Director of the Kinder Institute on Constitutional Democracy, University of Missouri, for including a symposium on my book manuscript as part of the 5th Annual Shawnee Trail Conference in March 2019. Panelists Sonu Bedi, Catherine Rymph, and Mark Storslee offered insightful remarks about the manuscript. Thanks also to Justin for the opportunity to present a draft chapter in an academic workshop sponsored by the Kinder Institute and, with Jim Fleming, to codeliver the 2015 Constitution Day Lecture. Thanks very much to Joseph Bacchi, Brad Baranowski, Chris Hamilton, Julia Harper, and Hanna Helwig, former and current editors of the *Boston University Law Review*, for publishing several of the commentaries from the UNAM and Kinder Institute book symposia and providing me a chance to respond to them.

At an early stage of this project, I was fortunate to give a lecture at the University of Richmond School of Law and to receive helpful faculty feedback, particularly from Corrina Lain, Henry L. Chambers Jr. and Meredith Harbach. I also benefited from sharing a draft chapter in the workshop series at Temple University's Beasley School of Law, and at Cardozo Law School, as part of the New York Family Law Scholars workshop series. The book benefited from feedback received at presentations made at the 2014, 2017, and 2018 annual meetings of the American Political Science Association and at the 2016 and 2018 North American Regional Conference of the International Society of Family Law.

Thanks to Rick Garnett, Paul Horowitz, and Nelson Tebbe for the chance to present various draft chapters in the Annual Law and Religion Roundtable, during meetings hosted at Washington University School of Law, Notre Dame Law School, and University of Pennsylvania School of Law. Thanks to Suzanne Kim for the chance to give a lecture on a draft chapter at the Center for Gender, Sexuality, Law & Policy at Rutgers University. Mark Graber's schmoozes at University of Maryland Francis King Carey School of Law on "Constitutional Democracy in Crisis" and on "Democracy and Constitutionalism" were a welcoming place to share draft chapters. At Dartmouth College, I benefited from comments by students in Sonu Bedi's Supreme Court Workshop and by

faculty and students in a lunch talk. I am also grateful to participants in conferences sponsored by Fordham Law School ("Fifty Years of *Loving v. Virginia* and
the Continued Pursuit of Racial Equality"), and Duke Law School ("Present
and Future of Civil Rights Movements: Race and Reform in 21st Century
America"). Thanks to Martha Albertson Fineman for the chance to present
work in a Vulnerability and the Human Condition Initiative workshop at Emory
University. Sharing a draft chapter, at George Thomas's invitation, at Claremont
McKenna's conference "The Future of Religious Liberty and Liberal Tolerance"
also helped this book.

Over the years, many friends and colleagues have provided moral support
and insightful comments as this book took shape. Some also commented on the
proposal as well as on drafts. In particular, I am grateful to Aziza Ahmed, Carlos
Ball, Sot Barber, Sonu Bedi, David Bernhardt, Carli Conklin, Rebecca Davis, Bob
Davoli, Justin Dyer, Bill Eskridge, Gillian Frank, Rick Garnett, M. Christian Green,
Clare Huntington, Jonathan Kahn, Daniel Kanstroom, Robin Bradley Kar, Ken
Kersch, Suzanne Kim, my former editor Elizabeth Knoll, Roberta Kwall, Steve
Macedo, Eileen McDonagh, Douglas NeJaime, Julie Novkov, Martin Oversby,
Jeffrey Pasley, Rachel Rebouché, Josh Rabinowitz, Emily Stoltzenberg, George
Thomas, the late Sydney Verba, Robin Fretwell Wilson, and Emily Zackin. At
BU, many colleagues provided instructive comments in faculty workshops over
the years, in particular Jack Beermann, Khiara M. Bridges, Julie Dahlstrom, Gary
Lawson, Karen Pita Loor, Nancy Moore, David Rossman, David Seipp, and Kate
Silbaugh. Conversations with David Lyons were especially informative.

This book would not have been possible without the enormous support of the
Pappas Law Library and its outstanding librarians. In particular, I want to single
out for special thanks my library liaison, Stefanie Weigmann, Associate Director
for Research, Faculty Services and Educational Technology, who provided crucial research help from this book's earliest stages to its publication. In addition,
several former and present BU Law students provided valuable research assistance. Gillian Stoddard Leatherberry patiently and capably slogged through a
mountain of historical materials referring to bigotry. As the chapters took shape,
Julie Aversa, Omeed Firoozgan, Katherine (Nina) Jones, Josephine Kovacs,
Melissa Kraus, Jessica Lees, and Stella Swartz provided capable research and editorial assistance. In the final stages, Caitlin Cooper, a graduate student in the
BU School of Education, commented on the entire manuscript. BU Law student
Brittany Hacker did triple duty, providing valuable research help, reading and
carefully commenting on the manuscript, and assisting with the index. Thanks
also to Bridget Donovan, Ben Morgan, and Tyler Gabrielski, Senior Program
Coordinators at BU Law, for assistance with manuscript preparation.

Thanks to my editor Dave McBride and to Emily Mackenzie, assistant editor,
at Oxford University Press, and to two anonymous reviewers, whose comments

have improved the book manuscript. I am grateful to Kelsey Hauck for giving permission to use the untitled artwork by the late Douglas Pedersen for the book's cover; thanks to Sot Barber for the gift of that artwork years ago.

Finally, thanks to my home team. My daughter Sarah McClain Fleming served as my accountability mentor, offering encouragement and inspirational artwork and Post-it messages along the way to "get the book finished!" My daughter Katherine Amelia McClain Fleming provided astute editing of several chapters. My biggest debt is to Jim Fleming, spouse, colleague, and sometime coauthor. In addition to being a wonderful and generous companion and life partner, he helped me immeasurably on this book both by having countless conversations with me about the rhetoric, and problem, of bigotry and by generously and con-structively editing and commenting on the book manuscript multiple times. As if that weren't enough, he also helped to prepare the index. I am grateful for conversations about the book's topics with my father, Robert C. McClain, and with my mother, Marilyn McClain-West, to whom this book is dedicated.

Portions of the following three law review articles appear in revised form: Linda C. McClain, "From *Romer v. Evans* to *United States v. Windsor*: Law as a Vehicle for Moral Disapproval in Amendment 2 and the Defense of Marriage Act," 20 *Duke Journal of Gender Law & Policy* 351 (2013) (in chapter 7); McClain, "The Civil Rights Act of 1964 and 'Legislating Morality': On Conscience, Prejudice, and Whether 'Stateways' Can Change 'Folkways,'" 95 *Boston University Law Review* 89 (2015) (in chapter 5); and McClain, "Prejudice, Constitutional Moral Progress, and Being 'On the Right Side of History': Reflections on *Loving v. Virginia* at Fifty," 86 *Fordham Law Review* 2701 (2018).

Who's the Bigot?

Puzzles about Bigotry

In September 1966, "Dear Abby" published an advice column titled "Bigots—They're More to Be Pitied Than Censured."[1] "Hurt" sought advice about the decision to remain silent rather than confront another guest who, in "casual conversation" at a cocktail party "in the home of some very prominent and respected gentile people," "made some very degrading remarks about 'the Jews.'" Hurt, who had a Jewish mother and non-Jewish father and "married a gentile," asked "if perhaps I should have said something. And if so, what?" Abby advised: "You cannot hope to educate a bigot with one short lecture at a cocktail party." Thus, "the best response is sincere (and silent) pity rather than uttered (and futile) censure." She added: "Bigotry and bad manners are boorish, whether perpetrated on one who is half-Jewish or 99.44% Chippewa."[2] (It was not the only time that Abby, who was Jewish, would condemn such bigotry in her column.[3])

More than fifty years later, the "Social Q's" advice columnist Philip Galanes published a letter from "Susan," who wanted to "step in" and "shut . . . down" another customer in a deli who "was screaming" that "a transgender woman, with a little girl" was "a piece of trash" and threatening to "beat her." Susan didn't dare, and the woman and child "left quickly" after paying. She asks Galanes: "Advice for next time?"[4] In a column titled "Bigotry, Defused," Galanes counseled: "Tangling with angry bigots is never your go-to move." The "better option is to support the woman": "Walk right up to her, as if a lunatic were not screaming at her, and help . . . get her out of that deli as quickly as possible." He explained: "In my experience of irrational hatred, engaging madmen and madwomen only gives them more room to seethe. Better to neutralize the ugliness by placing it alongside normal behavior." He concluded: "The only known antidote to hatred is love."[5]

In each incident, the advice columnist readily used the label "bigot" to characterize the person uttering hurtful or hateful remarks. Both advised that it was pointless to try to persuade or tangle with a bigot, but for different reasons. Dear

Who's the Bigot? Linda C. McClain, Oxford University Press (2020). © Oxford University Press.
DOI: 10.1093/oso/9780190877200.001.0001

Abby's advice that pity, rather than censure, is the best response suggests that the bigot cannot be educated. Then again, she links bigotry to bad manners and being a boor—conditions that one might (with effort) change. By comparison, in linking bigotry to irrational hatred and lunacy, and advising against engaging a madman, Galanes seems to rule out any possibility of education. Further, his concluding advice—that the only known antidote to hatred is love—is about how a bystander might aid the targets of such hatred, not how someone might cure the person who hates.

Calling out bigotry and arguing over whether a public figure is a bigot are visible and contentious features of daily public life. Bigotry is a fraught and contested term. The rhetoric of bigotry—how people use such words as "bigot," "bigoted," and "bigotry"—poses puzzles that urgently demand attention. Identifying, responding to, and preventing bigotry have engaged the efforts not only of advice columnists, but also of civil rights activists, clergy and religious groups, community groups, social scientists, politicians, lawyers, judges, and ordinary citizens. While Dear Abby and the Social Q's columnist readily used the label "bigot," assuming a shared understanding with their readers, people often disagree over *who* is a bigot and *what*, exactly, makes a belief, attitude, or action bigoted. People seem to share a conviction that bigotry is morally wrong, but they disagree about when the label applies. At times, it seems that people apply the term to describe any views or actions that they find "not only wrong but badly wrong."[6] When is the label "bigotry" necessary to express moral censure? When is it needlessly provocative, shutting down debate?[7] To put the question vividly, are you "morally obligated" to call out your bigoted relatives at Thanksgiving or does putting "political civility" on the Thanksgiving menu mean listening to and treating them with respect?[8]

Claims about bigotry are simultaneously backward- and forward-looking. Defining a belief or practice as bigotry may be possible only after society has repudiated it as wrong and unjust. Once there is general agreement that such past beliefs and practices were bigoted, it becomes hard for people to understand that anyone ever seriously defended them. Racial discrimination and segregation are powerful examples.[9] As chapter 5 explains, when some members of Congress argued that all Americans had a stake in passing the Civil Rights Act of 1964 and repudiating bigotry, prejudice, and racial discrimination, opponents strongly resisted charges that segregation was bigotry and flipped the charges, calling supporters of the act "anti-bigot bigots."[10]

Charges of bigotry are also forward-looking: past examples of bigotry on which there is consensus become the basis for prospective judgments about analogous forms of bigotry. People debate: Is this belief or practice bigotry because it is like forms of discrimination that we have disavowed? The stakes are high because people worry about failing to learn from the past. Further, a charge of bigotry carries heavy moral condemnation and a suggestion of bad moral character.[11] In the debate over same-sex marriage, opponents argued that their sincere religious belief that marriage is between one man and one woman was nothing like the racial bigotry of Jim Crow-era antimiscegenationists. They argued that comparing their religious opposition to same-sex marriage with religious opposition to interracial marriage wrongly "branded" them as bigots and was itself a form of bigotry.

In politics, the stakes are also high: learning from the past entails that our political leaders and institutions should condemn and prevent—not endorse—bigotry. Despite an evident agreement that bigotry in all its forms is wrong, political battles over bigotry are often sharply polarizing because politicians disagree over which views and actions are forms of bigotry.

The Rhetoric of Bigotry in Public Discourse

Charges, denials, and countercharges of bigotry are increasingly frequent in the United States. People turn to the language of bigotry in so-called culture war issues around marriage, such as whether a county clerk must issue a marriage license to a same-sex couple if doing so violates her religious beliefs or whether a baker with similar beliefs must bake a wedding cake for such a couple. The rhetoric of bigotry is also pervasive in controversies over race and immigration: whether public officials like President Donald Trump have encouraged or endorsed white nationalism, whether keeping statues of Confederate generals in public spaces reflects bigotry, and whether calls for "building the wall" stem from bigotry.

Growing political polarization and "intense partisan animosity"[12] suggest the high stakes in conflicts over who is a bigot and why. The 2016 presidential campaign saw a dramatic spike in references to bigotry on major television news networks.[13] The Republican and Democratic Party Platforms both denounced bigotry and various forms of intolerance, but their lists of those forms differed strikingly. In addition, the Democratic Platform explicitly condemned Republican nominee Trump for creating a "climate of bigotry."[14] Trump countered Democratic nominee Hillary Rodham Clinton's frequent charges that his campaign was "peddling" bigotry by labeling her as a bigot who "sees people of color only as votes."[15]

During Trump's campaign and continuing into his presidency, bipartisan warnings sounded that "bigotry seems emboldened" and "normalized."[16] Civil rights groups asserted that Trump's statements and his administration's policies have "tapped into a seam of bigotry and hate that have resulted in the targeting of American Muslims and other minority groups."[17] Critics linked such bigotry not only to anti-Muslim prejudice, but also to racism, anti-Semitism, nativism, populism, xenophobia, homophobia, misogyny, and sexism.[18] Some conservative commentators countered that critics of Trump and his supporters are "anti-Trump bigots" and that their "political correctness" is a form of bigotry.[19] Some political scientists even link the 2016 election to the possible death of democracy in the United States and elsewhere if core norms of "mutual toleration" erode, allowing "extremist demagogues" to go unchecked.[20]

In the 2018 midterm elections, the campaigns of some newly-elected Democratic candidates explicitly criticized the Trump administration for fostering bigotry.[21] An online poll taken in the week before those elections reported that 61% of Democrats and those leaning Democratic would use the terms "racist/bigoted/sexist" to "describe Republicans today"; 54% chose "ignorant," and 44%, "spiteful." Among Republicans and those leaning Republican, only half as many (31%) chose the terms "racist/bigoted/sexist" to "describe Democrats today"; 54% chose "spiteful," and 49%, "ignorant."[22]

The midterms also intensified concern over polarization. Commentators diagnose a new "tribalism," in which the Left believes it is the bigotry and racism of "right-wing tribalism" that is "tearing the country apart," while the Right believes it is the "identity politics" and "political correctness" of "left-wing tribalism" that is doing so.[23] Indeed, one provocative claim is that today, "the most pervasive form of bigotry" is political bigotry: intolerance toward people with different political opinions.[24]

Why is there so much controversy over bigotry when renouncing—and denouncing—it seems to be a shared political value with a long history? In 1790, President George Washington assured the Hebrew Congregation of Newport, Rhode Island, that "happily, the Government of the U.S. . . . gives to bigotry no sanction, to persecution no assistance."[25] In this significant founding-era statement, bigotry had a clear meaning: official intolerance and persecution of Jews and other religious groups. But what are bigotry's other forms? Common usage suggests that overt racism and anti-Semitism are clear instances. Both have the element of a repudiated history, so that people often claim that such bigotry is "un-American" or contrary to American ideals. We learn bigotry's meaning by looking to the past, but the past also reveals a shortfall in living up to such ideals.

What history teaches about bigotry and how to draw analogies between past and present, however, is often controversial. People have invoked Washington's disavowal of bigotry in battles over same-sex marriage and the rights of transgender persons. As another example, in support of a legal challenge by Muslim Americans to the Trump administration's executive orders limiting travel from several Muslim-majority countries (the "travel ban"), a group of constitutional law scholars filed a "friend of the court" (amicus curiae) brief quoting Washington's renunciation of bigotry to argue that the ban violated the First

Amendment's Establishment Clause. The brief argued that the ban, considered in light of Trump's numerous statements about the threat posed by Muslims and Islam, showed "animus" toward a "disfavored religious group."[26] The Trump administration, however, asserted that the ban would protect Americans from admitting foreign nationals who would "engage in acts of bigotry or hatred."[27] When a closely divided (5–4) Supreme Court upheld the ban, Chief Justice Roberts, writing for the majority, quoted Washington's language as illustrating that "our Presidents have frequently used [their extraordinary power to speak to fellow citizens] to espouse the principles of religious freedom and tolerance on which this Nation was founded," even though presidents have "performed unevenly in living up" to that task. Roberts rejected Trump's numerous remarks criticizing Muslims as a basis for striking down the ban, contending that it was "facially neutral toward religion" and rested on national security rationales.[28]

Past and present controversies about marriage and the scope of civil rights laws are illuminating windows into questions raised by the rhetoric of bigotry. Tracing this rhetoric across a set of earlier debates relating to interfaith and interracial marriage and the recent debate over same-sex marriage reveals contested understandings of bigotry. Those controversies also show recurring patterns of arguments, including appealing to conscience and sincere belief to counter charges of bigotry as well as denying and flipping such charges.

Because marriage is both an intimate, private relationship and a public institution reflecting important societal values, it provides a valuable lens through which to examine both the backward- and forward-looking dimensions of bigotry. The argument that any step toward racial desegregation would lead inevitably to interracial marriage played a key role in historic civil rights battles: resisting the Supreme Court's desegregation decisions, such as *Brown v. Board of Education*; opposing landmark federal civil rights legislation, such as the Civil Rights Act of 1964; and defending laws barring interracial marriage, the last of which were struck down in *Loving v. Virginia*.[29] Defenders of segregation appealed to history and tradition, asserting that to say racial segregation and restrictions on race mixing were immoral or bigoted was to say that "our Founding Fathers" were "immoral men and blasphemers against God."[30]

The public repudiation of racial segregation and racial restrictions on marriage now feature as markers of moral progress and of the United States better realizing, over time, ideals of liberty and equality. The repudiation of those practices as white supremacy and racial bigotry becomes a benchmark for contemporary civil rights struggles. I demonstrate how, in controversies over extending the fundamental right to marry to same-sex couples, *Loving* played a key supporting role. In controversies over religious exemptions to state anti-discrimination laws, participants mine this civil rights past to argue that today's struggles are similar or different. The rhetoric of bigotry plays a potent—but sometimes distracting—role in these conflicts. For it is not necessary to label a belief "bigoted" to uphold an anti-discrimination law limiting people's ability to act on their sincere religious beliefs when doing so harms or interferes with the rights of others.

Puzzles About Bigotry

The controversies over marriage and civil rights provide settings in which to take up several puzzles about the rhetoric of bigotry: whether it is the motive for or the content of a belief that makes it bigoted; whether bigotry is simply short-hand for beliefs that are now beyond the pale; and whether bigotry stems from a type of character, "the bigot," who has specific moral and psychological traits, or whether we all are vulnerable to being bigoted.

The first puzzle is whether a charge of bigotry concerns the *motivation* for a belief or act: is the appeal either to *sincere* religious belief or to *conscience* a defense to a charge of biogtry? The contrast drawn between the bigot motivated by hatred toward a group and the sincere religious believer seeking to follow conscience might suggest that the answer should be yes. People often draw such a contrast in debates over the evident conflict between LGBTQ rights and religious liberty. For example, in his dissent in *Obergefell v. Hodges*, in which the Supreme Court held that same-sex couples have the fundamental right to marry, Chief Justice Roberts contended that Justice Kennedy's majority opinion had "portrayed" as bigoted those people who, "as a matter of conscience, cannot accept same-sex marriage."[31] Kennedy nowhere said such people were bigots, but explained that there were limits to enacting "sincere, personal opposition into law" when doing so denies the basic liberties of others.[32]

In *Masterpiece Cakeshop v. Colorado Civil Rights Commission*, baker Jack Phillips drew on both the *Obergefell* majority opinion and the dissents, arguing that he was a "conscientious man of faith," inspired to "love and serve people from all walks of life"; his refusal to bake a wedding cake for a same-sex couple was based on his religious belief that marriage was the union of one man and one woman, not "invidious discrimination."[33] Many who filed "friend of the court" briefs on Phillips's behalf argued that sincere "men of faith" like him are nothing like the racist bigots of yesteryear who opposed interracial marriage.[34] If the Court ruled against Phillips, it would "tell him—and all traditional Muslims, Orthodox Jews, and Christians—that acting on beliefs central to his identity is wrong, benighted, even bigoted."[35] Some even reversed the charges of bigotry: the civil rights commissioners and judges who denied business owners like Phillips a religious exemption from state civil rights laws were the *real* bigots, "intolerant" toward his conscientious religious beliefs.[36]

Certainly, the impulse to link bigotry to hateful motivation tracks common definitions of bigotry: hateful beliefs about and actions toward a group are a worrisome form of bigotry. Philosopher John Corvino argues that bigotry is "stubborn, unjustified *contempt* toward groups of people."[37] Organizations that monitor extremist groups in the United States warn that there has been a surge in "white supremacy and hate-driven domestic terrorism" in the country; they argue that there is a link between Trump's bigoted rhetoric and this surge.[38]

Other common definitions of bigotry, however, link it not with religious insincerity or the absence of conscience, but with intolerance and prejudice toward a group's beliefs or actions or toward a group itself.[39] Equating bigotry *only* with hateful motives or actions, so that religious beliefs could never be bigoted, obscures the historical prominence of religious bigotry, or intolerance, and its role in shaping commitments to religious toleration. President Washington's quoted reassurance to the Hebrew Congregation of Newport was that the government would practice religious tolerance.[40] The United States would not establish an official religion, or favor one religion over others, no matter how sincere a particular religion's beliefs. Such favoritism seemed to concern Mitt Romney, who, while campaigning for the Senate, criticized the Trump administration's choice of a "religious bigot" to deliver the blessing at the opening of the US embassy in Jerusalem. Romney observed that Pastor Robert Jeffress had called Islam and Mormonism "heresy from the pit of hell," and said Jews "can't be saved." Jeffress responded that he and "millions of evangelical Christians around the world" could not be bigoted for espousing belief in a 2,000-year-old teaching that "salvation is through faith in Christ alone."[41]

People may hold bigoted beliefs sincerely, conscientiously, and zealously. A *sincere* white supremacist, anti-Semite, or anti-Muslim could still be bigoted. As philosopher Tara Smith explains, "a person's conscience might be sincere, though depraved," and sincerity is "no guarantee" against one's conscience advising actions that would harm others or violate their rights.[42] The religious disagreement over ending racial segregation, taken up in chapters 4 and 5, illustrates the problem with assuming that a belief rooted in conscience or sincere religious belief cannot be bigoted. In the 1950s and 1960s politicians and clergy invoked conscience, the Bible, and God's plan for the races as they vehemently denied that their defense of racial segregation was bigoted. They asserted that they were waging a war of morality and conscience, and that those who disagreed were poor students of the Bible—even heretics. At the same time, religious opponents of segregation appealed to conscience to argue that it was not only un-American but indeed unscriptural. For Dr. Martin Luther King Jr. and other clergy members fighting segregation, conscience was a powerful force to condemn bigotry and prejudice. A central premise of King's philosophy of nonviolent direct action was that such action aroused conscience and could redeem people from their prejudices.[43]

Bigotry clearly has a complex relationship to conscience and religious belief.[44] In these historical battles, some people appealed to conscience to indict bigotry and to help people overcome it, but other people invoked conscience to rebut charges of bigotry. Pioneering social scientists recognized long ago the paradox that religion both "makes and unmakes"—supports and condemns—bigotry and prejudice.[45] Drawing sharp contrasts between (1) today's conscientious believer who, based on scripture, believes marriage is between one man and one woman and (2) yesterday's segregationist who quoted the Bible to oppose integration and interracial marriage suggests that the latter simply used religion as a pretext for discrimination. But this ignores the fact that clergy and politicians defending segregation vehemently rejected the label of "bigot" and themselves appealed to religion and conscience.

A second puzzle concerns whether it is the *content* of a belief, not what motivates it, that invites the label bigotry. On some definitions, bigotry refers to an *unreasonable belief* about or an *irrational hatred* of a group.[46] The Social Q's columnist drew on such definitions in referring to the "irrational hatred" of the "angry bigot" at the deli counter.[47] A bigot, one dictionary explains, is "a person who has strong, unreasonable ideas, especially about race or religion, and who thinks anyone who does not have the same beliefs is wrong."[48] Defining bigotry as "*extreme* intolerance" also suggests unreasonableness.[49]

On such definitions, the *reasonableness* of a belief would counter a charge of bigotry. To return to Phillips, his supporters argued that his religious beliefs about marriage are not only sincere, but also reasonable: such beliefs rest on "decent and honorable religious or philosophical premises" (quoting Justice Kennedy's language in *Obergefell*).[50] Those supporters contrasted religious objections to interracial marriage as unreasonable: rooted in white supremacy, racist pseudo-science, and distortion of religion.[51]

Whether a belief is unreasonable is at the core of debates about whether being intolerant of certain beliefs is always morally blameworthy bigotry. William Ramsey illustrates this definitional puzzle with racism: beliefs in racial superiority and inferiority are "factually inaccurate" and "morally repugnant." But "by adopting a strong anti-racism stand, I am being quite hostile to the opinions of others, which for some is sufficient for bigotry."[52] Ramsey's example resonates with charges that political correctness is a form of bigotry because it is intolerant of certain views.

One lesson about the rhetoric of bigotry is that ideas about what is reasonable and unreasonable change over time. The various struggles over civil rights and marriage reveal that time is often critical to understanding contests over what is bigoted. These struggles show that what we "retrospectively judge evil was once justified as reasonable."[53] Before the 1960s, the expression of racism by white political leaders was "open," "brazen," and "unabashed"; after the 1960s, "what used to be common sense was now a cancer, a deadly sin."[54] This book uses the idea of generational moral progress to highlight that over time, people come to understand that practices once defended as natural, necessary, and just are unjust.

This temporal dimension of judging what is reasonable relates to a third puzzle about bigotry: is "bigotry" simply a term used to signal an anachronistic and now-reviled view? By calling someone a bigot, are we declaring that their position is not within the boundaries of civility or acceptable reasons for supporting or opposing laws or policies? Racism, again, is a frequent example: while inequality and implicit forms of prejudice persist, "blatant racism is out of the question for anyone wishing to be a respected member of public society."[55]

For that reason, conservative religious opponents of legalizing same-sex marriage warned that if courts and the public accepted the analogy between past legal restrictions on interracial marriage and present-day restrictions on same-sex marriage, their religious definition of marriage as only between one man and one woman would be treated as the moral equivalent of "racial bigotry."[56] Some Supreme Court justices shared that view. In dissent in *Obergefell*, Justice Alito argued that the "implications" of the race "analogy" will be "exploited by those who are determined to stamp out every vestige of dissent." He predicted that dissenters from the new "orthodoxy" about marriage would be branded as bigots.[57]

This puzzle about the role of time shows bigotry's backward- and forward-looking dimensions. Just as the boundaries of reasonable and unreasonable views shift over time, so, too, do society's understandings of permitted and proscribed forms of prejudice. Changing social and legal norms about expressing prejudice can "have a strong effect on people's tolerance for prejudice."[58] For example, that "overt bigotry" (such as "old-fashioned," blatant racism) is "widely considered socially unacceptable" is a signal achievement of the civil rights movement and the enactment of civil rights legislation.[59] People turn to the term "bigotry" to characterize views that have ceased to be acceptable.

This understanding of bigotry may explain the deep alarm many people experienced over how many young and college-educated white men were among the white supremacists marching, in August 2017, in Charlottesville, Virginia, wearing Ku Klux Klan and neo-Nazi regalia and chanting anti-Semitic and racist slogans to protest the removal of a statue of Confederate General Robert E. Lee.[60] When that protest spilled over into an act of terror killing a young counterprotestor (Heather Heyer) and injuring others, many urged President Trump to speak out unequivocally against the white supremacists and neo-Nazis, as did Virginia's governor, who said: "I am disgusted by the hatred, bigotry and violence these protestors have brought to our state over the past 24 hours."[61] When Trump read a statement that "we condemn in the strongest possible terms this egregious display of hatred, bigotry, and violence on many sides, on many sides," the qualifier "on many sides" drew swift condemnation from civil rights leaders, clergy, and politicians for the dangerous moral equivalence Trump seemed to draw between white supremacist marchers and anti-racist counterprotestors, giving "succor to those who advocate anti-Semitism, racism, and xenophobia."[62]

In the first of a cascade of resignations, Kenneth Frazier, the only African American CEO on Trump's American Manufacturing Council, resigned as "a matter of personal conscience," stating: "American leaders must honor our fundamental values by clearly rejecting expressions of hatred, bigotry, and group supremacy, which run counter to the American ideal that all people are created equal."[63] The idea that bigotry is properly repudiated and left in the past explains the urgency in appeals to conscience and to core American ideals to indict it. Trump's critics feared that his remarks could threaten crucial norms against public expression of intolerant and racist views, emboldening fringe "white bigots" to "come out of their closets," so that views that had become "widely reviled" could be redefined as "reasonable opinions—just part of the discussion."[64] Controversy over Trump's reaction to Charlottesville was part of a broader concern that he was not just using "dog whistles" that appealed to bigotry but making overt appeals to it.[65] Some black clergy related this to American "backsliding"—"the revenge of an American conscience that's never repented of its racist history."[66] As Reverend Thabiti Anyabwile told his congregation: "Things that were left smoldering, embers have caught a bit of wind from our current president, and from time to time we are seeing flashes of fire."[67]

This temporal dimension of bigotry also surfaces in rhetoric about wanting to be on the "right" rather than the "wrong" side of history. Such phrases suggest that the past teaches important lessons about discrimination. Political campaigns in some post-2016 state and federal elections, particularly in southern states, have employed such rhetoric.[68] Similar rhetoric also played a striking part in legal challenges by same-sex couples seeking the right to marry. For example, the Attorney General of Virginia expressed his desire to be on "the right side of history" as a reason for not defending his state's ban on same-sex marriage, by contrast with his predecessors, who chose to defend Virginia's ban on interracial marriage in *Loving* and its segregated schools in *Brown*.[69] In *Obergefell*, the Commonwealth of Virginia also stressed those parallels between past and present in filing a brief in *support* of same-sex marriage.[70] On the other hand, opponents of same-sex marriage rejected such parallels and asserted that the "truth about marriage" can never be on "the wrong side of history."[71]

That societies come to understand, over time, that certain historical beliefs, practices, and traditions are a product of prejudice and bigotry reveals the importance of experience and moral learning. People in the midst of a controversy over marriage or civil rights may worry about whether they accept a status quo that future generations will look back on as an obvious form of bigotry. Past examples of when people have been certain, but wrong, also provide reason to be skeptical or cautious about appeals to history, tradition, and conscience. This book explores this theme of insight and generational moral learning in multiple contexts: the scientific study of prejudice, controversies over desegregation and civil rights laws, disputes over marriage, and the Supreme Court's evolving approach to LGBTQ rights.

The fourth puzzle is whether the term "bigot" suggests a particular type of *character*, with distinctive psychological or moral traits. For example, people evaluate those who engage in bigoted acts, such as using a racial slur against a coworker, as having "poor moral character," and expressions of overt bigotry can trigger moral outrage.[72] On some definitions, the bigot holds views about a group inflexibly and obstinately, impervious to facts.[73] Such traits make it—as Dear Abby advised—futile to try to educate a bigot. Or does singling out the bigot as a distinct type having bad character miss that prejudice and stereotypes are the outgrowth of normal cognitive processes, like thinking in categories? Is it more accurate to speak about "the bigot in your brain" to refer to these processes, or even to say that we all are somewhat bigoted?[74]

From the earliest studies of prejudice, social scientists have wrestled with this question. In 1944, social psychologist Gordon W. Allport warned of a "significant battle being waged" in the United States between "the bigoted and the democratic character." The bigot lacked "insight" and was unable "to take another's perspective or correct one's misinterpretations based on new information about a group." Those traits made the bigot vulnerable to a "demagogue," who "justifies" the person's "hatreds" by blaming various minority racial and religious groups for his misfortunes.[75] In subsequent decades, other social scientists have offered similar psychological sketches.[76] The 2016 and 2018 elections brought renewed interest by social scientists in whether Republican voters supporting Trump had "authoritarian personalities" or were prone to "outgroup prejudices."[77]

In tension with this association of bigotry with fixed mental traits and bad character, however, is the scientific understanding of prejudice as the outgrowth of normal cognitive processes. For example, even as he diagnosed the bigoted personality, Allport observed that humans must think in categories, which set the stage for the study of stereotypes and social psychologists' emphasis, today, on how people have "implicit bias" despite their egalitarian ideals. Recent social psychology speaks of the "buried prejudice" to which ordinary people are prone because of the way the mind works.[78] Such work avoids the language of bigotry and moral blame in describing these processes, instead offering hope that it is possible for people to gain insight about these biases and overcome them.[79] Phrases like "good people with hidden biases" communicate that people who seek to address their biases are not doomed to be bigots.

Two incidents from the 2016 presidential campaign show these competing approaches to prejudice. When Democratic nominee Hillary Clinton placed "half of Trump supporters" into a "basket of deplorables" because of their many prejudices—"racist, sexist, homophobic, xenophobic, Islamophobic—you name it"—and added that some of them were "irredeemable," she drew on the idea of the bigot as a fixed type.[80] She swiftly apologized for grossly generalizing, clarifying that what was deplorable was Trump's building his campaign on "prejudice and paranoia" and "retweeting fringe bigots."[81] In rallies, Trump announced his shock at hearing Clinton "attack, slander, smear, demean [and] demonize" the "wonderful, amazing people" supporting him.[82] But some commentators countered that while Clinton's statement may have been politically incorrect, it was factually correct—whatever the specific percentage, "a genuinely deplorable cadre of bigots" had gained "real, outsized influence within the Republican Party."[83] Some Trump supporters related Clinton's remark to liberal "bullying" that branded as bigots good people whose opinions had been ruled out of bounds by "political correctness."[84]

Sociologist Arlie Hochschild's sympathetic portrayal of Tea Party members in Louisiana, in *Strangers in Their Own Land*, captured this sentiment that political correctness wrongly treats "good people" as bigots. They reject how liberals tell them they *should* feel about groups they perceived as "cutting in line in front of them" as they waited for an American dream that eluded them. She observes: "It was with joyous relief that many heard a Donald Trump who seemed to be wildly, magically free of all PC constraint. He generalized about all Muslims, all Mexicans, all women." Trump liberated his supporters from the constraint of pretending "sympathy" for such groups and from complaints about racism, sexism, and discrimination. As one person told Hochschild: "People think we're not good people if we don't feel sorry for blacks and immigrants and Syrian refugees. . . . But I am a good person and I *don't* feel sorry for them."[85] Cognitive science scholar George Lakoff offered a similar diagnosis of Trump's appeal: conservatives who perceive that "liberal anti-bigotry organizations" regard them as bigots and un-American for their views about immigrants, gays, and other groups, have felt "more and more oppressed by what they call 'political correctness.'" Trump "expresse[d] out loud everything they feel—with force, aggression, anger, and no shame." He made their "politically incorrect" views respectable and gave them "a sense of self-respect."[86]

In the second incident, candidate Clinton drew on the newer social science about implicit bias. In answering a question by debate moderator Lester Holt about whether police have racial bias, she described implicit bias "as a problem for everyone, not just police." However, some critics (including Trump's running mate, Governor Mike Pence) construed her remark as a charge that we are all racists and bigots.[87]

These incidents confirm the strong moral blame attached to a charge of bigotry, leading to the rejoinder that one is a good person, not a bigot. The move
to equate discussion of implicit bias with a charge of bigotry also suggests how
charged public discussions about bias are, even when they avoid the language of
bigotry. They raise questions about whether it is useful to refer to bigotry to discuss problems of prejudice. The contemporary study of prejudice suggests that
focusing on the bigot as a fixed type is less fruitful than focusing on why people
develop and hold prejudices and whether their beliefs can be changed. Similarly,
some caution against conflating a person's racist belief or action with a person
being a racist.[88] This is a "hate the sin, not the sinner" approach. What is more,
equating racism only with overt bigotry, which is now publicly condemned
and less pervasive than half a century ago, misses institutional and unconscious
racism.[89] In the context of LGBTQ rights, drawing a sharp contrast between
the homophobic bigot—akin to the segregationist—and the decent, sincere
religious believer obscures the fact that government may need to put limits on
acting even on sincere beliefs when doing so interferes with the rights of others.

My method in this book is to investigate such puzzles by tracing how people
understood and spoke about bigots and bigotry in a series of past and present
controversies over marriage and civil rights. These controversies enable us to
glimpse the language used in both legal and nonlegal settings, including debates,
speeches, and testimony in Congress, judicial opinions and dissents, arguments
made in landmark civil rights cases, pastoral counseling and psychology
journals, guidebooks on intermarriage, books and journals by social scientists,
and newspapers, magazines, and other forms of media. By looking at charges,
denials, and countercharges of bigotry in these different contexts, we see how
people argued during times of transition, when society had not yet reached a
settled consensus that racial segregation and discrimination were wrong and
should be prohibited. The recent legal and constitutional battles over same-sex
marriage and LGBTQ rights permit a similar glimpse at competing arguments
over what people have thought bigotry is and is not.

In concluding, I consider lessons for present and future controversies in
which people turn to the rhetoric of bigotry, such as the legal rights of transgender persons. I offer some thoughts about the current political climate, and
the debate over whether calling out bigotry helps to restore civility or hinders
it. The turn to bigotry to identify repudiated and unreasonable views explains
the heavy moral condemnation and strong emotional charge the term "bigotry" arouses. To call someone a bigot may stop a conversation because it marks
someone as beyond the pale, not reachable through dialogue or persuasion.[90]
The rhetorical retort of complaining that someone has been "branded a bigot"
can be as much a conversation stopper as actual charges of bigotry. I conclude
that the rhetoric of bigotry is sometimes necessary and appropriate, but at other

times, there are more constructive ways to talk about prejudice, intolerance, and discrimination. Rhetoric matters. Particularly if we care about moral learning and coming to new understandings about injustice and justice, we should pay careful attention to the rhetoric of bigotry.

An Overview

As a starting point, chapter 2 revisits pioneering and still-influential research on prejudice. During the post–World War II period, social scientists and civil rights groups fervently sought to understand the roots of racist and anti-Semitic prejudice—and bigotry—in order to eliminate it. Chapter 2 focuses on Gordon W. Allport's foundational work *The Nature of Prejudice* (1954), which introduced still-relevant concepts about prejudice, as well as contradictions and tensions with which social scientists continue to wrestle, including the relationship between religion and prejudice. This literature is particularly valuable because for much of the twentieth century, social scientists used people's reported attitudes about whether they would cross lines of race, ethnicity, and religion to marry— and how they judged those who did—as a measure of prejudice and bigotry.[91] As Allport concluded: "It is because intermarriage would symbolize the abolition of prejudice that it is so strenuously fought."[92] Allport and social scientists of his time argued that law should enlist conscience to close the gap between American ideals and discriminatory practices.

Chapter 2 then examines a second important point in the scientific study of prejudice: the late twentieth-century shift from asking people to report their attitudes to studying implicit biases through such techniques as the Implicit Association Test (IAT). This shift deals with the problem that although overt bigotry has declined, discrimination persists. One continuity with Allport's work concerns the role of *insight* (or conscience): when persons with egalitarian attitudes about race and sex equality are made aware that hidden biases may be shaping their behavior, the cognitive dissonance can motivate them to overcome such biases.

With this grounding in the scientific study of prejudice, I trace the rhetoric of bigotry through a series of past and present controversies over marriage and civil rights. Chapter 3 begins with interfaith marriage, in particular, "mixed marriage" (a marriage in which spouses from two different religious traditions retain them after marrying). Many religious traditions have proscribed such marriages, although they were never prohibited in criminal or civil law. In post–World War II America, Protestants, Catholics, and Jews were separated not only by socioeconomic and cultural barriers, but also "by suspicion, prejudice, and a lack of social contact."[93] As the rate of interfaith marriage began to rise, parents, religious leaders, marriage counselors, and social scientists who opposed such marriages sought to distinguish objections based on bigotry and prejudice (including religious intolerance) from objections based on legitimate sociological and theological concerns (including concerns of conscience). Experts opined that young people might seek an interfaith—or interracial—marriage as a protest against bigotry or to signal that differences should not matter. This earlier debate over interfaith marriage illustrates competing views about assimilation and "universal brotherhood" in a pluralistic society.

Studying interfaith marriage also illustrates that civil and religious law have distinct rules about who may marry. The same is true of same-sex marriage: in the United States, civil law now uniformly permits it, but religious denominations differ. In legal controversies over whether public officials or business owners with religious objections to same-sex marriage should be exempt from issuing marriage licenses or providing wedding-related goods and services, the example of interfaith marriage often arises: If the law should provide an exemption for persons who object to same-sex marriage, should it also do so for those who object to interfaith marriage?

Another valuable historical context in which to examine the rhetoric of bigotry is religious opposition to *Brown*, which overruled the legal doctrine of separate but equal in public education. Present-day controversies over religious objections to same-sex marriage frequently bring up religious objections to desegregation and to interracial marriage, to argue that those historical examples are either informative or inapt. Chapter 4 shows that opponents of *Brown* and of desegregation vehemently rejected the label "bigot"; they appealed to conscience, religious belief, and theological arguments about God's plan for the proper separation of the races. Segregationist ministers and politicians warned that any step toward desegregation—including federal civil rights law—would lead to interracial mixing and interracial marriage. Pro–civil rights clergy and activists who defended *Brown* appealed to conscience to condemn segregation.[94] Religious leaders spoke of redeeming the bigoted person who was trapped in irrational fears and prejudices.[95] Studying this religious and political rhetoric is a valuable window into ideas about how to free someone from prejudice and bigotry. Complicating this appeal to conscience is that segregationist ministers also appealed to conscience, stating with conviction that segregation was "pleasing to the Lord."[96] Indeed, they appealed to the same Bible verse, Acts 17:26, enlisted by clergy to oppose segregation.

Examining this rhetoric of conscience and bigotry in sermons, speeches, and political rhetoric is valuable because, in today's debates over marriage, civil rights, and religious liberty, participants enlist this civil rights past in different ways. Reviewing these competing appeals to religion casts doubt on arguments today that play down the extent of religious support for segregation and antimiscegenation laws or view such support as merely pretextual.

Chapters 5 and 6 study the rhetoric of bigotry and conscience in the context of two significant civil rights developments: the enactment of the landmark Civil Rights Act of 1964 (CRA) and the Supreme Court's 1967 decision, *Loving v. Virginia*, which struck down Virginia's law barring interracial marriage. Both are contested reference points for more recent battles related to marriage and anti-discrimination law, and the evident conflict between religious liberty and LGBTQ rights.

Lawmakers and witnesses who supported the CRA appealed to the nation's conscience. Some supporters enlisted the rhetoric of bigotry, calling the refusal of service by businesses based on race bigotry inconsistent with American ideals.[97] CRA proponents argued that Congress could—and should—legislate morality: though anti-discrimination law might not immediately change hearts and minds, it could stop discriminatory conduct. Many religious leaders testified in support of the CRA, appealing to religious conscience. But some testified against it, invoking religious convictions about the biblical origins of segregation and inequality.

Opponents of the CRA enlisted the rhetoric of bigotry in many ways, ranging from denying bigotry, to arguing that no law could end bigotry, to arguing that people had a right to be bigoted in the marketplace.[98] Some flipped the charges of bigotry—contending that it was supporters of the CRA who were the *real* bigots. Chapter 5 also considers debate over the famous "Mrs. Murphy" rooming house exemption from the CRA's public accommodations provision (Title II). Given the intense present-day controversy over whether for-profit businesses should have exemptions from state public accommodations laws, it is useful to revisit how lawmakers and witnesses discussed this exemption. The chapter also briefly revisits two cases in which the Court upheld Title II against challenge, both of which featured in *Masterpiece Cakeshop: Heart of Atlanta Motel v. U.S.* (1964)[99] and *Newman v. Piggie Park Enterprises, Inc* (1968).[100] I consider what lessons those prior controversies teach for present-day debates.

Chapter 6 turns to *Loving*, in which the Court struck down antimiscegenation laws as an unconstitutional "endorsement of the doctrine of White Supremacy."[101] I trace the rhetoric of bigotry, prejudice, and conscience in the briefs, oral argument, and opinion in that case. Virginia offered a modern rationale for its law by relying on a then-recent book by a rabbi and sociologist contending that interfaith, interethnic, and interracial marriages should be strongly discouraged because they posed problems, particularly for the children of such marriages.[102] The Lovings characterized Virginia's law as the "odious" relic of slavery and rooted in racial prejudice. Their amici contended that antimiscegenation laws violated freedom of conscience and that "race prejudice"—rather than interracial marriage itself—created problems for the intermarried.

Loving proved to be a crucial precedent in the constitutional battle over same-sex marriage and it features in ongoing struggles over the scope of anti-discrimination laws. In both contexts, participants have disagreed over the lessons of *Loving* for the present. Chapter 6 argues that *Loving* illustrates the theme of generational moral progress in our constitutional jurisprudence: laws once justified by appeal to nature, God's law and plan for the races, and societal well-being are repudiated as rooted in prejudice. Justice Kennedy drew on *Loving* in *Obergefell*: "The nature of injustice is that we may not see it in our own times."[103] The competing appeals to *Loving* in Kennedy's majority opinion and the dissents raise the question of when insight about prejudice is possible.

Chapter 7 charts the trajectory of the Court's evolving approach to the constitutional liberty and equality of LGBTQ persons and the role of moral disapproval as a basis for law, beginning with *Bowers v. Hardwick* (1986) and culminating in *Obergefell*. In *Romer v. Evans* (1996), the first of the Court's landmark opinions limiting the ability of majorities to discriminate on the basis of sexual orientation because of moral disapproval, the Court struck down a law that seemed "inexplicable by anything but animus," leading dissenting Justice Scalia to argue that there was no "animus" and that the majority was "disparaging as bigotry" the moral beliefs of Coloradans.[104]

The "animus versus morality" dynamic would recur over the next few decades, as the Court overruled *Bowers* in *Lawrence v. Texas* (2003) and, a decade later, struck down federal and state laws barring same-sex couples from marrying. Chapter 7 focuses on a curious dynamic in these cases: In none of the majority opinions does Justice Kennedy call those who morally disapprove of same-sex intimate association or extending marriage to same-sex couples bigots. Nonetheless, the dissenting justices argue that the Court has branded such people as bigots. What gives rise to these charges? One answer might be that a finding of animus is a charge of bigotry. But the dissenters also make such charges when the majority acknowledges the sincere moral and religious convictions of opponents of same-sex marriage. Chapter 7 shows that the Court oscillates in its approach, sometimes focusing on bad motives and sometimes on legal practices (however motivated) whose effect and social meaning are to deny equal liberties to groups like gays and lesbians who are morally worthy of the status of equal citizenship. *Obergefell* illustrates the latter approach. Chapter 7 highlights that religious groups weighed in on both sides in all of the major gay rights cases, a fact that suggests the limits of a framing that pits conscience and religious liberty against LGBTQ rights.

As chapter 8 details, *Obergefell* generated a fresh set of controversies, as same-sex couples sought to purchase wedding-related goods and services in the marketplace, and some merchants refused to provide them because of their religious convictions about marriage. One such controversy reached the

Supreme Court, in the highly publicized *Masterpiece Cakeshop* case: the baker
Jack Phillips argued that Colorado's anti-discrimination law, which prohibited
businesses from refusing goods and services based on a customer's sexual orientation, violated his religious liberty and freedom of speech by not exempting
him from creating wedding cakes for same-sex couples. Justice Kennedy's narrowly reasoned majority opinion did not resolve those controversies. The Court
did, however, suggest that rhetoric matters, in concluding that remarks by one
commissioner about the appeal to religion to justify discrimination showed
"hostility" and "animosity" toward Phillips's religion, instead of tolerance and
respect. Yet the Court also affirmed states' authority to protect gays and lesbians
against discrimination.

What is the best way to resolve the conflict between claims of conscience
and state anti-discrimination laws? Chapter 8 offers a close study of the rhetoric
and argument of the parties and their amici in *Masterpiece Cakeshop* to highlight their contrasting answers to this question. Phillips's amici denied the relevance of the civil rights past; as with debates over the CRA, some reversed the
charges of bigotry to apply them to the "intolerant" civil rights commissioners
and judges. Defenders of Colorado's law drew a direct parallel between past and
present, countering that history teaches important lessons about past assertions
of conscience and religious liberty to justify many forms of discrimination and
exclusion. They pointed out that the Court rightly rejected religious objections
by business owners to obeying the Civil Rights Act, even though they were genuinely held and widely shared. Many cited *Piggie Park*, in which a white restaurant owner argued that having to serve black customers violated his religious
belief that God intended that the races not mix.[105] They warned that opening the
door to religious exemptions based on conscience leads to every person being
"a law unto himself,"[106] and undercuts important gains in civil rights. The debate
over public accommodations law illustrates that the focus on bigotry and bad
versus sincere motives can be a distraction: "The question in a discrimination
case is not whether any particular person should face moral condemnation as a
bigot," but whether there is discrimination that has caused harm to a person.[107]

This book concludes, in chapter 9, by offering some lessons about the rhetoric
of bigotry, drawn from past and more recent struggles over marriage and civil
rights. I analyze one present-day example: controversies over the legal status of
transgender persons. As states have enacted or proposed laws requiring persons
to use bathrooms and other sex-segregated spaces that match their biological
sex at birth rather than their current gender identity (so-called bathroom bills),
some have criticized this as "bathroom bigotry," while others have retorted that
"biology is not bigotry." The Obama and Trump administrations have taken
sharply different approaches to this issue and how past civil rights struggles
apply to it. I also ask why sexism and misogyny do not feature more frequently

in accounts of bigotry. Finally, I ask whether Allport's warning of a battle between the bigoted and democratic character is pertinent today, in a climate of
increasing political polarization and antipathy. I conclude by relating conflicts
over calling out bigotry and renewing civility to the challenge of pursuing the
ideal of "e pluribus unum" in a diverse and divided polity.

A Note on Terminology

Several of this book's chapters revisit historical materials from the 1940s through
the 1960s about racial discrimination. Those sources use terms no longer used
today, in particular, "Negro" instead of black or African American. I use those
terms when I quote or paraphrase sources. The term "Negro" "tended to be used
as a term of reproach by Whites," but also, from the early twentieth century until
the late 1960s, was "the standard preferential term" used by blacks, associated
with "racial progress" and with leaving such terms as "colored" behind.[108] The
fact that earlier terms, "no matter how dignified they seem when first employed,
eventually sound like terms of contempt" reflects, Richard Rothstein argues, a
desire to forget the United States' history of exclusion of African Americans.[109]
In discussing the US Supreme Court's evolving approach to gay and lesbian
rights, I use the terminology employed in the parties' briefs and the justices'
opinions, rather than present-day terminology, such as LGBTQ.

From the Bigot in Our Midst to Good People with Hidden Biases

The Scientific Study of Prejudice

Chapter 1 posed a number of puzzles about the rhetoric of bigotry. This chapter turns to one helpful resource for grappling with those puzzles: how social scientists in the United States have wrestled with bigotry in their study of prejudice. To set the stage for later chapters' examination of how people have used the language of bigotry in conflicts over marriage and civil rights, this chapter asks about bigotry itself. What are bigotry's roots, and what can prevent or remedy it? Is "bigotry" just a synonym for "prejudice"? What underlies the intuition that to say that someone's attitudes about a group reflect bigotry carries more moral condemnation than to say that they reflect biases or stereotypes? Is the bigot a fixed personality, or are we all a bit bigoted? What light does this scientific study shed on the relationship between bigotry and conscience or religious belief? Can a religious belief that is sincere nonetheless be bigoted?

Two Moments in the Scientific Study of Prejudice

Social scientists in the United States have taken up questions about bigotry as part of the scientific study of prejudice and intergroup relations. Some of the earliest scientific efforts date back nearly a century.[1] This chapter focuses on two significant stages of that study. The first is the post–World War II period, when civil rights groups, scholars, and universities showed keen interest in studying prejudice as a "social disease" in order to "search for more effective ways to prevent or reduce the virulence of the next outbreak."[2] To represent that stage, I revisit psychologist Gordon W. Allport's classic study *The Nature of Prejudice* (1954),[3] published the year that the Supreme Court decided

Who's the Bigot? Linda C. McClain, Oxford University Press (2020). © Oxford University Press.
DOI: 10.1093/oso/9780190877200.001.0001

Brown v. Board of Education.[4] Introducing the twenty-fifth anniversary edition of the book, Kenneth Clark (whose work the Court cited in *Brown*) observed that it "established the parameters for a scholarly social science approach" to the "complex human problem of prejudice."[5] Fifty years after its publication, twenty-first-century social scientists describe Allport's book as providing a continuing foundation for the study of prejudice.[6] *The Nature of Prejudice* did not advance one single, unifying theory of prejudice but instead presented multiple perspectives that addressed cognitive processes, motivational influences, and sociocultural processes. Those different perspectives, as well as the tensions and contradictions within Allport's approach, have inspired diverse research agendas by subsequent generations of social scientists.[7]

The second significant stage is the shift, beginning in the late twentieth century, from studying prejudice by examining what people report concerning their (conscious) attitudes and beliefs about members of different groups to focusing on unconscious cognition and implicit bias. This newer focus is evident from the title of social psychologists Mazharin R. Banaji and Anthony G. Greenwald's *Blindspot: Hidden Biases of Good People* (2013). As they explain, problems of discrimination persist, even though—by comparison with Americans in studies from fifty to seventy-five years ago—"early twenty-first century Americans display low levels of explicit (overt) race prejudice in survey studies" and most "now express egalitarian racial attitudes." Testing for implicit bias through such measures as the Implicit Association Test (IAT) is a way to understand why.[8] One concern motivating this shift is that an "over-emphasis" in social policy on overt prejudice may be detrimental because it assumes that the problem is one of the *few* (the "malicious 'bad apples'") rather than the *many* (those with implicit biases).[9] Saying that "good people" have such biases avoids causing discomfort or suggesting that they are bad for having them. By comparison, speaking about overt bigotry or racism suggests strong moral condemnation.[10]

Looking at these two stages in the scientific study of prejudice reveals important points of continuity that are helpful in confronting puzzles about bigotry. One is the recognition, then and now, that the mind must think in categories, but that such categorization leads to problems of stereotyping and prejudice. Both approaches also share an optimism that with awareness of how the mind works, it is possible to recognize and remedy prejudice and bias. Allport wrote of the role of conscience, insight, and shame in emancipating people from bigotry and prejudice; Banaji and Greenwald write of the role of "discomfort" and "cognitive dissonance" in coming to terms with one's implicit bias.[11] A final shared premise is the "intergroup contact hypothesis" (advanced by Allport): one way to reduce bigotry, prejudice, or bias is through social contact between members of different groups on terms of equality.[12]

Stage One: The Post–World War II Scientific Study of Prejudice

The scientific study of prejudice in the 1950s, and Allport's work in particular, provide a useful avenue into puzzles about bigotry.

Revisiting Allport

One reason to revisit the earlier scientific study of prejudice is that the concern then to create a hate-free world finds echoes in present-day concerns about an evident rise in extremism and hate. As Allport explained, the premise for such study was understanding "the roots of prejudice" would help foster "hate-free values." To do so, universities gave "new prominence to this approach under various academic names: *social science, human development, social psychology, human relations, social relations*."[13] At Harvard University, for example, Allport, a professor of psychology, cofounded a new Department of Social Relations.[14]

To improve intergroup relations, civil rights groups and scholars viewed as urgent the task of understanding racial, ethnic, and religious prejudice and discrimination. The newly created Department of Scientific Research of the American Jewish Committee funded a "Studies in Prejudice" book series, which included such classics as *The Authoritarian Personality*.[15] In the wake of the horrors of World War II and the "mechanized persecution and extermination of millions of human beings in what was once regarded as the citadel of Western civilization," the series coeditors argued that "an aroused conscience is not enough if it does not stimulate a systematic search for an answer" to understand the personal and social aspects (or group dynamics) of prejudice and to help eradicate it.[16]

Another imperative for such study was understanding and ending racial discrimination against African Americans in the United States. Along with Allport, the other giant in the early scientific study of prejudice was Gunnar Myrdal, whose *An American Dilemma: The Negro Problem and Modern Democracy* (1944) helped put "race discrimination in the United States on the national agenda."[17] As chapter 5 will discuss, Myrdal's work provided an implicit frame for President Harry S. Truman's Committee on Civil Rights report, *To Secure These Rights*, proposing a robust civil rights agenda to end segregation.[18]

A second reason concerns the role of law. Present-day civil rights debates refer back to landmark civil rights laws as a fixed reference point. But opponents of such laws hotly challenged whether law could or should address problems of "human nature," such as bigotry and prejudice. Allport believed that the scientific study of important and enduring human problems like prejudice could— and should—contribute to law reform.[19] He argued that anti-discrimination laws could succeed, despite initial resistance, because they aligned with Americans' "conscience," or their sense of guilt about the gap between American ideals and racially discriminatory practices. Such laws also made it possible for members of different groups to have social contact on terms of equality, which, he predicted, could reduce prejudice.[20]

A third reason to revisit the scientific study of prejudice is its focus on attitudes about marriage in measuring prejudice and bigotry. That connection is pertinent to this book's look back at controversies over interfaith and interracial marriage. Social scientists asked about people's willingness to cross lines of faith, ethnicity, or race to marry and their views of whether others should do so. Like Myrdal, Allport observed the frequent use by the white bigot of the intermarriage question—"Would you want your daughter to marry a Negro?"—to oppose any step toward dismantling legally enforced racial segregation because it would lead to more social contact on terms of social equality and, inevitably, to interracial marriage.[21]

Fourth, Allport's work provided a pioneering look at the relationship between religion and bigotry. Allport puzzled over the "paradoxical situation" that "there is something about religion that makes for prejudice, and something about it that unmakes prejudice."[22] That paradox is helpful in wrestling with the puzzle of whether bigotry and sincere religious beliefs are opposites, or whether a sincere religious belief can be bigoted. In subsequent decades, studies of the psychology of religion have returned to that paradox and developed more complex models for understanding it.

Finally, Allport's work includes tensions of continuing relevance to understanding prejudice. One tension is between his analysis of prejudice as the outgrowth of ordinary cognitive processes versus an irrational antipathy related to weaknesses in personality. On the one hand, Allport argued that liberation from bigotry and prejudice was possible through conscience, education, and social contact. On the other, he also posited a "genuine bigot," with a certain personality structure, for whom such liberation might not be possible. That tension is important to the question of whether and how people can "break the prejudice habit."[23]

Allport's focus on ordinary cognitive processes has a modern counterpart in social psychologists' explanation of how thinking in categories gives rise to the "hidden biases of good people."[24] But instead of his focus on a distinctive bigoted or "prejudiced personality," his modern counterparts focus more on how social learning and social environment contribute to prejudice toward outgroups.[25] To introduce this idea of the bigot as a fixed, and worrisome, type, I begin with Allport's 1944 essay, "The Bigot in Our Midst." For the competing idea that people may be liberated from bigotry and prejudice, I compare Allport's other work, including *The Nature of Prejudice*.

The Bigot in Our Midst

In October 1944, Allport published "The Bigot in Our Midst" in *Commonweal*, contending that in the United States, a "significant battle is being waged" between "two types of character, the bigoted and the democratic." Noting that we have "always had bigots in our midst and probably [always] shall," he argued that "racial and religious tensions have a way of increasing" during and after wartime to a "dangerously high" level. Citing opinion polls, Allport reported that "85% of the population [is] ready to scapegoat some group or other"; "at least forty percent express prejudice against the Negro," "five to ten percent are violently anti-Semitic," and "perhaps forty-five percent are mildly bigoted in the same direction." A "large nucleus of people [are] aggressive Antis": anti-Semitic, anti-Negro, anti-Catholic, anti-Russian, anti-Protestant, and anti-labor. Allport worried that some "aggressive" Antis were "ready" to "start violent persecutions" and to "convert the wavering, mildly bigoted fringes."[26]

Allport defined the "mental dynamics of bigotry": "a BIGOT is a person who, under the tyranny of his own frustrations, tabloid thinking and projection, blames a whole group of people for faults of which they are partially or wholly innocent." As he described the bigot's mental life:

> Unable to feel its way accurately into the other fellow's nature, it regards him as a strange creature capable of sinister motives and deeds. The bigot loses perspective because he does not correct his misinterpretation as it grows. . . . No wholesome moment comes when he says to himself, "Halt! . . . This group of people is not all alike. It isn't responsible for my difficulties. I am reading into it some of the evil that lies in my own buried nature." The bigot's mind never doubts its own interpretation in the area of its prejudices.[27]

The bigot accepts "tabloid explanations" for his various wartime "irritations" and "worries" that target minority groups, pigeon-holing "a whole race of people" rather than thinking of them as individuals. Previewing his later work on how the mind must think in categories, Allport states: "Whenever it can do so the human mind stops its functioning on the broadest level of generalization."[28]

One example of tabloid thinking concerns hostility to interracial marriage as a gambit to oppose ending racial segregation:

> If our bigot is anti-Negro he will sooner or later treat us to his stereotyped thrust. "Well, would you want your sister to marry a Negro?" The irrelevance of this matrimonial query so startles us that we are abruptly silenced. . . . For him the question does not seem irrelevant. His

rejection is total. The Negro, if unacceptable as a brother-in-law, is un-acceptable as a colleague, neighbor, voter.

Allport counters that while the bigot is "entitled to choose his friends . . . and to marry according to his taste," he is "not entitled to prevent social inter-mingling among those who do not share his prejudices."[29]

Bigots attribute to or project upon others qualities about which they are "secretly ashamed." By blaming scapegoats for "our own sins and shortcomings," Allport explains, we allow our conscience to be at rest. As the example of Germany illustrated, the bigot may readily follow a "demagogue" who "justifies his hatreds for him, and through blandishments makes him feel smug and self-satisfied."[30]

Is the United States, Allport asks, vulnerable to the sort of "mass surrender of maturity" to bigotry taking place in Germany? He distinguishes between the "largely ineffectual" efforts to reach the *adult* bigot—through "[religious] appeals to brotherly love," scientific evidence, and "intercultural education"—and efforts to prevent children from becoming bigots. "No young child is ever a bigot." Instead, the child learns "the basic prejudices of his elders" and arranges people into hierarchical categories, with "his own kind" as "superior." The child does not learn that "diversity is compatible with equality." Allport asserts the crucial importance of mobilizing "our Christian-democratic-scientific ethos" in this "war" over influencing minds. "Education for democracy" has helped to train minds to be "self-critical" and to hold impulses in check, since there is a critical distinction between "*feeling* prejudice and *acting out* prejudice."[31]

Allport concluded his essay with a tone of urgency: people who "embrace fascist principles and techniques to protect their prejudices . . . seldom realize they are doing it," but will "invoke democratic symbols to justify their attacks (states' rights, private initiative, freedom of speech and the like)." This results in a battle over the meaning of "democracy" between "paranoid bigots . . . busily engaged in rousing hatred against this scapegoat or that, chiefly the Jews" and "much of the press, most of the churches, [and] many stalwart opinion leaders." Allport predicted that the latter would prevail, given the "resiliency" of American democracy, but the outcome was by no means certain: "The strain of the coming months and years will bring an added array of frustrations, bewilderments and demagogues. Bigotry is ever the easier way to respond to this particular combination of social and psychological pressures."[32]

Emancipation from Bigotry Through
Conscience and Insight

Allport repeated this conclusion that a lack of "insight" is "characteristic of the bigot" after he and Bernard Kramer, a Harvard colleague, surveyed college students about their attitudes concerning three minority groups—Negroes, Jews, and Catholics—to try to understand "the correlates of prejudice."[33] Bigots, they argued, "are peculiarly insensitive to the origin and nature of their own attitudes." By contrast to the "less prejudiced" students, the more prejudiced regarded their "ethnocentric views of the world" as "natural" and not acquired from other sources, such as parental attitudes.[34]

Instead of viewing the bigot as forever stuck, however, Allport and Kramer suggested that emancipation from bigotry was possible. Citing Myrdal's argument that "each American is susceptible to sharp conflict when his prejudices clash with his American Creed," they argued:

> Those who are aware of the conflict and who suffer guilt feelings from it are closer to freedom from prejudice than are those who repress their shame and suffer no conscious discomfort. Shame is thus one step toward emancipation from bigotry.[35]

For example, 60% of the students surveyed who said they know they have prejudices and are ashamed of them "fall in the less prejudiced half" of the survey, while 74% who say they have prejudices, but regard them as "natural and unavoidable," fall into the more prejudiced half. Indeed, the prejudiced person tends to view his "hostilities" as "fully justified by virtue of the misbehavior of the minority groups whom he dislikes."[36]

Personality, however, influences whether such emancipation is possible, since prejudice "is woven into the very fabric of personality" in a "style of life" in which "self-criticism, self-knowledge," and "self-blame play little or no part." By contrast, such qualities "play a prominent part" in "a personality relatively free from prejudice."[37]

Like Allport in "The Bigot In Our Midst," Allport and Kramer posit the bigot as a distinct personality type. While the earlier essay seems to write off adult bigots as beyond reach, they suggest that education could "lead our population" away from prejudice and bigotry. "Schools, artists, and leaders of opinion" should offer interpretations that expose "the fallacy of stereotypes" and "ethnic generalizations" and counter "the miasmic philosophy of the jungle"—that "the world is a hazardous place in which men are basically evil and dangerous."[38] In time, this could lead to "out-groups and in-groups" viewing one another "with less alarm, and with growing equanimity and fellow-feeling."[39]

Allport's *The Nature of Prejudice*

In 1954, Allport published *The Nature of Prejudice*. As mentioned earlier, several features of this work illuminate contemporary puzzles about bigotry. It also provides an important window into the connection between law and social science in the historical struggles over civil rights and marriage that I take up in later chapters. In this section, I focus on: (1) Allport's definition of prejudice and the tension between viewing it as stemming from normal cognitive processes or from an irrational hatred and weak personality structure; (2) the role of social contact in reducing prejudice; (3) his analysis of attitudes about and barriers to interracial marriage; (4) the role of law in aligning practice with conscience and combating prejudice and discrimination; and (5) the paradoxical role of religion in "making" and "unmaking" prejudice and bigotry.

Allport's preface to *The Nature of Prejudice* captures both the confidence and urgency with which he and other social scientists undertook the study of prejudice. Allport asserts that the "infant science" of conflict and the roots of prejudice had already undertaken more "solid and enlightening study . . . than in all previous centuries combined." Continuing this study was urgent: "Without knowledge of the roots of hostility we cannot hope to employ our intelligence effectively in controlling its destructiveness." Allport advised readers that by determining the causes of prejudice and discrimination, scientific study could aid in evaluating what concrete social and legislative steps could improve group relations.[40]

Prejudice: Result of Ordinary Cognitive Processes or Bigoted Personality?

In a volume reflecting on the fiftieth anniversary of *The Nature of Prejudice*, the editors observed that because Allport did not advance a "pet theory," his very "breadth" and "intellectual dexterity" led him to embrace "seemingly contradictory views." For example,

> Allport is the founder of the cognitive approach to prejudice, which views stereotyping and categorization as normal and inevitable byproducts of how people think. Yet he also viewed prejudice as a fundamentally irrational hatred, born of ignorance and the ego-defensive maneuvers of people with weak personality structures.[41]

Allport located a root of prejudice in normal human tendencies: "The human mind must think with the aid of categories. . . . Once formed, categories are the basis for normal prejudgment. We cannot possibly avoid this process. Orderly living depends upon it."[42] In *Blindspot*, Banaji and Greenwald quote this passage in crediting *The Nature of Prejudice* as "the recognized starting point for modern scientific understanding of stereotypes." Indeed, they use the term "*Homo categoricus*" in their own work on stereotypes and hidden biases.[43]

Allport explains that we categorize and prejudge in our daily living.[44] Human beings tend to separate into groups that tend to stay apart. This leads to exaggerations of differences between groups and to actual or imagined intergroup conflicts of interests.[45] When categorization applies to groups, prejudgments can be rational or irrational. The latter can reflect ignorance of the evidence about a group of people or a "much deeper and more baffling . . . irrational prejudgment that *disregards* the evidence."[46] Allport's important observation that prejudice can be "entirely normal"—the product of "prejudgment"—undermined "the view that prejudice is solely the product of sick motives"; it "anticipated" modern social psychology's appreciation that people "do not acknowledge their own biases" because of "the unconscious, automatic, implicit, [and] ambiguous nature of prejudgment."[47]

Allport also recognized that prejudice can be irrational. He argued that "few people know the real reason for their hatred of minority groups." The "inner conflict" and shame some people feel about their prejudices, when measured against the American Creed (as discussed earlier), could lead to insight and overcoming prejudice, but he posited that "a sizable group . . . totally lack insight."[48] However, as some commentators observe, rather than probing "the different reasons why" that group lacked "insight into, or even awareness of, their biases," he dismissed them as "genuine bigots."[49] This unresolved tension in Allport's work mirrors the present-day puzzle over whether to view the bigot as a fixed type or whether all people, with effort, can recognize and overcome prejudice.

Defining Ethnic Prejudice

Allport's book focuses primarily on racial or "ethnic prejudice," but he observes the historical prominence of religious rationales for "prejudice and persecution."[50] He mentions theological anti-Semitism and the appeal to the Bible to justify slavery. Over time, however, there was a shift to "the fiction of racial inferiority" to justify prejudice because its "biological finality" seemed to spare people "the pains of examining the complex economic, cultural, political, and psychological conditions that enter group relations."[51] Allport prefers the term "ethnic" prejudice to "race" prejudice because "ethnic refers to characteristics that may be, in different proportions, physical, national, cultural, linguistic, religious, or ideological in character."[52]

Ethnic prejudice has "two essential ingredients": (1) "definite hostility and rejection" and (2) "the basis of the rejection [is] categorical," and the person who is its target is "not evaluated as an individual." For example, a hotel has rooms available for a "Mr. Lockwood," but not for a "Mr. Greenberg." Ethnic prejudice, Allport argues, "is an antipathy based upon a faulty and inflexible generalization.... It may be directed toward a group as a whole [or an individual] member of that group." Prejudice includes both an *attitude* of favor or disfavor and also is "related to an overgeneralized (and therefore erroneous) *belief*."[53]

Beliefs may be rationally attacked and altered, but they "usually have the slippery propensity of accommodating themselves somehow to the negative attitude, which is much harder to change." For example, Mr. X asserts that "the trouble with the Jews is that they only take care of their own group," but when informed that Jews give more generously to general charities of the community than do non-Jews, he counters: "That shows they are always trying to buy favor and intrude into Christian affairs. They think of nothing but money; that is why there are so many Jewish bankers."[54]

Prejudice also grows out of distinctions people draw between members of the "in-groups" with which they identify (the "we") and members of "out-groups" (the "they"). One's in-group begins with family, Allport explains, and extends to include "geographical region, occupational groups, social (club and friendship) groups, religious, ethnic, and ideological memberships." While loyalty to in-groups "does not necessarily imply hostility toward out-groups," many people "think a great deal about out-groups [and] worry about them." There are a range of ways of acting out one's prejudice in rejecting out-groups, from verbal rejection to discrimination, including segregation, by custom or law, and to physical attack.[55]

Discrimination, as Allport defines it, is "any conduct based on a distinction made on grounds of natural or social categories, which have no relation either to individual capacities or merits, or to the concrete behavior of the individual person."[56] In the United States, he identifies numerous forms of public and private discrimination against ethnic minorities. While one limitation of *The Nature of Prejudice*, as commentators observe, is that Allport did not analyze sexism as a form of prejudice, it is notable that one example of in-group discrimination concerns men's views of women. For some people ("misogynists among them"):

> Women are viewed as a wholly different species than men, usually an inferior species. Such primary and secondary sex differences as exist are greatly exaggerated and are inflated into imaginary distinctions that justify discrimination.[57]

Allport then debunks various rationales for prejudice, such as racial and ethnic differences, by presenting evidence from the scientific study of group differences. He distinguishes genuine versus perceived differences, noting that certain visible markers of evident difference between in-group and out-group (e.g., skin color) contribute to categorization and to prejudgment.[58]

Stereotypes

The Nature of Prejudice explains the role that *stereotypes* play in rationalizing positive prejudice in favor of some groups and negative prejudice against others.[59] Describing stereotypes as "pictures in our heads," Allport explains that a stereotype acts both as a device to justify "categorical acceptance or rejection of a group" and as "a screening or selective device to maintain simplicity in perception and in thinking." To illustrate, he draws on studies of the many "pictures" people hold of "the Jew" and "the Negro," adding (as in his essay on bigotry) that for some people, these stereotypes may be a "projection" of "unacceptable" qualities within themselves.[60] But stereotypes, he explains, can weaken over time as social support for them changes, whether due to education, mass media, or simply evolving social and political conditions.[61] An additional cause, discussed in the next section, is social contact.

In recent decades, advances in social psychology have sustained Allport's argument that stereotypes act as a "justificatory device," although "in many more ways than Allport could have anticipated."[62] For example, he focused on the individual, while more recent work shows how stereotypes justify systems by rationalizing the status quo. Stereotypes "provide legitimacy for institutional forms," such as segregation (a contentious issue in Allport's time) or "heterosexual marriage" (more recently contentious). A significant insight is that "forms of stereotyping and prejudice" that justify systems "render cultural practices and institutions legitimate, rational, and sometimes even necessary and noble."[63] As later chapters will show, this notion that what once seemed natural, necessary, and noble could be a source of injustice is a key theme in Supreme Court cases affirming the constitutional liberty and equality of gays and lesbians. In such cases, LGBT rights advocates have argued that institutional discrimination against LGBT people in criminal and civil law rests on prejudice rooted in stereotypes and irrational fears.

Social Contact on Terms of Equality and Attitudes about Intermarriage

One of Allport's most significant contributions concerns the impact of social contact on prejudice: "Prejudice (unless deeply rooted in the character structure of the individual) may be reduced by equal status contact between majority and minority groups in the pursuit of common goals." He adds that the "effect" of such contact "is greatly enhanced if [it] is sanctioned by institutional supports (i.e., by law, custom or local atmosphere), and provided it is of a sort that leads to the perception of common interests and common humanity between members of the two groups."[64] In studying college students, for example, Allport and

Kramer found that "the more numerous the equal-status contacts" students re-ported "in school, at work, in recreation, as neighbors, [and] as friends," "the less the prejudice" they held toward minority groups such as Jews. By con-trast, "merely casual" contact "may engender prejudice": "a person who has no knowledge, or only casual knowledge, of a minority group becomes easy prey to second-hand stereotypes and short-cut formulations" and is "suggestible" to "derogatory epithets" when no firsthand experience counters them.[65]

In *The Nature of Prejudice*, Allport further develops the intergroup contact hypothesis, supporting it with examples such as racially integrated military units in the army, which brought "the two races together into close contact *on an equal footing in a common project* (of life and death importance)." Based on experience in such units, white soldiers "were more favorably disposed" to association with "Negro soldiers" than white soldiers who did not directly work with them.[66] Allport also discusses racially integrated employment and housing (to which I shall return).[67]

The intergroup contact hypothesis remains a fixture in the scientific study of prejudice between groups and how to reduce it.[68] Subsequent generations of social scientists have tested and confirmed Allport's hypothesis in many areas "beyond the ethnic and racial domain for which it was originally formulated."[69] In a recent study, Thomas Pettigrew (a former student of Allport) and Linda Tropp concluded: "Over the last several decades, literally hundreds of studies have shown that intergroup contact can reduce prejudice."[70] One of the most "striking" findings is the impact of such contact in reducing prejudice and fostering more positive attitudes toward gays and lesbians.[71]

The impact of social contact on reducing prejudice also bears on interfaith and interracial marriage. As chapter 3 explains, a common narrative in the 1950s and 1960s was that more opportunities for people of different religions to have social contact on terms of equality inevitably led to a rise in intermarriage. As chapters 4 and 5 detail, defenders of legal segregation and antimiscegenation laws gave, as a reason to oppose desegregation in schools and other areas of daily life, the "inevitability" of interracial marriage if there were social contact on terms of equality between white and African American children.

Racially integrated public housing is another example that Allport offers for the social contact hypothesis: "White people who live side by side with Negroes of the same general economic class . . . are on the whole more friendly, less fearful, and less stereotyped in their views than white people who live in segregated arrangements." "Integrated housing policies," he argues, "remove barriers to effective communication," encourage "knowledge and acquaint-anceship," and reduce "hostility."[72] Of note is how Allport connects these gains through social contact to the "fraught" issues of interracial marriage and racial bigotry.

Allport observes that along with the "net gain in friendship" in integrated housing come "realistic obstacles" to close relationships: the "mingling of adolescent boys and girls brings with it the possibility of mixed marriages *which in our present culture constitute a serious problem for the couples involved.*" Given the "state of social opinion" about interracial marriage, he argues, "such an eventuality is viewed quite realistically as fraught with potential suffering for the children."[73] Racial bigotry or prejudice, in other words, will cause such "suffering." For example, a white mother reports that she likes living in an interracial housing project and describes her "Negro" neighbors as "wonderful" people, who "should be given every opportunity, the same as whites." She wants her children "to grow up unprejudiced," but is "worried about" her daughter, who, at twelve, "has grown up so that she doesn't see any differences between Negro and white people." Because the daughter lives around "a lot of fine Negro boys," she is "likely to just naturally fall in love with one":

> It would be such a mess—people are so prejudiced—she'd never be happy. I don't know what to do—it would be all right, I guess, if everybody wasn't so prejudiced against mixed marriages. I've been thinking a lot about it—I'll probably move out before [my daughter] gets much older.

Allport points to this mother's dilemma as illustrating the conflict between "social pressure" posed by in-group prejudices and "personal conviction" that resists such views.[74]

Allport observed that prejudice toward an interracial married couple and their children makes "intermarriage" impractical, under current social conditions. At the time he wrote, many states had antimiscegenation laws that barred such marriages. Where such marriage was legal, he noted, it was "rare" and "bedeviled by social complications that create grave problems even for the most devoted couples." He opposed antimiscegenation laws and argued that they lacked any "biological grounds." By contrast, a "rational," but seldom stated, ground for objecting to interracial marriage was the "handicap and conflict" it would cause "both parents and offspring in the present state of society." But to state opposition in those terms, he argued, "would imply that the present state of society should be improved so that miscegenation can safely take place."[75] This, in turn, plays into the use by the "bigot" or "prejudiced person" of the intermarriage question—"but would you want a Negro to marry your sister?"—to end "most discussions of discrimination." If "even the most tolerant person may not welcome intermarriage—because of the practical unwisdom in a prejudiced society"—then the bigot can justify maintaining all barriers and forms of racial discrimination. Allport concludes that "the intermarriage question (actually so

irrelevant to most phases of the Negro question) is forcibly introduced to protect and justify prejudice."[76]

Allport emphasizes the symbolic role played by intermarriage: "It is because
intermarriage would symbolize the abolition of prejudice that it is so strenuously fought."[77] To appreciate this symbolic role would be a "distinct gain" because it would allow clearer perception of "the real problems in race relations."
And, he added, "the abolition of segregation" would help greatly to achieve this
gain.[78]

The Paradoxical Relationship Between Religion and Prejudice

Another contribution relevant to present-day puzzles about bigotry is Allport's
identification of and attempt to "unravel" a paradox about religion: "It makes
prejudice and it unmakes prejudice."[79] He used the image of a woven cloth: "Two
contrary sets of threads are woven into the fabric of all religion—the warp of
brotherhood and the woof of bigotry."[80] He speaks of religion not in any "ideal
sense," but "as it actually exists historically, culturally, and in the lives of individual men and women."[81] He argues that the "seeds of bigotry" can be found
in the theological, sociocultural, and personal-psychological dimensions of
religion.[82]

The "paradox" Allport identified remains a subject of scientific study.[83] Indeed,
one researcher observes that "during the half century since" Allport "famously"
wrote of religion's paradoxical role in prejudice, "a large amount of research has
been conducted" on that relationship and "has generally found that religious involvement was positively correlated with various forms of prejudice."[84] For example, a 2010 meta-analytic review of past studies involving "White Christians
in the United States" confirmed the "paradox of religious racism," and observed
that one factor may be religious ethno-centrism: because religion "tends to be
practiced within race," people of other races "may appear to belong to religious
out-groups."[85] Allport's identification of this paradoxical role of religion is important to this book's consideration of the role of religious arguments on both
sides of historical and present-day battles over marriage and civil rights laws.

How, on Allport's view, does theology both make and unmake prejudice
and bigotry? On the one hand, "plentiful supports for brotherhood are found
in nearly all systems of theology."[86] In *The Nature of Prejudice*, Allport gave the
example of those who are "motivated by the demand of their religion that they
love their neighbor" and "know that whatever absolute differences exist, they
are partially offset by common affirmations—including the doctrine of the
brotherhood of man."[87] In a 1966 essay, "The Religious Context of Prejudice," he
wrote of the religious motivations of many of those battling "for civil rights, for

social justice, for tolerance and equi-mindedness—in short, for brotherhood," referencing Dr. King, and "recent pronouncements from nearly every major religious body."[88]

On the other hand, Allport wrote, such evidence "does not cancel the fact that members of Christian churches are on the average more bigoted than nonchurchgoers."[89] As a contemporaneous example of "the contamination of universalistic religion with ethnocentric attitudes," he pointed to the "Jim Crow churches in the United States." He states that "through most of America's history the Church has been a preserver of the status quo in race relations rather than a crusader for improvement."[90] Allport gave other historical examples of theological justifications for bigotry that are in tension with religious strands of universalism, such as the long history of Christian anti-Semitism and Catholic persecution of Jews.[91]

Allport theorized that the problem of religious bigotry is not with theology or religion as such, even though various religions have "irreconcilable differences." Instead, "most of what is called religious bigotry is in fact the result of a confusion between ethnocentric self-interest and religion, with the latter called upon to rationalize and justify the former." The fusion of religion with the pursuit of ethnocentric self-interest, for example, leads to the merger of religion and prejudice, evident in "ethnocentric slogans like, 'white, Protestant, gentile, American.'" "Nothing is easier," he concludes, "than to twist one's conception of the teachings of religion to fit one's prejudice."[92] This charge of twisting religion to fit prejudice is echoed in debates over racial segregation (as chapters 4 and 5 will discuss) and in recent debates about religious exemptions to anti-discrimination laws prohibiting discrimination on the basis of sexual orientation (as chapters 7 and 8 will discuss).

Religious bigotry, Allport argues, stems from the fusion of religious creed with the dynamics between in-groups and out-groups, such as "irrelevant considerations of caste, social class, national origin, cultural differences, and race." He concludes:

> If one looks at the matter closely, it becomes doubtful whether bigotry ever is or can be exclusively religious. . . . Bigotry enters only when religion becomes the apologist for in-group superiority and overextends itself by disparaging out-groups for reasons that extend beyond deviation in creed.[93]

Pettigrew studied this dynamic in Little Rock, Arkansas, concluding that segregationist ministers who opposed school desegregation appealed to a "creed of segregation" that intersected with the American creed (as chapter 4 will discuss). The "sociocultural context" of religion, Allport also argues, contributes to bigotry. Congregations are "an assemblage of like-minded people" and represent "the ethnic, class, and racial cleavages of society, over and above denominational cleavages." This supports parishioners' ethnocentrism.[94] In the mid-1950s, the theologian Reinhold Niebuhr also diagnosed such ethnocentrism in religion.[95]

Allport offered various theories about why, on average, churchgoers report higher levels of prejudice than nonchurchgoers. One was that for certain people, both "prejudice and religion" fill psychological needs.[96] But he also distinguished among churchgoers: "one type . . . tends to be prejudiced," while another is "relatively unprejudiced."[97] This he relates to another puzzle: the "double influence of religious teaching."[98] Some of the college students whom Allport and Kramer studied, for example, viewed the impact of their religious training as "negative," teaching them "to despise other religious and cultural groups"; others viewed it as "positive," teaching such messages as "we are all equal and . . . there should be no persecution, for any reason, of any minority groups."[99]

Allport tackles these puzzles about the "contradictory directions" in which religion's influence on prejudice runs by distinguishing different religious orientations, which he calls "institutionalized" (or "extrinsic") versus "interiorized" (or "intrinsic").[100] Someone who has an institutionalized approach to religious affiliation may attend religious services irregularly and more for the "benefits of communal contact" than for spiritual association.[101] He writes: "Belonging to a church because it is a safe, powerful, superior, in-group is likely to be the mark of an authoritarian character and to be linked to prejudice."[102] He also hypothesized that some people with an extrinsic approach to religion held an extreme political ideology that "invariably harbors" bigotry against groups, such as "Negroes, Jews, Catholics," and immigrants, who are viewed as "menacing" to their (lost) idyllic way of life.[103] By comparison, for "religiously motivated" people who seek "spiritual association" and have a more interiorized outlook, "belonging to a church because its basic creed of brotherhood expresses the ideals one sincerely believes in, is associated with tolerance."[104] Allport expresses hope that his findings, "when understood by clergy and laity, may lead to a decrease in bigotry and to an enhancement of charity in modern religious life." His practical prescription to clergy is that "to reduce prejudice we need to enlarge the population of intrinsically religious people."[105]

In subsequent decades, researchers have pointed out limitations of Allport's distinction between extrinsic and intrinsic orientation as an explanation for religiously linked prejudice. In particular, while religions may proscribe certain forms of prejudice (such as racial prejudice against African Americans, e.g., especially since the passage of the Civil Rights Act of 1964), they may prescribe others (such as prejudice against Arabs or Muslims or negative views of homosexuality).[106] Researchers have found, for example, that "stronger endorsement of orthodox Christian beliefs and higher intrinsic religiosity were related to higher prejudice against lesbians and gay men but to lower racial/ethnic prejudice."[107] As chapter 8 discusses, this finding is relevant to current battles over objections to same-sex marriage rooted in religious beliefs: such believers insist that their sincerely held views are nothing like odious racist views or opposition to interracial marriage.

Stateways Can Change Folkways: The Role of Law in Bolstering Conscience and Reducing Prejudice

Finally, a component of *The Nature of Prejudice* of continuing relevance is Allport's positive view of the role of law and public policy in prohibiting discrimination, assisting conscience, and reducing prejudice.[108] He challenges the famous assertion by Charles Graham Sumner, a Yale University sociologist and Episcopal minister, that "stateways cannot change folkways," and its modern variant: "You cannot legislate against prejudice."[109] Allport observes that in the late nineteenth century, the Supreme Court "justified its conservative decisions" (such as *Plessy v. Ferguson*, which upheld racial segregation on common carriers under the infamous "separate but equal doctrine") "on the grounds that the law was powerless to counter 'racial instinct.' "[110]

Allport gave several arguments against the "weak" premise that you cannot legislate against prejudice. First, since discriminatory laws likely "*increase* prejudice," he reasoned that anti-discrimination laws would "*diminish* prejudice." Since "Jim Crow laws in the south ... in large part *created* folkways," anti-discrimination laws can create new folkways. For example, he looks at the World War II-era Fair Employment Practice Committee (FEPC), which established fair employment laws through executive order, and some state law counterparts.[111] Allport offers a decidedly optimistic view about the power of anti-discrimination policies to set new norms of equality, creating new folkways:

> It turns out that few employers are confirmed in their prejudice; they
> are merely following what they assume to be accepted folkways. They
> are cooperative when they are assured that customers, employers, and
> the law prefer, or at least expect, a condition of no discrimination to
> prevail. It turns out that when equality is practiced, there is little ob-
> jection. Often there is not even any awareness that change has taken
> place.[112]

Such laws do not aim directly at prejudice, but instead at "its open expression" through discriminatory practices. Nonetheless, "as a by-product of the improved conditions," people "gain the benefits that come . . . from equal status contact and from normal acquaintance."[113] Law facilitates social contact on terms of equality.

Similar to his argument that shame spurs insight and emancipation from bigotry, Allport argues that conscience supports anti-discrimination law. He asserts that "most Americans have a deep inner conviction that discrimination is wrong and unpatriotic," and "deep inside their consciences do approve civil rights and antidiscrimination legislation."[114] He echoes Myrdal's diagnosis of the "moral dilemma of America" with respect to the unequal status of African Americans—the "ever-raging" conflict between the high national precepts of the "American Creed" and the conditions of actual life, including "group prejudice."[115] Law can help to remove this conflict:

> While their own prejudices may make them squirm and protest in opposition to proposed laws, they may sigh with relief if the law, in accord with their "better nature," is passed—and enforced. People need and want their consciences bolstered by law, and this is nowhere more true than in the area of group relations.[116]

As I explain in chapter 5, members of Congress similarly appealed to conscience to justify enacting the Civil Rights Act of 1964, while opponents countered that Congress should not attempt to legislate morality. Establishing a new "legal norm," Allport contends, "creates a public conscience and a standard for expected behavior that check *overt* signs of prejudice."[117] For example, under the new norm established by the CRA, expression of overt racial bigotry/explicit racism became "increasingly proscribed" and beyond the bounds of civility as "people became more accepting of the spirit of the civil rights laws."[118]

At the time when Allport was writing, some argued that education must pave the way for anti-discrimination legislation. He agreed to a point, but appealed to "the basic habit of democratic society" to argue that passing the law itself would convert most people: "After free, and often fierce, debate, citizens bow to the majority will. *They do so with a special kind of willingness if the legislation is in line with their own private consciences.*" Law "often breaks into a vicious circle so that a process of healing starts to occur." He also appealed to the Constitution as expressing the country's "official" morality and to federal laws as leading and guiding folkways.[119] Allport tempered the argument that people will obey laws that are "in line with" their conscience with the caveat that they will do so "if they are tactfully administered" and are not "felt to be imposed by an alien will." Noting the "legendary resistance" by the South to "Yankee interference," he concedes: "Even a law otherwise acceptable may be resisted if it is felt to be a personal (or regional) affront."[120]

The Nature of Prejudice went to press while the Supreme Court was considering *Brown*. Thus, it remained to be seen whether the Court would overrule *Plessy*'s "separate but equal" doctrine and its "false assumptions," as Allport put it, "in light of modern social science."[121] In fact, in *Brown*, Allport and thirty-one other social scientists and medical doctors coauthored a consensus document, "The Effects of Segregation and the Consequences of Desegregation: A Social Science Statement," submitted by appellants in support of their challenge to racially segregated public schools and the doctrine of "separate but equal."[122]

In the preface to the 1958 edition of his book, Allport commented on the Court's 1954 and 1955 decisions in *Brown* and the declaration of "massive resistance" by "at least seven states." He reiterated his earlier arguments about the role of law in aligning with conscience. Desegregation "comes about most easily in response to a firmly enforced executive order"—"most citizens accept a forthright fait accompli with little protest or disorder . . . because integrationist policies are usually in line with their own consciences (even though countering their prejudices)." He applied this "line of reasoning" to *Brown*:

> It probably would have been psychologically sounder for the Supreme Court to have insisted upon prompt acquiescence with its ruling of 1954. "Deliberate speed" does not fix an early and inescapable date for compliance. . . . No firm and consistent course of action is agreed upon; leadership falters; countermovements flourish.[123]

Introducing the twenty-fifth edition of Allport's book, Kenneth Clark called these words "prophetic."[124] Chapter 4 explains that when lawmakers and clergy defended their resistance to desegregation, they appealed to conscience and denied that they were bigots.

Gauging Prejudice Through Attitudes Concerning Intermarriage and Other Social Contact

It may be striking to readers today to see how centrally people's attitudes about intermarriage featured in the scientific study of prejudice. That study is valuable background for this book's historical chapters on the rhetoric of bigotry in objections to interfaith and interracial marriages. Well into the second half of the twentieth century, the primary research method used by social scientists to measure attitudes about race and other intergroup relations—and, thus, prejudice—was the survey method: researchers asked questions and people surveyed gave answers, or "self-reported" their racial attitudes. As Banaji and Greenwald observe, such self-reporting was "very useful in the earliest studies of prejudice," in part because, "unlike present-day Americans, early twentieth-century Americans apparently had no qualms about openly expressing their racial and ethnic attitudes."[125] In the early 1920s Emory Bogardus, a sociologist, "was the first to study prejudicial attitudes scientifically," using what he called a "social distance scale."[126] Listing forty different races, Bogardus asked Americans if they would "willingly admit members of each race (as a class, and not the best I have known, nor the worst members)" to various "classifications," beginning with "close kinship by marriage." The classifications include other personal connections, "my club as a personal chum," and "my street as my neighbor," and then move to more distant connections, "employment in my occupation in my country," "citizenship in my country," "as visitor only to my country," ending with "would exclude from my country."[127] The social distance studies showed clear hierarchies: "Most of Bogardus's respondents were ready to welcome Americans to 'marry into my family'" (followed by "English"); they were least willing to admit as kin members of the "Turkish" and "Negro" groups.[128]

Present-day Americans, Banaji and Greenwald explain, would refer to most of Bogardus's forty races as "nationalities" or "ethnicities," not races.[129] Now-discredited "race science" of the 1920s and 1930s led to this multiplying of racial categories and also shaped laws barring interracial marriage. By the late 1930s the majority of states in the United States had laws barring interracial marriage; the list of races named in such laws "was so complex and convoluted that its logic was apparent to no one."[130] When, in 1948, the California Supreme Court struck down California's antimiscegenation law (two decades before *Loving v. Virginia*), one ground was the law's "vague" and "uncertain" definitions of race.[131]

When social scientists surveyed people's attitudes about intermarriage they asked not only about interracial marriage, but also about interfaith and interethnic marriage, particularly marriage to Catholics or Jews. When Allport and Kramer studied "the roots of prejudice" by surveying college students' views of Catholics, Negroes, and Jews, they asked if a student agreed or disagreed with the statement: "I can imagine myself marrying a [Jewish person/Negro/a Catholic person]."[132] In a 1949 article, "Dimensions of Prejudice," Kramer took stock of the many instruments used to measure different dimensions of prejudice.[133] One cluster of questions aimed at discerning prejudice in "direct personal relations," such as marriage and close friendship.[134]

To assess attitudes about these direct personal relations, survey instruments asked persons to agree or disagree with positive or negative statements about intermarriage. Some of these survey statements echo expressed views about interracial and interfaith marriage that I examine in later chapters. Statements about interracial marriage included, for example: "Racial intermarriage should be prohibited by law"; "There should not be a law forbidding the marriage of whites and Negroes"; "The doctrine of evolution proves that Negroes and whites should not mate"; "Racial intermixture is biologically injurious"; and "Racial intermixture is not biologically injurious but has bad social consequences."[135]

Hypothetical questions about interracial marriage, in particular, reveal the challenges an interracial couple would face in a segregated society. One survey asks the interviewee to imagine that "in the community where you live a Negro marries a white girl," and offers two responses: "You fight for the maintenance of the color line" or "you do nothing about it." Another asks: If "your sister takes a friendly interest in an educated and unmarried Negro boy," do you "commend her for her broad-mindedness" or instead "warn her of the possible consequences of her behavior"?[136]

Surveys testing people's opinions about interfaith marriage included such statements as, for example: "Although each person should decide for himself, in general, marriage between Christians and Jews should be discouraged"; or "Intermarriage should not be allowed to take place whether or not the parties agree."[137] They also assessed people's openness to such marriage, for example: "I can imagine myself marrying a Jewish person" or "I can hardly imagine myself marrying a Jew." As with questions about interracial marriage, surveys inquired about how people would evaluate interfaith marriage decisions made by others: Would someone approve or disapprove of a non-Jewish woman's intention to marry a Jewish man despite her friends' urging her "to break off the relationship"?[138]

These surveys also assess attitudes about social equality in a range of daily activities: willingness to cross ethnic, racial, and religious lines in close social relations other than marriage. These questions are of interest because of the premise (discussed in chapters 3 and 4) that as young people crossed those lines more frequently, an inevitable result would be more intermarriage. The fear that social equality could lead to intermarriage comes through in such survey statements as: "If the line of intermarriage need not be crossed, if it can everywhere be preserved intact, I wish that social equality in equally cultured circles, might be accorded the Negro."[139]

People were asked to agree or disagree with accepting statements about interracial social contact, particularly involving children: "I would be willing to have Negro young people as social equals for my adolescent sons and daughters"; "Negro and white children should be educated in the same schools"; or "Both groups would profit from more social intermingling." Other survey questions used rejecting statements about association with Jews or blacks to measure prejudice: for example, "I would not invite a Jewish person to my home"; "Most hotels should deny admittance to Jews, as a general rule"; "Negroes should not be allowed to mingle with whites in any way"; or "Under no circumstances should Negro children be allowed to attend the same schools as white children."[140] One survey question presented Booker T. Washington's famous disavowal of social equality: "In all things purely social the two races should be as separate as the fingers on the hand, but in all things that make for the public good they should be as united as the hand."[141]

Stage Two: The Hidden Biases of Good People

By the 1970s, social psychologists became more aware of the limits of question-asking methods as a way to study prejudice. One problem was "impression management"—research subjects might give untruthful answers because they desired "to present themselves in ways that would be looked upon favorably by others."[142] Such concerns multiplied on "highly charged topics" such as racial attitudes, especially as public norms about the acceptability of discrimination shifted.[143] Even by the early 1950s, when researchers tried to replicate pioneering studies from the 1930s of racial stereotypes held by college students, some students protested against "the unreasonable task of making generalizations about people—especially those they had hardly ever met."[144] The Civil Rights Movement, landmark civil rights laws of the 1960s, and Supreme Court opinions striking down forms of racial discrimination changed the "normative climate" in the United States so that public expression of overt or "old-fashioned racism"— so pervasive at the time Allport wrote—was no longer acceptable; and yet forms of racial inequality and disadvantage have persisted.[145] For these and other reasons, researchers in the late twentieth century developed newer methods of studying bias, including hidden or implicit bias. What light do these newer scientific approaches shed on puzzles about bigotry?

The Bigot in Your Brain: Bad News, Good News

In 2008, *Scientific American* featured a story, "Buried Prejudice: the Bigot in Your Brain," with a disconcerting teaser: "Deep within our subconscious, all of us harbor biases that we consciously abhor. And the worst part is: we act on them."[146] The opening anecdote quoted Reverend Jesse Jackson, a "committed black civil-rights leader," sharing the acute pain he feels when he walks down a street, hears footsteps, starts "thinking about robbery," but then "I look around and see somebody white and feel relieved." The article used Jackson's confession to introduce the problem of implicit biases: "People unwittingly hold an astounding assortment of stereotypical beliefs and attitudes about social groups: black and white, female and male, elderly and young, gay and straight, fat and thin." It illustrated implicit biases with a drawing of a person's brain divided into categories (black, female, old, strong, white, male). It cautioned that while people may assume that implicit bias cannot be as serious a concern as the "overt, or explicit, prejudice that we associate with . . . the Ku Klux Klan or the Nazis," research shows that it is much more prevalent. Furthermore, "its effects can be equally insidious" and even lethal when, for example, police making split-second decisions are more likely to mistake a harmless object like a cell phone for a gun if a "black face accompanies it." "Unconscious racial bias," the article suggests, may shape daily social interactions, sway hiring decisions, and even "infect" critical medical decisions so that doctors take black patients' health complaints less seriously.[147]

The article connects Allport's work to the more recent research of social psychologists such as Mahzarin Banaji and Anthony Greenwald.[148] Just as Allport traced the problem of prejudice to ordinary processes of cognition, these later researchers stress that "implicit biases grow out of normal and necessary features of human cognition, such as our tendency to categorize, to form cliques and to absorb social meanings and cues." After many disheartening examples of implicit biases found even in preschoolers, the article offered "some good news." Although researchers once believed it was virtually impossible to change one's implicit associations, more recent work suggests that "people who report a strong motivation to be nonprejudiced tend to harbor less implicit bias."[149]

This bad news/good news message is a frequent feature in social psychologists' writings about prejudice. It suggests the "bigot in [the] brain" of people who believe they are free of bias does not doom them, unlike the "genuine bigot" about whom Allport worried. As Susan Fiske explains the bad news: "Our brains and our impulses all too often betray us," despite our good intentions and egalitarian ideals. Now, the good news: "Our prejudices are not inevitable; they're actually quite malleable, shaped by an ever-changing mix of cultural beliefs and social circumstances."[150] Importantly, Fiske distinguishes between overt or "barefaced bigotry"—"your grandparents' prejudice"—and "modern prejudice." Of the former, she writes: "Most estimates suggest such blatant and wrongheaded bigotry persists only among 10% of citizens in modern democracies." Such "blatant bias does spawn hate crimes, but these are fortunately rare (though not rare enough)."[151] "Our own prejudice," she writes, takes a "more subtle, unexamined form." She explains neuroscience findings about how prejudgments take place in "the blink of an eye": people are able to "identify another person's apparent race, gender, and age in a matter of milliseconds," and "in that blink of an eye," "a complex network of stereotypes, emotional prejudices, and behavioral impulses activates." "These knee-jerk reactions do not require conscious bigotry," although "they are worsened by it."[152]

Fiske explains how culture and social conditions shape and can worsen prejudice: "Years, even generations, of explicit and implicit cultural messages— gleaned from parents, the media, first-hand experiences, and countless other sources—link physical appearances with a host of traits, positive or negative."

Roots can "stretch back centuries," as with racism. "Such messages are absorbed, accepted, and perpetuated, often unconsciously, by our culture's members and institutions."[153] The good news, however, is that social conditions and "the right social engineering" can reduce prejudice, showing that "our biases are not so hardwired." Fiske frames the fight against prejudice as one we can and must win: if we are informed and persistent in understanding "how automatically people fear difference, dehumanize the less fortunate, and demonize the Other," we can understand how such "forms of segregation can perpetuate themselves, and why we must fight against them."[154]

Implicit Bias and the 2016 Presidential Campaign

An episode during the 2016 presidential campaign illustrates some of the challenges in discussing implicit bias publicly and distinguishing it from overt prejudice or bigotry. In the first presidential debate between Democratic nominee Hillary Rodham Clinton and Republican nominee Donald Trump, moderator Lester Holt asked Clinton, "Do you believe that police are implicitly biased against black people?" She answered:

> Lester, I think implicit bias is a problem for everyone, not just police. I think, unfortunately, too many of us in our great country jump to conclusions about each other. And therefore, I think we need all of us to be asking hard questions about, you know, "Why am I feeling this way?"

Clinton then suggested some de-biasing tasks that police departments could undertake, such as implicit bias training.[155]

Clinton identified implicit bias as a problem for everyone, but critics read her answer as an attack on police and a charge of racism and bigotry. Thus in the vice presidential debate, Governor Mike Pence referred to Clinton's remarks as using "a broad brush to accuse law enforcement of implicit bias or institutional racism."[156] As journalist William Saletan observed, Clinton's statement "triggered a backlash on the right," with charges that she had suggested "everyone is bigoted" and had called "the entire nation racist."[157] Such critics, he argued, "reject the whole idea of implicit bias" and "equate it with 'guilt,' 'bigotry,' and 'racism' writ large." They "find it absurd, to the point of self-refutation, that Clinton calls this bias 'a problem for everyone,'" for "how can all of us be bigots?" As he aptly noted, conflating implicit bias and bigotry misses the point of shifting to talk about implicit bias: "The reason why it can fairly be attributed to everyone—is that it's not an accusation of guilt or bigotry," but instead "an acknowledgment of the human condition."[158] Of course, this conflation of implicit bias with bigotry may simply be an example of the tactic of objecting that one is being branded a bigot, even when there is no explicit charge of bigotry. Or perhaps it illustrates a more general problem: people bristle at any charge of bias, whether explicit or implicit, because it seems to suggest that they are bad people.

The Hidden Biases of Good or Good-ish People—and How to Fight Them

In their book *Blindspot*, Banaji and Greenwald try to avoid this problem by speaking of the hidden biases of "good people"—people who, "along with their other good traits, have no conscious race preference" and "regard themselves as egalitarian." But when the same people take the Implicit Association Test (IAT) to assess implicit bias, the results indicate an "automatic White preference" (for example, more quickly associating pleasant words with White faces than with Black faces).[159] Banaji and Greenwald consciously avoid referring to implicit bias as racism or bigotry. Thus, they differ from social psychologists who use the term "aversive racism" to capture the conflict experienced by "good people" who consciously endorse "egalitarian principles," but unconsciously harbor "negative feelings and beliefs about blacks." Today's "aversive" racist is not the "old-fashioned," "blatant" racist who "acts out bigoted beliefs [and] represents the open flame of racial hatred." Instead, John Dovidio and Samuel Gaertner argue that the conflict between egalitarian principles and those "negative feelings" is a new form of the "American dilemma."[160] They stress that these negative feelings and beliefs are "rooted in normal, often adaptive psychological processes," rather than emphasizing "the *psychopathology* of prejudice." What is striking about their framework is their hope that its emphasis on normal processes might "avoid the stigma of overt bigotry."[161]

Banaji and Greenwald, however, prefer to speak about "uncomfortable egalitarians," who experience "discomfort in interracial interactions" and discriminate by "in-group favoritism" toward their own group, rather than by actively hating or wishing ill will to out-groups.[162] As they explain, these forms of discrimination involve "no open expressions of hostility, dislike, and disrespect" taken to be characteristic of prejudice, and yet they have practical consequences (as the *Scientific American* article reported) in a wide range of contexts.[163] Banaji and Greenwald not only examine race, but also detail how automatic gender stereotypes and in-group favoritism disadvantage women.[164]

Why do we have implicit biases? Explanations range from evolutionary theories about the importance of snap judgments about in-groups and out-groups to survival, to the primacy of "feeling" before "thinking" in our "righteous minds," to thinking "fast and slow."[165] Banaji and Greenwald, for example, use the idea of "mindbugs," errors the mind makes, to capture how people use membership in social groups as a "cue" that generates an "unconscious social inference" about particular people and how to treat them.[166] Whatever the theory as to the "why," the good news, most scientists suggest, is that it is possible to *do* something about these biases. Consider a fruitful analogy to an earlier generation's urgent quest to remedy the problem of prejudice. Allport stressed the role of conscience, insight, and shame as paths to "emancipation" from prejudice and bigotry. Banaji and Greenwald focus on insight in the form of cognitive dissonance and discomfort when a person confronts the gap between egalitarian ideals and evidence that one's implicit biases may be shaping one's behavior. A vivid example is the "creepy, dispiriting, devastating moment" that biracial writer Malcolm Gladwell experienced when his Race IAT test result revealed a "moderate preference for White people."[167]

By analogy to the role Myrdal and Allport envisioned for the troubled conscience closing the gap between American ideals and unjust practices, the IAT results confront the test-taker with the gap between egalitarian ideals and automatic mental processes about race, sex, or sexual orientation. Banaji reported that her own "failing" IAT score—her automatic White preference—was "sharply inconsistent with the egalitarian race attitude that she holds in her own reflective mind"; this "gap" would "not have been unveiled *without the insights the test inflicted*."[168] In other words, "the IAT's role is to reveal" such "mental dissonance." But this "real discomfort" can supply the motivation to "use that knowledge to move beyond dismay and to find ways to understand hidden biases and, if desired, to neutralize them before they translate into behavior." Banaji and Greenwald express optimism about being able to do so: the "self-knowledge achieved by taking the IAT" provides "power," for the "reflective, conscious side of the brain" is "more than capable of doing the necessary work" to seek change.[169]

One criticism of this focus on self-knowledge as the path to change is that its centering on the individual suggests what Jonathan Kahn calls a kind of "DIY Antiracism: 10 Ways You Can Fight Implicit Bias from the Comfort of Your Own Home!" This focus on self-work, he argues, may fail to address broader issues of structural or institutional racism. He contrasts this DIY de-biasing with efforts of civil rights leaders, in the 1950s and 1960s, to confront structural injustice.[170] As chapter 5 will explore, such efforts used nonviolent direct action to arouse the nation's conscience.

To be fair, some experts on hidden or unconscious bias offer a broad agenda for how "good-ish" people can fight bias in their everyday lives and in the institutions around them. Social psychologist Dolly Chugh speaks of good-ish people—people who believe in equality, diversity, and inclusion, but also will sometimes make mistakes—rather than good people to move beyond a binary of good/bad, racist/nonracist and instead focus on the "hard work"

of using the insights of science to act in a "bias-packed world."[171] One important method for addressing implicit bias is familiar from Allport's time: social
contact. Changing our daily experiences is one way to alter impressions and
associations that happen (as Gladwell puts it) in "the blink of an eye" and contribute to prejudice and discrimination. Gladwell writes that for whites to have
"as positive associations with blacks" as they have with whites requires "more
than a simple commitment to equality." It requires changing one's life to encounter minorities on a regular basis, so that "when you want to meet, hire,
date, or talk with a member of a minority, you aren't betrayed by your hesitation
and discomfort."[172] This prescription might have been written in Allport's time.
The *Scientific American* article also concludes with social contact as one way to
"thwart biased attitudes."[173]

An important factor in the rapid increase in public acceptance of gays and
lesbians and of same-sex marriage is personal contact. An "overwhelming
number of Americans (87%) say they know someone who is gay or lesbian,"
a dramatic increase from just twenty years ago.[174] By comparison, even though
the United States is "more diverse than ever," it remains racially segregated in
neighborhoods, schools, and other areas of daily life, which limits opportunities
for social contact.[175] Other forms of geographical sorting, such as by political
ideology, limit social contact and contribute to growing mistrust and contempt
across lines of political party. Indeed, some diagnose interparty prejudice as the
most pervasive present-day form of bigotry.[176]

Conclusion

This account of two stages in the scientific study of prejudice suggests several
answers to puzzles about bigotry. First, in classic studies of prejudice, bigotry
sometimes was just a synonym for prejudice, as when Allport talked about the
role of religion in making and unmaking bigotry and prejudice. At other times,
scientists referred to the bigot as a distinct personality type who is stuck in
their prejudices. Allport's own work reflects this tension, even as he stressed
(in words that may resonate today) the urgency of educating for democracy
to avoid succumbing to demogogery and bigotry. Second, more recent scientific study of prejudice distinguishes old-fashioned, overt bigotry from the
more common form of prejudice today—unconscious or hidden bias of good
or good-ish people. While calling this problem "the bigot in your brain" may
be catchy for a magazine headline, social psychologists generally avoid the
language of bigotry—and sometimes even racism—for the reasons discussed
here, including the strong moral condemnation associated with such language.
Certainly, the persistence of overt racism and an alarming rise in extremist

rhetoric and hate crimes should not be ignored. The good/bad binary, however, focuses too narrowly on bad apples with bad motives, missing that "all people hold prejudices, especially across racial lines in a society deeply divided by race."[177] A third conclusion is that an impulse linking Allport with social psychologists more than a half century later is that science helps us understand prejudice as a first step to remedying it.

Interfaith Marriage as a Protest Against Bigotry?

Debates in the 1950s and 1960s

> What is the real nature of interfaith marriages? Why are parents, relatives, friends, churches, and students of marriage so uniformly opposed to them, or at least skeptical of their chances of success? Does it mean that these people are narrow-minded and guilty of an intolerance which we Americans are taught to shun?
> —James H. S. Bossard and Eleanor Stoker Boll,
> *One Marriage, Two Faiths* (1957)

> Idealistic youngsters may be determined to do what they can to change a sorry world, and bigotry is one of its meaner aspects. What better way to protest against it than to marry a victim of prejudice?
> —Russell O. Berg, "The Minister and Mixed Marriage" (1962)

Revisiting the rhetoric of bigotry in controversies in the 1950s and 1960s over interfaith marriage helps make sense of present-day controversies. Historically, social scientists measured bigotry and prejudice by surveying people's attitudes about whether to cross lines of faith, ethnicity, and race to marry (as chapter 2 showed). Common definitions of bigotry have included religious beliefs. For example, a bigot is "obstinately and unreasonably wedded to a particular religious creed, opinion, or ritual."[1] In this chapter, I depict the debate over whether objections to interfaith marriage were due to bigotry—an intolerance at odds with the "American creed" of tolerance and equality—or whether there were legitimate, reasonable grounds for such objections. One puzzle posed in chapter 1 is relevant here: whether conscience or sincere religious belief is a defense to charges of bigotry. Some arguments against interfaith marriage appealed to threats to the conscience of those who intermarried. Participants in these debates also pondered whether people who crossed lines of faith to marry did so to protest *against* bigotry. I focus on objections to interfaith marriage, but

Who's the Bigot? Linda C. McClain, Oxford University Press (2020). © Oxford University Press. DOI: 10.1093/oso/9780190877200.001.0001

include some comparison with those to interracial marriage (taken up more fully in later chapters). Looking at these forms of intermarriage together brings out notable similarities and differences in arguments about why they were both increasing and viewed as problematic.

The debate over interfaith marriage is also instructive for present-day controversies (taken up in chapter 8) over the legal recognition of same-sex marriage and whether there should be religious exemptions from state laws requiring that business owners providing goods and services (including for weddings) not discriminate between customers. The fact that religious traditions have prohibited or strongly discouraged interfaith marriage, while civil law permits it, illustrates that civil and religious law are not identical. If people are able to accept this gap with respect to interfaith marriage, they may more readily accept it concerning same-sex marriage. If we agree that it is unreasonable for a business open to the public to deny a good or service because the owner objects to interfaith marriage, is the same true when the objection is to same-sex marriage? The chapter concludes by observing how the rhetoric of bigotry still bubbles up in today's debates over interfaith marriage in an environment in which such marriages are more common and involve more religious traditions than half a century ago.

Making Sense of Motives for Mixed Marriage

On July 24, 1960, a *New York Times* story reported that "one of the major concerns of American parents" has been the "tremendous growth" in "interfaith" marriages: "Inexperienced young people increasingly disregard the warning" by "both churchmen and marriage specialists" that "interfaith marriage is risky. . . . They feel that their love for each other can overcome all obstacles." Older people also increasingly "embark on interfaith marriage."[2] By the early 1970s, a Gallup poll reported that public "tolerance" of mixed marriage (interfaith and interracial) was steadily climbing.[3] In 1951, "54% of Americans had told Gallup that 'two young people in love who are of different religious faiths—Protestant, Catholic, or Jewish—should not marry.'"[4] Two decades later, large majorities approved of marriages between Jews and non-Jews (69%) and between Protestants and Catholics (72%). Gallup also reported an upward trend in public approval of interracial marriage (still much lower than for interfaith marriage). By 1972, 29% approved of marriage between "whites and blacks."[5]

As interfaith marriage increased, of particular concern was the mixed marriage, in which spouses from different religious traditions retained those affiliations rather than forming a household united by one faith. Why did clergy and "marriage specialists" warn against interfaith marriages? What obstacles did they believe such marriages faced? Why did young people enter such marriages despite these obstacles?

Looking back at the rhetoric of bigotry gives insight into how people understood the motives of young people for entering interfaith marriages and the motives of parents for objecting to them. Both religious leaders and secular experts asked: Did opposition to intermarriage reflect bigotry or intolerance at odds with American ideals?[6] While they urged parents to examine their motives for objecting to a child's marriage to make sure they did not stem from bigotry, they reassured parents that there were legitimate grounds to discourage such marriages. They pointed to statistics showing higher rates of unhappiness and divorce among religiously mixed couples. Seasoned marriage counselors warned that young people failed to appreciate that mixed marriages attempted to combine not just two religions, but two entirely different cultures in one household.[7] Secular and religious authorities drew on the "science" of marital compatibility to advise that "like marries like" was the best, time-tested formula for marital success.[8] Appealing to the risk of marital unhappiness and divorce allowed parents to oppose such marriages with a clear conscience, even if their own liberal principles about equality and tolerance would seem to support intermarriage.

Bigotry also was relevant to young people's motives for crossing lines of faith to marry. Reverend Berg, the marriage counselor quoted at the beginning of the chapter, suggested that "to protest against bigotry" might be one motive.[9] On this view, intermarriage reflected an embrace of important American values about equality and "brotherhood" and a conviction that differences did not—or should not—matter. It was a path to achieve greater tolerance and to fight prejudice and discrimination. Opponents of intermarriage argued that it was not a sound path to "universal brotherhood," but a rejection of an important group identity and a proper pride in one's group and its perpetuation.[10]

Mixed marriage, experts counseled, also posed threats to religious conscience. In the 1950s, before Vatican II (an important reform council initiated by Pope John XXIII), official statements by Protestant denominations warned against marrying Roman Catholics because of the premarital promises required for the mixed marriage to be valid. Clergy cautioned that Protestants in such a marriage would be at risk of violating duties of conscience concerning their own faith and their responsibility for the religious education of their children. Protestant denominations complained of the "intolerance" and authoritarianism of the Catholic Church and cautioned their members not to enter into agreements that would violate conscience and religious liberty.

This chapter's analysis of the interfaith marriage debate uses certain ideas introduced in chapter 2, such as social distance and the intergroup contact hypothesis. In the post–World War II era, Protestants, Catholics, and Jews were

separated not only "by differences in ethnic background, tradition, and socioeconomic standing," but also "by suspicion, prejudice, and a lack of social
contact."[11] There were strong social controls against interfaith as well as interracial marriage, and there were also legal controls against interracial marriage in
many states in the 1950s and in a minority until 1967 (when *Loving v. Virginia*
invalidated the remaining laws).[12]

Many secular and religious commentators attributed the increase in intermarriage to more "intergroup contact" on terms of "social equality." As young people
of different faiths, races, and ethnicities met in college or the workplace, this
proximity increased the possibility of intermarriage. As new laws and changing
social practices put limits on discrimination on the basis of race, national origin,
and religion in various settings, one result was increased opportunities for young
people to meet and intermarry.[13] How people talked about mixed marriage
reveals competing views concerning pluralism.

I begin with two case studies by a 1950s marriage counselor concerning an
interracial and an interfaith marriage problem. I highlight two influential books
from the 1950s to show how prominent Protestant leaders and secular marriage
experts assessed the rise in interfaith marriages and the perils such marriages
posed. Such texts debated whether there were bases other than bigotry and intolerance for opposing such marriages. I compare Jewish debates about interfaith marriage, focusing on concerns similar to but distinct from those over
inter-Christian mixed marriages. The chapter concludes with recent analyses
of interfaith marriage that consider whether the increase in such marriages is
a useful measure of a decline in prejudice and a rise of a more religiously integrated society.

Two Case Studies on Interracial and Interfaith Marriage Problems

In 1951 and 1952 Dr. Maurice J. Karpf, a marriage counselor practicing in
Beverly Hills, California, published case studies presenting "three aspects of
inter-marriage: an inter-racial problem (Negro-white); an inter-faith problem
(Catholic-Jewish); and an intercultural problem (different social and economic
backgrounds)."[14] The first two problems reveal common and distinctive themes
about (1) why young people desired such marriages; (2) why parents opposed
them; and (3) how the marriage counselor viewed young people as naive in
thinking difference did not matter. These cases illustrate a theme prevalent in
marriage counseling at that time: marital happiness had dimensions of personal satisfaction along with communal obligations, which sometimes were in
tension.[15]

Karpf's First Case: An Interracial Problem

The case of an "interracial problem" came to Dr. Karpf "through the girl's father, Mr. X, a lawyer of broad, liberal views on social and economic questions,
interested in good race relations, and active in several organizations promoting
them," including the NAACP and the Urban League. The father had successfully
transmitted his values to his daughter, Z, a college senior with a "fine social conscience" who "oppos[ed] discrimination" and showed "considerable interest in
minority groups." She "mingled freely with white and colored classmates of both
sexes, and brought them home with the encouragement of her father . . . until
she announced that she was in love with a colored boy, a first year graduate student in chemistry, and intended to marry him." This problem, Karpf observes,
has disturbed a "happy and tranquil" family. The mother, who "foresaw trouble"
when the daughter "associated" with African American boys and girls, blames
the father and "insists that if this marriage goes through she will not be able to
face her friends and relatives." The father fears the marriage may "cause his wife's
nervous collapse or a rupture in their own marriage."[16]

Despite their shared liberal values, father and daughter disagree about why
he objects to the marriage. The father tells Karpf "he had no objection to racial
intermarriage on principle," except that "he does not believe that [Z] will be
happy, as society is not so constituted at the present as to make it possible for
such a couple to be happy." The father is "deeply hurt" that Z now believes he
was "insincere" in his "activities in favor of racial understanding and good will."
"Like all good conservatives," she contends, "he draws the line at intermarriage."
He believes that Z's relationship has become a "cause" for her and doubts the
"depths" of her love for her intended.[17]

Karpf reports on his several interviews with Z. At first, Z, "attractive, high
spirited, intelligent and somewhat impulsive," was "aggressively hostile" because
she anticipated efforts to talk her out of the marriage. Karpf tells her that he
shares neither her father's fears nor her mother's conviction that the marriage
would "wreck her life." He had "known several intermarriages which turned out
quite happy." In subsequent interviews, they focus on a "different problem": the
impact of her plans on her family. They explore whether Z has a "right to her own
happiness" and "whether her parents had a right to deny it to her by interfering
with her intended marriage." She answers the first question in the affirmative,
but isn't certain she could pursue her happiness at her parents' expense. In the
past, she admits, their concerns were usually rooted in her "best interests" and
they were "usually right." However, she questioned their objectivity in this case,
because they saw only "difficulties for her" and "heartbreak for themselves."[18]

Karpf steers Z toward considering "the problems . . . involved in intermarriage
in general and this type of intermarriage in particular," suggesting she "read up

on the subject." After doing so, Z realizes that "this type of intermarriage is much more serious in its implications and consequences" than other marriages. She "had not realized before that she would be practically limited to living in a colored area [and] would virtually have to give up her white friends and associates, or . . . be prepared to face a life in which she would always imagine herself being pitied or considered peculiar." She expresses concern about the impact of the marriage on her intended and about "the color of the children born in the marriage." Would she be able to deal with the prejudice? While she still resented society "for imposing restrictions and handicaps upon people simply because of the color of their skin," Z now "wondered whether the best way of fighting this discrimination was by flying in the face of society or whether she could accomplish more by fighting discrimination without being charged with having an axe to grind."[19]

Z now has "more objectivity," viewing her intended spouse as a "person in his own right" rather than an "embodiment or personification of his unfairly persecuted race." And yet her intended never appears as a person in his own right in this case study. Karpf opts not to include him in the discussion because he questions her intended's degree of emotional involvement and motive ("marrying a white girl of good family with all its implications").[20] When Z expresses the wish to be able to "look into the future and see what it holds," Karpf proposes to let her see what "life in a Negro environment . . . would be like." After graduation, she will find living quarters in Harlem while preparing to enter graduate study at Columbia University and try to "live as normal a life as the circumstances would permit." Her boyfriend tries to "dissuade her," but his fears that the experiment will end their relationship "strengthen her resolve" to go through with it. Z does move, and the experiment's outcome, as her boyfriend "expected," is that Z found that "she just did not have the courage" or "pioneering spirit which such a marriage required."[21]

Karpf summarily attributes Z's seeking an "alliance with a Negro" to a "neurotic element" in her makeup.[22] (In the 1950s and 1960s, some writings about black–white marriage theorized that people entered into them due to neurotic motives and "psychological sickness of various sorts."[23]) In explaining his handling of the case, Karpf reiterates that he has "no prejudice against interracial marriages," but only requires that "social and psychological factors" be in place to make a "happy and successful marriage."[24] He ponders whether extensive analysis and therapy could have directly addressed Z's "neurotic trend," or whether it was better to "treat" the situation on the conscious level, as he did. The postscript is that Z obtained her doctoral degree, teaches in a junior college, has married (the reader infers, a white man), and is combining teaching and motherhood "without any neurotic trait having manifested thus far."[25] She has, in other words, made a successful "marital adjustment."[26]

The happy ending—of what one commentator on Karpf's case study describes as an "outstanding example of helping an engaged girl to help herself' "—is that a young white woman does not enter an interracial marriage.[27] No doubt the reading that Karpf provided her about intermarriage stressed the challenges that couples face in making a successful adjustment when like does not marry like. By the early 1950s, the axiom that like should marry like was a "shorthand way for marriage counselors and clergy" to advise that "too many differences in family background, education, or religion would cause problems for a couple."[28]

Based on her reading about intermarriage and her experience in Harlem, Z realized that she lacked the courage to endure the racial prejudice and loss of status and white privilege that an interracial marriage—in 1951—would bring.[29] Historian Rene Romano confirms these likely consequences: "Contrary to the traditional understanding of interracial marriage as an avenue for assimilation for the minority partner, in many black–white marriages in the forties and fifties, it was the white partner who assimilated into the black community." Karpf speculated that the motive of Z's boyfriend was social mobility, but while white male–black female couples were sometimes able to "live quietly in white neighborhoods," because "the race of the 'head' of the family helped determine the acceptability of couples among whites," that partial acceptance would not extend to a black male–white female couple like Z and her intended.[30]

Karpf's Second Case: An Interfaith Problem

Dr. Karpf's companion case, an "interfaith problem," shows a family sharply divided over assimilation and Jewish identity in America.[31] A, "a Jewish girl" of twenty-two, intended to marry "B, a Catholic young man of Italian parentage" and a fellow graduate student in A's department. A's father, "shocked beyond words" by her plans, pleads for Karpf's help. In a description that seems to echo stereotypes about Jews (though Karpf himself was Jewish), Karpf says that A's father is "a wealthy manufacturer," "the president of his synagogue, of middle class attitudes and convictions, self-made, inordinately proud of his status in his community and ready to pay any price within reason to maintain and raise it."[32]

A's father has concerns that B will be unable to support A "in the manner and style to which she was accustomed." B's parents have a "fruit market," are of "very modest means," and have "a very large family." The father's "principal worry," however, is that B is "non-Jewish" and A will face problems "in making a happy life for herself with a non-Jew." The marriage's impact on "his own status in the community" also concerns the father, leading him to broach with his daughter whether B would convert to Judaism. Unlike Z's mother, A's mother is unwilling to "stand in her daughter's way," even though she "would have preferred a Jewish boy."[33]

In the past, A condemned her younger brother, who "insist[s] that religion, religious practices, prescriptions and differences are of the past and have little place in American life," for "his indifference to the cause of Zionism." A had previously embraced Zionism, arguing that establishing a "Jewish State in Palestine" was the "only hope for a solution of the Jewish Problem in Nazi Germany and Fascist Italy" and that "it was one's duty to be concerned about one's people." Now, A is "lukewarm or indifferent to Jewish nationalism" and "convinced that the best interests of American democracy lie in the direction of a social and biological intermingling of the peoples and cultures making up the American people."[34]

When A meets with Karpf, she doesn't explicitly call her father a bigot, but describes his objections as "due to prejudice and outworn racial and nationalistic pride which had no place in 20th Century America." When Karpf asks how she reconciles her prior criticism of her brother with her present view on intermarriage, she answers that she and her fiancé have concluded, after many discussions, that "there isn't much sense in maintaining Jewish separatism, especially on a nationalistic basis, for American Jews." Further, "since neither she nor her fiancé is very religiously inclined their religious differences would have little influence on their happiness together."[35] As the counseling continues and events unfold, readers learn that A's view is naive.

Karpf asks A if she has "given any thought" to "the problems that may arise from religious and cultural differences" in religious intermarriage and to the "prospects" for marital success and happiness "under such circumstances." A has not, and initially takes marital happiness "for granted where the marriage partners loved each other and were free from religious observances." She becomes "confused and uneasy," however, after reading up on "cultural and religious factors in marriage."[36] Such reading likely stressed the formula of like marries like for marital adjustment and success and cautioned about the higher divorce rate when partners differed in religion.

Karpf also presses A to learn B's "position on religious matters" and how B's announced intention to conform to his parents' "sensibilities" will affect A, as a Jew marrying a Catholic. B has not yet seen his priest "because of his awareness of the seriousness with which the Church looked upon such deviation." After educating herself about the requirements of the Catholic Church with respect to mixed marriage, she learned that her options were to (1) "accept Catholicism"; (2) "give a binding pledge to rear her children in a religious belief which was not hers"; or (3) "abandon the idea of marrying a Catholic who was loyal to his parents or Church or both." Initially "outraged" by B's lack of "frankness or courage," she confronts him and learns that he will "have to abide" by the

Church's requirements "for the sake of his family and his future" academic ca-
reer (with which the Church may help). She breaks off the engagement after
he claims that "she misled him by misrepresenting her true feelings about her
religion" and tells her that once she understood Catholicism, she would "find it
so much superior to Judaism" that she would gladly "embrace it," removing "the
only obstacle to their happiness." In A's words, while she "was willing to abandon
her religion for a broader humanism," she would never do so for Catholicism, "an
even more restricted" and "limited" religion than Judaism. Nor could she bring
her children up in a faith "that would alienate them from her."[37]

A is "quite bitter" about her experience, but comes to see that she had
been "immature in her attitudes toward her father, her religion, her previous
convictions, [and] her fiancé." A "has since married a young man of her own faith
who entered her father's manufacturing establishment, and from all accounts
she is very happy."[38] As with Z, Karpf detects a "neurotic tendency," manifest in
her "seeking a liaison with someone outside her own faith."[39]

It bears noting that both Z and A met their intended spouses in college, a place
allowing for social contact between diverse people on terms of equality—one
factor associated with intermarriage. Another factor was a belief, among college
students, in universalism and that religious and other barriers separating people
must be broken down to end prejudice and bigotry.[40] Z may have viewed her
marriage as consistent with her commitment to fighting discrimination, but had
not realized how such discrimination would affect her personally. A's marriage
plans ended with the rude awakening that her fiancé did not share the universalism they had professed, or at least that he was not free to act on the premise
that religious differences do not matter.

Pastoral Counseling: Protesting Bigotry as a
Motive for Mixed Marriage

Clergy also counseled young people and their parents about contemplated interfaith marriages. One brief blueprint for such counseling, *The Minister and
Mixed Marriage*, illustrates how concerns about bigotry might arise in assessing
both parental motives for objecting to interfaith marriages and the motives of
young people for entering them. The author, Russell Berg (quoted at the beginning of this chapter), explains: "To determine what ministers can do about
all this, we must first understand why so many youngsters marry outside their
own faith." He notes several structural factors, such as assimilation, increasing
interfaith contacts, and lessening anti-Catholicism and anti-Semitism. He also
discusses "classes of motives." One class concerns "getting away from something,"

including marrying "to protest against bigotry": "idealistic youngsters" determined to change "a sorry world" might do so by marrying a "victim of prejudice." Or, a person who belongs to a group that is "looked down upon" (e.g, "Italians, Mexicans, Puerto Ricans, or Jews") might marry to "escape" that culture or religion and join an "accepted' group." Berg comments that many of those motives "intertwine . . . social, national, cultural, and religious factors" and are "not valid, healthy excuses for crossing lines between faiths to marry."[41] By comparison, "love" is the "healthiest motive" for an interfaith marriage. If a couple is made aware of the "difficulties in a mixed marriage," but is deeply enough in love to face such difficulties, this "may lead to a union as happy as any other."[42] (To make the couple aware of such difficulties, the minister—like Karpf—urges "any youngster" considering mixed marriage to "read everything he can find on the subject."[43])

Berg also urges ministers to probe parents' motives for opposing their children's marriage plans, which may include valid ones, such as "genuine concern for the youngster's happiness," as well as invalid ones, such as *"mere prejudice."* Berg advises: "If this [prejudice] is the parents' motive, the adolescent will sense that it is weak, which strengthens his side of the case." Hence, "in counseling with the teen-ager" seeking to marry, "the minister may suggest that the parents just might be right—if their motives are based on knowledge rather than bigotry."[44]

Problems of Prejudice and Conscience in Interfaith Marriage

What type of knowledge might a parent or clergy invoke in opposing a young person's interfaith marriage to make sure that their opposition did not rest on mere prejudice and bigotry? To understand the case that religious leaders and social scientists made against such marriages, I look at two well-received books offering guidance: *One Marriage, Two Faiths: Guidance on Interfaith Marriage* (1957), by sociologists and counselors James H. S. Bossard and Eleanor Stoker Boll, and *If You Marry Outside Your Faith: Counsel on Mixed Marriages* (1954), by James A. Pike, Episcopalian priest (and later Bishop).[45] As Bossard and Boll frame the issue: "Why are parents, relatives, friends, churches, and students of marriage so uniformly opposed to [interfaith marriages], or at least skeptical of their chances of success? Does it mean that these people are narrow-minded and guilty of an intolerance which we Americans are taught to shun?"[46] The authors answer that final question with a general "no," while admitting traces of bigotry in particular instances. The authors enlist religious teaching and social science to argue that this uniform opposition rests on concerns over marital happiness, religious conscience, and child well-being.

Increasing Social Contact, Increased Intermarriage

In *If You Marry Outside Your Faith*, Pike observes that "fifty years ago it would not have been particularly important that any such book as this be written," since there were "few mixed marriages," but "now the mixed marriage is one of the most common phenomena of our time."[47] Similarly, Bossard and Boll observe the "striking" extent to which "our young people, and older ones too, are constantly crossing economic, social, and religious lines in their marriages," such that "we have come to accept this as part of the American creed of tolerance and social opportunity."[48]

The problem of interfaith marriage, both books explain, grows out of dynamics of immigration, assimilation, and the "working of the melting pot."[49] At the turn of the twentieth century, Roman Catholic immigrant groups were "marked off from their neighbors in terms of means, education, economic opportunity and cultural advantage," and "the Jews in America by and large were still in a religious and cultural ghetto," while people of "Anglo-Saxon Stock," earlier arrivals in the United States, enjoyed better opportunities for education, leisure, and culture. Social contact outside of one's group was low; people might find "Cinderella stories" entertaining, but were "personally upset" when such scenes were acted out "in their own families."[50]

By the early 1950s, however, the opportunity for social contact was much higher: second and third generation families enjoy "widespread economic and educational opportunities," "Jews graduate from Harvard," "Roman Catholics belong to the best clubs," and suburbia hosts people "of all backgrounds and religions."[51] Groups may mingle freely in "many aspects of life," contributing to "the common heritage," while religious and other freedoms allow "each group . . . to retain and exercise its own ways and values." As "young people of all elements" meet in "school, play, work, and national service," and see their commonalities, they "tend to marry without reference to the less obvious intangible differences between them," particularly "traditional religious faith."[52]

Young people, Bossard and Boll argue, apply the "American creed of personal rights and individual development" to the realm of marriage, particularly as increased mobility disrupts the "solidarity" and influence of the extended family. Rather than seeking the counsel of family or of "pastor, priest, and rabbi," young people assert "the sole right to choose" to marry whom they please. Told that "this is the secular age in marriage and family life," they reject "the old, the traditional, the tried, the true, the time honored."[53] Despite opposition to interfaith marriage, rooted in accumulated wisdom, experience, and scientific views, Pike observes, youth insist: "Love will find a way!"[54]

Why Are Interfaith Marriages a Problem? Broken Homes and Cultural Differences

The "clear fact," Bossard and Boll argue, is that interfaith marriages "present personal and family difficulties of varying kinds and degrees" that cannot be "waved away by the magic wand of wish."[55] Opposition is not simply intolerance at odds with the American creed. One problem concerns the greater risk of separation and divorce. Pike discusses the 1938 "Maryland study," which found that a higher percentage of children in mixed marriages were in "broken homes"—homes affected by divorce, desertion, or separation—than in homes with "religious homogeneity."[56] He cites one particular chart, which had long "provided American rabbis and ministers with a means of illustrating the dangers of marrying outside the faith."[57] The chart indicates the percentage of broken homes based on parents' religious affiliation, showing that where both parents were Protestants, 6.8% of the parents were separated and, where both were Roman Catholic, 6.4%. By comparison, 15.2% of mixed marriages "represent broken homes." Pike comments: "This differential of 2¼ to 1 as to the chance of success is not an unimportant consideration!"[58]

Both books assert that mixed marriages are problem marriages from a social science perspective. The influential framework of marital adjustment explained why. The difference in interfaith marriage is not simply that of "two people who have been in the habit of going to, or professing allegiance" to, different churches. Rather, Bossard and Boll assert, "it is a union of two different cultures."[59] A religion is a culture—"a way of doing and . . . thinking." Culture, social scientists teach, "penetrat[es] into every phase of our lives," including "intimate aspects . . . that are fundamental in the marital relationship" and child rearing. Because marriage itself is "the most . . . pervasive relationship in life," in mixed marriages, marital partners have to make adjustments that "reach out into every aspect of life." Bossard and Boll offer numerous illustrations of the challenges of "cultural union and adjustment," ranging from the role of religious codes in sexual behavior to different norms about drinking and permissible recreation, to family meals. Whether or not cultural differences lead to separation or divorce, they will be grist for tension, conflict, and unhappiness.[60] In *The Minister and Mixed Marriage*, Berg echoes that prediction: because religion "may determine one's attitudes on almost anything from A to Z—from Alcohol (which devout Methodists don't use) to Zola (whose books obedient Catholics don't read)," a "different-faith couple may discover they live in a whole orchard full of apples of discord."[61]

Based on "experience," Bossard and Boll conclude, "all of our major religions have come to see the frequent dangers to family unity and stability resulting from interfaith marriages" and to advise that religious unity contributes to marital success. The authors quote a 1956 Methodist Church statement drawing on social science about like marrying like: "Recent research has emphasized the importance of common cultural and religious backgrounds as the foundation for successful marriage."[62] Bossard and Boll counter the "lay reaction" that we should be guided by science by observing: "Scientists may oppose mixed marriages as much, or even more, than do the churchmen."[63]

Threats to the Family's Role in Cultural Transmission and Group Preservation

Religious groups also oppose intermarriage, Bossard and Boll explain, because of its impact on the family's core role in preserving and perpetuating a religion. This objection highlights both the home as a place of religious observance and the role of parents in social reproduction, including transmitting religious values. "Most religions," they explain, "look upon marriage and the family" as the "ideal" unit in which "the living of a good life as prescribed by the church can best develop and flourish." Rearing children is the "basis of church maintenance and growth," and "related in many ways to the values stressed by religious teaching." Many children born to mixed marriages, however, are "sure to be lost to the church of one of the parties" and often to those of both.[64]

In emphasizing the importance that religious groups place on passing religion along to the newer generation, Bossard and Boll presuppose that a group's pride about its "cultural heritage" is appropriate, rather than intolerant or bigoted. They observe that "every group desires to extend itself into the future by bearing [children]" and "rear[ing] those children in the ways of doing and thinking of the particular group." They analogize from national to religious identity: people "who are proud to be Americans" would not send their children to Great Britain or Russia "to be reared," because they "want their children to . . . act and think like Americans." So, too:

> Any group with pride in itself, that thinks its way of life is right, feels this way. It wants to pass its culture and heritage down to its children so that it will survive and so that the children will have the best possible heritage.[65]

But "a family in which parents are of different faiths cannot easily fulfil the function of cultural transmission."[66]

Threats to (Protestant) Conscience in a Protestant-Catholic Mixed Marriage

Another objection to mixed marriage that the authors treat as legitimate is that such marriages pose threats to the conscience of marital partners of different faiths and of any children. Pike asserts that children, "even unborn . . . are entitled to be protected against a divisive spiritual atmosphere." A "unity of conviction in the household enables a child to grow in grace on the basis of his respect and love for his parents." Protecting children from "spiritual injury is not easy in a mixed marriage."[67] Bossard and Boll explicitly reject the argument that a "unified cultural training" will lead to "narrow-mindedness and bigotry in social relationships," explaining the injury to conscience from a *lack* of such unity.[68]

Addressing the question whether a child "kept in a circle of Catholic social relationship" will be "intolerant" of "the attitudes and behavior of non-Catholics," Bossard and Boll counter that such a child "may seem narrow to those of another way," but suffers no inner conflict: he "is certain and sure," has "no decisions to make, and no pangs of conscience if he follows 'the straight and narrow path.' "[69] By comparison, there is "no such certainty" for the child whose parents "represent two ways of life," argue about "the right way of living," and "attempt to pull him back and forth"—"no matter which way he goes, a haunting pang of conscience follows him for deserting the other way." The authors continue: "Conflict and guilt feelings are the essence of the neurotic personality," and "like the bigoted person, the neurotic is not always successful in his social relationships." The implication is that a unified religious home avoids these problematic personality types.[70]

As an adult, the child of the mixed marriage also has to sort out which tradition (if either) to pass on to their own child.[71] Pike emphasizes perils for the conscience of non-Roman Catholics who marry Roman Catholics. At the time, a Catholic seeking to marry a non-Catholic had to receive a "dispensation." For a mixed marriage between a Catholic and non-Catholic to be "valid" and performed by a priest, the non-Catholic spouse had to promise in an antenuptial agreement: (1) that he or she will "not in any way hinder or obstruct" the Roman Catholic spouse "in the exercise" of his or her religion; (2) that "all children of either sex born of [the] marriage shall be baptized and educated in the Catholic faith and according to the teachings of the Catholic Church"; and (3) that the non-Catholic will marry "only according to the marriage rite of the Catholic Church." In some dioceses, an additional promise was that contraceptive devices would not be used contrary to the teachings of the Catholic Church. Furthermore, the Roman Catholic party to the agreement must promise "to do all in his power by word and example, to bring about the conversion of the non-Roman party."[72]

A non-Catholic who signed such an agreement risked conscience in several ways, Pike argues. First, while the Roman Catholic position on birth control forbids all methods other than the "rhythm method" or abstinence, some Protestant "ethics of birth control" emphasize the role of "conscientious" decision by the couple about whether to have a child "at this point in their married life."[73] The non-Catholic may be agreeing to abide by "an ethical outlook" in "direct conflict" with his or her own. If, instead, the non-Catholic agrees, but the parties secretly plan not to honor the agreement, the Catholic will be committing a mortal sin, under Catholic teachings, and this may strain his or her faith.[74]

A second threat to conscience concerns religious education of any children. For example, Pike asks, "if [a devout] Lutheran is convinced that Lutheranism is right and Catholicism wrong, how can he conscientiously sign an agreement permitting his children to be reared in what he considers a false and erroneous creed?"[75] To agree would be a "sin."[76] Pike cites "official statements" by various Protestant denominations proclaiming that "the religious education and spiritual training of their children . . . is a paramount duty of parents and should never be neglected nor left entirely to others."[77]

The rhetoric of these Protestant statements is vivid. They describe the Catholic premarital agreement as reflecting discrimination, intolerance, and authoritarianism, threatening the non-Catholic spouse's civil and religious rights. A 1950 resolution by the American Baptist Convention "repudiate[s] the Roman Catholic claim to authoritarianism in marriage and declare[s] it an invasion of the principles of religious and social freedom." It urges Baptist pastors to inform young people of "the menace to their freedom" of this "imposed authoritarianism" and the "dictated rules regarding the raising of offspring of mixed marriages in the Roman Catholic Church" and about "their civil and religious rights under our Baptist standards of religious liberty."[78] Even more emphatic is a 1953 resolution by the Lutheran Church-Missouri Synod: the contract required by the Roman Catholic Church "involves a sinful promise or oath; violates the Christian conscience; condemns unborn children to the soul-destroying religion of the Antichrist; and is diametrically opposed to the eternal truths of God."[79] Protestant denominations also asserted that the "young Protestant" agrees to terms that "threaten conscience" and the "peace and stability of the home" in a context in which they act under the "emotional compulsion of romantic love."[80]

Pike aims to dispel "prejudice," ignorance, and confusion about the Catholic position on mixed marriage, such as believing that the agreement is "un-American" and denies the non-Catholic's "religious freedom."[81] Even so, he uses the provocative term "'Jim Crow' situation" to describe the circumstance when one party to the marriage is Roman Catholic and the other party "has complied with the demands of the Roman Catholic Church about the 'promises.'" He elaborates: the fact that the non-Catholic spouse was willing to consent to raising the children as Roman Catholic may be interpreted by the Catholic spouse and any children to mean that the non-Catholic spouse did not regard his religious heritage as "worth preserving for his children," which may lead to "contempt" toward that heritage as a "'second-rate' religion." The non-Catholic spouse may counter this "sense of superiority" by the Catholic spouse with "distrust" of the Catholic Church and contempt for its religious practices.[82]

One Catholic reviewer praised Pike's book for making a "solid contribution to the dispelling of ignorance on the Catholic position" and thus help "to prevent mixed marriages" and the "notion that the non-Catholic suitor or sweetheart is trapped by last-minute revelations of what the ante-nuptial promises really mean." But the reviewer regretted that passages about Jim Crow had "sowed some more seeds of misunderstanding" and, thus, may have "helped to develop new prejudices or buttress existing ones."[83]

Bigotry and Prejudice in Attitudes Toward Interfaith Marriage

Not all objections to interfaith marriage were benign or framed as resting on science about marital happiness. The Catholic reviewer's concerns illustrate the place of prejudice in objections to interfaith marriage. In the post–World War II period, there were "tensions between Protestants and Catholics, Christians and Jews, and among members of different denominations." In "popular Protestant discussions," Catholics were "blind followers of a totalitarian system, apparently not unlike the Nazi or Soviet regimes." Protestants thought the Catholic laity "rejected all churches but their own as false religions." By comparison, Protestants conceived themselves as "thoughtful, conscientious practitioners of democratic government." In turn, some Catholics denounced Protestants as bigoted toward Catholicism.[84] Some Catholic leaders proclaimed the Catholic Church "the greatest democracy on earth."[85]

Protestants cultivated Jews as "important allies" in "the drive against Catholic hegemony," but popular "misgivings about Jews and instances of overt anti-Semitism were never far from the surface." Religious leaders "tended to take for granted" that anti-Semitism was engrained in "American culture" and "was likely to persist until Jews themselves became more like non-Jews."[86]

Such prejudices likely deterred interfaith marriages and shaped objections to those that did occur. Writing in 1954, Pike cautions that while the "present generation" is "more likely to discount prejudice than their elders," it is important not to dismiss the role it may play and its effects on the happiness of marriages. The "religious problem" with interfaith marriage may be solved satisfactorily, but the "sociological issues" may remain. As an example, Pike reports that the mother of Josephine, a Congregationalist, commented about Josephine's proposed husband, Nathan, a Jew who currently practices no religion and is considering conversion: "But he wouldn't be welcome at the country club with us!" Pike observes that economic, social, and cultural differences still existed between groups, notwithstanding assimilation, and that "the operation of prejudice of this type is too widely known—and experienced—to labor the discussion." (By comparison, society's use of the general, "undiscriminating" term "Protestant" relieves "the social barriers and ease[s] the prejudices" entering into "reactions of relatives and friends" to a marriage between persons of different Protestant denominations.)[87]

As with objections to interracial marriage (discussed in Karpf's first case), otherwise liberal-minded parents may couch objections to interfaith marriage in generalities that do not admit the role of bias and prejudice. Pike describes "Mrs. Teale," who, as trustee of her college, "had fought vigorously for the removal of all racial and religious barriers in the admission policy" and "elimination of restrictions in the college's social clubs." Her daughter was surprised "to find her mother nevertheless shocked when she announced her attachment to a Jewish student." The mother "took refuge in generalities such as 'I don't think it is wise,' and 'I don't think it would work out.'"[88] Prejudice also features in reactions from an interfaith couple's social circle. Their "friends and business associates," Pike mentions, often "became quite 'cool,'" impairing "future ties" and memberships in clubs and resorts.[89] Bossard and Boll also detail the loss of friendships when a couple who married thinking "religion is not too important because both are 'tolerant' individuals" finds that "not everyone has the same attitude." "Some [friends] may have to be counted off" as not "true friends," but as bigoted. Some couples, including "many interracial unions," choose a strategy of "relative social isolation" to insulate "their home life against . . . hurts and invidious comparisons."[90]

Should an interfaith couple give credence to these social objections and prejudices? It depends, Pike argues. If they have not solved the "religion problem," then "these other factors will loom much larger in their destructive effect upon the peace and fruitfulness of their relationships." But if they have a "positive and mutually held religious faith as a basis of their new union," that "centripetal force" should "hold things together in spite of the centrifugal forces represented by family opposition and social restriction." Indeed, if they have this solution and "are in love, it would be unworthy of them to rate these factors so high as to be a barrier to the marriage."[91]

What's the Best Solution to the Interfaith Marriage Problem?

Pike argues that there is only one satisfactory solution for "two sincere people of different religious backgrounds" who "respect" the "integrity of each other's religious convictions" but "recognize the impasse which a mixed marriage would involve." Each must endeavor to learn about the other's faith tradition and any other faith tradition which they might jointly adopt. If they can come to the "same Church allegiance," this solves the problem of a mixed marriage.[92]

Bossard and Boll are less prescriptive, offering an inventory of "solutions that have worked." These forms of marital adjustment range from one partner accepting the other's faith, to each maintaining their faith but reaching agreements about how to rear children, to a religious neutrality. The first approach works well if the partner who makes the change does not strongly identify with his or her religion and may be eager to escape it. Agreements to maintain two religious affiliations but to rear the children in one may result in a stable, happy marriage, though they may lead to the person with the "losing" religion regretting the decision or secretly exposing the children to it. Compromise solutions tend to work well, the authors find, with highly educated couples.[93] The "path" to whatever happiness is possible in mixed marriage, they conclude, must be through "understanding, tolerance, compromise, and mutual respect."[94]

Relieving Burdens of Conscience and Exploring Ecumenical Unity

After the Second Vatican Council (1962–1965), the Catholic Church developed a revised approach to mixed marriage, culminating in Pope Paul VI's apostolic letter, *Matrimonia Mixta*, announced in 1970.[95] The non-Catholic would no longer be required to make promises regarding the rearing of children, but would be "made aware" of the Catholic party's "promise to do all he or she can to have the offspring baptized and educated in the Catholic faith."[96] One impetus for this change seemed to be recognition of the "intolerable burden" on conscience that the required promises presented for non-Catholics.[97] The new position reflected both the Vatican's emphasis on "human conscience" in religious freedom and the "ecumenical movement," which expressed a "new spirit of brotherhood and friendship" and sought a "restoration of unity" among all Christians. Another reason was recognition that many couples resolved the burden on conscience by dispensing with religious marriage, resulting in an "ever-increasing number of mixed marriages contracted in a way considered not valid from the point of view of the Catholic doctrine."[98] This new approach, commentators argue, shows respect for "each person's conscience," but "real hardships" often remain "when a Catholic and a non-Catholic partner" who each have strong religious beliefs cannot reach agreement on "religious matters."[99]

Could mixed marriages be harbingers of greater Christian unity? A 1967 news article reported on the "180-degree change of attitude" toward mixed marriage expressed at an "ecumenical meeting between Roman Catholic and Presbyterian-Reformed churchmen," evident in the cochair's statement: "If two people of different faiths can live together in deep love and understanding, then we have something pointing to the great church of the future."[100] The story observes that "few" Protestant-Roman Catholic couples "who have lived happily through the years despite the arguments of their churches, clergy and lay friends *that they were 'outside the pale'*" had "dreamed that they might end up considered as key bridges to the eventual reunion of the Christian Church."[101] (This bridge to Christian reunion would not, one infers, extend to Christian–Jewish intermarriage.)

Matrimonia Mixta takes a more skeptical view: "Precisely because they admit differences of religion and are a consequence of the division among Christians, [mixed marriages] do not, except in some cases, help in reestablishing unity among Christians." The "Christian family" is the "living cell of the Church," and so "diversities in matters of religion, especially with regard to . . . the education of the children," make fulfilling the Gospel teachings in the family more difficult.[102] Some Catholic commentators argue, nonetheless, that couples in mixed marriages "who try to share their common spiritual heritages while being faithful to their own consciences" provide a "living sign of hope" of the "pilgrimage toward greater unity."[103]

Jewish Debates about Interfaith Marriage: Threat to Jewish Survival or the Price of Living in an Open Society?

In the early 1960s rates of interfaith marriage by American Jews were still low, compared with other forms of interfaith marriage.[104] Even so, Jewish religious leaders, Jewish organizations, and social scientists concluded that rates were rising with each new generation and warranted attention. A sampling of those discussions reveals concerns both similar to and distinct from those about inter-Christian mixed marriage. Similarities include narratives about the structural and personal factors contributing to the rise in intermarriage and queries about whether parents, clergy, and experts could oppose them in good conscience in light of a commitment to tolerance and the American creed. Some differences reflect the complexity of Jewish identity as being a religious minority in a majority

Christian nation, and the fact that anti-Semitism was about not only religion, but also ethnicity (and perceived race).

This section focuses on the following themes: (1) interpreting intermarriage as an inevitable outcome of assimilation and living in an open society; (2) assessing the motives of Jews who intermarry and parents who oppose such marriages; (3) addressing why intermarriage was perceived as a problem; and (4) debating how best to respond to intermarriage. The book *Intermarriage: Interfaith, Interracial, and Interethnic* (1964) by Albert I. Gordon, a rabbi and a trained sociologist, will inform the discussion.[105] Gordon argues against intermarriage in general—interfaith, interracial, and interethnic. Moreover, as chapter 6 explains, Gordon's book played a central role in *Loving v. Virginia*, when the attorney general of Virginia relied on it as a "scientific treatise" offering modern support for Virginia's ban on interracial marriage.[106]

What Explains Intermarriage? Assimilation and Amalgamation

The basic narrative explaining the rise of Jewish intermarriage echoes Bossard and Boll and Pike's analyses in relating intermarriage to immigration, assimilation, and increasing intergroup social contact, but with some twists.[107] In a 1963 study, sociologist Erich Rosenthal explained that American Jews, "mostly of recent immigrant origin," participate in the "sequence" affecting all immigrant groups in the United States, which "starts with competition and conflict among groups upon initial contact and which ends, after an intermediate phase of accommodation, in assimilation and amalgamation." Intermarriage is "the final stage in this process" or "race relations cycle." While Jews have achieved "high levels of acculturation"—measured by "class mobility and educational attainment"—they have resisted intermarriage.[108] Rosenthal and others point both to involuntary segregation, such as discrimination in housing markets and employment, and to voluntary efforts, such as living in predominantly Jewish neighborhoods and working in common occupations.[109]

Some sociologists linked the rise in intermarriage to an inconsistency between "conservative attitudes toward marriages" and activities creating conditions favorable to intermarriage, including fighting to end discrimination:

> Sending children to public schools and to centers of higher education away from home, struggling against restrictive covenants, job discrimination, and quota systems, participating in interfaith activity, are but a few representative practices which lead inevitably to intergroup contacts and subsequently to love and marriage.[110]

Rabbis also assumed an "inevitable" link between greater social, intellectual, and economic equality and "a greater number of social contacts between people of different faiths," leading to "a greater number of mixed marriages."[111] In 1965, Judah Cahn, a Reform rabbi active in civil rights, described such marriages as "part of the price that we must pay for the freedom we have gained."[112] Other rabbis spoke of the possibility that Jewish children "may desire to marry persons of another faith" as "the inevitable price we pay for living in an open society."[113]

Intermarriage, nonetheless, posed a "bitter dilemma," argued Marshall Sklare of the American Jewish Committee. Jewish survival in a "free society" is threatened, "not by Gentile hostility but by Jewish indifference." Recognizing that such survival "literally depends on each individual Jew" should lead, Sklare hoped, to a new "consciousness" about one's responsibilities concerning the "highly personal" issue of marriage.[114]

Could Parents Object in Good Conscience
to Intermarriage?

These discussions raised the question whether liberal Jewish parents could, in good conscience, oppose Jewish-Gentile marriages since they seemed to flow from the very principles of equality and "the transitory character of the differences" between people that they instilled in their children.[115] Was opposition to intermarriage inconsistent with the "American ethos" and simply a reflection of prejudice? Sklare described the dilemma of the liberal Jewish parent who "must ask himself if the Gentile is any less worthy of the Jew than the Jew is of the Gentile" and whether the parent's teachings are "in some way" responsible for their child's choice.[116] The young person brings the "egalitarian, universalist principles upon which he had been nurtured" to bear in picking a mate: "that people should be judged by their personal merits, not by race or religion."[117]

The parent may feel he cannot "oppose the match," since he probably "believes that love is the basis of marriage, that marriage is the uniting of two individuals rather than two families, and that the final determination of a mate is his child's prerogative." Although these ideas run "contrary to the norm, if not practice, of traditional Jewish society," Sklare observes, each successive generation in America has embraced them more. Thus, the parent falls back on "the argument of happiness," appealing to experience and statistics about higher divorce rates in "exogamous marriage." By doing so, the parent evades "the need to confront the painful contradiction in his own position," and "can oppose his child's intermarriage with a good conscience."[118] That parents point to the risk of "marital discord and unhappiness" instead of invoking "the religious prohibitions," other authors observe, suggests that they recognize their disapproval is at odds with the American ethos, which places "primary emphasis on the individual—his will, his choices, his personal wellbeing."[119] The Jewish parent's appeal to the risk of unhappiness and divorce statistics resembles the objections by Z's father to interracial marriage and the enlisting of science by Pike and Bossard and Boll to show why objecting to interfaith marriage is not narrow-minded intolerance.

Rabbi Gordon's book strongly resists an argument that opposition to intermarriage stemmed solely from intolerance. I highlight his book because he included both interfaith and interracial marriage in arguing that intermarriage must "be regarded as a threat to both personal and group happiness."[120] He insists that parents who "attempt to dissuade their children from intermarrying are not selfish, intolerant people, as their children are wont to say." Instead, they know "intuitively" and from experience that when "opposites in color or religion" marry, they are "far less likely to be as successful in their marriages as are persons of the same color and religion."[121] Intermarriage "is also a threat to the children": "It may tend to make them marginal in their relationships to parents, their faiths or their races" because they may find it "difficult" and sometimes "impossible" to identify with their parents or their parents' "way of life."[122] Similar to the guidebooks on interfaith marriage by Pike and Bossard and Boll, Gordon argues that a mixed religious household denied children the secure sense of identity they needed and subjected them to "inner conflict."[123]

Gordon also appeals to group pride to reject the argument that people who opposed intermarriage are "per se prejudiced." Similar to Bossard and Boll, he argues that "the desire to perpetuate one's own religion or to prevent its assimilation is understandable and reasonable." He also refers to the legitimate desire of races and ethnic groups to "perpetuate themselves." Similar to the tactic of flipping charges of bigotry to say that those who allege bigotry are the real bigots, Gordon flips the charge of prejudice: "The tendency to classify all persons who oppose intermarriage as 'prejudiced' is, in itself, a prejudice."[124] On this view, there are good reasons to oppose intermarriage.

Young People's Motives for Intermarriage

Studies offered a slew of psychological and social reasons for why Jewish persons picked non-Jewish spouses. Canvassing older explanations for intermarriage, such as "pathology" (recall Karpf's description of A as neurotic for choosing a Catholic fiancé), Sklare concluded that these "outmoded" reasons were insufficient. He instead identified the "marked rise in egalitarianism on the college campuses following World War II," which promoted a "climate in which dating" and sometimes "marrying outside one's social group" was "no longer regarded as deviant behavior, and on the more 'advanced' campuses even confers some degree of status."[125] Gordon found that some college students who espoused a universalism viewed interfaith marriage as a way "to prove once and for all that this is or ought to be one world."[126]

Resonant of Bossard and Boll, Gordon also found that youth's "tendency to 'rebel' against the ideas, opinions and practices of their elders" was particularly "manifest" with respect to traditional religious opposition to intermarriage in favor of in-group marriage.[127] Furthermore, "today's" parents are less likely to disown or impose sanctions on a child who intermarries.[128] Another factor, Gordon argued, was the emphasis on "romantic love" rather than an earlier day's emphasis on matches arranged by parents and marriage brokers.[129]

Not all students shared the egalitarian, universalist ethos supporting intermarriage. Gordon found that 50% did not favor "marriage to a person of another religion" and 91% disfavored "marriage to a person of another color."[130] He identified "prejudice and bias against other peoples and religions" as "an important factor" limiting intermarriage.[131] He found "prejudice and intolerance" by white students toward African Americans and the persistence of "stereotypes and prejudices" toward Catholics and Jews. Even so, Gordon predicted the dynamic of more social contact leading inevitably to more intermarriage.[132]

Other studies found that Jewish men intermarried at a higher rate than Jewish women. As to why, Sklare argued that "bright middle-class Gentile girls" at the better colleges who are "'emancipating' themselves" are attracted to the "political liberalism characteristic of Jewish students or by their equally characteristic avantgardism in intellectual and aesthetic matters."[133] Other researchers argued that because fostering the "Jewish ethos" in the Jewish male made him "serious-minded, hard-working, ambitious, and intellectual," such qualities made him an attractive potential mate for the Gentile girl.[134] Cahnman painted a less attractive picture of the impact of Jewish household dynamics and gender role socialization to explain both the Jewish young man's motives for intermarriage and why Jewish women were less attractive marriage partners. Nonetheless, if Jewish boys "prefer Gentile girls," Cahnman argues, Jewish girls should learn to "compete more effectively"![135]

What to Do About Intermarriage

In the 1930s, Mordecai Kaplan, a pioneer of Reconstructionist Judaism, stated: "Jews must be prepared to reckon frankly and intelligently with intermarriage as a growing tendency which, if left uncontrolled, is bound to prove Judaism's undoing."[136] Discussions in the 1960s echoed that view. How, then, should Jewish religious leaders, community leaders, and parents respond to increased intermarriage? Contrasting Gordon and Cahnman reveals significant points of agreement but also significantly different conceptions of preserving Jewish heritage and important democratic ideals.

Gordon rejects the view that intermarriage might be a path to realizing human brotherhood. He treats interracial and interfaith marriage alike as threats to the duty to preserve important forms of difference:

> It is the duty of men and women of different faiths, colors, and nations to learn to live together in peace and amity while maintaining their differences. . . . The elimination of all differences in religion or color could only lead to blandness and is, therefore, not to be mistaken for a blessing to mankind but rather as a serious threat to the welfare of individuals and the society of which they are a part.

Because such differences are so important, Gordon rejects the sentiment that intermarriage would end intolerance and prejudice:

> Universal brotherhood, freedom from prejudice, intolerance and hatred of the unlike will hardly be purchased at the price of giving up all group personalities. None of the great prophetic voices of the past ever proposed that national or religious groups, however different from their own, should cease to exist in order to achieve universal brotherhood.[137]

"The major religious bodies" and "national ethnic and racial groups," Gordon asserts, view intermarriage as a "betrayal" of their "ideals and values." It also injures group "pride" because "families, friends, religions and races, knowing that their 'values' differ from those of others, believe that their unique way of life is somehow endangered when mixed marriage occurs."[138] (Bossard and Boll, discussed earlier, similarly defended a *religious* group's pride and desire for cultural transmission, but did not include racial groups.) These and similar passages from Gordon (as chapter 6 discusses) were quoted by Virginia in *Loving* to defend its antimiscegenation law.

Gordon, however, argued that avoiding social contact by segregation is not the answer: "The voluntary or forced isolation and insulation of any minority group behind ghettolike walls is not only undesirable but spells danger . . . to the social and political philosophy of America."[139] Instead, he argued that the remedy rests with education, instilling in children "a genuine love" of their religious heritage through better religious schools and better homes providing "rich and meaningful religious experiences" for children. A child with such an education and parental example is less likely to be lost "to another religion."[140]

Like Gordon, Cahnman focuses on preserving Jewish homes, but rejects any analogy to racial pride or heritage. Drawing on Kaplan, he argues that interfaith marriage will be "no problem" for a Jewish partner confident about Judaism and willing to make it "the civilization of the home."[141] A "confident" Judaism can compete and even recruit. Historically, Judaism was open to converts and, in a democratic society, the concept of "peoplehood" must be "kept free of racist implications." It is "defined by common heritage, common interests, common hopes."[142] Kaplan asserted that an "unqualified refusal" to intermarry was "contrary to the ideal of cultural and spiritual cooperation"; openness to intermarriage, so long as the couple establishes a Jewish home, rebuts charges of "racial pride" and "tribalism." For "what is valuable is the Jewish social heritage, or civilization and not physical descent."[143] By contrast to Gordon, Cahnman does not treat, as similar, objections to interracial and interfaith marriage. Notably, he criticizes the lack of acceptance by the "organized Jewish community" of "racially mixed married couples," arguing that this "discrepancy" between "liberalism professed and illiberalism practiced" must be resolved.[144]

Interfaith Marriage as a Proxy For Religiously Integrated Lives?

As this chapter has explained, in the 1950s and 1960s, religious leaders and social scientists viewed increased interfaith marriage as an inevitable outcome of more social contact and less prejudice, but also as a significant problem. Both interracial and interfaith marriage departured from the formula of like marrying like. Secular and religious writers highlighted both greater risks of marital unhappiness and burdens on conscience posed by interfaith marriage and a legitimate desire to pass on one's religion to counter concerns that objections rested on intolerance inconsistent with American values. Even so, they recognized that some objections to interfaith marriage stemmed from bigoted and prejudiced views about group differences.

The story of interfaith marriage continues to be one of generational change. Do such marriages still register as problem marriages for parents and religious communities? Examining interfaith marriage in the early twenty-first century, Naomi Riley observed that poll data indicates that "the importance placed on avoiding intermarriage has been falling among Americans for decades," with higher percentages of people saying it was more important to *their parents* that they marry within their faith than it was to them that *their children* do so. They also recognized that their attitude was out of step with the importance their religious tradition placed on marrying within the faith. Riley concludes that interfaith marriage is joining those issues (such as "divorce or abortion or pre-marital sex") about which "people may be aware of their faith's teachings and yet choose not to pay much attention to."[145]

Commentators continue to describe the rise in interfaith marriage as the inevitable result of intergroup contact. In *American Grace: How Religion Divides and Unites Us*, social scientists Robert D. Putnam and David E. Campbell interpret the "gradually increasing rates (and acceptance) of religious intermarriage" as evidence of the "glacially slow" and yet "momentous . . . lowering of interfaith barriers" in the United States. "Roughly half of all married Americans today are married to someone who came originally from a different religious tradition . . . and a bit fewer than one third of all marriages remain mixed."

One clue, they argue, about when this shift toward tolerance of intermarriage occurred is that by 1982, Gallup stopped asking people whether they approved of marriage between a Catholic and Protestant or a Jew and non-Jew. In 1951, 54% of Americans said that "two young people in love who are of different religious faiths—Protestant, Catholic, or Jewish—should not get married"; by 1982, "nearly 80%" polled *approved* of such intermarriage. Another clue is the declining percentage of people answering "very important" to the question, "How important are shared religious beliefs to a successful marriage?"[146]

Interfaith marriage, Putnam and Campbell conclude, is a "reasonable proxy for interfaith integration in other spheres." If we "crossed religious boundaries to find our mate," we are "very likely to have crossed those same boundaries to find our friends." In short, "Americans now live in a more religiously integrated society."[147] In addition, while earlier discussions of interfaith marriage focused particularly on combinations of Protestant, Catholic, and Jew, discussions today recognize that such marriages also include Buddhist, Hindu, Muslim, Sikh, and other religious traditions.[148] Commentators in the 1950s and 1960s debated whether interfaith marriage grew out of an embrace of the American creed or ethos—ideals about equality, cooperation, and the insignificance of difference—and might even be (as Reverend Berg put it) youth's "protest against bigotry." This discussion still resonates as interfaith marriage occurs amidst today's more religiously pluralistic environment. For example, in 2005, Robert Wuthnow found that couples in interfaith marriages connected their choices to American ideals and values about the worth and legitimacy of diversity, difference, and pluralism. They disdained the alternative of being influenced by racism or prejudice.[149]

Conclusion

Do mixed marriages today pose the same challenges to conscience and to preservation of religious identity that worried earlier commentators? In some households, clashes between faiths may not arise because a growing number of Americans identify as "nones," saying their religion is "nothing in particular" or they are atheist or agnostic.[150] Most mixed marriages today are more intercultural than interfaith. As Roberta Kwall observes, we "rarely" hear about how intermarried couples "seek to bridge theological differences." Instead, the issue is blending the "cultural trappings of the two religions," for example, celebrating Christmas and Chanukah. On the other hand, "raising children in a home where a couple has theological differences is likely to be a huge challenge." As did Gordon and Pike decades ago, clergy often recommend that interfaith couples "pick one theology for the home."[151]

In 2015, two young women, one raised Jewish and the other Catholic, asked the rabbi at their Boston-area synagogue to officiate their wedding. The rabbi explained that she could not: the problem was not that the Jewish partner wanted to marry a woman, but that "she wanted to marry a non-Jewish woman." This refusal might seem "paradoxical" to many, journalist Mark Oppenheimer observed: "If clergy can embrace same-sex marriage, why can't they marry a Jew to a non-Jew?" One rabbi, active in marriage equality for gay couples, explained the conundrum: with gay marriage, it was clear that there was an "ethical obligation" for Jewish tradition to evolve; it was not clear that "the same logic" applied to the longstanding tradition against rabbis performing interfaith weddings.[152]

Thus, debates over interfaith marriage continue in an era of civil marriage equality for same-sex couples. While the future brides in Oppenheimer's story had confidence that they could integrate their two religions in an "eccentric fusion," social scientists and clergy still caution that interfaith marriages that remain mixed pose significant challenges that a couple may not anticipate.[153] To answer the questions posed by Bossard and Boll at the beginning of this chapter, these voices of caution insist that their objection is neither bigoted nor intolerant, but rooted in religious concerns (such as blending two faiths) and social concerns.[154] Is a clergy member who takes such a stance, in 2020, a bigot?[155] Most people probably would answer no, but might answer differently if the objection were to interracial marriage. We now reject theological defenses of racism and racial separation, while we accept differences among religions. But, to anticipate chapter 8, consider the marketplace: What if a business owner, obligated by law not to discriminate on the basis of religion, declined to serve an interfaith couple due to sincere religious opposition to such marriage? How about the interfaith, same-sex couple described here? Should that be more permissible than declining to serve an interracial couple?

Finally, burdens of conscience may be a distinctive concern for two religious people in an interfaith marriage, while there is no obvious parallel threat to conscience in an interracial marriage. As this chapter showed, the bigger concern for interracial marriage was the discriminatory social conditions that interracial couples and their children faced. Yet, as the next few chapters discuss, during the 1950s and 1960s, defenders of racial segregation and of legal bars on interracial marriage deflected charges of bigotry by appealing to conscience and religion, as well as to science. By contrast, secular and religious voices in the civil rights movement argued that segregation and the ban on interracial marriage lacked any sound theological or scientific basis and violated the conscience of those seeking to marry.

You Are Waging a Fight of Morality and Conscience

Competing Theologies of Segregation and Integration

> Racial segregation is a blatant denial of the unity which we have in Christ. Segregation is a tragic evil which is utterly un-Christian. . . . The Church can help by showing that the continual outcry of inter-marriage is a tragic distortion of the real issue. It can show that the Negro's primary aim is to be the white man's brother, and not his brother-in-law.
> —Dr. Martin Luther King, Jr., "The Role of the Church in Facing the Nation's Chief Moral Dilemma" (1957)

> We confidently affirm . . . since Christ and the Apostles demonstrated that the principles of charity and Christian brotherhood could be made operative in all the relations of life without involving revolutionary changes in the social, economic, or political order, there is certainly no valid ground for the charge that segregation is inherently wrong, contrary to the will of God, and essentially un-Christian. Many well-meaning civil and religious leaders who now endorse the policy of integration in schools, churches and other areas of life seem to ignore . . . that the question of intermarriage and complete racial integration is necessarily involved, and is bound to overshadow all other issues in the minds of people whose children will be forced to serve as guinea pigs in this dangerous experiment in race relations.
> —Reverend G. T. Gillespie,
> "A Southern Christian Looks at the Race Problem" (1957)

In 1957, Reverend G. T. Gillespie, president emeritus of Bellhaven College in Jackson, Mississippi, put "the question of intermarriage" at the center of his religious defense of racial segregation.[1] That same year, Dr. Martin Luther King, Jr.'s religious condemnation of racial segregation countered that segregationists' "outcry" about intermarriage distorted the issue.[2] While Gillespie invoked "reason and conscience" along with scripture to rebut the charge that segregation rested on "blind and unreasoning prejudice," King urged that the Church

Who's the Bigot? Linda C. McClain, Oxford University Press (2020). © Oxford University Press.
DOI: 10.1093/oso/9780190877200.001.0001

must help to address the "suspicions, fears, and misunderstandings" that un-derlie "race prejudice," hindering realization of ideals of "brotherhood."[3]

This chapter retrieves the rhetoric of bigotry and conscience in arguments by clergy like Dr. King, who condemned racial segregation, and Reverend Gillespie, who defended it. These competing appeals to conscience illustrate the paradox-ical role of religion in—as Gordon Allport put it—"making and unmaking" prejudice and bigotry. How did religious and political leaders battling over de-segregation understand the relationship between conscience and bigotry? What accounts for Reverend Gillespie's confidence that segregation is not "essentially un-Christian" and Dr. King's conviction that it is? Might people be confused about whether they have correctly understood the "dictates" of conscience or whether their judgment is, instead, clouded by prejudice or bigotry? I address those questions by looking at segregationist and integrationist theology in the years following *Brown v. Board of Education,* drawing on official positions taken by religious denominations, speeches by politicians, and sermons, public addresses, and writings by clergy.[4]

The battle over segregation was between two competing versions of "Southern civil religion," with both sides appealing to America's founding texts, principles, and heroes and claiming "God on our side."[5] Indeed, sometimes both sides appealed to the same Bible verse.[6] Studying these competing appeals to religion in the civil rights past may shed light on present controversies in which religious liberty and civil rights conflict. As Jane Dailey observes, American historians, for the most part, "have subscribed to King's version of the sacred his-tory of the civil rights movement," stressing his view of segregation as "heresy" and religion's role in the civil rights movement's challenge to the "existing order of segregation."[7] Few historians have "reckoned seriously with the substance of segregationists' religious beliefs"; most have downplayed "the theological beliefs of white southernors" and considered segregationists "dupes at best."[8] As later chapters show, some conservative opponents of civil marriage equality for same-sex couples and anti-discrimination laws that protect LGBT persons similarly downplay religious arguments for segregation, either minimizing their prevalence or portraying them as pretextual, wicked, or simply mistaken interpretations of scripture.[9] They insist that today's sincere religious believers who oppose gay and lesbian rights have nothing in common with religious segregationists, and that to suggest they do is to brand them as bigots. By con-trast, arguments defending modern anti-discrimination laws and resisting broad claims for religious exemptions commonly analogize religious justifications for sexual orientation discrimination to now-repudiated religious arguments for race and sex discrimination.

In view of these competing appeals to the civil rights past, it is instructive to look back to a time before *Brown* became a canonical text embodying the "declared position of the whole government" on ending race discrimination.[10] When Gillespie and King offered their competing theologies, *Brown* still faced "massive resistance" as an unwarranted departure from the "declared position" supporting segregation and "separate but equal." Careful attention to the "theology of segregation" enables us to see the "titanic struggle waged by participants on both sides" of the civil rights conflict "to harness the immense power of the divine to their cause."[11]

For example, on March 25, 1957, Representative William M. Tuck (Virginia) shared with his fellow members of Congress an address given by Representative John Bell Williams (Mississippi) to the Defenders of State Sovereignty and Individual Liberties in Richmond, Virginia. Williams assured his audience that they were "fighting a war of morality and conscience" in resisting the school desegregation ordered by *Brown* so that "children of both white and colored races may be permitted to enjoy participating in a society unsullied by amalgamation and unstained by moral disintegration." He asserted that "race consciousness" was a "virtue," not bigotry or "race prejudice."[12] Observing that race consciousness "is being preached as anti-Christian," he countered that "there is nothing in the Bible or its teachings that can be cited . . . to support the theories recently advanced that segregation, per se, is anti-Christian." "Eminent southern clergyman," he insisted, "tell me that the Bible deals with miscegenation and interracial marriages in no uncertain terms, holding this to be contrary to the principles of godliness, and in contradiction to the teaching of Christianity."[13]

A few months later, Representative Williams shared with his colleagues a "southern Christian" defense of segregation by Reverend G. T. Gillespie, written as a "reply" to statements made by "numerous church leaders and ecclesiastical bodies denouncing segregation as unjust, sinful, wicked, displeasing to God, and essentially un-Christian." As mentioned earlier, Gillespie "confidently" refuted such charges by appealing to reason and conscience and "broad" biblical principles.[14]

What prompted Williams and Gillespie to offer a religious defense of segregation and critique of *Brown*?[15] Major Christian denominations had issued statements denouncing racial segregation and supporting *Brown*. Religious leaders appealed to "Christian conscience," prophetic Judaism, as well as to democratic and constitutional ideals to reject racial and religious bigotry and prejudice and to support universal brotherhood. These pro–civil rights religious arguments appealed to the demands of "Christian citizenship" and described the South as a "laboratory" for testing "both Christianity and democracy."[16]

In the 1957 address quoted at the beginning of the chapter, Dr. King argued that racial segregation was "utterly un-Christian" and that the "chief moral dilemma" was the failure to make "our Nation a brotherhood." He argued that Christian churches "*must*" help conquer segregation and misunderstandings that underlie "race prejudice."[17] Churches could also counter the "the continual outcry of inter-marriage [as] a tragic distortion of the real issue" by showing that "Negroes . . . simply want the right to live as first-class citizens, with all the responsibilities that good citizenship entails."[18] King called for "courageous leadership" from white "moderates" in the South.[19]

By 1957, as King acknowledged, along with black ministers, some white ministers and rabbis in the South *had* summoned that courage and declared support for *Brown* and integration. Some also had decried the strategic use of intermarriage to justify resistance to desegregation and civil rights. Like King, many called for the integration of religious congregations as an expression of universal brotherhood, lest churches fail to "practice what they preach." Building on Gunnar Myrdal's arguments in *An American Dilemma* (discussed in chapter 2), such clergy argued that the "most decisive opponent of the segregationist is his own conscience."[20]

This chapter explores how pro-civil rights ministers and rabbis sought to make the theological and moral case for civil rights and desegregation.[21] How could they, as Dr. King urged, help people to conquer their prejudices? How did clergy articulate a civil religion to reach the undecided "moderate middle"?[22] Was it possible to persuade a bigot by the appeal to conscience? King and other clergy stressed the need to redeem the segregator and the role of conscience in freeing people from prejudice, hatred, and bigotry. I also draw on an illuminating case study by Ernest Campbell and Thomas Pettigrew (a student of Allport) of clergy's competing responses to the 1957 crisis in Little Rock over implementing *Brown*,[23] and why the majority of ministers who supported *Brown* had only limited success in taking the mantle of leadership urged by King.

Shortly after *Brown*, one prominent Southern Baptist ethicist who laid out the theological case against segregation worried publicly that "a lot of our Baptist people" are going to be on the "wrong side" of the issue.[24] That worry proved prophetic. Yet some historians argue that by the late 1960s and early 1970s, awakened by conscience, a "new South" emerged that was not premised on segregation and white supremacy.[25] Once-"mainstream" theological justifications for segregation and white supremacy were now publicly "extreme."[26] Not all segregationists abandoned their religious beliefs in segregation as scriptural and God's plan, but they recognized the risk of being labeled a racist or bigot if they aired those beliefs publicly.[27]

The Theology of Segregation

How did Representative Williams, Reverend Gillespie and others defend the theology of segregation? What were their proof texts as they denied that opposition to desegregation rested in prejudice and bigotry?

Not Bigotry or Intolerance, but Morality and Conscience

By 1957, while some of the states affected by *Brown* had taken steps to integrate their public schools, eight states in the Deep South continued their "Massive Resistance."[28] In his 1957 Richmond address (quoted earlier), Representative Williams explained this resistance as a "fight of morality and conscience." In 1955 he, along with Senator James Eastland and Judge Tom P. Brady, drafted Mississippi's "interposition" resolution, declaring that *Brown* was a dangerous "abrogation of the sovereign rights of the States" and that Mississippi had no constitutional obligation to comply with it.[29] In 1956, Eastland and Williams were among the nineteen Senators and seventy-seven Representatives who joined the "Southern Manifesto," declaring *Brown* an "unwarranted exercise of power," "contrary to the Constitution," and "destroying the amicable relations between the white and Negro races . . . created through 90 years of patient effort by the good people of both races."[30]

Traces of segregationist theology are evident in Williams's address. He claims to be on the side of conscience, "noble ideals," and a "fight" for "our great American institutions." On the other side are "modern carpetbag enemies" and a "once-respected United States Supreme Court," whose recent decisions depart from "separate but equal" as a "firmly fixed principle." Williams praises the Virginia Supreme Court for resisting, in *Naim v. Naim* (1955), a "directive" of the US Supreme Court concerning a challenge to Virginia's antimiscegenation law.[31]

Williams dismisses the label *bigot*: "All these facts the liberals brush off as the bigoted rantings of Southern race baiters and demagogues." He charges that "statements favoring segregation by Southern leaders are deliberately distorted to make the author appear as a bigoted fool." News accounts "ridicule" Southern religious beliefs and "make it look as if we in the South hold our Negro friends and neighbors in utter contempt . . . contrary to all of the teachings and traditions of the southern people." Williams distinguishes bigotry from a virtuous race consciousness:

> Is it bigotry to hold that race consciousness is a virtue, as distinguished from race prejudice? Race consciousness is neither prejudice nor intolerance. It is an innate awareness of a birthright being held in trust for posterity. . . . [A] majority of us have been taught, and we understand, how it came about that Israel became a great nation, while Edom faded into oblivion. We recall the downfall of every great empire when it became infiltrated with immorality and was reduced to mongrelization through racial intermarriages and intermingling.

Williams invokes the words of English statesman Benjamin Disraeli, a favorite of segregationists: "No man will treat with indifference the principle of race, for it is the key to history."[32]

Williams argues that "church leaders who adopt the pious attitude that interracial marriage and the resulting mongrel offspring are acceptable in the light of Christian teachings assume unto themselves the divine power to rewrite the meaning of the Gospel" and "invade the realm of politics."[33] By contrast, southern clergy assure him that the Bible *does* hold interracial marriage to be contrary to "godliness" and "the teachings of Christianity." Williams reassures his audience that "our hopes and prayers are with you as you seek to turn back the evil forces of centralization, miscegenation, and racial amalgamation" and that with the guidance of "the same God that watched over" and "inspired" Jefferson to "swear eternal hostility against tyranny," "we shall not fail."[34]

Reason and Conscience, Not Blind and Unreasoning Prejudice

Reverend G. T. Gillespie's essay "A Southern Christian Looks at the Race Problem," entered into the Congressional Record by Representative Williams, offers a fuller account of the theology of segregation. Gillespie responds to the frequent "charge" that "white people of the South are so blinded with prejudice and so filled with enmity against the Negro race that they cannot see the race problem in its true perspective."[35] Gillespie's rebuttal stresses the *reasonableness* of segregation, including opposition to intermarriage.

Aware of denominational statements supporting *Brown*, Gillespie counters that "Southern Christians, generally, feel that [*Brown*] was a tragic mistake."[36] He explains that the "crux of the whole racial problem" is the intermarriage and "amalgamation" that will "inevitably" follow if the "experiment" of enforced school integration succeeds. Gillespie asks:

> Is it desirable that social relations leading normally to intermarriage and ultimate racial amalgamation should be encouraged and approved; or, is it more desirable . . . that racial intermarriage should be discouraged or prohibited, and that each race should be enabled to preserve its own racial integrity?[37]

Clearly, he and the "30 million or more southern Christians" on whose behalf he writes view the second approach as more desirable. Intermarriage "overshadows all other considerations in the minds of parents in typical southern communities." It explains their "uncompromising opposition" to "integrated schools," and also "the traditional southern attitude with respect to social intermingling of the races in homes, churches, hotels, public assemblies, recreation, transportation and other public facilities."[38] Forbidding social equality in all these areas of daily life is necessary to prevent the social contact that would lead to intermarriage.

Gillespie appeals to several forms of authority to support "the principle of segregation": "scientific, historical, and Biblical data," "moral and ethical grounds," and consistency with "the principles of Christianity and the great traditions of American democracy." Thus, "intermarriage between widely different racial groups is unnatural, unfair to offspring, and prejudicial to human progress." It is contrary to "an instinct" with which God has "endowed His living creatures" to "mate only with their own kind." This principle, which Gillespie finds evident in birds and cattle, applies with "even greater force" to "the mating of human beings of widely different types and cultural backgrounds." The "offspring" are "generally unstable, eccentric, ill-adjusted, unpredictable, [and] unhappy"; if the "experiment" extends "over successive generations," the result is "a retarded or decadent civilization." Gillespie contrasts the "remarkable virility of the cultures of the Hebrews, the Greeks, and the English-speaking peoples, all of whom kept their racial stocks pure," with the "retarded or decadent civilizations of India, Egypt, Spain, [and] Portugal, who allowed their racial stocks to become mixed with the diverse peoples with whom they came in contact."[39] On the importance of avoiding intermarriage, Gillespie cites a 1913 report by "the late Dr. Charles W. Eliot, president of Harvard University," on "the effect of race mixtures in the Orient."[40]

As for "Biblical data," Gillespie argues that "the principle of segregation is in harmony with the purpose and will of God as revealed in His Word, and is consistent with the teaching and spirit of Our Lord Jesus Christ."[41] One proof text is Genesis 11 concerning the Tower of Babel. At a time when "the whole world had one language," the people sought to build a city "with a tower that reaches to the heavens." When "the Lord" saw this, he came down and "confuse[d] their language so they would not understand each other" and "scattered them from there all over the earth."[42] This story indicates, Gillespie contends, that God "thwarted the first manmade plan of integration." It shows that "divine providence" is responsible for "linguistic differences" and "other factors which have served to keep the peoples of the earth segregated into tribal, national, or racial groups, from prehistoric times down to our day."[43]

A further proof text is that by "divine decree," Abraham and his descendants "were separated from all the other peoples of the earth" and Israel "existed" for 1,500 years as "a strictly segregated nation." God forbade them "to mingle socially, to intermarry, or to amalgamate with the nations around them," on penalty of death.[44] In a 1954 address on "A Christian View on Segregation," Gillespie offered as proof that in Genesis, Noah's three sons "became the progenitors of three distinct racial groups" who were dispersed across the earth.[45] Prior religious justifications for slavery drew on the curse that Noah placed on one of his sons, Ham, for observing him naked and intoxicated: that Ham's son, Canaan, "shall be a servant of servants."[46] While theological arguments against segregation cited the Parable of the Good Samaritan, Gillespie insists that while the parable condemns "narrowminded intolerance" and shows the duty to "love our neighbors," Jesus "did not ignore or denounce racial distinctions, [or] set plans on foot to abolish them or to bring about amalgamation of the Jews with the Samaritans or other races." Because Jesus and the Apostles did not comment on racial integration or segregation, the question is left to "the reason and conscience of the individual."[47]

Invoking reason and conscience, Gillespie rebuts the charge that segregation rests on "blind and unreasoning prejudice." Instead, reason, "experience," and "the broad principles" in the Old and New Testaments show that church leaders who condemn segregation as "displeasing to God" and "essentially un-Christian" are "in error." Christian "brotherhood" does not require "revolutionary changes in the social, economic, or political order." Segregation is a "well-considered and time-tested American policy," "consistent with the principles of true Americanism" and incorporated in seventeen state constitutions.[48]

Gillespie concludes with Booker T. Washington's famous 1895 address, stating that "agitation of questions of social equality is the extremist folly," and that "in all things that are purely social, we can be as separate as the fingers, yet one, as the hand, in all things essential to mutual progress." Washington's "wise" Christian leadership, Gillespie asserts, shows that helping "the Negro . . . improve his lot" should be done "within the framework of a segregated society."[49]

Segregationist Theology as a Civil Religion

These remarks by Williams and Gillespie highlight several characteristic features of appeals to religion to defend segregation and oppose *Brown*: (1) the appeal to the Bible to identify God as the author of racial difference, as segregating the races, and as prohibiting intermarriage and amalgamation; (2) the positing of a God-given natural instinct in human beings to preserve racial purity; (3) the argument that neither Jesus nor the New Testament explicitly condemned racial segregation; and (4) the appeal to conscience and morality to refute charges that support for segregation rests on bigotry or unreasoning prejudice. This theology of segregation melded the appeal to scripture with other forms of proof: (1) the study of civilizations revealed that the most successful maintained their racial purity, while those who mixed declined; and (2) segregation is in keeping with American history, traditions, and constitutional principles.

Prominent Southern clergy agreed with politicians that "our Southern seg-regation way is the Christian way" and that the Bible taught that God was "the original segregationist."[50] To integrate the races in school was to "foster misceg-enation, thereby changing God's plan and destroying His handiwork."[51] The "widely reprinted and distributed" pamphlet, *God the Original Segregationist*, written by Carey Daniel, pastor of First Baptist Church of West Dallas, Texas, articulated a "folk theology of segregation [that was] recycled through letters to editors, newspaper columns, and frequently in private correspondence."[52] That theology referred to the Bible verses discussed here and various punishments imposed for violating God's "sacred law of segregation," and insisted that Jesus "never specifically repudiated" segregation, putting the burden of proof on those arguing against it.[53]

A striking example of interpretive differences is the competing appeals defenders and opponents of segregation made to Acts 17:26. If the "pro-civil rights religious literature" shared "a common Bible verse," it was this: "Of one blood has God made all nations for to dwell on all the face of the earth, and hath determined the times before appointed, and the bounds of their habitation."[54] While they emphasized the first part of the verse, however, segregationists countered with the second. As Paul Harvey observes: "For biblical literalists such as most Southernors were, passages such as Acts 17:26 correlated to the specific social customs of God's Zion, the American South," and indicated that "the plan of God is for diversity of races to continue through earthly time and into eternity."[55]

Such religiously infused defenses of segregation illustrate a form of Southern *civil* religion, fusing "civil and religious legitimations" for segre-gation and the Southern "way of life."[56] For example, Tom Brady, Baptist lay-person and Mississippi circuit judge—whose book *Black Monday: Segregation or Amalgamation. America Has Its Choice* was published by the Association of Citizens' Councils—linked defending segregation to preserving "our God-given American way of life."[57] Preventing "mongrelization" was part of that way: "We have, through our forefathers, died before for our sacred principles. We can, if nec-essary, die again. . . . You shall not mongrelize our children and grandchildren."[58] Although *Black Monday* expressed "the sentiments of the South's most rabid segregationists," Brady's "angry and defiant" perspective "represented a strain of thought that was shared by a large segment of Southern Baptist conservatives."[59]

Brady drew his "facts" about God as the author of segregation from "archaeologists, anthropologists and scientists,"[60] including the "scientific racism" he learned at Yale in the 1920s about the superiority of Caucasian (par-ticularly, Anglo-Saxon) civilization.[61] Although support for eugenics waned in the United States after the horrors of the Nazi regime, it was pervasive in the United States through the 1930s and left its traces. Eugenics included both a "profound . . . rejection of the basic principle of human equality" and the view that "whole classes of people denominated races were . . . categorically inferior to others."[62] Thus, in a 1954 address to a Citizens' Council about *Black Monday*, Brady charged: "This Supreme Court [in *Brown*] seeks to set aside all the laws of eugenics and biology!"[63]

On this view, white civilizations were superior, but threatened by integration. Governor Ross Barnett similarly warned that "there is no case in history where the Caucasian race has survived social integration."[64] Appeals to the superiority of the white race and civilization were not uniquely Southern. In 1957, New York City-born and Yale-educated William F. Buckley, founder of the conservative journal *National Review* and the "face of the mainstream, respectable, non-fringe postwar Right," wrote in support of resisting school integration: "The white community in the South" was "entitled to take measures . . . necessary to prevail, politically and culturally," because, "for the time being, it is the advanced race."[65]

Another element of this civil religion was invoking the nation's heroic past in resisting charges of bigotry. As one White Citizens' Council asserted: "If we are bigoted, prejudiced, un-American, etc., so were George Washington, Thomas Jefferson, Abraham Lincoln, and other illustrious forebears who believed in segregation. We choose the old paths of our founding fathers and refuse to appease anyone."[66]

In this civil religion of segregation, the superior white race is strikingly vulnerable to racial mixing and ruin. On the one hand, the basic laws of God and nature include racial instincts to associate and mate only with one's kind. On the other, such "normal, natural, human instincts" may be overcome if forced "commingling" in schools destroys each race's "established usages, customs, and traditions," so that white children may intermarry.[67] Children in integrated schools may also be indoctrinated by instruction about equality and belonging to one human family. Gillespie's article illustrates this tension: because social contact on terms of equality in education inevitably weakens the natural instinct to preserve racial purity, any step toward integration will lead to intermarriage. To avoid the sin of miscegenation and divine punishment, segregation was necessary both in public spaces, like schools, and private spaces, including churches and families.

How did such accounts deal with the gap between denunciations of race mixing and the undeniable fact of interracial sexual contact, made illicit by antimiscegenation laws, and of white men's sexual and reproductive exploitation of black women during and after slavery? As W. E. B. DuBois wrote, in response to the "cry" of "Southern Gentlemen" to "deliver us from the vision of intermarriage," "legal marriage is infinitely better than systematic concubinage and prostitution." And to such Gentlemen's cry about black "vagabonds" violating white women, DuBois responded: "The wrong which you gentlemen have done against helpless black women in defiance of your own laws is written on the foreheads of two millions of mulattoes, and written in ineffaceable blood."[68] Williams obliquely acknowledges this reality: "In every group, white and Negro, there are individuals who, despising their birthright, have violated that trust."[69]

A sermon by W. A. Criswell, pastor of a large congregation of the First Baptist Church in Dallas, Texas, illustrates both segregationist theology's appeal to civil religion and the gendered nature of the fear of race mixing.[70] He preached that the rights to segregate in educating children represented "America," "freedom," and "spiritual democracy." Raising the specter of intermarriage of southern daughters (including his own), Criswell pled:

> Don't force me by law, by statute, by Supreme Court decision ... don't force me to cross over in those intimate things where I don't want to go. ... Let me have my friends. Let me have my home. Let me have my family. And what you give to me, give to every man in America and keep it like our glorious forefathers made it—a land of the free and the home of the brave.[71]

In this appeal, segregation was a "sanctified" part of America. Criswell's plea captures "the link between race and sex that haunted white Southern conservatives" and animated segregationist theology: "Only a proper ordering of the races would maintain the white Southern purity against defilement."[72] Preserving "white purity" focused on white girls and women—as Brady put it, "the loveliest and purest of God's creatures."[73]

The Theological Case Against Segregation

What was the theological case against segregation? What were its proof texts and principles? How did clergy understand the role of conscience in rescuing people from bigotry and prejudice? How did they enlist American ideals? Two helpful sources are official resolutions and statements by religious denominations and the sermons and speeches of clergy and civil rights leaders.

Statements Condemning Racial Segregation and Supporting *Brown*

Denominational statements insisted that "the practice of racial segregation is a blight on the Christian conscience."[74] In 1959, social scientists Campbell and Pettigrew observed: "There is no reasonable doubt that the major religious bodies of America believe that the church must condemn race separation."[75] While Gillespie stressed keeping churches, schools, and families segregated, these statements appealed to conscience to end segregation not only in public facilities, but also within churches.[76] Only a few statements explicitly challenged racial barriers to marriage.[77]

Some statements urged the church to lead in condemning racial segregation. Issued in 1954, shortly after *Brown*, the General Assembly of the Presbyterian Church's Report of the Council on Christian Relations refers "to two dynamic forces at work [in diminishing racial segregation], the Federal Constitution and the Christian conscience."[78] The report reasons that if segregation is "not merely the separation of two peoples, but the subordination of one people to another," the courts are ahead of the church. If the church does not keep pace with its own principles, it will "be in the embarrassing position of having to adjust its sense of morality to measure up to the morals of the state."[79] A subsequent statement asserts that "the Christian conscience cannot rest content with any legal or compulsive arrangement that brands any people as inferior," and *Brown* must be "recognized [and obeyed] as the law of the land."[80]

Initially, in 1954, the Southern Baptist Convention (SBC) (historically, white Baptists) declared that *Brown* was "in harmony with the constitutional guarantees of equal freedom to all citizens, and with the Christian principles of equal justice and love for all men."[81] However, many Baptist laypersons and some ministers criticized the SBC's declarations and were among those who mobilized for "massive resistance" to *Brown*.[82]

The statement by the National Baptist Convention (historically, black Baptists) observed the gap between America's claim of "Democracy and Christianity" and "the treatment America permits to be accorded her minority peoples," leading "Negroes" to be "puzzled as to the attitude they should adopt regarding the sincerity of the American claim of . . . 'Justice to all and special privilege to none.'" *Brown* led "the race" to take heart and "justified the faith, the hope and the love they exercise toward this country."[83]

The 1958 Statement of the Roman Catholic Bishops of the United States, "Discrimination and Christian Conscience," appeals to scripture and papal instruction to reject the theology of segregation.[84] Insisting that "the heart of the race question is moral and religious," it stresses the "universal" nature of the Christian faith, which "knows not the distinctions of race, color or nationhood." It states that "discrimination based on the accidental fact of race or color . . . cannot be reconciled with the truth that God has created all men with equal rights and equal dignity."[85] "Enforced segregation" imposes "a stigma of inferiority," contrary to papal instruction that "God did not create a human family made up of segregated, disassociated, mutually independent members." The Statement declares: "Every man has an equal right to life, to justice before the law, to marry and rear a family under humane conditions" (an evident critique of antimiscegenation laws).[86]

The 1958 Statement compares the "bigoted ill-treatment" and "discrimination" directed at "Negroes, Indians, and also some Spanish-speaking Americans" with that directed, "some decades back," against "the immigrant, Irish, Jewish, Italian, Polish, Hungarian, German, Russian." Just as "the immigrant, fortunately, has achieved his rightful status in the American community," enjoying "economic opportunity" and "educational equality," "Negro citizens seeks [sic] these same opportunities."[87] Black civil rights leaders similarly located desegregation within the broader framework of assimilation of minority groups in the United States.[88] Racial segregation hindered normal processes of social contact, inclusion, and assimilation (what commentators analyzing interfaith marriage referred to as the "race relations cycle" or the "melting pot," as discussed in chapter 3).

Sermons and Speeches: Universal Brotherhood and Christian Conscience

Two post-*Brown* speeches by prominent Protestant ministers illustrate scriptural and theological arguments for compliance with *Brown*, appealing to the demands of Christian conscience.[89] Each speaker responds to the claims by segregationists that the Bible forbids integration and intermarriage. They enlist science as supporting scriptural truths about the unity of humankind and debunking myths of racial difference.

What does the Bible have to say? and *"What should Christians do?"* In his address "I Have Not a Demon," delivered in 1955 at the Southern Baptist Convention's Christian Life Conference, Dr. Thomas Buford Maston, a leading Baptist ethicist who "devoted considerable energy to the civil rights movement," addresses "the teachings of the Bible concerning race and relations." He echoes the scientific study of prejudice: being prejudiced is not "innate," but part of our "social heritage," something we "catch" as a result of exposure to an environment "highly charged with racial prejudice." When children play in communities with "those of different racial groups," they do not have an "aversion" to playing or freely associating, but as they age, "their associates, and sometimes their parents, and shame on us, sometimes even Sunday school teachers and church workers tend to build these prejudices in too."[90]

The race problem, Maston argues, is "basically a moral and spiritual problem" and should not be brushed aside as "a political problem." In the United States, the "most acute" race problems are the "white-Negro problems we have in the South," including the "increase in pressure and tension" due to *Brown* leaving implementation of school desegregation up to local communities and federal courts. This problem, he observes, is "American Christianity's test case," implicating not just the "American Dilemma" identified by Myrdal but also "our Christian ideals." He contends: "our practice has fallen short of our theory"—of both American and Christian ideals.[91]

When Maston examines what the Bible says about "these race issues that we face," he cautions that there is nothing in the Old or New Testament with "anything parallel to the problem that we have in our country in the relationship of white and Negro." The Bible, however, does have "some tremendously significant principles" that can and should be "applied to the race problem." Such "fundamental principles" are more important than "any specific Scriptures that we can find."[92]

One principle is: "All people and races come from one family stock." Maston starts with Acts 17:26, which, as noted earlier, was also used to support segregation: "And he made from one every nation and man that live on all the face of the earth having determined allotted periods and boundaries of their habitation."[93] Observing that Paul made this statement in Athens (where Greeks drew "a sharp distinction" between Greeks and barbarians) and "put a Jew on the same plane as a Greek," Maston asks what application Paul would make if speaking in Birmingham, Dallas, or Jackson. Rejecting racial hierarchy, Maston concludes that *all* persons are on the "same plane" (i.e., level) because God is the "Creator of all" and determines the "status" of all nations.[94]

Maston argues that scripture and science generally agree that "all men sprang from the common stock." He notes that anthropologist Ruth Benedict cites Genesis as expressing "the same truth that science has shown today"—"that all people of the earth are a single family and have a common origin." Maston derives from Bible verses a basic unity in the human family and the equal worth and dignity of all human beings. Thus, "men of all nations of all races—of all colors" were created in God's "image" (Genesis 1:27) and "Christ died for all men." He cites another frequent proof text in integrationist sermons: as stated by Peter in Acts 10:34, "God is no respecter of persons" and "shows no partiality."[95] Maston also reasons that while Jesus "did not have any contact with . . . the Negro," his positive attitude toward the Samaritan suggests his "attitude toward any of the outcasts of society—or racial group."[96]

Maston asks, "What should Christians do concerning the race question in general and the segregation issue . . . in particular?" He begins with what Christians should *not* do: "become identified with those who have set aside our Constitution," say that the Supreme Court is a "bunch of Communists," or "be stirred up by political or religious demagogues."[97] Notably, Maston resists the strategic use of intermarriage: "the main boogerboo is intermarriage," but "we're not going to let that scare us away from doing what we ought to do as Christians."[98] In a pivotal moment, Maston states: "We will be on the side of those who defend our public schools ... we will not be a party to any program to eliminate them." When he does not "hear an amen," he expresses concern "that a lot of our Baptist people including some of our Baptist preachers are going to be on *the wrong side of this whole issue*."[99] Subsequent developments would validate his concern.[100]

Neither scripture nor science supports our kind of segregation. Another significant address was given a few months after *Brown* by Reverend Benjamin E. Mays, an ordained Baptist minister and President of Morehouse College (where he was a major influence upon Dr. King). Speaking to the World Council of Churches, Mays reported on the results of this ecumenical body's study of Christianity and race. He states that since "the Church gets its authority from the Bible, we have searched Scriptures anew—both the Old and the New Testament—to see whether there is anything there to justify our modern policy of segregation based on race, color, or ethnic origins."[101] He reviews scriptures expressing objections to intermarriage, but concludes that "in the Old Testament, the lines are definitely and sharply drawn" on the basis of religion, not race. For example, in Deuteronomy 7:2–4, when Moses exhorts the Jews not to marry in the new land, the text makes clear that the objection is religious—intermarriage will lead to "turn[ing] away" from God and "serv[ing] other gods." Mays explains that "the nations that surrounded Israel belonged to the same racial stock as Israel"; what made them unacceptable was that "they served their own gods." He concludes: "We search in vain, therefore, if we expect to find in the Old Testament support for our kind of racial or color segregation." Nor is there support for a "pure" Jewish race, since, "throughout its history, Israel made proselytes from other nations and races."[102]

Turning to the New Testament, the study found that it proclaims a "religion that was supra-racial, supra-national, supra-cultural, and supra-class." Mays adds: Jesus's "doctrine of God as father embraces the human race and makes us all children of the same God."[103] He distinguishes forms of segregation practiced by Jews and Jewish Christians from "modern segregation based on caste, color, and race." While a non-Jew could become a Jew by "meeting certain conditions," and non-Jews could become Christians, "in our time, when segregation is based on race or color, there is nothing one can do to qualify."[104]

Mays discusses other New Testament scriptures frequently cited by pro–civil rights clergy, such as Peter's experience with Cornelius and the birth of the church at Pentecost, when "Jews and proselytes" of "some fifteen different nations were assembled." In Galatians 3:28, Paul declares: "There is neither Jew nor Greek, there is neither slave nor free, there is neither male nor female; for you are all one in Christ Jesus." Such passages show, Mays explains, that "in Christ all divisions are unified, and racial and ethnic groups become one."[105] The "modern race problem" dates to the seventeenth century, with the period of European "overseas exploration and expansion into Africa, Asia, and America" and forms of racial exploitation.[106]

Mays next contrasts present-day scientific understanding about race with that of "forty or fifty years ago," when scientists were divided over the question of inherent racial superiority and "hundreds of volumes were written to justify a denial of equal opportunity to some peoples on the ground that they were inferior and that God had made them that way." There is no longer such disagreement among "the top scientists." Indeed, a "recent UNESCO publication" concludes that "available scientific knowledge provides no basis for believing that the groups of mankind differ in their innate capacity for intellectual and emotional development." A UN publication likewise found no scientific justification for discrimination and rejects "views of racial inequality which have been based on ignorance and prejudice."[107] Once again, Acts 17:26 plays a role: citing Paul's declaration that God "made of one blood all nations of men," Mays concludes that "science," at long last, "has caught up with religion."[108] He also calls for a "non-segregated" church, arguing that "to proclaim one thing and act another is sheer hypocrisy."[109]

These illustrative speeches deny any valid scriptural or scientific grounds for racial prejudice and race discrimination. They diagnose a shortfall between Christian and constitutional ideals and social practice.

Living by Conscience, Not Prejudice

By what strategies could religious leaders exhort their hearers to live by the demands of conscience rather than prejudice? What might prevent them from acting on conscience? In a sermon delivered the first Sunday after *Brown*, Reverend Charles P. Bowles, a minister at Dilworth Methodist Church in Charlotte, North Carolina, addressed such questions. He reported that after he spoke at a men's club meeting immediately after *Brown*, the man sitting next to him—"an average American and an average Methodist"—said: "I know it is not Christian to be opposed to [de]segregation, but I am opposed to it just the same." He told his congregation that this man "represents the thought of many Christians in our churches," who "know what is right," but "prefer to follow our prejudices." Similar to Maston, Bowles urged his congregants to act from "rational judgment" and "Christian intelligence," rather than their prejudices, and from a "warm heart of love" like the Good Samaritan.[110] He implored his congregation not to "give over to the hysteria of hate," but to focus on the Christian principle of "human brotherhood" and "show the world that a Christian democracy can and will work."[111]

A remarkably frank speech, in which a minister deploys conscience to indict his own prejudice, is "This I Believe," delivered by Dr. Haywood N. Hill in Trinity Presbyterian Church in Atlanta, Georgia. Explaining that he was "born and raised in Southern towns with their rigid racial patterns and their typical Southern prejudice," Hill lists his "likes," including racial, social, and intellectual segregation in church, school, neighborhood, and recreation, while having the benefit of black employees to "take the drudgery out of living for myself and my family."[112] He states: "I do not want my daughter to marry a Negro. I like the racial status quo. I am a Southernor."[113]

"But," Hill pivots, "I am also a Christian." He then lists beliefs that he "must" have: "God created all men" and "all men are equal in the sight of God"; "all men are my brothers and are children of God, and . . . I am my brother's keeper"; and Jesus "meant what he said when he commanded me to love my neighbor as myself and when he commanded me to do unto others as I would have them do unto me." In a critical passage, he contends: "As a Christian and as a scientist, I am obligated to act on the basis of what I know and believe and not on the basis of what I like. I must live by conviction and by *conscience* rather than by preference and by *prejudice*." Devoted to "the pursuit of objective truth," he "must know that . . . there is no such thing as racial inferiority." He must "regard every man, rich or poor, black or white, as a child of God and as a person, not as some kind of subhuman being or animal or even as an inferior." He must also "welcome . . . on the same basis that I would welcome any other individual" a "Negro who wants to worship in or join my church."[114]

Returning to intermarriage, Hill states:

> I must not only accept the efforts of the Negro to achieve his legitimate aspirations, but I must help him achieve them, and I believe that the church must do the same if it is a truly Christian church. I must do this, even though it goes against my deepest prejudices and even though it threatens my superior and isolated position in the community and even though it entails the risk of intermarriage.[115]

Rather than dismissing the "risk of intermarriage" as a segregationist "boogerboo," he argues that Christians must accept the risk. Through this self-examination, Hill may have voiced views shared by some of his listeners, including apprehension over intermarriage. He also pointed the way to replace prejudice with a commitment to the full political, civil, and social equality of African Americans.

Rescuing the Segregator from the Poisonous Fangs of Prejudice and Bigotry

A striking argument in many post-*Brown* sermons and speeches was that the bigoted or prejudiced person needed to be rescued from bigotry and prejudice. Like his teacher, Dr. Mays, Dr. King stressed that segregation harms ("scars the soul") of "both the segregator and the segregated."[116] A central tenet of King's philosophy of nonviolent resistance was that it was the "most potent" weapon for arousing the conscience of the oppressor, and his sense of shame or guilt, as a step toward reconciliation and redemption.[117]

Such sermons stressed the environmental causes of prejudice, cautioning to hate the sin ("segregation, racial prejudice, and injustice"), not the sinner. So urged Baptist minister and King associate C. K. Steele, who spoke of loving "our white friends" who "are victims in need of rescue from the poisonous fangs of racial customs and traditions that have grown up out of the hotbed of ignorance and prejudice."[118] Civil rights activist Rabbi Baumgard counseled that "it is too easy to call [the average] Southerner intolerant and prejudiced," without realizing that he is "caught in the tentacles of habit." Using the examples of his own mother and school teacher, Baumgard stated that they face the necessary but difficult task of "admitting that [their] entire life"—premised on white superiority—"has been a lie."[119]

In an address to his Nashville congregation, Reverend Merrimon Cuninggim appeals to the "troubled conscience of the Southerner," which "may be deeply hidden beneath layers of custom and rationalization, but . . . is there." He spoke of the need to educate and redeem—rather than "annihilate"—the person who clings to his prejudices like "idols." He observes: "Even the fury of the fanatic racist . . . which seems so sure and unambiguous, is the more frenetic because it covers an anxious insecurity or hides a deep alienation from self." He grants that "the 'fanatic racist' often succeeds in his cover-up," but "we know within our own hearts the conviction of sin and the need for repentance."[120]

Some sermons and speeches expressly referred to bigotry. Bigotry, Reverend William B. Selah argued, "robs the bigot himself of peace; for prejudice and the peace of God cannot dwell together in the same heart."[121] He described "racial bigotry" and "religious bigotry" (e.g., the Klan's anti-Catholicism) as a "denial of Christian brotherhood."[122] Segregationist ministers attributed *Brown* and the civil rights movement to Communist influence and "outside agitators," but Selah and others flipped the argument: racial and religious bigotry are a "threat to freedom" and play into the hands of Communism by dividing the nation "into contentious groups."[123] For example, author and civil rights activist Lillian Smith criticized Southern preachers and politicians for "spreading bigoted talk" about "the Catholic menace" and "the false fear of 'intermarriage of the races.'" Asking how "intelligent men [can] tell our people . . . the greatest danger facing the South and this nation is the danger that a few white people and a few Negroes may possibly marry each other," Smith retorts that "our greatest hazard" is that "the Communist powers may win the admiration and allegiance" of the "new nations" emerging in Africa and Asia "while we are still clinging to a past gone forever."[124]

The strategies for rescuing people from their prejudices track the methods detailed by social scientists of the era for "breaking the prejudice habit" (recall chapter 2). Both stress the role of conscience, or gaining insight about one's prejudice. They also include education and social contact between white and black persons on terms of equality.[125] Because "people come to believe in the things they perform regularly," religious leaders also urged "practicing equality"— acting "as if" our constitutional commitment to the "equality of all men" is true.[126]

Finally, the rhetoric of bigotry appears in descriptions of acts of violence against civil rights supporters, such as church and synagogue bombings. Rabbis and ministers urge their audiences not to "pull the covers of silence over our conscience" because of the violence committed by bigots.[127] Even if the consciences of such perpetrators cannot be reached, such violence, particularly that directed against nonviolent, peaceful demonstrators, could stir the consciences of others.

Christians in Racial Crisis in Little Rock: Competing Appeals to Conscience

In 1959, social scientists Ernest Campbell and Thomas Pettigrew observed that "the Protestant ministry is potentially the most effective agent of social change in the South" in the coming decade.[128] A 1958 poll in the journal *Pulpit Digest* seemed to support such a role: "Four out of five Protestant ministers in the seventeen Southern states are in favor of compliance with [*Brown*]." Only 12% agreed that "the Negro is different from other races in ways so basic that distinctions between him and others, in law and other public regulations, are realistic and necessary"; 82% "said that the Negro 'is no different from any other human being in any essential respect, and therefore no law or public agency should make any distinction whatever based on race.' "[129] Why, then, did not more white clergy act as agents of social change?

In *Christians in Racial Crisis: A Study of Little Rock's Ministry*, Campbell and Pettigrew offered a "scientific analysis" of the "failure of religious leadership" in Little Rock during the Central High School desegregation crisis in the fall of 1957.[130] Why did the Protestant ministry not take a unified stand in support of integration despite the fact that most of the community's "denominational clergymen view racial integration as morally right and desire to do something" about it?[131] Because the authors interviewed ministers on both sides of the issue, their study sheds light on the different ways clergy appealed to scripture and conscience to justify their contrasting positions.

By 1957, Little Rock's school board had announced a desegregation plan to comply with *Brown* and admit a small number of black students to Central High School in the fall. On September 3, however, Governor Orval Faubus called in the Arkansas National Guard to prevent the students from entering the school.[132] He stated that "negroes have been integrated [peacefully] into the public school[s]" where it was "acceptable to the majority." But "forcible integration of the public schools in Little Rock against the overwhelming sentiment of the people of the area" and by federal court order was likely to "bring about widespread disorder and violence." He cited Arkansas's "Resolution of Interposition," adopted in response to *Brown* to reassert state "sovereignty" over education.[133] Earlier that year, the state legislature passed laws prohibiting school integration.[134] Faubus asserted that he was calling in the Guard to "maintain or restore the peace and order of the community," stating that he had reached the decision "prayerfully."[135]

After a federal district court ordered Faubus to cease interfering with the integration of Central High, he withdrew the Guard and nine African American students entered. However, an angry mob's protest led to removing the children from the school under police escort. President Eisenhower finally ordered federal troops to enforce the federal court order, warning of the global impact of the incident.[136] The students returned under military escort, and military units "remained on guard until the close of the school year in the late spring of 1958." In fall 1958, Little Rock closed its public high schools to avoid continued racial integration.[137]

Little Rock's Ministers in Conflict

In the months leading up to the expected integration of Central High, very few white ministers preached directly against segregation "on moral and religious grounds." One notable exception was Reverend Marion A. Boggs, the "highly respected 'dean' of Little Rock's Protestant ministers."[138] On the Sunday closest to July 4, Boggs preached: "I am not going to give aid and comfort to segregationists . . . by failing to speak out on a matter I know to be right"—that "enforced separation of the races is discrimination which is out of harmony with Christian theology and ethics."[139] He voiced his conviction that "the church of Jesus Christ must rise to its full height of moral and ethical leadership." He asked: "Are we prepared to remove from our minds the prejudices and from our statute books the legal hindrances that stand in the way of full citizenship for our Negro citizens?" That is the "crucial test of Christian Citizenship."[140]

Faubus's calling in the Guard was the "crisis" that prompted contrasting ministerial responses. A group of local ministers representing six major Protestant denominations released a statement "to strongly protest" Faubus's action, followed shortly by a statement by another group of ministers supporting him for enforcing Arkansas's law requiring racial segregation in public schools.[141]

Open conflict between ministers—and laypersons—arose after President Eisenhower sent in the military escort. Various Citizens' Councils issued resolutions challenging all ministers who supported forced school integration "to integrate their churches by publicly inviting the colored people to their services." On the other side, the Episcopal bishop of Arkansas wrote a letter to Little Rock's Episcopal Churches, citing a 1952 Episcopal resolution establishing the policy of "consistently opposing and combating discrimination based on color" and declaring that physical violence at Central High "forces us to our knees in shame over our inability to exert an adequate Christian leadership in this hour."[142]

Dueling prayer services developed after the Episcopal bishop held a meeting, attended by Representative Brook Hays (also president of the SBC), to plan a citywide prayer service on Columbus Day. Interested black ministers were not invited to attend the planning meetings. An effort was made to make the service "neutral" on desegregation, but "vigorous segregationists, ministerial and otherwise," declined to participate in what they perceived as "merely an attempt to promote integration under a veneer of prayer." In a newspaper advertisement, the League of Central High Mothers declared that the clergy planning the service had engaged in "well known" activities "toward race-mixing." They challenged such clergy to fight out the integration question "on its merits" rather than sidestepping the issue to say, "Brethren, Let Us Pray."[143]

News stories announced an alternative prayer service with an explicitly segregationist aim, to be held the night before the Columbus Day service. A call for prayer at Central Baptist Church, signed mostly by pastors of small, Missionary Baptist churches, declared that returning the black children to (all-black) Horace Mann High School, "where they legally and morally belong," was the only path to "real and lasting peace."[144] A *New York Times* story reported: "Citizens could take their choice whether to attend a Friday night prayer service sponsored by 24 Baptist pastors who are avowed segregationists, or wait for Saturday's meeting when the praying will be neutral." With such competing calls to prayer, Campbell and Pettigrew observe, "the effort of ministers in the city's major churches to serve as agents of reconciliation was frustrated."[145]

The Central Baptist Church prayer service, sponsored by segregationist ministers, was "filled to capacity" (between six and seven hundred people), with an overflow crowd on the lawn. In explaining the need for a separate service for "those who are conservative in their beliefs about the deity of Christ," the "host pastor" disparaged the way that Jews, Catholics, and most Protestants pray (as "modernists"). Themes included that "the use of federal troops is unconstitutional," "Governor Faubus is a preservator of peace," and "Negroes who are Christians" and "our brothers and sisters in the Lord" are "not causing the trouble."[146]

By comparison, while "the larger and more prominent churches" in Little Rock "presented an essentially solid front" in participating in the Columbus Day prayer services, many sponsors found the attendance "disappointing." The service's stated objectives included "the support and preservation of Law and Order" and "casting out of rancor and prejudice in favor of understanding and compassion." However, in keeping with the objective of neutrality, there were no "moral imperatives" or "community goals."[147]

After the prayer services, "religious participation in the integration dispute declined sharply," with an important exception. "Dissident segregationists" became "more vocal than ever" and were supported in a steady stream of "Letters to the Editor."[148] Campbell and Pettigrew argue that the role of these "dissident segregationists" in giving voice to widely held public support for segregation— including by members of churches whose ministers condemned it—is critical to understanding why so many Little Rock ministers who supported integration failed to do so publicly.

Segregation as Pleasing to the Lord: Melding the Creed of Segregation with the American Creed

Not all Protestant bodies or their ministers condemned segregation and supported *Brown*. A prominent dissenting voice in the Little Rock crisis was the Arkansas Missionary Baptists, a "fundamentalist" group who linked desegregation in education to racial "mongrelization" and offered scriptural and theological arguments to support segregation.[149] An instructive text is their "Resolution on Integration," published in a local newspaper, which states that God has "taught in the Bible that segregation of the races was and is His desire and plan, Israel being a notable example," since God forbade Israelites to marry "with the black races of Canaan."[150]

The resolution affirms that Baptists are "law-abiding citizens," with "genuine love for all humanity," who oppose the use of physical force "either to hinder or to promote the integration of free men everywhere." Nonetheless, "the integration of Negroes and whites in our schools and society [is] a threat to the security of our nation and contrary to the teachings of God both in the Bible and in nature." The Supreme Court rulings and "the use of Federal troops" to enforce them are "deplorable, *unscriptural*, and not in harmony with previous decisions of that body" or with "the beliefs and purposes of the God-fearing and democratic-minded men who at the first drafted the Constitution of the United States of America."[151]

Ministers adhering to such beliefs defended their support for segregation with a "clear conscience," Campbell and Pettigrew argue, despite the emphasis on Christian conscience in condemning segregation. They could do so because they adhered to an "elaborate and extensive *creed of segregation* which bisects, contradicts, and interprets the American creed in ways both devious and intricate." Its tenets are: "Racial integration cannot be American since segregation is pleasing to the Lord and America is a Christian nation"; "Were segregation un-Christian, then all of the major Christian bodies would not have established segregated churches"; and "Americans should establish their own racial policies based on God's Will," not foreign "reactions." Furthermore, if segregation were "un-constitutional," a competent Supreme Court "could not have delayed discovery until 1954 [in *Brown*]." Segregation is "mutually desirable to both races," responsible for more "substantial" progress on the part of "the Negro" than "for any comparable period in the history of man."[152]

Particularly striking is such ministers' "basic certainty and assurance." Anticipating readers' suspicion that segregationist ministers were "struggling to legitimize a shaky position," Campbell and Pettigrew write: "Our impression is strongly to the contrary. All evidence indicates that the arguments were given with assurance and conviction, in the spirit of those who have a sense of mission." Consider one minister's statement: "Just as sure as I know my own name, I know that separate facilities for white and Negroes [are] pleasing to the Lord.' "[153] Such ministers "have a feeling of unequivocal support from the Bible which the integrationist ministers fail to find for their position."[154] Indeed, the "small sect minister" can "explain the minister who favors integration only by defining him as a poor student of the Bible."[155] The public support that segregationist ministers received for their views contributed to their confidence. Many reported that churchgoers who disagreed with the integrationist position of their own ministers had joined the segregationists' churches.[156]

Campbell and Pettigrew conclude that segregationist ministers gave "religious legitimization" to efforts to maintain racial segregation, defended as God's will rather than hatred or prejudice:

> The status quo need not be defended or explained because it is customary, economically feasible, psychologically functional, nor because of hatred or prejudice; it must be defended by those who claim to obey God's will. A Christian . . . supports [segregation] for the highest of motives. God who made the races separate intends them to remain that way. Those who wish His favor must follow His dictates.[157]

These ministers expressed a "value common to many white southerners in all walks of life." Such ministers "effectively neutralized the denominational minister's effort to aid the cause of integration by appealing to the Christian conscience."[158] Christian conscience dictated support *for* segregation.

The Paradox of the Churches

Campbell and Pettigrew argue that what theologian Reinhold Niebuhr called "the paradox of the churches" helps explain why the Protestant ministers who favored integration failed to be more effective leaders of peaceful change. This dynamic resembles what Allport called the paradoxical role of religion in both "making" and "unmaking" prejudice and bigotry. Niebuhr argued that despite official proclamations of universal brotherhood at the denominational level, brotherhood at the congregational level degenerated into a "sanctified sense of kind, whether of race or class or neighborhood." Paradoxically, the very "democratic" feature of Protestant self-governance in local churches "sacrifices leadership to lay prejudice."[159]

Campbell and Pettigrew apply this analysis to the "Protestant dilemma" in Little Rock. A minister's professional success is measured by increased financial support and growing membership. The minister is supposed to be a "cohesive force" rather than to divide members.[160] A minister who alienates his congregation by speaking out forcefully against segregation risks losing financial support and members—even though such a stance reflects the official denominational position. While Little Rock parishioners could not reasonably expect such ministers to speak out in defense of segregation, they did expect their ministers to keep silent and not dwell on "political" issues. That expectation "had real teeth": "decreased contributions, lowered attendance, and even removal of particularly offending clergymen."[161]

Niebuhr contrasted the "exceptional achievement of the Catholic Church in breaking down the walls of [racial] partition" and desegregating Catholic schools. He suggests that such success may be due in part—ironically—to its "undemocratic" structure. While "many clergymen in the Protestant churches have been as right and as heroic as the Catholic priests," "the [Catholic] bishops have supported the priests while Protestant congregations have been free to dismiss their clergy when they were critical of the 'Southern way of life.'"[162]

What, then, of the appeal to Christian conscience? Individual church members may sense the conflict between religious principles and their own personal preferences but, Campbell and Pettigrew conclude, would "prefer for the church to compromise in those realms of life (like race) in which they have strong emotional involvements counter to religious doctrine."[163] Recall the average Methodist described by Reverend Bowles who announced that he was opposed to desegregation even though he knew that such a position was not Christian.

Law, Conscience, and the Problem with the Myth of Moderation

In 1960, Pettigrew revisited the problem of Protestant religious leadership on desegregation in the address "Religious Leadership and the Desegregation Process," delivered at Fisk University, Nashville, Tennessee, when the "sit-in" movement was drawing growing attention—and religious support.[164] He suggests that a major problem is "the myth of moderation": that "a God-fearing Christian" should be moderate—a "middle of the roader." If that myth were not so "all pervasive" among "some of the clergy, and particularly among the laity," other constraints would not be such a great deterrent to "effective social action." The "white man in the South who feels that he is obligated to hold this middle of the road position" sees "extremists" on both sides: on one side, the Klan and Citizens' Council, "shooting at him, burning crosses, and blowing up buildings"; on the other, the "NAACP, the Southern Regional Council, etc.," whom he views as also "extremists [and] very much like the Citizens' Council," even though they sought only to enforce *Brown*.[165]

In challenging this myth, Pettigrew excoriates the moderate: "The moderate abhors violence, but . . . invites it unwittingly by saying that time is the only solution. The moderate is tireless in the belief that the hearts and minds of men are not changed by law and the traditions cannot be changed overnight." The moderate "agrees with the racist in feeling that the 1954 Supreme Court decision was not based on legal precedent" and predicts violence if "you make us integrate through the federal courts." Moreover, he "feels the church has no business in racial matters. He advocates reconciliation without repentance."[166] Indeed, by 1963, King would state that he had "almost reached the regrettable conclusion that the Negro's greatest stumbling block in his stride toward freedom is not the White Citizens' Counciler or the Ku Klux Klanner, but the white moderate . . . who constantly advises the Negro to wait for a 'more convenient season.'"[167]

Pettigrew challenges the myth of moderation by insisting (as did Allport) that "the hearts and minds of men *are* changed by law."

> This is one of the best principles established in social science study of race relations today. . . . Laws do change attitudes and behavior. . . .

In race relations typically, and particularly in the South, you change behavior first.[168]

Pettigrew offers a local example: "I am sure white attitudes toward integrated lunch counters in Nashville have already changed," but they changed "because you had them integrated."[169]

In summing up why "we could get along handsomely" *without* moderation, Pettigrew shares an anecdote revealing that even the most "ardent segregationist minister in Little Rock" worried about the judgment of history. One such minister observed that 100 years ago, in the same church, he would have delivered "some of the best defenses of slavery you have ever heard or could imagine." He continued: "Today, if I got up in that pulpit and delivered those brilliant defenses of slavery, they would laugh me out of the church." He added: "This is what worries me. If anybody a hundred years from now in that same pulpit got up and tried to deliver my brilliant defenses of segregation, they will laugh him out of the pulpit."[170]

That minister's concern about the judgment of history reflects Reverend Maston's concern, in 1955, that "a lot of Baptists" (including preachers) would be on "the wrong side on this whole issue."[171] Forty years later, in 1995, the SBC issued its "Resolution on Racial Reconciliation," "unwaveringly denounc[ing] racism, in all its forms as deplorable sin."[172] It cited the Bible verses invoked by clergy decades earlier to condemn segregation and affirm the unity of the human family. It recognized the "profoundly distort[ing]" effect of racism on understanding the demands of "Christian morality." It acknowledged both the defense by many Southern Baptist forebears of slavery and, later, the failure of many Southern Baptists to support legitimate civil rights initiatives for African Americans. The resolution apologizes to African Americans for "condoning and/or perpetuating individual and systematic racism in our lifetime" and genuinely repents of "racism of which we have been guilty, whether consciously or unconsciously."[173] In 2017, however, the SBC declined to adopt a resolution introduced by a prominent black pastor denouncing white supremacy and the "retrograde ideologies, xenophobic biases and racial bigotries of the so-called alt-right," leading some to note the SBC's "history of being on the wrong side of history."[174]

Conclusion

This chapter presented contrasting appeals to conscience, scripture, science, and US constitutional ideals in the competing theologies for and against racial segregation. A sobering lesson is that the appeal to conscience is no guarantee against being on the wrong side of moral issues. These competing theologies continued to feature in political battles, as Congress took up civil rights legislation in the 1960s. As chapter 5 details, by 1963 in Birmingham, the tactic of nonviolent resistance—and the violent reactions to it—would prove crucial to arousing the moral conscience of the nation and spurring Congress to pass long-overdue civil rights legislation.

Our Spirit Is Not Narrow Bigotry

Debating the Civil Rights Act of 1964 and Legislating Morality

> Discrimination in public accommodations is not simply a matter of
> economics, it is a matter of morality and of constitutional right. Until
> such indignities are eliminated, there can be no clear conscience for
> any of our citizens who seek to fulfill the spirit of America. Our spirit
> is not narrow bigotry.
>
> —Sen. Thomas Kuchel,
> 110 Cong. Rec. 6557 (March 30, 1964)

> Time and again those of us who oppose this outrageous legislation
> have been called prejudiced and bigoted, but it seems to this Senator
> that those terms apply much more accurately to those who would
> cram [the public accommodations bill] down the throats of Americans
> without really understanding its whole meaning.
>
> —Sen. Russell Long,
> 110 Cong. Rec. 12315 (June 1, 1964)

In 1947, President Harry S. Truman's Committee on Civil Rights issued a report, *To Secure These Rights*, proposing a robust civil rights agenda and an end to
segregation. Echoing Gunnar Myrdal's analysis of the "American dilemma," the
report identified the "gulf between our civil rights principles and our practices"
and proclaimed that "the greatest hope for the future" was "the increasing awareness by more and more Americans" of that gulf and the imperative of narrowing
it.[1] Truman was "profoundly troubled by the reports of violence inflicted on returning African American veterans" and of acquittals of the wrongdoers by "all-
white southern juries" and was determined to "do something" to advance civil
rights.[2] Race discrimination, the report declared, was morally wrong, harmed
the economy, and impaired US foreign relations. For reasons of "conscience, self-
interest, and survival in a threatening world," it was "time for action."[3] Pointing
to positive experiences with integration in the military and in housing, the report contended that the "separate but equal" doctrine "has institutionalized

Who's the Bigot? Linda C. McClain, Oxford University Press (2020). © Oxford University Press.
DOI: 10.1093/oso/9780190877200.001.0001

segregation and kept groups apart despite indisputable evidence that normal contacts among these groups tend to promote social harmony."[4] It urged all states to enact laws prohibiting racial discrimination in "public accommodations" (businesses open to the public and providing goods and services).[5]

In 1948, Truman delivered to Congress a ten-point plan based on the report's recommendations, but he correctly perceived that the measures would be received "coldly."[6] From 1948 until the early 1960s, members of Congress introduced a number of civil rights bills, but most failed; filibusters and amendments weakened the few that passed.[7] During that period, the Supreme Court issued opinions chipping away at legally compelled segregation and racial inequality in various spheres of daily life. One opinion, *Brown v. Board of Education*, motivated both massive resistance to desegregation and further efforts toward dismantling segregation (as chapter 4 described).[8]

In the summer of 1963 President John F. Kennedy proposed an ambitious civil rights bill, similarly justified on moral, economic, and foreign policy grounds. After Kennedy's assassination in November 1963, President Lyndon B. Johnson urged that passing the bill would be the most eloquent way to "honor" Kennedy.[9] On July 2, 1964, Johnson signed into law the Civil Rights Act of 1964 (CRA), which Congress passed after an "epic" battle.[10]

Supporters of the CRA insisted that the national conscience demanded such a law because discrimination posed an urgent moral crisis. One spur to arousing conscience was the increased national visibility of the peaceful nonviolent direct actions undertaken by the civil rights movement. In May 1963, public shame over televised broadcasts of Sheriff Bull Connor and his police force unleashing dogs and turning fire hoses on African Americans engaged in a civil rights march in Birmingham—and the consequent demand that the government do something—had a "transformative effect."[11] In June, President Kennedy addressed the nation, calling civil rights a "moral issue . . . as old as the scriptures and . . . as clear as the American Constitution." He invoked the Golden Rule, asking "whether we are going to treat our fellow Americans as we want to be treated."[12] Kennedy called on religious leaders to support the bill, as did Johnson. Religious leaders testifying before Congress in support of the CRA appealed to "the religious conscience of America" and condemned racism as "blasphemy against God."[13]

This chapter traces the rhetoric of bigotry and conscience as Congress considered whether it could or should legislate morality by passing a broad federal civil rights bill. I focus primarily on the debate over Title II, the public accommodations section, which prohibits discrimination based on race, religion, color, and national origin in hotels, restaurants, gas stations, and entertainment venues.[14] How did supporters of Title II view the problem of bigotry and law's role in addressing it? How did opponents challenge the claim that the national conscience demanded such a law to end bigotry?[15]

In insisting that all Americans had a stake in doing what conscience required, proponents of the CRA enlisted the rhetoric of bigotry. When President Johnson urged Southern Baptists that they had a "greater responsibility" than any other group of Christians to support the bill, he observed, "I have seen first-hand how basic spiritual beliefs and deeds can shatter barriers of politics and bigotry."[16] As quoted at the beginning of the chapter, Senator Thomas Kuchel (R-California), one of the floor leaders of the Senate debate, argued that "our spirit is not narrow bigotry," and that until the "indignities" of discrimination in public accommodations "are eliminated, there can be no clear conscience for any of our citizens who seek to fulfill the spirit of America."[17] Those who opposed the bill "out of prejudice or bigotry," some legislators argued, were "trying to hold back the tide of human progress."[18] As Dr. Martin Luther King, Jr. later put it, neither "the powers of bigotry or Bull Connor" could prevent a "new order" that "was destined to be born."[19]

Opponents of the CRA met these appeals to conscience and condemnations of bigotry in different, and sometimes contradictory, ways. One striking response, evident in the remark by Senator Russell Long (D-Louisiana) quoted at the beginning of the chapter, was to reverse the charge of bigotry to apply to those trying to "cram" the bill "down the throats of Americans."[20] Religious opponents of the bill claimed the moral high ground: they objected to presidential requests to clergy to support the bill because of their "deep moral and religious convictions that integration of the races is morally wrong and should be resisted." Drawing on the "creed of segregation" discussed in chapter 4, they asserted that clergy who argued otherwise were "blasphemers" against God, "immoral," "apostate," and communistic.[21] Opponents also insisted that God was the author of natural inequality and racial difference.

A contrasting response did not deny charges that refusing service to a customer because of race was bigoted, but maintained that private citizens had a right to be bigoted, unreasonable, and "nasty" when dealing with their private property.[22] Opponents also insisted that legislating morality would fail. Law—and certainly federal law—could not solve conflicts of human nature, and eradicate bigotry, until people were willing to follow the Golden Rule.[23]

Recovering this rhetoric is valuable to addressing puzzles about bigotry, including both the appeal to conscience to indict bigotry (as chapter 4 revealed) and the significance of time in assessing charges, denials, and countercharges of bigotry. Today, the CRA stands as a landmark civil rights law and a frequent point of reference in civil rights debates. Yet when Title II was debated, opponents challenged the claim that the bill presented a great moral issue and disputed the authority of a majority to impose its view of "fair and decent and good morals" on a minority.[24] A good illustration of this shift is arguments in *Masterpiece Cakeshop v. Colorado Civil Rights Commission*, discussed in chapter 8.

Opponents of Colorado's public accommodations law contrasted it unfavorably with Title II. In a brief filed in 2017, Texas and other states whose senators and representatives opposed Title II in 1964 now praised it as the model of a narrowly tailored and justified civil rights law. They also asserted that "public-accommodations concerns of past eras are not present" in today's disputes, such as conscience-based refusals by business owners to provide goods and services to same-sex couples.[25] Amici supporting Colorado's law disagreed, finding close analogies between past and present "concerns" from which we should learn, including the appeal to religious beliefs to oppose public accommodations laws.[26] This chapter's revisiting of the rhetoric and arguments in the debate over Title II provides a foundation for evaluating these competing views of the civil rights past.

Congress Can and Must Legislate Morality

Supporters of the CRA made several arguments concerning why Congress should legislate morality by passing the bill: (1) conscience and morality demand passage of the CRA and repudiation of racism and bigotry; (2) ample precedent exists for Congress passing legislation to address moral issues; (3) while legislation cannot do everything, such as change hearts and minds or prejudicial attitudes, it can at least regulate behavior and prohibit discriminatory conduct; and (4) experience with other anti-discrimination laws and common sense indicate that such laws can change behavior and may, eventually, change attitudes. I also discuss the argument that the public accommodations law, through the "Mrs. Murphy" boarding house exception, preserved freedom of choice in private social relations, and the competing argument that law—as matter of moral principle—should not include such an exception.

Proponents of the CRA expressed convictions about the proper role of law in combating prejudice and bigotry that parallel those of post–World War II studies of prejudice (discussed in chapter 2). One conviction challenged the assertion that "stateways cannot change folkways" and, thus, that you cannot fight prejudice by attempting to legislate morality.[27] Invoking Myrdal, for example, Gordon Allport contended that most Americans "deep inside their consciences do approve civil rights and antidiscrimination legislation" because they feel a sense of shame at the gap between American ideals and discriminatory treatment of African Americans in the United States.[28] Another conviction was that social contact on terms of equality can diminish prejudice and that legislation can bring about that contact.[29] Supporters of the CRA appealed to "common sense" and "experience" under state and local anti-discrimination laws to insist that such laws can and do change behavior.

Conscience and Morality Demand Passage of the CRA and Repudiation of Racism and Bigotry

Proponents of the CRA argued that Congress could and should legislate morality to close the gap between conscience and practice in the United States. Dr. King argued that with "resolute presidential leadership," Congress could pass meaningful civil rights laws to end racial discrimination, "America's greatest moral dilemma."[30] Marking the gap between America's "professed beliefs and our actual practices," New Jersey Senator Clifford P. Case asserted:

> Most Americans want the Congress to act to right a wrong that has persisted for too long. The hypocrisy in which all of us have had a part has had a corrosive effect on the national conscience. Discrimination is debasing, not just to those discriminated against but to those who discriminate.[31]

Likewise, Senator Kuchel appealed to conscience—and the "American spirit"—as requiring the rejection of "narrow bigotry," arguing that "discrimination in public accommodations" was a matter of "morality and of constitutional right," not simply "economics." He proclaimed: "Our spirit is not to refuse service to a fellow human being because God provided him with a different skin pigmentation than our own."[32]

Attorney General Robert F. Kennedy contended that "the need for this country to live up to its ideals" clearly outweighed "the right of privately owned public service enterprises to insult large sections of their public by refusing to serve them, for no reason than the arbitrary and immoral logic of bigotry."[33] Because the latter was "plainly a right to commit wrong," "surely, in the balancing, there can be no question on which side the scales [of justice] must fall."[34]

Racial discrimination in public accommodations, Kennedy argued, is "morally offensive to us all," and requires "Negroes to suffer humiliation and deprivation that no white citizen would tolerate," adding that such discrimination "has been the source of more than 65% of the 1,580 civil rights demonstrations that have taken place since May [1963]."[35] Key speeches by bill sponsors also stressed that "monstrous humiliations" were the "evil" that the public accommodations law would address, and "freedom from indignity" was the freedom the CRA would advance.[36] Dr. King's "Letter from a Birmingham Jail" wrote of "being humiliated day in and day out by nagging signs reading 'white' and 'colored'" and by the denial of goods and services.[37] In Congressional hearings, religious groups testified that the "sting and pain" of daily humiliation that African Americans faced was something that "no conscientious person" could defend.[38] A coalition of Jewish religious bodies and civic groups condemned the unjust humiliation, indignity, and insult "to which the Negro is constantly subjected," noting Jews' own experience with being "turned away" from facilities "supposedly open to the public."[39]

Examples of the explicit rhetoric of bigotry. Similar to Senator Kuchel, a number of legislators stressed the stake all American citizens have in ending such bigotry. Representative Fred Rooney (D-Pennsylvania) argued that Pennsylvanians supported Title II "not only for the sake of the American Negro, his dignity and his future, but for the sake of all Americans who, knowingly or otherwise, sell their free birthright by practicing prejudice or bigotry."[40] A representative from Connecticut argued that "our self-respect should dwindle with each indication of bigotry and racism."[41]

The rhetoric of bigotry also featured in the argument that the CRA addressed the unfinished business from Emancipation. One dramatic example is Senator Wayne Morse's (D-Oregon) appeal to President Lincoln's rhetoric to argue that the issue was "whether this country will remain half free and half slave":

> So long as a Negro in this country does not have exactly the same rights of constitutional enjoyment that every white person has . . . he is enslaved . . . to the bigotry, the prejudice, and the bias under which he has suffered ever since the Great Emancipator uttered those historic words in the form of the Emancipation Proclamation a hundred years ago.[42]

Some legislators turned to the language of bigotry to rebut the argument that the civil rights bill was not necessary because of the "paternalistic" and "kindly" treatment of "the American Negro" by "the white segment of our society." Thus, Representative John B. Anderson (R-Illinois) expressed "sympathy" that passing "this legislation will spell the end of the last vestiges" of such treatment, but continued: "The record in this case contains irrefutable evidence that amid the paternalism and the kindliness are . . . glaring and even shocking examples of discrimination and ill treatment which has been born and bred out of hatred and bigotry."[43]

Some supporters argued that bigotry might be a motive for opposing the CRA. A senator from Ohio asserted: "Those who for selfish reasons, or out of prejudice or bigotry . . . are standing in the way of constitutional rights for the Negroes of America are, in a sense, to be pitied." He argued that such opponents "are trying to hold back the tide of human progress, to halt the relentless force of the strength of the human spirit."[44] In the House, a representative from California also contrasted bigotry with moral progress: "In the debate over this bill the representatives of these backward States plus a few others have sought to defend a system of bigotry and racism with moth-eaten ideas already declared unlawful or out of step with the 20th Century."[45]

Another argument was that constitutional objections to Title II were a pretext, since opponents could not openly "defend prejudice or bigotry" or contend that "racial discrimination" in the market was a "worthwhile American tradition."[46] Reversing the charges that the bill's supporters played into the hands of Communists, some argued that the people in the various states "opposed to delivering the Constitution to the Negroes of America" were just as "subversive" as Communists because applying their "biases, prejudice, and bigotry" would "destroy government by law."[47]

These examples of speeches employing the rhetoric of bigotry indicate that lawmakers often referred to bigotry as a synonym for racism, racial prejudice, and hate; they believed that a civil rights law prohibiting discrimination could properly limit "practicing" bigotry. Because bigotry was contrary to American ideals and to progress, they suggested that opponents of the bill hid their bigotry by offering arguments that were pretexts.

The appeal to religious conscience. Religious leaders testified that "the religious conscience of America condemns racism as blasphemy against God." In a hearing before the Senate Committee on Commerce, a Catholic priest (Father Cronin), rabbi (Rabbi Blank), and Presbyterian minister (Dr. Blake) made an "historic" joint appearance to deliver that message, with which over thirty-three other religious groups asked to be identified.[48] Explaining the groups' concern with "the moral principles that indicate the necessity of enacting" the civil rights legislation, Cronin referred to statements by major religious bodies "specifically condemn[ing] racial discrimination, segregation, and prejudice as incompatible with the principles of faith in God." He also appealed to one of America's hallowed texts: "Racial discrimination and segregation still continue to deny persons basic human rights in this country 100 years after the issuance of the Emancipation Proclamation."

One ecumenical document Cronin cited, "Appeal to the Conscience of the American People," adopted in January 1963 by the National Conference on Religion and Race, called for a "renewed religious conscience" on the "serious moral evil" of racism. The appeal mourned the fact that despite *Brown* and "the heroic nonviolent protests of thousands of Americans," segregation "remains entrenched everywhere—North and South, East and West."[49] It urged Americans to "seek a reign of justice" in which "public facilities and private ones serving a public purpose will be accessible to all." Cronin testified that because many religious bodies held their meetings only where public accommodations were open to all, they were unable to find adequate places to

meet. He argued: "Neither law nor morality sanction the concept of the absolute right of property."[50]

Other religious statements in support of the public accommodations provision insisted that the religious case against discrimination was undeniable. The
Council for Christian Social Action insisted: "Anyone who takes seriously the
principles underlying our Judeo-Christian heritage must admit that discrimination against the members of any group whom God has created is a sin against
God and a corruption of whatever religious faith we profess."[51]

Along similar lines, Senator Hubert Humphrey (D-Minnesota) found particularly "moving" a letter by "435 southern Presbyterian ministers, educators,
and laymen" stating: "The voice of filibuster has for too long been regarded as
the most authentic southern voice. It is not. The South's most authentic voice
is the voice of conscience and of faith." The group, A Fellowship of Concern,
supported passage of a "strong and effective civil rights bill," which would "have
the effect of righting cultural and civic wrongs too long extended and ignored."
It praised President Johnson's challenge "to southern churchman to support the
civil rights bill and to encourage its effective translation into the customs of community life."[52]

The praise of nonviolent direct action in some of these religious statements
reflects the embrace of methods of "engaging the public conscience" that extended beyond resolutions and statements to support direct action. Not all
churches agreed with this "growing engagement of clergy in civil rights activism,"
as discussed later in this chapter.[53]

A national law helps people follow conscience. Legislators and witnesses argued
that most Americans wanted to follow conscience and do the right thing, but
needed the help of a strong national law. For example, Walter Reuther, President
of the United Automobile Workers (UAW), testified:

> There is great good will in Americans in all parts of the country to do
> the right thing. The Deerfield prejudice of Illinois suburbia is just as evil
> as the Bull Connor prejudice of the South. Down deep in the hearts of
> most Americans there is the desire to do the right thing—but the right
> thing will not be possible in Chicago or Birmingham unless there are
> strong laws backed up by the Federal Government.

Based on experience with "strong labor laws," Reuther argued that "strong civil
rights laws" would also be welcomed.[54] Another union president testified that
without such a law, "the man who wants to do the right thing" is "not free to follow
his conscience, because he fears the competition of a man who is doing the wrong
thing." "Decades of experience," he contended, show that legislation resting "on
our avowed ideals" "frees the rightdoer" and "check[s] the wrongdoer."[55]

Congress Can Legislate Morality

Lawmakers and witnesses also argued that ample precedent existed for Congress to "require by law what is demanded by morality."[56] Missouri Senator Edward Long observed:

> Most of our criminal laws are fundamentally moral. The minimum wage law, the child labor law, and many others are founded in morality. The civil rights legislation before us today seeks to do no more. . . . It merely seeks ways and means to help make the guarantees of our Constitution, the law of the land, a reality for all Americans.[57]

Witnesses offered the specific example of enacting prior anti-discrimination laws:

> It is also too late in the day for anyone to argue seriously that this type of legislation is undesirable because you cannot legislate morality. That is an argument that one finds wherever important social legislation is developed. . . . But we have had such legislation now for almost 20 years.[58]

The Kennedy and Johnson administrations as well as legislators stressed the acute need to right a moral wrong and defended the propriety of Congress passing legislation to do so. They made the strategic choice to emphasize Congress's power to regulate interstate commerce as the constitutional underpinning for the CRA more than its power to enforce the Thirteenth or Fourteenth Amendments.[59] The moral conviction was clear, however, when the Supreme Court, in *Heart of Atlanta Motel v. United States*, heard an unsuccessful challenge to Title II by a motel operator.[60] When Solicitor General Archibald Cox emphasized that Title II was "addressed to a commercial problem of grave national significance," Justice Goldberg pressed him: "Isn't there [a] moral problem, also?" Cox answered that Congress was also "keeping faith" with the promise that "all men are created equal," and that "the failure to keep that promise lay heavy on the conscience of the entire nation, North as well as South, East as well as West."[61] In upholding Title II, the Court's opinion in *Heart of Atlanta Motel* observed that Congress had often regulated commerce to reach activities that are "moral wrongs."[62]

Realism About What Civil Rights Legislation Can Achieve: Changing Behavior, If Not Hearts and Minds

Could a civil rights law prevent bigotry—or at least its overt expression? Even though proponents of the CRA appealed to the nation's conscience to insist that

the urgent moral problem of racial discrimination necessitated civil rights legislation, they called for realism about what law could do. Legislation "can help although
it cannot do everything."[63] Law could reach discriminatory behavior, though it
might not transform underlying attitudes. For example, one senator argued:

> As Martin Luther King said: "Morality cannot be legislated; but behavior can
> be regulated. The law may not change the heart, but it can restrain the heart-
> less." We have seen this in so many areas where we know we can't change the
> heart of man, the mind of man, but we can regulate his behavior.[64]

An NAACP officer testified: "This is not going to be any cure-all . . . but it is going
to be a cure-some."[65] He elaborated: "Whether a person wants to do right or not,
if he is prohibited from doing wrong by the power of the law, he is not going
to flout it to the extent that he does now."[66] Civil rights law, supporters argued,
could limit people's ability to *act on* their prejudices when doing so harms other
American citizens or the nation.[67]

Republican Representative William M. McCulloch (R-Ohio), an author
of the CRA, stressed the difficulty of legislating in the field of "morals and the
thinking and attitudes of human beings." Legislation was "only a persuasion and
a proper urging" and could not alone "solve this most troublesome domestic
problem." But it was necessary to try, because the CRA's proponents are "on the
side of the angels."[68] The success of the law, another lawmaker argued, would depend on appealing to individuals' "civic pride" and "morality": "the people must
do that which they feel is righteous."[69]

Enacting a civil rights law that applies to everyone, Michigan Senator Philip
A. Hart asserted, would allow society to get "accustomed" to the idea and "learn to
live with it."[70] Some witnesses argued that such a law *could* eventually change hearts
and minds, as people internalized it. Reuther predicted such a process would follow
Congress's passage of a strong, comprehensive federal civil rights "code" that ful-
filled the "promise of our forefathers" that "all men are in fact equal beings":

> Someday, after this code has been accepted by all Americans, prejudice
> will end and the code will fall into disuse. Such a code . . . will have set a
> standard of conduct that will make fair practices in all walks of life not
> only a rule of conduct but a condition of mind and of heart.[71]

The Appeal to Experience and Common Sense:
Law as Educational

Many legislators and witnesses pointed to experience with anti-discrimination
laws to counter the argument that attempting to legislate morality would fail.

Like Allport, they stressed the impact of law on educating people and changing behavior. Responding to the argument that racial discrimination "must be eliminated by friendly persuasion, by education, not law," the Christian Social Action Council pointed to the impact of a public accommodations law in Washington, DC, where racial discrimination went from being "accepted as the standard and normal pattern of society" to being "rare and unexpected."[72] Some witnesses testified that the passage of a state or local public accommodations law was "educational . . . for many people who had discriminated before" because it "reflected a will of the community."[73]

Witnesses and legislators also drew on experience to show that people's anticipated reaction to a new anti-discrimination policy often differs from what they actually do.[74] Witnesses pointed out that the public accommodations laws in thirty states and the District of Columbia "have brought none of the grave evils in their train that have been so freely predicted."[75] Richard Bennett, of the American Friends Service Committee, testified:

> In the process of acting without discrimination, people's attitudes change. Further, experience has shown the difference between how people say they will act in advance of some proposed change in hiring or housing or school patterns and what they actually do when the change comes.[76]

The Senate Report on Title II also noted this dynamic, citing Richard Marshall, an attorney from El Paso, Texas:

> Many of the theaters and restaurants welcomed with relief the passage of the ordinance, since they had the force of law behind their natural desire to serve all patrons without causing arguments on their business premises. I do not think that even the most fervent . . . opponents of the ordinance among the restaurants and hotel people would today be able to state that this legislation had either harmed their business, taken any of their property or profits from them, deprived them of any of their liberties, or created any super police power in the community.[77]

Economic historian Gavin Wright's study of the actual effects of the CRA found that businesses' fear of economic ruin and loss of white customers failed to materialize and that integration in fact proved beneficial for businesses. The CRA brought about a learning process, as businesses learned that white customer reaction was not as severe as predicted, and white customers learned that desegregation was "not as bad as they had feared."[78]

In hearings on Title II, several governors pointed to successful experience with public acceptance of state public accommodations laws to predict that the federal law could succeed.[79] Governors also emphasized that passing a law was not enough: "firm enforcement" was necessary to "close the gap between the principle and practice of nondiscrimination."[80] The Japanese-American Citizens League observed that "once compliance becomes the accepted and automatic order, the tensions and questions of the transitional stage pass away."[81]

Exemptions: Debating Mrs. Murphy and Her Boarding House

Given the intense present-day controversy over whether for-profit businesses should have exemptions from state public accommodations laws, it is instructive to consider how lawmakers and witnesses discussed justifications for the "Mrs. Murphy" boarding house exception to the CRA. Legal scholar Robin Fretwell Wilson bluntly contends that "everyone understood that the fictional Mrs. Murphy was a bigot," who rejected would-be African American boarders solely because of their skin color.[82] When asked what justified the exclusion, Attorney General Kennedy—who condemned the "immoral logic of bigotry"—said that government was not "attempting to become involved in social relationships." Public accommodations law did not affect those "who own small rooming houses and live on the premises themselves and just have a few rooms to rent" because "it becomes virtually a social operation."[83] Other defenses of Mrs. Murphy's right to refuse accommodation "for any reason—good, bad, or indifferent—that strikes her fancy" stressed freedom of association, the right to privacy, and the sanctity of one's home.[84] Wilson suggests that one important reason for the exemption was simply "political expediency," breaking the "logjam" over Title II by adding a "sweetener" to overcome some southern senators' opposition to it.[85]

Notably, some religious leaders and groups testified *against* the Mrs. Murphy exemption. The National Community Relations Advisory Council urged that "the coverage of this bill not be limited under the guise of concern for private property" and argued that "an exemption for bona fide private clubs" was "sufficient to protect the legitimate interests of free association." By contrast, "other establishments, open to the public and often licensed by the State are properly within the coverage of this bill."[86]

Father Cronin, on behalf of his religious colleagues, contended: "Morally speaking, the discrimination that makes an American a second-class citizen is intolerable and untenable, regardless of whether this is the reputed Mrs. Murphy's boarding house or the largest hotel in the United States." Senator John Pastore (D-Rhode Island) pressed Cronin on whether the administration's public/private ("social") line was justifiable: it was a "disgrace" that "along route 40 . . . African Ambassadors of emerging nations in Africa, or any other race or color, American or otherwise, should be denied access to these public facilities," but was it a different case if "a widow . . . has a large house and inadequate income and seeks to take lodgers"? Might not Title II's requirements, without an exemption, "put her in a position where she may run into social difficulties that make it impossible for her to make a living?" Cronin, however, would not distinguish based on size "once a facility is open to the public." Mrs. Murphy "has every right to insist that people who come to her private home are well-dressed, well-behaved, mannerly, the type of person that she would like to associate with. But I cannot morally accept the decision that color is the basis for discrimination."[87] Rabbi Blank suggested that it would clarify issues to "think of Mrs. Murphy . . . as we thought of Typhoid Mary": "Once these facilities are made available to any segment of the public, that there is the possibility of spreading the evils of discrimination and subjecting our citizens to shame and degradation which they should not be subjected to."[88]

Arguments Against Legislating Morality Through Civil Rights Law

Members of Congress and witnesses made various, and sometimes conflicting, arguments against Title II. On the one hand, they argued that Congress should not and could not legislate morality, stressing law's limited ability to change human nature. Such legislation might instead make the problem of bigotry worse. On the other hand, they defended segregation and racial inequality as rooted in moral principles and the divine order, not bigotry. Opponents of the CRA also appealed to constitutional principles, such as liberty, self-determination, freedom of choice and association, and control of private property. Notable was the argument that people had a right to be wrong (and bigoted) and to discriminate. Some instead applied the label "bigot" to the bill's supporters. Opponents also made federalism and prudential arguments: state and local governments knew better how to address discrimination. Even better were nonlegal approaches, such as persuasion, or racial minorities building their own support networks of businesses, schools, and social institutions.

Segregation of the Races in Social, Business, and Religious Life is of Divine Origin

Traces of the theology of segregation discussed in chapter 4 appear in the Congressional debates about the CRA. One example is the testimony of

Dr. Albert Garner, President of the Florida Baptist Institute and Seminary. On June 17, 1963, President Kennedy met with a number of ministers, appealing to them to form a biracial committee to support voluntary integration of businesses and to urge Congress to support the administration's civil rights bill. Dr. Garner objected, telling Kennedy that "seeking to use the American clergy and the churches as agencies of political action was inappropriate" and "in conflict" with Kennedy's prior expression of belief in "the separation of church and state."[89] Garner also said that "segregation is a principle of the Old Testament" and that "racial integration that would lead to intermarriage was against the will of their Creator."[90]

In July 1963, in a hearing on Title II, Garner's statement in opposition was entered into the Congressional Record. He stated that he was a member of the Race and Civil Rights Committees of the American Baptist Association, an association of "some 31,000 congregations with almost a million members."[91] Two features of Garner's statement warrant attention. First, it included a recent resolution of the Florida State Baptist Association of Churches expressing "deep moral and religious convictions . . . that integration of the races is morally wrong and should be resisted" and that "federal efforts to force integration as a new social pattern of life is morally wrong, un-Christian, and in conflict with the word and will of God as well as historic Christianity." The resolution stated that "the Negro should be afforded greater opportunities for achievement and encouraged to win respect for himself in public life," but not through racial integration (such as in public schools, pursuant to *Brown*). The resolution's "findings" include that: (1) "segregation was the social pattern of life of the Old Testament Hebrew People . . . given and administered by divine command"; (2) "prior to this century, neither the Hebrew religion, the Christian religion, nor any denomination of the Christian religion ever held that integration of the races was necessary to obey God, to follow the teachings of Jesus Christ"; and (3) "our Nation became the greatest and most respected Nation in the world under the pattern of segregation in social life."[92] Garner's statement elaborated that "we hold that moral principles never change and that segregation of the races in social and religious life is still of divine order." The proposed civil rights bill conflicted with "historic Hebrew and Christian religious concepts on social and business affairs" and instead embodied "social reforms based upon anti-Christian and atheistic social philosophies." Garner called President Kennedy's statement that "race has no place in American life or law" a "flagrant affront to the social facts of life in this country" and an "atheistic concept."[93]

Second, Dr. Garner expressly "register[ed] disagreement" with the testimony by Father Cronin, Rabbi Blank, and Dr. Blake in support of the CRA. He stated that "if segregation which they refer to as 'racism' in social, business, and religious life is immoral and blasphemy against God, our Founding Fathers and the fathers of these gentlemen were . . . immoral men and blasphemers against God." Their testimony, he asserted, "is a classic example of apostate Christian and Hebrew concepts, designed to revolutionize and remold the social, economic, business, and religious life of America along the lines of a new social order of atheistic and anti-Christian religious views."[94]

Garner's insistence that moral principles do not change over time was echoed in a comment by Senator Richard Russell of Georgia, who challenged clergy's efforts in support of the CRA because it presented a "moral issue." Russell asserted: "If it is a great moral issue today, it was a great moral issue at the ratification of the Constitution of the United States," implying that the clergy "were two centuries late."[95] While clergy supporting the law insisted that conscience demanded that it right wrongs "too long ignored," Garner and Russell denied that there were such wrongs: what was reasonable at the founding remained reasonable in 1964.

Senators and Representatives who opposed the CRA introduced statements by southern clergy and lay people to show that there was not one unequivocal religious voice in support of it. In effect, the argument was that there were decent, sincere people on both sides. South Carolina Senator Strom Thurmond read letters from various southern churches that adopted resolutions stating that ministers and laymen who appealed to conscience in support of the "so-called civil rights bill" did not "speak for" them. Like Dr. Garner, they associated such positions with atheism and communism, not Christianity.[96] On June 9, 1964, West Virginia Senator Robert Byrd cited a news item reporting that the American Council of Christian Churches, "representing 15 denominational groups with a total of more than 20 million members, wired President Johnson today protesting the civil rights bill." Byrd called the Council "a highly reputable religious organization, one which is composed of good citizens genuinely interested in the welfare of humanity and deeply determined to live up to the terms of the Christian code."[97] Given that "the churches representing each side can justly claim to [be] the ultimate repositories of the public morals," he asked how to "reconcile these two widely divergent positions."[98]

Some lay witnesses also asserted the divine origin of segregation: God was the original and "greatest" segregationist. Samuel J. Setta, Chairman of the Referendum Committee of Easton, Maryland, argued:

> You are bucking a law which was never enacted by any legislature when you pass a law like this, the law of nature. God himself was the greatest segregationist of all time as is evident when he placed the Caucasians in Europe, the black people in Africa, the yellow people in the Orient and so forth, and if God didn't see fit to mix people who are we to try it?[99]

Setta found further justification in the life of Jesus: "Christ himself never lived an integrated life, and although He knew His life on earth would be a model for all mankind, when he chose His close associates, they were all white." Neither Christianity nor Judaism had "integrate[d]," he added, and the thirty states that have anti-discrimination laws are "just as segregated as the 20 that don't." Setta, a "motel owner and operator," countered Attorney General Kennedy's emphasis on the "immorality of discrimination" with the immorality of a law that would destroy businesses by compelling people to deal with "the Negro socially." Setta urged Congress not to "try to outdo God in the makeup of the world."[100]

Equality is Not a Characteristic of Either Nature or Human Nature

A related argument was that inequality and racial difference were features of nature and natural law. This argument may reflect traces of the eugenic theories (dominant earlier in the twentieth century) about a hierarchy of races that should not intermix; such theories strongly rejected "the basic principle of human equality" (as discussed in chapter 4).[101] If Congress forced integration and social mixing, it would harm the structures of both black and white societies and destroy the nation. North Carolina Senator Sam Ervin explained:

> I think that people segregate themselves in society on the basis of race
> in obedience to a natural law which is that like people seek like people,
> and I think one of the most precious rights of all Americans, of all races,
> is the right to be allowed to select their own associates and associates
> for their immature children.[102]

Some witnesses credited God as the author of racial difference and inequality. R. Carter Pittman, an attorney from Georgia, attacked the "specious propaganda" underlying *Brown* and the civil rights bill, "that all men are created equal, and that there are not such differences between whites and Negroes as are significant for education and social purposes."[103]

Some opponents of the CRA appealed to inequality as a feature of nature and human nature to challenge the use of government and laws to promote equality—despite the language of equality in US founding documents. Senator John Tower (R-Texas) entered into the record a sermon, "The Problem of Equality," delivered by Dr. Walter R. Courtney, of the First Presbyterian Church, in Nashville, Tennessee, which contrasted the words of the Declaration of Independence—"All men are created equal"—with the lack of evidence in nature for equality—whether among plants, animals, nations, or races. Although the "raucous sounds of conflict" in Birmingham and elsewhere show that "equality has intoxicated the modern world," Courtney insisted: "Between individuals, races, groups and nations there are broad differences, and equality is not a characteristic of either nature or human nature." Jesus "talked of love and neighborliness, but not equality."[104]

Government, Courtney argued, cannot solve "the problem of equality." Insisting on full equality leads to communism, while insisting on liberty with "a fair portion" of equality points to democracy. In a showdown between the two, the "Christian way" is to "choose liberty and . . . hope and work for equality." Thus, he criticized "slogans" voiced by church leaders that "appear . . . Christian" but are not, such as "human rights, not property rights." Property rights, he responded, "form the seedbed in which human rights mature."[105]

As did opponents of *Brown*, some opponents of Title II of the CRA asserted that racial integration would lead to "mongrelization" through intermarriage—and to national ruin. Mississippi Governor Ross Barnett warned: "I don't [think] they ought to integrate in the schools. They start dancing together, playing together, now and then intermarriage between the Negroes and the whites, and it has never worked in any country. It has always ended up in a mongrel race."[106] C. Maurice Weidemeyer, Delegate to the Maryland General Assembly, doubted that the United States could survive integrated, claiming that "foster[ing] integration"[107] has hindered the progress of many great nations.

Cultural and moral differences were another argument against integrating public accommodations. Representative Albert Watson (D-South Carolina) predicted: because the two races are separated by cultural and moral differences, the "innumerable establishments throughout the South such as public theaters, restaurants, and . . . fairs . . . will lose business as soon as integration occurs."[108]

Some opponents of the public accommodations bill appealed to natural differences to support an idea of parallel, but equal societies; others clearly linked difference with moral or other inferiority. Senator Ervin argued that the goal should be to

> provide the opportunity for each American, Negro or white or oriental or any other kind, to have free access and free opportunity to move wherever his talents, his ability, his money, and his tastes will permit him to go, within the rights of other people to live their lives as they want to do so[109]

A related argument was that racial minorities could correct any "injustices" by catering "to their own people." Weidemeyer asserted: "They have the same opportunity to go into business and to conduct a hotel or restaurant or other types of businesses, just as much as any other citizens who have previously done so."[110]

Alabama Governor George Wallace contended that forcing integration harmed African Americans by "brand[ing]" them as "inferior." He attacked *Brown's* "message": "If I were a Negro I would resent [*Brown*] because that decision, in effect said, 'You are inferior, and you cannot get a good education and you cannot develop unless you mix with whites.'" Segregation, far from being "synonymous with hatred," was in the best interest of all parties.[111]

Thus, opponents of the CRA appealed to religion and to nature (itself following certain divine laws) to defend segregation. Because inequality was natural and Christian, governmental efforts to secure equality were both "un-Christian" and doomed to fall. Moreover, a decade after *Brown*, the cry of intermarriage still sounded to oppose any federal efforts to dismantle racial subordination, even in places of public accommodation.

Government Should Not Legislate Morality—People Have a Right to Discriminate and Be Bigoted

Opponents of the CRA argued that government *should not* legislate morality—to do so violated rights—and *could not* do so—any such effort would fail.[112] The different ways these opponents enlisted the rhetoric of bigotry are striking. Some legislators viewed bigotry as part of the conflicts of nature, but insisted that "no manmade law [can] guarantee universal brotherhood."[113] Instead of curing "intolerance and bigotry," Senator Tower argued that the law would "substitute the force of the state for the voluntary choices of the citizen." "Prejudice and bigotry cannot be eliminated until the hearts and minds of the southern people are prepared for it," he asserted.[114] Southern people—who are "good-hearted," "kind, warm, and hospitable" and "not cruel people basically"—know that "we cannot overturn the mores of a whole society overnight," and they "wish to see the genuine resolution of these difficulties . . . in a peaceful, orderly, and lasting manner." Instead, the proposed law "discriminate[s] against white Peter in favor of colored Paul. And it makes a mock[ery] of the work of the churches for more than 2,000 years because it turns God's work over to Caesar."[115]

This idea echoes arguments that "coercion" through law could not end discrimination. As Senator Frank Carlson (R-Kansas), asserted: "The end of discrimination and inequality of treatment among our citizens will come only when all of us are willing to lay aside bigotry and prejudice and give full credence to the Golden Rule."[116] As an attorney from Louisville, Kentucky put it:

> The plain truth of the matter . . . is that men cannot be forced to love and respect their fellow men by even the most stringent governmental edict. If moral changes could be effected so easily, let me assure this

committee that I would be the first to applaud the enactment of such laws.[117]

A different argument was that although there may be a "moral argument" for a federal public accommodations law, principles of freedom of choice and private property rights should prevail, even if that meant shielding bigotry. This libertarian argument took several forms. For example, Senator Spessard Holland (D-Florida) argued:

> And doesn't a Negro family on a long trip get as thirsty, hungry, and sleepy as a white one? But in a stable society we must be governed by principles of law. In principle, the owner of a private business ought to be able to serve or exclude anyone he pleases, for whatever reason. He may be a bigot; or he may be guided by the knowledge that if he does not restrict his clientele he'll go bankrupt.[118]

Federal laws already on the books, others argued, had failed to end "discrimination, intolerance, and bigotry"; more laws would not bring us "any nearer to the solution of this problem." Discrimination persisted because human beings like "their right of choice—their right to associate with whom they like . . . to work and worship as they choose [and] even to be wrong in their judgment." [119]

Individuals had a "right to discriminate" and a "right to be wrong," asserted James J. Kilpatrick, editor of the *Richmond News Leader* and vice chairman of the Virginia Commission on Constitutional Government. He argued that "the American system" rests on the individual's "right in his personal life to be capricious, arbitrary, prejudiced, biased, opinionated, unreasonable." Without such a right, "the whole basis of liberty is destroyed."[120] Kilpatrick was not alone among conservatives in "expressing deep concern about the threats that the civil rights movement posed to the American constitutional order."[121]

Laurence H. Eldredge, a Pennsylvania attorney who testified against Title II, used the rhetoric of bigotry to make a similar point in an editorial, "The Right to Be Nasty," which was entered more than once into the Congressional Record.[122] He expressed sympathy for "the efforts of the Negro race" to "eliminate in our public life the gross injustices which they have suffered in the past," acknowledging that past and present treatment of them "flagrantly violates our fundamental ideas of equal justice and equal rights for all citizens." But the solution should not be a federal law compelling people engaged in providing goods and services to do so "without any discrimination, under threat of criminal sanction." "Anglo-Saxon tradition" about property ownership gives "private citizens" a "right to lead their own lives as they see fit, to make utter fools of themselves and to incur community condemnation, and to be eccentric, unreasonable, *bigoted*, and nasty."[123] Eldredge drew a line between common law burdens on innkeepers and common carriers and what he considered "private businesses," which the proposed law would (dangerously) treat as "public." Shopkeepers must be free to exclude would-be customers for good reasons and "less rational" grounds. As Eldredge uses "bigoted" here, it signals an unreasonable position, but one that people are entitled to act upon. Indeed, he also argued that the fact that, in 1964, "decent people" intensely disputed whether nondiscrimination *should* be the "national standard," eliminating the right to exclude, was a sufficient reason to oppose the CRA.[124]

A famous—or infamous—argument against the majority legislating morality through the proposed public accommodations law was Yale Law School professor Robert Bork's *New Republic* article "Civil Rights—A Challenge."[125] Senator Olin D. Johnston (D-South Carolina) asked to have Bork's "outstanding article" printed in the Congressional Record.[126] Bork feared "the danger . . . that justifiable abhorrence of racial discrimination will result in legislation by which the morals of the majority are self-righteously imposed upon a minority." Like Eldredge, Bork granted the "ugliness of racial discrimination." He distinguished, though, between the use of law to compel racial discrimination and the use of laws like Title II to tell people that "even as individuals they may not act on their racial preferences in particular areas of life." Of the latter, Bork wrote that the "the principle of such legislation" was one of "unsurpassed ugliness."[127] He challenged the "moral position" of civil rights demonstrators, stating that they were "part of a mob coercing . . . other private individuals in the exercise of their freedom," akin to Carrie Nation's invading saloons.

This line of thinking countered Robert Kennedy's argument that living up to the nation's moral ideals must outweigh protecting the "immoral logic of bigotry." Bork questioned whether the "moral preference" against racial or religious discrimination "deserves elevation to the level of the principle of individual freedom and self-determination."[128] On this view, libertarian concerns for freedom must outweigh the federal government's imperative to combat bigotry.

A Federal Law Will Make the Problem of Bigotry Worse; Local, State, and Nonlegal Solutions Are the Best

One striking argument against the CRA conceded that bigotry was a problem, but asserted that passing the civil rights bill would make it worse. Senator Johnston used resistance to *Brown* to make the point: "Instead of promoting peace and harmony between the races, as a result of this decision we have seen racial violence, intolerance, bigotry, and hatred compounded and multiplied." He concluded that "whenever government decrees a social policy for people when the people are not behind such a policy, one can only expect as a result such violence and trouble."[129] Some senators enlisted the earlier words of their former Senate colleague Lyndon B. Johnson to argue that the public accommodations bill would stir up bigotry:

> When we of the South rise here to speak against this resolution, or to speak against the civil rights proposals, we are not speaking against the Negro race. We are not attempting to keep alive the old flames of hatred and bigotry. We are instead trying to prevent those flames from being rekindled. We are trying to tell the rest of the nation that this is not the way to accomplish what so many want to do for the Negro.[130]

What was the better way than a federal law? Kilpatrick, for example, argued for nonlegal methods:

> You go about it through the churches; you go about it through persuasion, through the ordinary arts of human relations, and that this is how things are corrected, with an occasional nudge here and there from economic pressure. You correct it by a sense of shame.[131]

Appealing to conscience, North Carolina Representative L. H. Fountain asserted that in his "home state and throughout America," "responsible local people of both races" were "solving the problem with a spirit and a will, with courage, conviction, conscience, and with commonsense and judgment that cannot be legislated."[132] His colleague Representative Basil L. Whitener referred to his participation in local "programs and efforts" contributing to "better race relations and opportunities for our Negro friends"; by comparison, "the legislation before us would breed further discontent and friction."[133] South Carolina Representative William Jennings Bryan Dorn argued that the "fantastic progress" states had made on race relations proved that "legislation of this nature" is "best handled at the local and the State level."[134]

In predicting the CRA's failure to regulate morality, opponents analogized the bill to the prior failure of Prohibition. Mississippi Representative William M. Colmer observed: "We got everybody all stirred up and we passed a national prohibition law," and then "turned around and repealed it," because "we recognized that we could not legislate on the question of temperance."[135] After that "unfortunate experience with . . . a moral question," Dorn noted, Congress "returned" the issue to the States.[136] Colmer predicted a similar lack of success with federal civil rights law: "You are attempting to tell people how they have to treat their fellow man in their social, economic, and other contacts with him. . . . Everybody in this room knows that you cannot do it that way."[137]

Denying and Reversing the Charge of Bigotry

Finally, some legislators denied that there was a problem of bigotry that warranted a federal solution. Some, like Senator Long, even reversed the charge of bigotry. As quoted at the beginning of this chapter, he asserted that the terms "prejudiced and bigoted" were better applied to supporters of the public accommodations law.[138] Senator Byrd argued that the label "bigot" intimidated people from voicing their opposition to the CRA and instead applied to the bill's supporters:

> Anyone who opposes a civil rights bill is labeled anti-Negro, a racist, and a bigot. The antibigot bigots in this country have so intimidated many men that they will not stand up and resist demands made in the name of civil rights.[139]

He also condemned Title II as giving "special treatment," not simply "equal treatment" (a slogan that would resurface in debates over gay rights, as chapter 7 discusses).

Another tactic was to appeal to past American heroes to rebut charges of bigotry. For example, while supporters of the bill related it to the unfulfilled promises of the Emancipation Proclamation, opponents also appealed to Abraham Lincoln, "the great liberator." They argued that because Lincoln recognized "there are physical differences among the races," they could not be deemed a racist or bigot for also doing so.[140] Such insistence is similar to Dr. Garner's or Senator Russell's insistence that moral principles don't change. It does not admit that understanding of what is reasonable and of what constitutional commitments require evolve over time, or that there can be a shortfall between principles and practices that requires government to act.

Challenge and Resolution: We Must All Overcome the Crippling Legacy of Bigotry and Injustice

Within hours of the CRA's enactment, Moreton Rolleston, motel operator and restaurant owner in Atlanta, challenged Title II, asserting that the law violated his property rights and was a form of involuntary servitude prohibited by the Thirteenth Amendment. In a companion case, Ollie's Barbeque challenged Title II. In December 1964, in *Heart of Atlanta Motel v. United States* and *Katzenbach v. McClung*, the US Supreme Court upheld Title II.[141] President Johnson stated that "the nation has spoken with a single voice on the question of equal rights and equal opportunity," now that the Court had upheld the public accommodations section of a law "proposed by two Presidents" and "overwhelmingly adopted by Congress." Johnson said he was "heartened by the spirit with which the people of the south have accepted the Act even though many were opposed to its passage" and expressed hope for "reasonable and responsible acceptance" of the act "now that the Supreme Court has also ruled."[142]

This idea of speaking with a unified voice and of acceptance of the CRA illustrates themes of generational moral progress. The passage of the CRA set a new baseline about the proper role of federal anti-discrimination law in seeking to eradicate prejudice: the United States was taking steps to realize the promises of the Emancipation Proclamation and the Reconstruction Amendments.[143] The CRA, followed by the Voting Rights Act and the Fair Housing Act, also changed the perception of the United States by the foreign press and foreign leaders. In 1963, Bull Connor's violence in Birmingham seemed to show US hypocrisy as a moral leader. Two years later, international reaction to the violence of Alabama state troopers against peaceful civil rights activists marching from Selma to Montgomery to support voting rights was different: Selma was viewed not "as an example of the character of American democracy," but instead as "the rearguard action of white supremacists doomed to defeat."[144]

President Johnson himself sounded this theme of moral progress and thus is an interesting moral protagonist in this story of enlisting law to fight bigotry. Despite his arguments, as a senator, that civil rights bills would not solve problems of bigotry and would only make them worse, once he became president, he threw his weight behind passing the CRA. He drew on his own identity as a "son of the South" to highlight his awareness of the difficulties of overcoming the legacy of racial prejudice. In 1965, after the violence by police against the civil rights campaign for voting rights in Selma, Johnson gave a speech calling for swift passage of the Voting Rights Act. He drew on the rhetoric of bigotry not to lay charges against particular people or states but to characterize the problem as "an American problem" about which everyone should care. Once again, he referred to his own personal history in granting "how agonizing racial feelings are" and "how difficult it is to reshape the attitudes and the structure of our society." He referred to unkept promises since the Emancipation Proclamation in saying that "the time for justice has now come." Johnson turned to a key phrase from the civil rights movement in speaking of the need to overcome bigotry:

> What happened in Selma is part of a far larger movement which reaches into every section and every state of America. . . . It is not just Negroes, but really it's all of us who must overcome the crippling legacy of bigotry and injustice. And we shall overcome.[145]

This speech "anchored the meaning of the crisis" in Selma "with the constitutional past" by invoking Lincoln and the Emancipation Proclamation. The way forward was a "collective commitment to the civil rights movement," so that the "'we' in 'We Shall Overcome' was becoming 'We the People of the United States.'"[146] Rather than label particular people bigots, Johnson acknowledged every American's stake in overcoming bigotry, just as Kuchel urged that "our spirit is not narrow bigotry."

Looking back at the CRA also reveals competing views about the relationship between conscience and law. The CRA, in prohibiting discrimination, attacked a moral evil and expressed moral values, commitments, and ideals. Similar to social scientists studying prejudice, supporters predicted that a law that bridged the gap between conscience and practice would gain support, even if there were initial resistance. Opponents countered that the CRA enacted a controversial morality in violation of other's rights. The bill's agenda of "forcing" integration was contrary to nature, to God's own design, and to social harmony and racial progress.

It bears emphasizing the appeals to natural law, divine law, and unchanging moral principles in this opposition. In present-day arguments about the proper scope of civil rights laws, those who seek religious exemptions bristle at the notion that religious resistance to racial integration is of any relevance to present-day controversies, suggesting either that such religious objections were a pretext or simply not a reasonable position (as I will discuss in chapter 8). Those who caution against such exemptions point out that religious beliefs about segregation were not "fringe" in the mid-1960s and were sincerely and widely held. In 1964, even after the Court's unanimous upholding of Title II in *Heart of Atlanta* and *McClung*, Maurice Bessinger, a white restaurant owner, refused service to three black customers on the same terms as whites, arguing that to compel such service would violate his "sacred religious beliefs" about segregation. His religious beliefs were "relatively mainstream" and he later "became a statewide political figure."[147] In the ensuing case, *Newman v. Piggie Park Enterprises*, the federal district court rejected his First Amendment objection to Title II, explaining that a business owner did not have an "absolute right to exercise" his religious beliefs "in utter disregard of other rights"; the US Supreme Court also described his First Amendment objection to Title II as "patently frivolous."[148] As chapter 8 will discuss, that case became a central reference point for the parties, their many amici, and the Supreme Court in *Masterpiece Cakeshop*.

Prejudice, Moral Progress, and Not Being on the Wrong Side of History

The Legacy of Loving *for the Right to Marry*

> It was 1967, nearly two centuries after the Constitution was adopted, before the Supreme Court struck down state laws prohibiting interracial marriage. . . . Now, nearly 50 years later, the arguments supporting the ban on interracial marriage seem an obvious pretext for racism; it must be hard for those who were not then of age to understand just how sincerely those views were held. When observers look back 50 years from now, the arguments supporting Florida's ban on same-sex marriage, though just as sincerely held, will again seem an obvious pretext for discrimination. Observers . . . will wonder just how those views could have been held.
>
> —Judge Robert L. Hinkle
> *Brenner v. Scott*, 999 F. Supp.2d 1278, 1281 (N.D. Fla. 2014)

> It is becoming increasingly clear to judges that if they rule against same-sex marriage their grandchildren will regard them as bigots.
>
> —Professor Andrew M. Koppelman
> (quoted in Adam Liptak, "A Steady Path To Supreme Court as Gay Marriage Gains Momentum in States,"
> N.Y. Times, Feb. 13, 2014, at A1)

Loving v. Virginia (1967) is a landmark civil rights case, decided by the Supreme Court just a few years after the passage of the Civil Rights Act of 1964.[1] The poignant story of Mildred Jeter (half-African American, half-Native American) and Richard Loving (white), who grew up together in Central Point, Virginia, fell in love, crossed state lines to marry, and brought a famous legal challenge to Virginia's antimiscegenation law, is "part of mainstream culture."[2] It inspired both an HBO documentary (*The Loving Story*) and a Hollywood film (*Loving*). After a sheriff invaded their bedroom and told them that their marriage license was no good in Virginia, they faced prosecution and accepted a trial judge's suspension

Who's the Bigot? Linda C. McClain, Oxford University Press (2020). © Oxford University Press.
DOI: 10.1093/oso/9780190877200.001.0001

of a one year prison sentence if they left the state for twenty-five years. In 1963, news of the civil rights bill then being debated in Congress spurred Mildred Loving to write to Attorney General Robert F. Kennedy, seeking help to be able to return to Virginia—if not to live, at least to visit family and friends. Represented by an ACLU eager to bring a challenge to the remaining state antimiscegenation laws as the last relic of state-enforced racial segregation, the Lovings prevailed in the US Supreme Court. In a unanimous opinion, Chief Justice Earl Warren called such laws an unconstitutional "endorsement of the doctrine of White Supremacy."[3]

Loving and its meaning, over fifty years later, are crucial to understanding puzzles about the rhetoric of bigotry, especially bigotry's backward- and forward-looking dimensions. No Supreme Court case proved more vital to the constitutional battle over same-sex marriage than Loving. Participants, however, disagreed over the analogy between legal restrictions on interracial marriage and those on same-sex marriage. In Obergefell v. Hodges (2015), the majority drew on Loving repeatedly to support its holding that the fundamental right to marry extends to same-sex couples.[4] Disagreements over Loving's legacy continue in controversies over whether state laws prohibiting discrimination in public accommodations based on sexual orientation or gender identity violate the First Amendment rights of those with religious objections to same-sex marriage. In Masterpiece Cakeshop v. Colorado Civil Rights Commission, as chapter 8 will illustrate, baker Jack Phillips and his amici sought to distinguish the bigotry and odious racism behind antimiscegenation laws from the "decent and honorable" religious convictions of "sincere" and "reasonable" people who conscientiously object to same-sex marriage. Defenders of state anti-discrimination laws, in response, invoked Loving to show the long history of religious arguments to justify racial discrimination and to argue that discrimination "justified" by history, tradition, or religious convictions, however sincere, should not prevail in the marketplace.[5]

Loving illustrates generational moral progress in our constitutional jurisprudence: laws once justified by appeals to nature, God's law and plan for the races, and the well-being of children and society are repudiated as rooted in prejudice. On the fortieth anniversary of Loving Mildred Loving herself sounded the theme of generational progress, stating that "the older generation's fears and prejudices have given way."[6] In Obergefell, Justice Kennedy invoked Loving to show the role played by "new insights" about injustice and what the Constitution's commitments to liberty and equality demand.[7] He also wrote: "As the Constitution endures, persons in every generation can invoke its principles in their own search for greater freedom."[8] As Justice Ginsburg expressed it, in United States v. Virginia (VMI), an important gender equality case, "the history of our country is the story of the extension of constitutional rights to people once ignored or excluded."[9] The notion of moral progress embraces a "moral reading" of the Constitution: its guarantees of liberty and equality reflect commitments to "abstract aspirational principles" that we seek to realize over time, as contrasted with originalist understandings that fidelity to the Constitution requires following the understandings and expectations of the founders.[10] In interpreting the Constitution, we aim to redeem its promises.[11]

When are new insights about objectionable discrimination possible? For people not alive when *Loving* was decided, federal judge Robert L. Hinkle (quoted at the beginning of the chapter) observed, "it must be hard" to "understand just how sincerely" views against interracial marriage were held. Instead, they seem "an obvious pretext for racism." Fifty years hence, he predicted, people may have the same view about arguments supporting bans on same-sex marriage.[12] As Professor Andrew Koppelman quipped, judges may worry that "if they rule against same-sex marriage their grandchildren will brand them as bigots."[13]

The Commonwealth of Virginia is an interesting moral protagonist in the story of *Loving*'s legacy and puzzles about bigotry and time. Contrast the Virginia attorney general's stance in *Loving* with that taken by the Virginia attorney general in litigation over the state's ban on same-sex marriage. In *Loving*, Virginia denied that the antimiscegenation law rested upon prejudice by appealing to "modern" social science—Rabbi Albert Gordon's book *Intermarriage*, introduced in chapter 3—supposedly showing the problems posed by intermarriage, particularly for children. Virginia downplayed, however, that prejudice itself was at the root of these "problems." The Lovings characterized such laws as the "odious" relics of slavery—the final vestige of legally sanctioned segregation—and as rooted in racial prejudice. Their amici contended that antimiscegenation laws violated freedom of conscience and that "race prejudice" was the problem, not interracial marriage itself.

Nearly fifty years after *Loving*, same-sex couples challenged Virginia's ban on same-sex marriage. Concern for the judgment of history is evident in the decision of Virginia's Attorney General, Mark Herring, not to defend the ban because "it is time for the Commonwealth [of Virginia] to be on the right side of history and the right side of the law."[14] As an example of being on the wrong side, he pointed to his predecessors who defended Virginia's antimiscegenation law in *Loving*. In *Obergefell*, Virginia filed a brief supporting same-sex marriage, pointing out parallels between the rationales offered for prohibiting it and those advanced to justify antimiscegenation laws. Some other southern states filed amicus briefs in support of bans on same-sex marriage, insisting that "odious" antimiscegenation laws had *nothing in common* with laws preserving the traditional definition of marriage. Similarly, some conservative commentators reject the notion that defenders of traditional marriage are on the "wrong side of history," insisting that bans on interracial marriage were "historical anomalies" based on prejudice, while limiting marriage to one man and one woman is based on "reason" and "truth."[15] *Loving* also featured prominently in *Obergefell* itself.

Prejudice and Moral Progress: Arguments in *Loving*

In *Loving*, the trial court appealed to the theology of segregation to justify Virginia's antimiscegenation law:

> Almighty God created the races white, black, yellow, malay and red, and he placed them on separate continents. And but for the interference with his arrangement there would be no cause for such marriages. The fact that he separated the races shows that he did not intend for the races to mix.[16]

On appeal, the Virginia Supreme Court rested on its 1955 decision in *Naim v. Naim*,[17] which cited an "unbroken line of decisions"—except for *Perez v. Sharp* (1948)[18]—upholding state antimiscegenation laws and read the Fourteenth Amendment as not denying Virginia the power to regulate marriage to prevent a "mongrel breed of citizens" that would "weaken or destroy the quality of its citizenship."[19] *Naim* quoted US Supreme Court rhetoric from *Maynard v. Hill* (1888) declaring that marriage has "more to do with the morals and civilization of a people than any other institution"; it also attempted to distinguish *Brown* on the ground that while education is "the very foundation of good citizenship," intermarriage "is harmful to good citizenship."[20]

When *Loving* reached the US Supreme Court, Chief Justice Earl Warren (writing for the Court) concluded that "no legitimate overriding purpose independent of invidious racial discrimination" justified Virginia's antimiscegenation law. The supposed "legitimate purposes" to which the *Naim* court referred (preserving citizens' "racial integrity" and "pride" and preventing "the corruption of blood") were "obviously an endorsement of the doctrine of White Supremacy."[21] Warren quoted, but did not comment on, the trial judge's theological rationale. The Court also ruled that the law violated the Due Process Clause by restricting the fundamental right to marry.[22]

Arguments in Defense of Virginia's Antimiscegenation Law

Not prejudice, but preventing problem marriages. The brief filed by the attorney general of Virginia in *Loving* argued that the antimiscegenation law did not violate the Fourteenth Amendment because the "Framers" intended to exclude such laws from its terms.[23] Therefore, any "judicial inquiry into the wisdom, propriety or desirability of preventing interracial alliances" was "completely inappropriate"; if the Court did inquire, it would find "conflicting scientific opinion."[24] The brief quoted excerpts from several decades of such "opinion" warning against racial mixture, but appealed to Rabbi Albert I. Gordon's book *Intermarriage: Interfaith, Interracial, Interethnic* (introduced in chapter 3), as "the most recent scientific treatise upon the propriety or desirability of interracial marriages from the psychological and sociological point of view."[25] At oral argument, Assistant Attorney General McIlwaine argued that Virginia's law "serves a legitimate legislative objective of preventing the sociological and psychological evils which attend interracial marriage."[26]

Virginia recast its antimiscegenation law as rooted not in racial bigotry and prejudice, but in "modern" concerns over how marital "differences" make marital "adjustment" difficult and lead to divorce and harm children. At oral argument, the justices repeatedly questioned McIlwaine about whether Virginia's law was anything other than "the result of the old slavery days, the old feeling that the white man was superior to the colored man, which was exactly what the Fourteenth Amendment was adopted to prevent."[27] McIlwaine urged that the issue was whether the specific provisions at issue were "justifiable" in 1967. The justification, he contended, stemmed from the psychological and sociological problems posed by interracial marriages. Virginia chose to deal with these "problems" by preventing such marriages.[28]

To support Virginia's contemporary rationale, McIlwaine stated that "our proposition on the psycho-sociological aspects of this question is bottomed almost exclusively" on Gordon's book.[29] It is instructive, therefore, to look closely at the state's strategic use of the book. Not only did Virginia brush to the side Gordon's arguments against interfaith marriage, introduced in chapter 3; it selectively quoted from his discussion of why interracial marriage is harmful for children.

Not racial inferiority or superiority, but racial difference. Virginia related its prohibition of interracial marriage to its legitimate interest in the marital success of its citizens:

> Text writers and judicial writers agree that the state has a natural, direct and vital interest in maximizing the number of successful marriages which lead to stable homes and families, and in minimizing those which do not. It is clear . . . that intermarried families are subjected to much greater pressures and problems than are those of the intramarried.[30]

McIlwaine argued that "the State's prohibition of racial intermarriage" stood on the "same footing" as its prohibition of polygamous, incestuous, or underage marriage. What is more, "there's far more evidence of the reasonableness of a ban against interracial marriage" than against those other marriages.[31]

In its brief, Virginia contended that Gordon's book gives "statistical form and basis to the proposition that, from a psycho-sociological point of view, interracial marriages are detrimental to the individual, to the family, and to the society."[32] The state characterized Virginia's laws as being about "difference" rather than prejudice. It quoted Gordon's rejection of "the argument that persons who oppose intermarriage—religious or racial—are per se 'prejudiced'" and his retort that "*the tendency to classify all persons who oppose intermarriage as 'prejudiced' is, in itself, a prejudice.*" Some people's opposition may rest in prejudice, Gordon acknowledged, but "neither races of man nor religious or ethnic groups need offer apologies for their [understandable and reasonable] desire to perpetuate themselves."[33]

At oral argument, however, the state could not deny the role of prejudice in creating problems for persons in interracial marriages. The justices pressed McIlwaine on whether "one reason that marriages of this kind are sometimes unsuccessful is the existence of the kind of laws that are in issue here and the attitudes that those laws reflect." He shifted the focus away from law, quoting Gordon: "It is the attitude which society has toward interracial marriages" that "causes a child to have almost insuperable difficulties in identification." McIlwaine added that "the problems which the child of an interracial marriage faces are those which no child can come through without damages to himself."[34] He contended that if the state has an interest in "protecting the progeny of interracial marriages from these problems," there is "clearly" scientific evidence that such children do suffer. As in the brief, he noted Gordon's reference to such children as the "victims" or "martyrs" of intermarried parents. The higher divorce rate and harm to children, he argued, arises from racial difference, not racial "inferiority" or "superiority."[35]

At oral argument, Chief Justice Warren observed that some people have "the same feeling about interreligious marriages" and asked whether the state could prohibit such marriages. McIlwaine responded: "I think that the evidence in support of the prohibition of interracial marriages is stronger than that for the prohibition of interreligious marriage."[36] When questioned about the basis for his statement, he rested "principally" on the "authority" cited in the attorney general's brief, "particularly" Gordon's book.[37] Had Warren pressed McIlwaine on whether Gordon's book actually supported singling out interracial marriage for prohibition, he would not have been able to offer a persuasive answer. Although Virginia's brief cited Gordon on the importance of "like marrying like" as a formula for marital happiness and divorce prevention, Gordon applied that formula to religion as well and devoted far more of his book to the problems posed by interfaith marriage.[38] Indeed, his criticism of both forms under the term "intermarriage" is evident even from the passages Virginia quoted in its brief and Appendix. For example, Gordon warns that intermarriage introduces "major differences"—whether of religion or race—that make marital success less likely. He concludes that "intermarriage is unwise for most individuals and must, therefore, be regarded as a threat to both personal and group happiness." He does not differentiate among forms of intermarriage, since all deviate from the formula that like should marry like: "The chances of happiness in marriage are greatest for those who are culturally, socially, educationally, temperamentally, ethnically, nationally, racially, and religiously more like than they are different."[39]

Virginia also quoted Gordon's insistence that there was no evidence that intermarriage might be a path toward realizing "universal brotherhood, freedom from prejudice, intolerance, and hatred of the unlike"—in other words, away from bigotry. This passage, however, makes clear that Gordon viewed *all* forms of intermarriage as "a threat to society."[40] He insisted: "It is the duty of men and women of different faiths, colors, and nations to learn to live together in peace and amity while maintaining their differences."[41] Although Gordon's immediate concern was to sound the alarm about assimilation by Jews leading to more intermarriage, these passages lump together race and religion in speaking of intermarriage as a "betrayal" and an injury to group "pride."[42]

Perhaps Virginia's attorneys thought that Gordon's appeal to group pride and a duty to preserve differences lent support to its "modern" defense of Virginia's law. Certainly, earlier defenses of antimiscegenation laws appealed to furthering racial pride and purity for both whites and "Negroes." However, Gordon also asserted that there was no biological basis for ideas of a "pure" race or of racial superiority and inferiority; in a passage not quoted by Virginia, he argued that the persistence of support for such ideas is a "pretext" for prejudice.[43] When describing various "controls" against intermarriage, Gordon acknowledges antimiscegenation laws, but takes no normative position on them. He reports: "Under the impression that the preservation of our society depends upon such methods," "over half of the States in the Union have such laws on their books."[44]

Why are interfaith and interracial marriages problem marriages? The impact of prejudice. By quoting selectively from Gordon's book, Virginia emphasized problems children suffered due to intermarriage, while largely ignoring the role of racial prejudice as a cause of that suffering. The attorney general framed the problems as stemming from societal "attitudes" toward interracial marriage, but a closer look at Gordon's book makes clear that "attitudes" is a euphemism for racial prejudice. Gordon writes of the harms of interracial marriage for children: "The children born of Negro-white marriages in the United States are,

I believe, among the most socially unfortunate persons in all the world if they seek or expect acceptance by the white community."[45] In language that unwittingly mirrors Virginia's interpretation of its antimiscegenation law (the "one drop rule"), Gordon takes the baseline of racial prejudice as a given, rather than a problem demanding remedy:

> To date there is no evidence that persons with even one drop of Negro blood will, knowingly, be accepted as whites. . . . He must find his roots within the Negro community or remain unaccepted and unacceptable to the white community. It will do no good to argue whether whites are correct in taking such an attitude. It is far more important to know that, realistically speaking, this unfortunately is their attitude.[46]

The lack of acceptance will be particularly difficult for children, Gordon predicts. He adds: "The subsequent resentment built up by children of interracial marriages . . . must be regarded as unhealthy and even dangerous."[47] Virginia includes none of this, although it does quote a brief paragraph in which Gordon mentions that children born of interracial married couples face "complex and emotionally frustrating problems," while the white partner in such a marriage often "imagines" that a child born of the marriage "is really white" and will be able to "pass" as such.[48]

For Gordon, the social fact of racial prejudice and discrimination provides a moral argument *against* interracial marriage. Published in 1964, as Congress debated what became the Civil Rights Act of 1964, *Intermarriage* does not credence the possibility of moral progress through the protection of civil rights laws:

> Unless a miracle occurs that will eliminate discrimination from our society—and that does not seem probable—we may expect such children to suffer the same indignities as do their parents. Whether people, however much they may love each other, have the moral right to create such a problem for a child is, of course, debatable. It is my belief that interracially intermarried parents are committing a grave offense against their children that is far more serious and even dangerous to their welfare than they realize. The Negro in the United States suffers greatly. . . . The children of Negro-white marriages are thus easily hurt, even by their well-intentioned parents.[49]

Omitting this passage, Virginia's brief quotes Gordon's conclusion that "the chances for the success of an interracial marriage are, according to my research, even less than that for an interfaith marriage."[50] It also omits Gordon's explanation of why:

In the latter case, parents, the family, the Church and Synagogue play significant roles in militating against marital happiness. In the former case, obvious difference in skin color makes for an unfavorable attitude toward the intermarried. Public opinion generally opposes such marriages.[51]

Gordon asserts: "If interfaith marriages require great courage, then interracial marriages may be said, *under present conditions in our society*, to require even greater fortitude."[52] He contends (in language echoing *Prince v. Massachusetts*): "The institution of marriage certainly does not require that we make martyrs of ourselves and of our children."[53] Had the attorney general included these passages in his brief, he would have had to admit that white resistance and prejudice were the primary reasons interracial marriages were "problem" marriages.

The attorney general's brief invokes Allport's characterization of Gordon's book as the "definitive book on intermarriage."[54] Gordon's acknowledgments thank Allport for "inspiration, guidance, and counsel."[55] In *The Nature of Prejudice* (as seen in chapter 2), Allport acknowledged that prejudice made intermarriages "practical[ly] unwis[e]" under current conditions, but he argued for dismantling legal segregation and working for conditions that would make those marriages feasible. He concluded: "It is because intermarriage would symbolize the abolition of prejudice that it is so strenuously fought."[56]

The Lovings' counsel engaged Virginia's reliance on Gordon's book only briefly. At oral argument, Bernard Cohen read the following passage from *Intermarriage* (not quoted by Virginia): "Our democracy would soon be defeated if any group on the American scene was required to cut itself off from contact with persons of other religions or races. The segregation of any group, either voluntarily or involuntarily, is unthinkable and even dangerous to the body politic."[57]

Arguments in Opposition to Virginia's Antimiscegenation Law

Neither the Lovings nor their five amici use the term "bigotry" to characterize the motives for Virginia's antimiscegenation law. However, they use synonyms, such as "racial intolerance," "race prejudice," and "modern day racism." The rhetoric of conscience features in arguments that the laws reflect the "guilty conscience" of white supremacists and violate freedom of conscience of those barred from marrying. While arguing that the Court need not address the supposed scientific bases for Virginia's law, they presented modern science rejecting any basis for the law. These briefs also offer narratives of moral and constitutional progress.

Racial intolerance and a guilty conscience underlie Virginia's antimiscegenation law. The Lovings urged the Court to take this "appropriate opportunity to strike down the last remnants of legalized slavery in our country."[58] Virginia's legislation was "motivated primarily by racial intolerance and antagonism directed against the Negro, and sought to preserve only the integrity of the so-called 'White Race' for reasons intellectually analogous to Hitler's goal of creating a Super Race." The history of antimiscegenation laws made clear that they were "both relics of slavery and expressions of modern day racism which brands Negroes as an inferior race." The multiple roots of such prejudice include religion, economic self-interest, and eugenic pseudo-science.[59] The NAACP Legal Defense and Educational Fund ("Fund") amicus brief described the rationales for Virginia's law (such as preventing a "mongrel breed of citizens") as turning on "the amalgam of superstition, mythology, ignorance, and pseudo-scientific nonsense summoned up to support the theories of white supremacy and racial 'purity.'" Nor would a theological argument, such as the *Loving* trial judge's appeal to "the Almighty" separating the races, suffice: "The Fourteenth Amendment places it entirely beyond the power of the state courts to implement racial discrimination, whatever the rationale."[60]

The Lovings' brief also highlights the interplay of racial prejudice and white men's "sore conscience" under the "illicit conditions fostered by the miscegenation laws." Interracial mixing took place in the South "almost entirely in the context of illicit exploitative sexual intercourse." They quote Gunnar Myrdal on white men's sexual exploitation of "the Negro female" and "fixation on the purity of white womanhood."[61]

The "evil" of such laws, the Lovings argued, is the "indignity" they inflict, by casting nonwhite persons as "not good enough to marry a 'white person.'" The laws had broader effects: "the dread of 'intermarriage'" functioned to "justify" widespread "discriminations" that reinforce "social segregation." The Lovings stress the harmful social meaning of such laws: they are the "paradigm" of measures expressing "the subordinate status of the Negro people and the exalted position of whites" and "functioning chiefly as the State's official symbol of a caste system."[62]

Constitutional and moral progress. The Lovings and their amici argued that striking down antimiscegenation laws would be an important marker of constitutional and moral progress. Antimiscegenation laws "are legalized racial prejudice, unsupported by reason or morals, and should not exist in a good society."[63] This appeal to "morals" and a "good society" is striking, given the repeated quotation in defenses of antimiscegenation laws (including in *Naim*, as discussed above, and in Virginia's brief in *Loving*) of *Maynard*—that marriage has "more to do with the morals and civilization of a people than any other institution."[64] Moral progress, on this view, requires abandoning such laws.

The Japanese American Citizens League (JACL) also situates the striking down of Virginia's law within a narrative of moral and constitutional progress, asserting that "the torchlight of the Constitution has been wielded to expose and burn away these remaining shackles to individual liberty."[65] Stressing the right to marry as "fundamental, basic and highly personal," JACL highlights the "shocking outrage" of interjecting a "racial principle" into this choice. Their brief debunks the idea of a pure race and argues that Virginia's law is "readily exposed as a racist, 'white supremacy' law."[66]

The JACL brief's reference to interfaith marriage is worth quoting, given Virginia's reliance on Gordon's book: "No one would seriously contend" that bans on marriage based on differences—such as "between Protestants and Catholics"—"could be constitutional." As with religion, so with race: "Whatever differences may exist between these groups can not provide proper bases for fixing public policy."[67]

Children, harm, and the new science about race. Virginia asserted that preventing harm to children born into interracial marriages was a reason to prohibit such marriages. By contrast, the Lovings stressed the "immeasurable social harm" stemming from Virginia's prohibition: the "outrageous civil effects" of declaring their "miscegenetic marriage" void, including rendering their children "illegitimate," preventing spouses from inheriting from each other, and allowing the husband to desert the family without any consequences.[68]

To show the absence of any rational basis for Virginia's law, the Lovings and their amici enlisted modern scientific understanding of race, including the 1952 UNESCO "Statement on the Nature of Race and Race Differences," which found that "no biological justification exists for prohibiting intermarriage between persons of different races."[69] Such modern science, the Fund brief argued, established "that there is no rational or scientific basis upon which a statutory prohibition against marriage based on race or color alone can be justified as furthering a valid legislative purpose."[70] Countering the supposed harm of miscegenation for children, the Lovings asserted that no anthropologist at any major US university supported "the theory that Negro-white matings cause biologically deleterious results."[71] Chief Justice Warren asked McIlwaine (counsel for Virginia) his opinion about "the findings of this great committee of UNESCO where . . . about [twenty] of the greatest anthropologists in the world joined unanimously in making some very cogent findings."[72] McIlwaine responded that the UNESCO report was not without its critics and doubled down on the argument that the "sociological evidence" in Gordon's book justified Virginia's law.[73]

Freedom of conscience and society's race prejudice. The only amicus brief filed in *Loving* by religious groups, that of the National Catholic Conference for Interracial Justice, the National Catholic Social Action Conference, and several Catholic Bishops and Archbishops in southern dioceses (NCCIJ brief), argued that bans on interracial marriage violate the freedom of conscience of those seeking to marry.[74] The brief also argued that it is societal prejudice—not interracial marriage itself—that is the problem. It warrants attention because, while Catholic groups opposed antimiscegenation laws, they later weighed in to support state and federal DOMAs and conscience-based exemptions from anti-discrimination laws protecting against discrimination on the basis of sexual orientation.

Virginia's laws, the NCCIJ brief argues, violate "freedom of conscience" because "marriage is a fundamental act of religion," holding a sanctified place in the theology of various denominations. Such laws "prohibit the free exercise of religion guaranteed by the United States Constitution" and also unconstitutionally deny "the right to beget children."[75] While the free exercise of religion is not "absolute," to restrict it, there must be "grave and immediate danger to interests which the state may lawfully protect."[76] The "preservation of a racially segregated society" is not such a lawful interest. The brief contrasts polygamous marriages, which the Supreme Court concluded were "inherently objectionable" because of their threat to "the principles on which the government of the people . . . rests": interracial marriages "do not constitute [such] a threat." (Recall that Virginia argued that the case for barring interracial marriages was *stronger* than that for banning polygamous marriages.) And while some "anthropological studies" indicate that polygamy is harmful to the family structure, no similar proof has been offered that "an interracial marriage, *because of the nature of the marriage*, is likely to engender similar harmful effects."[77]

The NCCIJ brief argues, moreover, that third parties' "race prejudice" creates suffering for "parties to an interracial marriage" and their children, not "anything inherent in the family structure of the marriage."[78] Government, however, may not allow the racial prejudice of third parties to justify restrictions on the freedom to marry. The brief quotes the California Supreme Court's opinion in *Perez*, which, two decades earlier, concluded that the state's antimiscegenation law unconstitutionally restricted the right to marry (and, a concurring justice argued, the right to religious freedom): "It is 'no answer to say that race tension can be eradicated through the perpetuation by law of the prejudices that give rise to the tension.' "[79] This argument bears a striking resemblance to the Supreme Court's statement about racial prejudice seventeen years later, in *Palmore v. Sidoti* (1984): "Private biases may be outside the reach of the law, but the law cannot, directly or indirectly, give them effect."[80] This premise—that law should not give effect to prejudice—would later reverberate in litigation over LGBT rights and same-sex marriage, as chapter 7 discusses.

Resistance, Acceptance, and a National Forgetting

Given the widespread conjuring of fears about the inevitability of interracial marriage as a reason to oppose all forms of integration, it is notable that *Loving,* unlike *Brown,* did not engender "massive resistance."[81] One possible reason is that by 1967, when the Supreme Court ruled in *Loving,* the outcome seemed "almost preordained" after the gradual extension of *Brown*'s reasoning to other laws mandating segregation.[82] Between 1959 and 1967, for example, the number of states with antimiscegenation laws dropped from twenty-nine to sixteen; however, in the Deep South, state courts "repeatedly upheld antimiscegenation statutes" in the years after *Brown.*[83] In the sixteen southern states whose laws *Loving* struck down, there was neither "massive resistance" nor "instant compliance."[84]

The role of clerks in those sixteen states merits brief discussion, given present-day controversies over whether clerks opposed to same-sex marriage should have to issue marriage licenses to same-sex couples. Clerks "gradually began to change their practices" as "the legal authority of *Loving* took hold."[85] Sometimes that change required a judicial order.[86] In Virginia, county clerks simultaneously issued marriage licenses to interracial couples *and* handed out "pamphlets telling applicants that interracial marriage was illegal" until one of the attorneys for the Lovings requested the state's attorney general to confirm the Court's ruling in a formal opinion.[87]

Despite such initial resistance, historian Peggy Pascoe argues that a remarkable feature of *Loving*'s legacy was a national "forgetting" of the "three-century-long history of bans on interracial marriage."[88] *Loving* became part of a narrative of generational moral progress. "In little more than a generation," she observes, "most White Americans somehow managed to forget how fundamental they had once believed these bans to be and . . . to persuade themselves that they, and their government, had always been firmly committed to civil rights and racial equality." Racial classifications seemed "deeply un-American," despite the United States' long history of legally enforced segregation.[89] Chief Justice Warren, who authored *Brown* and viewed *Loving* as the "culmination" of the Court's "judicial campaign against racism in the law," contributed to this progress narrative. In *Loving,* he wrote that "over the years," the Court had "consistently repudiated" race-based classifications as "odious to a free people whose institutions are founded upon the doctrine of equality."[90] Yet the Court's own "long history of countenancing segregation" contradicted that narrative; the very case Warren cited for that consistent repudiation *upheld* a war-time restriction on Japanese-Americans.[91] Moreover, to show the "rigid scrutiny" that racial classifications warranted, Warren cited another infamous case upholding such restrictions, *Korematsu v. United States.*[92]

Another factor in the national "forgetting" was replacing the "notion that white supremacy was an acceptable public policy" with "the notion that marriage was a private choice."[93] By framing marriage—including across the color line—as a fundamental right and a matter of private choice, not a matter "suitable for public regulation," *Loving* "forever changed the terms of the debate among whites about intermarriage." A 1967 *New York Times* editorial about the case, for example, stated that "choosing a husband or wife lies in the inviolable area of personal freedom that government may not enter."[94] The idea that racial prejudice and bigotry were not valid reasons to oppose people choosing to marry across racial lines came through clearly in press coverage, in 1967, both of (1) the high-profile wedding of Secretary of State Dean Rusk's eighteen-year-old white daughter, Peggy Rusk, to Guy Gibson Smith, a twenty-two-year-old black man in the Air Force Reserves, and (2) the celebrated film about white and black parents grappling with their children's announced marriage plans, *Guess Who's Coming to Dinner?*[95]

Pascoe argues that in "what must be regarded as one of the most dramatic shifts of public opinion in American history," within a few generations, "the majority of Whites had come to believe that laws against interracial marriage were clearly, irrevocably wrong." *Loving*'s striking down legal barriers, however, did not mean the end of social disapproval by friends and families, but that, too, diminished over time. In 1958, "91% of southern Whites and 79% of northern Whites told pollsters that 'Negroes and whites marrying' would 'hurt in solving the Negro-white' problem"; by 1999, "65% of all Americans had come to believe that 'interracial marriages are good because they help break down racial barriers.'"[96] When the question was framed in terms of a relative crossing racial lines to marry, progress seems slower: as recently as 1990, 63% of "nonblacks" said they "would oppose a relative marrying a black person"; by 2016, however, that dropped to 14%.[97]

Virginia (quoting Rabbi Gordon) challenged the "mistaken" premise that intermarriage could lead to universalism and more tolerance but, decades later, that premise persists. In a recent full-page ad by the dating website tinder.com celebrating the creation of new emojis representing "71 combinations of interracial couples," the ad spoke of "more awareness, tolerance, and acceptance" and proclaimed that "the rates of interracial marriages and relationships are a direct reflection of a society evolving and breaking down walls between cultures."[98] Many dating websites and apps, however, make breaking down such walls harder by asking users to identify their race and allowing them to screen and exclude potential dates on the basis of race.[99]

By the early twenty-first century, Pascoe observes, it became harder for the "dwindling minority of mostly older Americans" who still disapproved of interracial marriage to "make a public case for their views." Young Americans "found it difficult to believe that intermarriage had ever been illegal."[100] Yet, some Virginians experienced a jolting reminder of that past recently when they applied for a marriage license and were asked to identify their race from a list of more than two hundred racial categories. A member of one couple, Brandyn Churchill, described the long list of outdated, obscure, and offensive categories as "born out of a place of deep bigotry," and asked why Virginia was still requiring disclosure of race today. Virginia's Attorney General agreed that it was "not readily apparent" why, and therefore instructed clerks to issue a license even if people declined to answer while a lawsuit brought by Churchill, his fiancé, Sophie Rogers, and several other couples proceeded. A federal district court ruled that requiring such "personal data" of marriage applicants burdened the fundamental right to marry, citing *Loving*. The court described the law as a "vestige of the nation's and of Virginia's history of codified racialization" and dividing humans into a taxonomy with "Caucasians" as the "ideal form of humanity."[101]

As the opening quotation from Judge Hinkle shows, parties and courts enlist *Loving* to argue that a similar generational shift will occur in viewing legal restrictions on marriage by same-sex couples.

Prejudice and Moral Progress: The Legacy of *Loving* for the Right of Same-Sex Couples to Marry

Nearly fifty-years after *Loving*, same-sex couples in Virginia challenged the Commonwealth's ban on same-sex marriage. This next section highlights the role played by *Loving*, as well as ideas of constitutional moral progress and not being on the wrong side of history, in that lawsuit. I then examine *Loving*'s crucial but contested role in *Obergefell*.

On Seeing and Not Seeing Analogies

The first legal challenge by same-sex couples to state marriage laws came in 1970, just three years after *Loving*.[102] In such early challenges, courts rejected the analogy to *Loving*.[103] In *Baker v. Nelson*, for example, two men in Hennepin County, Minnesota, who were denied a marriage license analogized the "White Supremacy" Virginia attempted to maintain by its antimiscegenation laws to the "heterosexual supremacy" Minnesota sought to maintain by its prohibition on two men or two women marrying.[104] The Minnesota Supreme Court rejected that analogy, holding that Virginia's law reflected "patent racial discrimination," and a distinction based "merely upon race," while Minnesota's law was based upon "the fundamental difference in sex."[105] "The institution of marriage as a union of man and woman, uniquely involving the procreation and rearing of children within a family," the Court stated, "is as old as the Book of Genesis."[106] This religious reference is notable, given the repeated appeals to the Bible to justify antimiscegenation laws. In 1972, in a one-sentence ruling, the US Supreme Court dismissed the couple's appeal "for want of a substantial federal question."[107]

Decades later, this summary dismissal featured prominently when defenders of the federal Defense of Marriage Act (DOMA) and state defense of marriage laws (state DOMAs) cited *Baker* as evidence that the fundamental right to marry acknowledged in *Loving* simply did not entail the right of two men or two women to marry. But Justice Ginsburg observed that *Baker* dated from an era before the Court decided "that gender-based classifications get any kind of heightened scrutiny" and when "same-sex conduct was considered criminal in many states."[108]

Even before *Obergefell*, a number of state courts considering constitutional challenges by same-sex couples accepted the analogy to *Loving*. In *Goodridge v. Department of Public Health* (2003), the Supreme Judicial Court of Massachusetts looked to the "long history" in many states (including Massachusetts) during which "no lawful marriage was possible between black and white Americans." That history, Chief Justice Marshall observed, did not prevent the California Supreme Court (in *Perez*) and, subsequently, the US Supreme Court (in *Loving*) from striking down such laws as unconstitutional. Likewise, in the case of the bar on same-sex couples marrying, "history must yield to a more fully developed understanding of the invidious quality of the discrimination."[109] Marshall situates these and other precedents striking down race and sex discrimination in a narrative of constitutional moral progress (quoting Justice Ginsburg in *VMI*): "The history of constitutional law 'is the story of the extension of constitutional rights and protections to people once ignored or excluded.' "[110] *Goodridge*'s moral reading (of commitments to liberty and equality as abstract moral principles, not limited to framers' understandings and expectations) provided a template for Justice Kennedy's opinion in *Obergefell*.[111] A concurring opinion in *Goodridge* drew on *Loving* for another constitutional argument against Massachusetts's one man–one woman definition of marriage: it restricts who may marry using a sex-based classification, by analogy to Virginia's law using a race-based classification.[112]

In 2013, in *United States v. Windsor*, the Court struck down a portion of the federal DOMA defining marriage for purposes of federal law as the union of one man and one women, but did not reach the issue of whether the fundamental right to marry extends to same-sex couples. Kennedy's majority opinion, however, cited *Loving* for the proposition that "state laws defining and regulating marriage, of course, must respect the constitutional rights of persons."[113] After

Windsor, a flurry of lower federal courts invoked *Loving* in ruling in favor of same-sex couples' challenges to restrictive laws. A particularly valuable illustration is the constitutional challenge to Virginia's DOMA. The litigation highlights the different views the opposing parties and the judge took of *Loving's* relevance and the lessons we should learn from history and from the civil rights past about prejudice and moral progress.

Litigating Virginia's Ban on Same-Sex Marriage: Not Being on the Wrong Side of History

> I have lived long enough to see big changes. The older generation's fears and prejudices have given way, and today's young people realize that if someone loves someone they have a right to marry. . . . Not a day goes by that I don't think of Richard, and our love, our right to marry, and how much it meant to me to have that freedom to marry the person precious to me, even if others thought he was the "wrong kind of person" for me to marry. I believe all Americans, no matter their race, no matter their sex, no matter their sexual orientation, should have that same freedom to marry. Government has no business imposing some people's religious beliefs over others. . . . I support the freedom to marry for all. That's what *Loving*, and loving, are all about.
> —Mildred Loving (statement on fortieth anniversary of
> *Loving v. Virginia*)

Shortly after *Windsor*, Timothy Bostic and Tony London (a male couple) sued in federal court after a county clerk in Norfolk, Virginia, denied them a marriage license. A second couple, Carol Schall and Mary Townley (two women), sued because Virginia would not recognize their marriage legally entered into in California.[114] These plaintiffs challenged Virginia's statutory and constitutional bans on permitting or recognizing their marriages.[115] Virginia's legislature passed a DOMA, which also prohibited civil unions or "partnership contracts" between persons of the same sex.[116] In 2006, Virginia voters ratified an amendment to the state constitution providing that "only a union between one man and one woman may be a marriage valid in or recognized by this Commonwealth."[117]

In January 2014, the newly-elected Attorney General, Mark Herring, made national headlines when he concluded that Virginia's marriage bans were unconstitutional and announced that his office would side with the plaintiffs. He used the rhetoric of Virginia having been on the wrong side of history and the law in prior civil rights cases such as *Brown v. Board of Education* and *Loving*, and gender discrimination cases such as *VMI*.[118] Although his office argued against Virginia's marriage bans, attorneys for the county clerks defended the laws.

The oral argument: competing views of Virginia's marriage tradition. In the oral argument, Virginia Solicitor General Stuart Alan Raphael reiterated Herring's stance of not wanting to be on the wrong side of history. He related the county clerk's argument that "there is no traditional right to same-sex marriage" to "the same argument" made by the attorney general in *Brown* (about segregated schools) and then in *Loving* (arguing that "Virginia had banned interracial marriage since colonial days").[119] *Brown* and *Loving*, however, "teach that tradition is not the basis for determining the right that is at issue here," the principle of "equality of right." Raphael saw that same principle at work in Justice Kennedy's trio of majority opinions on gay rights, *Romer v. Evans*, *Lawrence v. Texas*, and *United States v. Windsor*.[120]

The Solicitor General also pointed out parallels between (1) the arguments made by his predecessor in defending Virginia's antimiscegenation law and (2) those made in support of Virginia's same-sex marriage ban, such as the state's power to limit who could marry and social science arguments about child well-being.[121] He noted that on questioning from Chief Justice Warren, his predecessor could not offer a "limiting principle" for a state's power to restrict interracial, but not "interreligious," marriage.[122] His predecessor, he argued, could have chosen *not* to defend Virginia's antimiscegenation law and other laws discriminating on the basis of race (such as *Brown*) or sex (such as *VMI*), but instead chose to defend them. This past indicated the need to make a "courageous decision" not to defend the laws under challenge. Raphael argued that although "all of those cases were really controversial when they were decided," the legal principle of equality was not; the controversy concerned "how that principle applied at that time in history."[123]

The attorneys for the county clerks appealed to history and tradition, stressing the "antiquity" of Virginia's marriage law. Bans on same-sex marriage, they argued, went to the core of what marriage is: the union of one man and one woman. By contrast, *Loving* struck down a racial restriction on marriage. For support, David Brandt Oakley, counsel for one clerk, quoted the Minnesota Supreme Court's analysis in *Baker* in contending that "this historic institution" of marriage is "more deeply founded" than the "contemporary concept of marriage" that the plaintiffs offered.[124] Austin Nimocks, counsel for another clerk, contrasted the "extreme novelty of same-sex marriage" with "over 400 years" of public policy.[125]

These analyses ignored the central role of *racial* difference in most of those centuries of Virginia's marriage law, claiming instead that the law was about recognizing and celebrating *sex* difference—the "unique complementarity and fundamental differences between men and women."[126] This picture of centuries of unchanging marriage law has no place for moral progress as the law of marriage better realizes ideals of liberty and equality. Nimocks inaptly recasts the common law system of coverture that the colonies inherited from England—with married women's loss of legal identity and acquisition of various legal disabilities—as a policy "celebrating" sex difference. Missing is any account of how Virginia's marriage law, over time, repudiated such sex inequality.

Also missing in Nimocks' projection back to the 1600s of the "responsible procreation" and optimal child rearing arguments for Virginia's law—"we have marriage laws because we have children"—is that arguments about procreation and children were central to defending Virginia's antimiscegenation laws.[127] As the Supreme Court of Virginia put it in *Naim*, such laws justifiably regulated "the marriage relation so that [Virginia] shall not have a mongrel breed of citizens."[128] In *Loving*, Virginia also asserted (relying on Gordon) social and psychological harms to children born into an interracial marriage.

By comparison, moral progress in constitutional interpretation featured centrally in the arguments against Virginia's DOMA. Theodore Olson, arguing for the plaintiffs, countered the portrait of centuries of unchanging tradition with one of progressive realization of ideals of "equality, openness, and nondiscrimination" as "we move one barrier of official discrimination after another."[129] Olson also appealed to Justice Ginsburg's statement in *VMI* (quoted earlier) about the United States' unfolding "story" of extending constitutional rights.[130] Noting the appeal to tradition to justify segregation, antimiscegenation laws, and sex discrimination, Virginia's Solicitor General argued that applying the "equality of right" principle had led to recognizing "that those practices were wrong." He argued that Justice Kennedy's declaration about generational progress (in *Lawrence*)—that "the constitutional framers knew that times can blind us to certain truths and later generations can see that laws once thought necessary and proper in fact only serve to oppress"—was "exactly what's going on here."[131]

Olson countered the argument that Virginia's centuries-old marriage policy reflected no history of discrimination: "Virginia erects a wall around its gay and lesbian citizens excluding them from the most important relation in life because of their sexual orientation and labels their intimate personal relationships as second rate, in[f]erior, unequal, unworthy, and void."[132] Drawing on *Windsor's* analysis of the federal DOMA, he argued that the "the purpose and effect" of Virginia's DOMA was "to demean, humiliate and put our citizens into a separate subordinate status."[133] Olson injected a personal note, as a Virginian: he expressed great pride in Virginia, with its storied founders, but added that "Virginia has had it [egregiously] wrong from time to time [and] it's wrong now."[134]

The federal district court opinion in Bostic. The federal district court opinion holding Virginia's marriage laws unconstitutional also offers a narrative of generational moral progress in realizing the Constitution's ideals and overcoming prejudice. It seems appropriate to note that the judge, Arenda Wright Allen, was the first black woman to be a federal judge in Virginia.[135] Her opinion opens with the statement by Mildred Loving on the fortieth anniversary of *Loving* (quoted at the beginning of this section).[136] Observing that America's ongoing "journey to make and keep our citizens free" and equal is at times "painful and poignant,"

Judge Allen stresses that one of the judiciary's "noblest" roles is to "scrutinize laws" rooted in "unlawful prejudice."[137] She eschews any explicit reference to bigotry as a motive for Virginia's past or present marriage laws, while gently but firmly explaining that history, tradition, and "heritage" cannot justify denying citizens the right to marry.

Virginia's marriage laws, Judge Allen observes, "are endowed with" a "faith-enriched heritage," but have "evolved into a civil and secular institution" with "protections and benefits extended to portions of Virginia's citizens." *Loving* shows that "extension of those protections and benefits has sometimes occurred after anguish and the unavoidable intervention of federal jurisprudence." She notes that "the parties before this Court appreciate the sacred principles embodied in our fundamental right to marry," but disagree concerning "who among Virginia's citizenry may exercise [that right]." Same-sex couples are not seeking "a new . . . right," but "simply the same right that is currently enjoyed by heterosexual individuals." She associates marriage with conscience: the "loving, intimate, and lasting relationships" gay and lesbian individuals form "are created through the exercise of sacred, personal choices" that, like those "made by every other citizen, must be free from unwarranted government interference."[138]

Loving features in Judge Allen's insistence that extending the right to marry should not be construed as "any dilution of the sanctity of marriage." "Similar fears," she observes, "were voiced and ultimately quieted after Virginia unsuccessfully defended its antimiscegenation laws by referring to a need 'to preserve the racial integrity of its citizens' and to prevent 'the corruption of blood,' 'a mongrel breed of citizens,' and 'the obliteration of racial pride.'"[139]

Judge Allen also enlists *Loving* in countering the county clerks' assertion that traditional marriage is "ancient because it is rational."[140] The "ancient lineage of a legal concept does not give it immunity from attack for lacking a rational basis."[141] Nor does the fact that beliefs are "dearly held." The example of *Loving* striking down Virginia's ban on interracial marriage shows that "other profound infringements upon our citizens' rights have been explained as a consequence of heritage, and those explanations have been found wanting."[142]

The court similarly turns to *Loving* in evaluating the appeal to tradition to justify the laws at issue. Legislators drafted Virginia's bans on same-sex marriage "in response to fears" about "homosexual marriage" weakening the institution of marriage, obscuring "moral values," and devaluing "the status of children." The court connects concerns about same-sex marriage to "nearly identical concerns" about the "significance of tradition" expressed when defending Virginia's ban on interracial marriage. Yet "the *Loving* court struck down Virginia's ban . . . despite [its] existence since 'the colonial period.'" Judge Allen acknowledges the value in "cherishing . . . many aspects" of our "heritages," but observes: "The protections created for us by the drafters of our Constitution were designed to evolve and adapt to the progress of our citizenry."[143] What unites past and present challenges to marriage laws is evolving understandings of our constitutional commitments.

Even in analyzing the prejudice evident in Virginia's DOMA, Judge Allen avoids the express rhetoric of bigotry. The parties disagree, she notes, about "the extent of animus that has been directed toward gay and lesbian people." Citing *Lawrence*'s observation that "for centuries there have been powerful voices to condemn homosexual conduct as immoral," Allen finds that such "moral condemnation" is manifest in Virginia to this day. "This record alone . . . gives rise to suspicions of prejudice, sufficient to decline to defer to the state on this matter."[144]

Judge Allen's opinion ends with rhetorical flourish about moral progress toward fuller realization of constitutional ideals: "Justice has often been forged from fires of indignities and prejudices suffered." Virginia's marriage laws are "steeped in a rich, tradition- and faith-based legacy," but government's "interest in perpetuating traditions" must "yield to this country's cherished protections that ensure the exercise of the private choices of the individual citizen regarding love and family." She situates her ruling in the nation's "uneven but dogged journey toward truer and more meaningful freedoms for our citizens" and a "deeper understanding" of the Constitution's reference to "We the People."[145] Strikingly, in the recent decision finding Virginia's inquiry on marriage license applications about race unconstitutional, another federal district court offered a similar vision about confronting Virginia's mixed history in light of constitutional commitments: "The Commonwealth of Virginia is naturally rich in its greatest traditions. But like other institutions, the stain of past mistakes must always survive the scrutiny of our nation's most important institution . . . the [US] Constitution."[146]

Prejudice, Moral Progress, and Time: The Legacy of *Loving*

Like Judge Allen's opinion, some other federal district court opinions striking down state DOMAs also offered narratives of generational moral progress. One example is *Brenner v. Scott*, in which federal district court judge Robert Hinkle observes that securing "the blessings of liberty" mentioned in the Constitution's preamble has "come more slowly for some than for others."[147] As quoted earlier, Hinkle reached back to 1967, and looked forward fifty years from the present, to emphasize the significance of time and generational change in evaluating beliefs about marriage.[148] In ruling that Florida's bans on permitting or recognizing same-sex marriage violated the US Constitution, Hinkle explicitly links such laws to bans on interracial marriage. Each involves a restriction on constitutional liberty in which later generations have had—or will have—difficulty in believing that the arguments offered for such restrictions were "sincerely held" rather than "an obvious pretext."[149]

Judge Hinkle does not label present-day opposition to same-sex marriage as bigotry, but contends that Florida's ban "stems entirely, or almost entirely, from moral disapproval," even though Florida offers "make-weight arguments" (like the responsible procreation justification) that "do not withstand analysis."[150] Judge Hinkle draws on *Loving* in observing that the Supreme Court recognized that the fundamental right to marry applied across racial lines, despite the fact that state laws forbidding such marriages were "widespread and of long standing."[151]

Competing Views of *Loving* in *Obergefell*: Is the Present Like the Past?

As the Supreme Court evaluated federal constitutional claims against state DOMAs in *Obergefell v. Hodges*, the parties and their amici advanced sharply conflicting arguments about the legacy of *Loving*. Some offer narratives of generational moral progress in constitutional interpretation that link the striking down of antimiscegenation laws and defense of marriage laws as the continual realization of constitutional ideals. They argue that prejudice, not legitimate state purposes, unites these two types of laws. By contrast, other amici distinguish *Loving*, which rightly struck down a law that was an odious relic of slavery, from laws which correctly defend a universal definition of marriage rooted in sound rationales, not bigotry, hatred, or animus. The US Catholic Conference of Catholic Bishops argued in *Bostic* (in the Fourth Circuit) and *Obergefell* that the one man–one woman definition of marriage was rooted not in hatred, bigotry, or animus, but in sexual conduct, common sense, and child well being; it made only passing reference to *Loving*.[152]

Most striking is the competing uses of *Loving* in the briefs filed by various states, including states whose antimiscegenation laws *Loving* struck down. Louisiana, along with thirteen other states, filed an amicus brief criticizing judicial opinions, like that of Judge Allen in *Bostic*, for relying on *Loving* and "repeatedly" drawing "a direct analogy between the white supremacist laws correctly invalidated in *Loving* and the man-woman marriage laws challenged here."[153] The brief also criticizes such opinions for quoting Mildred Loving's "extrajudicial" statement about the parallel between her situation and that of same-sex couples. Enlisting *Loving* this way, the brief argues, is a "troubling misapplication of a landmark decision" and denigrates citizens of states which "decline to adopt the novel institution of same-sex marriage" as "irrational, ignorant, or bigoted." In other words, the brief infers a charge of bigotry merely from drawing an analogy to *Loving*. Citizens who vote for state DOMAs, the brief insists, are "not voting to roll back the achievements of the Civil Rights movement."[154]

Loving "rightly" invalidated laws that were "odious" and "racist relics of slavery," Louisiana argues, but those laws have "nothing—nothing—to do with" the state DOMAs under challenge in *Obergefell*.[155] Notably, Louisiana's present-day assessment of antimiscegenation laws as odious repeats what the Lovings said about them decades earlier, when Louisiana (and several other states on its *Obergefell* brief) still had such laws, and had not (unlike some states) repealed them in the wake of *Brown*.[156] Citing *Baker*, Louisiana tries to distinguish *Loving* as simply striking down "invidious racial discrimination" in marriage laws; by contrast, the one man–one woman definition of marriage rests on the "fundamental difference in sex."[157]

The amicus briefs filed by the State of South Carolina and the Governor of Alabama similarly object to the use of *Loving* to challenge state DOMAs. South Carolina argued that *Loving* should be read simply as barring racial discrimination in marriage; indeed, *Loving*'s language about the fundamental right to marry is "dicta" that "does not suggest anything about same-sex marriage."[158] The Governor of Alabama argued that if the Supreme Court struck down state DOMAs, it would "usurp state sovereignty over the family"[159]—echoing arguments made in defense of Virginia's antimiscegenation law decades earlier. States have authority, he asserted, to "affirm the millennia-old institution of marriage," that is, "natural marriage."[160] As with the defense (in *Bostic*) of Virginia's "centuries-old" marriage law, Alabama's appeal to history ignores the long history of the state's ban on interracial marriage on the ground that it was "unnatural."[161]

By contrast, Virginia filed a brief invoking *Loving* to support striking down the state DOMAs challenged in *Obergefell*.[162] It expounded on moral progress, much like Judge Allen did in *Bostic*: Virginia, home of many "Founding Fathers," is "proud" of its contribution to America's constitutional democracy; but "it is also self-evident that the scope of the equality of right principle that these Virginians shared with the world and helped enshrine in our Constitution was not fully recognized in their day." National failures to recognize constitutional principles include slavery, lack of female suffrage until 1920, and the Court's upholding of state-sponsored segregation. In Virginia, such failures of recognition include defending segregated public schools (in *Brown*), prohibiting interracial marriage (in *Loving*), and excluding "female cadets" from Virginia Military Institute (in *VMI*). The brief links past and present, contending that "the arguments offered to defend those unjust laws are the same arguments offered by marriage-equality opponents today": federalism (state prerogatives to regulate marriage and education) and "history and tradition." The brief insists: "Virginia's government was wrong then, and the four States that reprise modern-day versions of those failed arguments are wrong here."[163]

Because of their role as amici in support of the Lovings, the NAACP and the NAACP Legal Defense & Educational Fund's amicus brief deserves mention on the issue of when insight about injustice is possible. The brief argues that the "primary theories" offered in support of state DOMAs "echo those advanced by proponents of antimiscegenation statutes and rejected by the Supreme Court in *Loving*."[164] It observes that "historically, courts and opponents of interracial marriage argued that such unions harmed children," but *Loving* rejected such theories as "unfounded, post-hoc rationalizations" and "it has become even clearer how blatantly offensive and preposterous these theories really are." The brief links past and present: "Today's arguments about purported harm to children, families, and heterosexuals are as offensive as they were in 1967. They are also patently wrong."[165] It maintains not only that such arguments were "wrong then, wrong now," but also that the wrongness has become more evident with the passage of time.[166]

The *Obergefell* Opinion: *Loving* as Showing New Insights About Unjustified Inequality

Loving plays a central role in Justice Kennedy's majority opinion in *Obergefell*, which takes up some of the themes just discussed. He states: "The nature of injustice is such that we may not always see it in our own times." As examples of how "new insights" have transformed the institution of marriage, Kennedy discusses the Court's striking down antimiscegenation laws and laws embodying gender hierarchy in marriage.[167] Generational progress is important to this view: "The generations that wrote and ratified the Bill of Rights and the Fourteenth Amendment did not presume to know the extent of freedom in all of its dimensions, and so they entrusted to future generations a charter protecting the right of all persons to enjoy liberty as we learn its meaning."[168] *Loving's* invalidation of "bans on interracial unions" provides an example of how "a claim to liberty" must be addressed when "new insights" reveal "discord" between the Constitution's commitments and "a received legal stricture."[169]

Loving also features in support of the Court's broad reading of the fundamental right to marry and its cautioning that history and tradition are not the only sources relevant to defining that right. Kennedy appeals to *Loving's* twin Due Process and Equal Protection holdings to argue that looking at liberty and equality together helped to make "the reasons why marriage is a fundamental right . . . more clear and compelling."[170] While Chief Justice Warren's opinion in *Loving* did not stress harm or humiliation, Kennedy argues that viewing liberty and equality together revealed "a full awareness and understanding of the hurt that resulted from laws barring interracial unions."[171] He links *Loving* to important Supreme Court opinions striking down "invidious sex-based classifications in marriage," arguing that these precedents show "the Equal Protection Clause can help to identify and correct inequalities in the institution of marriage, vindicating precepts of liberty and equality under the Constitution."[172]

Kennedy acknowledges the Court's failure to see injustice. The Court's summary dismissal in *Baker* is evidence that "the Court, like many institutions, has made assumptions defined by the world and time of which it is a part," including its presumption that the right to marry involves "a relationship involving opposite-sex partners." *Loving* is among those "other, more instructive precedents" that express "constitutional principles of broader reach" in defining the right to marry.[173] Indeed, *Obergefell* overrules *Baker*.[174]

Kennedy also enlists *Loving* in arguing that the "principles and traditions" that "demonstrate" why "marriage is fundamental under the Constitution apply with equal force to same-sex couples." For example, in articulating the first principle, that "the right to personal choice regarding marriage is inherent in the concept of individual autonomy," Kennedy argues that *Loving* invalidated "interracial marriage bans" because of this "abiding connection between marriage and liberty." Marriage is a bond that allows persons to find other freedoms; just as *Loving* stated that the freedom to marry cannot be restricted based on race, so too, two men or two women should be free to form that bond free of state interference.[175]

Moral progress in understanding constitutional commitments is evident when Kennedy discusses the fourth principle: that marriage is a "keystone of our social order," a "great public institution," and a "building block of our national community." "This idea," he writes, "has been reiterated even as the institution has evolved in substantial ways, superseding rules related to . . . gender and race once thought by many to be essential."[176] Citing *Loving* and *Lawrence v. Texas* (concerning the right of gays and lesbians to intimate association), he argues: "If rights were defined by who exercised them in the past, then received practices could serve as their own continued justification and new groups could not invoke rights once denied."[177] Kennedy stresses the harm, stigma, and injury suffered by same-sex couples "locked out" of "a central institution."[178] He concludes: "The limitation of marriage to opposite-sex couples may long have seemed natural and just, but its inconsistency with the central meaning of the fundamental right to marry is now manifest."[179]

The *Obergefell* dissenters found the majority's invocation of *Loving* inapt. They argued that the Court's summary affirmance in *Baker* just a few years after *Loving* showed its consistent adherence to the traditional understanding of marriage. *Loving*, Chief Justice Roberts argued, did not alter the "core definition of marriage" as the union of one man and one woman.[180] The dissenters rejected the majority's approach to how new insights and generational moral progress should inform constitutional interpretation of the scope of the right to marry. Justice Alito warned that comparing traditional marriage (excluding same-sex couples) to "laws that denied equal treatment to African Americans and women" in marriage would lead to "labeling as bigots" those who "cling to old beliefs" and express them in public.[181]

Chapter 7 more fully addresses Justice Kennedy's opinion as well as these dissents and their charges about bigotry. In assessing those charges, it is important to note some differences between *Loving* and *Obergefell*. *Loving* never said that the trial court's theological defense of segregation or "the doctrine of White Supremacy" underlying Virginia's law was "decent" or "honorable" and deserved the Court's "respect." By contrast, in *Obergefell*, Kennedy stated that "decent and honorable religious or philosophical premises" were the basis for many persons' opposition to same-sex marriage, even as he explained why such beliefs could not justify a discriminatory law.[182]

Conclusion

As parties and courts enlist *Loving* in newer battles over constitutional rights and anti-discrimination laws, a complicated part of *Loving's* legacy is the question of when insight about the gap between constitutional principles and unjust practices is attainable. In 1948, two decades before *Loving*, it was possible for the California Supreme Court to see—and rule—that California's antimiscegenation law erected "barriers of race prejudice" that infringed on the fundamental right to marry.[183] Virginia's attorney general, in 2014, contended that it should have been possible for his predecessor, who chose to defend Virginia's interracial marriage ban in 1967, to see that ban's violation of constitutional principles. In *Obergefell*, Justice Kennedy enlisted *Loving* in support of his declaration that "the nature of injustice is that we may not always see it in our own times." This could mean that such insight is not yet attainable, or that we simply fail to see because prejudice mars our vision. Mildred Loving's statement on the fortieth anniversary of *Loving* suggests that fears and prejudice made it harder for the older generation to see what is clearer to the newer ones. So too, newer generations may have difficulty seeing that beliefs now rejected as inconsistent with our constitutional commitments—such as racist religious beliefs—were once sincerely and widely held. Looking back at *Loving* and its legacy illustrates that what is taken for granted as reasonable distinctions in marriage law versus what is "odious" and "invidious" discrimination—bigotry—changes over time. Even so, the Lovings perceived those distinctions as odious at the time, raising the question of when insight is possible and what accounts for a failure to see. Similarly, even as the trial court appealed to segregationist theology and Virginia appealed to modern science, some religious group amici argued then that antimiscegenation laws violated conscience and reflected prejudice, just as other amici showed the limits of the science of race on which Virginia relied.

Sincere Believers, Bigots, or Superstitious Fools?

Motives and Morality in the Supreme Court's Gay Rights Cases

On May 2, 1977, journalist William Raspberry published an editorial, "Anita Bryant and Gay Rights: Bigotry or Prudence?," posing a question about Bryant's "passionate efforts" to overturn Miami-Dade County's gay rights ordinance through a voter referendum. He asked: "How could any non-bigot be opposed to a law prohibiting discrimination in housing, public accommodations and employment on the basis of 'affectional' or sexual preferences?"[1] Bryant, a popular singer, the face and voice for advertising Florida orange juice, and an evangelical Christian mother and wife, had organized the "Save Our Children" campaign against the ordinance.[2] Initially, Raspberry thought the answer was clear: "Miss Bryant's crusade was a campaign of bigotry." After talking with Bryant, he became less certain: Was it *really* "ignorance and bigotry at work" or "mere prudence"? Would it not be prudent, as she argued, to protect "our children" from being taught in schools by "*flaunting* homosexuals"—who would "be able to stand up and say 'I'm homosexual and I'm proud of it,' implying to our children that they have another legitimate choice open to them"? Bryant assured Raspberry that she believed in "live and let live" with respect to people's private lives, but "dr[ew] the line" at bringing things "out in the open." She denied it was a "civil rights issue," objecting that "in the name of human rights, vice is becoming virtuous."

Raspberry observed that many shared Bryant's fear about influence on children. What's more, he no longer believed that her "red-flag warnings about homosexuals teaching impressionable children" were "on a par" with a racist's "would you want your daughter to marry one?" argument against racial integration. Nor was there evidence that discrimination against gays and lesbians in Miami-Dade was as clear and widespread as was the discrimination blacks have

Who's the Bigot? Linda C. McClain, Oxford University Press (2020). © Oxford University Press.
DOI: 10.1093/oso/9780190877200.001.0001

experienced (as in the segregated Mississippi of Raspberry's own experience). People feared that while the gay rights ordinance aimed at a "largely theoretical problem," it would "trigger a very real one: the subversion of their children's sexuality." Raspberry concluded that if he lived in the area, he probably would vote against the voter referendum, but "with a lot less certainty."[3]

Voters did overturn the ordinance, and by a large margin. Bryant declared: "Tonight the laws of God and the cultural values of man have been vindicated."[4] Gay rights activists did not share Raspberry's uncertainty about whether to use the label bigotry. The leader of the unsuccessful effort to save the ordinance commented that "the bigotry and discrimination expressed by our opponents" brought many people without prior political experience "out of the closet" to fight similar efforts elsewhere in the country.[5] Bryant's rhetoric also set up a stark, polarizing tension between "gay and Christian," as she became an "icon" of an "ardently religious" backlash against gay people.[6]

Fifteen years later, local ordinances protecting against discrimination on the basis of sexual orientation triggered another successful referendum campaign stressing threats to children. Using the slogan "equal rights—not special rights" and spreading false information about the "homosexual lifestyle," Colorado for Family Values persuaded voters to amend the Colorado constitution to repeal such ordinances and prevent any other protection without a constitutional amendment.[7] In 1996, in *Romer v. Evans*, the Supreme Court (in an opinion by Justice Anthony Kennedy) struck down the amendment as unconstitutional, concluding that it did not further any "legitimate state interests" and "seems inexplicable by anything but animus toward the class it affects."[8] In dissent, Justice Scalia countered that what the Court labeled "animus" was simply "moral disapproval of homosexual conduct," which, just ten years earlier, in *Bowers v. Hardwick*, it had ruled was a legitimate reason to uphold a state's criminal sodomy law. Scalia accused the majority of "disparaging as bigotry" "traditional attitudes" about sexual morality.[9] Gay rights, conservative religious critics warned, were on a collision course with religious liberty and traditional marriage.

Romer launched the "morality versus animus" dynamic that would culminate, two decades later, in the Court's two landmark marriage opinions, *United States v. Windsor* (2013) and *Obergefell v. Hodges* (2015). Each time, Justice Kennedy wrote the majority opinion striking down the federal or state law restricting marriage to the union of one man and one woman, and each time, Justice Scalia and other conservative justices dissented, charging the majority with branding those with traditional moral and religious beliefs about marriage as bigots. In none of the opinions, however, did Kennedy use the term "bigot." Curiously, the dissenters sounded these charges whether Kennedy attributed support for laws defending traditional marriage to animus (as in *Windsor*) or to beliefs about marriage held "in good faith by reasonable and sincere people," resting on "decent and honorable religious or philosophical premises" (as in *Obergefell*).[10] While animus might seem akin to bigotry, "decent and honorable" beliefs do not. The dissenters' charges of bigotry seem to be strategic volleys in the culture war rather than rooted in fair readings of Kennedy's opinions.

The legal concept of animus is complex.[11] Sometimes the flaw lies in motives for a law—such as impermissible bias toward a particular group—and sometimes in a law's purposes or effects. The Court's analysis has subtly shifted from condemning bad motives—animosity—to condemning practices whose social meaning is to deny equal liberties to groups who are worthy of the status of equal citizenship. This shift is evident in *Obergefell*. Kennedy does not "disparage" the sincere beliefs of those who oppose same-sex marriage, but explains that to put the state's "imprimatur" on them by enacting them into law would demean or stigmatize same-sex couples "whose own liberty is denied."[12] In other words, it is not necessary to label supporters of a law bigoted to conclude that the law is unconstitutional because of its effects on others. Even so, the dissenters contended that the majority's analogies to race and sex discrimination "tar" with the "brush" of bigotry.[13] Although Kennedy drew such analogies to show (as chapter 6 explained) the evolution of marriage and of understandings of constitutional guarantees of liberty and equality, he never treated beliefs about same-sex marriage as the moral equivalent of racism.

This chapter traces the Supreme Court's evolving approach to the constitutional rights of gays and lesbians, focusing on whether moral disapproval is a sufficient basis for laws denying their basic liberties and equal status. Because of this historical focus, I use the terminology that the justices used in the majority opinions and dissents, rather than present-day terms, such as LGBTQ. I begin with the Court's seventeen-year trajectory from *Bowers* (1986) to *Lawrence v. Texas* (2003), in which the Court initially upheld and subsequently struck down state criminal laws punishing sodomy. I next turn to the Court's holding, in *Romer*, that an attempt to block gay and bisexual people from civil rights protections violated the Constitution. Finally, I take up marriage. Shortly after *Romer*, Congress passed the Defense of Marriage Act (DOMA) to "honor and reflect" a "collective moral judgment" in favor of heterosexuality and "heterosexual-only marriage laws" and disapproving homosexuality.[14] Seventeen years later, the Court held, in *Windsor*, that DOMA denied equal protection to gays and lesbians. Finally, in *Obergefell*, the Court ruled that state DOMAs violated the fundamental right to marry.

I analyze the rhetoric and arguments in briefs and the majority and dissenting opinions in these cases. Often, arguments defending the laws took the form "it's not A, it's B": it's not animus or bigotry, it's traditional moral judgments or sincere beliefs. As the Court cast doubt on moral disapproval as a sufficient basis for discriminatory laws, arguments shifted: marriage restrictions rest not on animus, bigotry, or *mere* moral disapproval, but on prudence, sound public policy, and preserving marriage. Arguments against such laws countered, "it's A, not B": such laws rest on animus or bigotry, not morality; and, in any event, moral disapproval alone—however sincere—is not enough. Understanding the patterns of argument sheds light on puzzles about the rhetoric of bigotry, including the charge of being branded as a bigot. This sets the stage for chapter 8's analysis of *Masterpiece Cakeshop*.

Criminal Sodomy Laws: From *Bowers to Lawrence*

Bowers v. Hardwick: Morality versus Animus

In *Bowers v. Hardwick*, a 5–4 majority rejected Michael Hardwick's argument that Georgia's law criminalizing sodomy violated his fundamental right to privacy. It also rejected his argument that "the presumed belief of a majority of the electorate in Georgia that homosexual sodomy is immoral and unacceptable" was not a sufficient rationale to support the law, commenting that "the law . . . is constantly based on notions of morality." Justice White's majority opinion ignored the fact that Georgia's criminal law prohibited *all* sodomy, defined in terms of "a person" committing *acts* (oral or anal sex). Treating the law as focused on "homosexual sodomy," the Court found "no connection" or "resemblance" between the rights protected in its prior cases about privacy—cases about family relationships, procreation and abortion, marriage, and child rearing and education—and "homosexual activity."[15] To argue for a "fundamental right to commit homosexual sodomy"—given the "ancient roots" of state criminal laws prohibiting sodomy—was "at best, facetious."[16]

Is the appeal to morality enough to support criminal law? Chief Justice Warren Burger appealed in concurrence to "millennia of moral teaching" to show that "condemnation of sodomy" is "firmly rooted in Judeao-Christian moral and ethical standards."[17] One of Burger's sources, also cited by Michael Bowers, Georgia's attorney general, was Derrick Sherwin Bailey's *Homosexuality and the Western Christian Tradition*.[18] Burger's citation to Bailey was an "odd choice": although Bailey established that Christian teaching regarded homosexual sexual behavior as immoral, he argued *against* using the Bible as a basis for criminal prohibition. Instead, his book was "a supporting treatise for the movement to repeal sodomy law in Great Britain."[19] Bailey served on the Wolfenden Committee, whose 1957 report recommending decriminalization led to such repeal a decade later.

In fact, Burger and his colleagues had ample indication that by the 1980s, many religious denominations in the United States shared Bailey's criticism of criminal sodomy laws. The Presbyterian Church, along with several other denominations, filed an amicus brief emphasizing the "strong agreement, even among those who deem [sexual unorthodoxy, homosexual or heterosexual] objectively immoral, that consensual unorthodox sexual acts should be decriminalized."[20] The brief included an appendix with statements from several religious bodies calling for civil rights legislation to end discrimination on the basis of sexual orientation in "housing, employment, business services, or public accommodations."[21] In 1977, the United Church of Christ issued a resolution deploring "the use of scripture to generate hatred, and the violation of civil rights of gay and bisexual persons." It stated that the voter referendum championed by Anita Bryant "represents a new reactionary movement which may eventually erode the civil liberties of all."[22] Such briefs resisted a "gay rights versus religious liberty" framing.

Religious amici also drew an analogy to the trial judge's religious defense of antimiscegenation laws in *Loving v. Virginia*. But, *Loving* teaches, a "majoritarian moral preference" is not enough for states to "interfere with private and consensual sexual association."[23] Furthermore, a democratic majority's appeal to "public morality" is insufficient.[24] Hardwick argued that this amicus brief raised "grave doubt" about Georgia's claim that its criminal sodomy law "implements universal morality." In fact, "state after state" had decriminalized sodomy.[25]

Bowers insisted that Georgia had the power to prohibit an "immoral" act. "Homosexual sodomy" was "an unnatural means of satisfying an unnatural lust . . . declared by Georgia to be morally wrong."[26] Decriminalizing that act would threaten the family and marriage. No religious denomination filed a brief supporting this use of the criminal law, but several conservative religious organizations did. The Rutherford Institute argued that "monogamous marriage and the family unit" are the foundation of our institutions; legitimizing sodomy would undermine that foundation and open the door to legalizing "all private consensual activities.'" Appealing to the religious roots of sodomy laws (also citing Bailey's treatise) and the long history of prohibition in the United States, it urged the Court to "steer" the right of privacy back onto the "historical path" and to reject the lower court's analogy between the intimacy of marriage and same-sex sexual intimacy. In extolling the "tether of history," the brief makes no mention of situations where the nation has broken with history, as in *Loving*.[27] Amici also asserted that a "new constitutional right to practice homosexual sodomy" would imperil the "operational freedom of religious and quasi-public private associations."[28]

Competing appeals to conscience and choice. The parties and their amici invoked conscience in competing ways. Bowers contended that ruling in favor of Hardwick would ignore "the traditions and collective conscience of our Nation."[29] Recognizing "homosexual sodomy" within the "right of intimate association" would lead to a slippery slope challenging other legal prohibitions, from polygamy to incest, bestiality, and necrophilia.[30]

Amici for Hardwick stressed individual conscience and moral choice. The Lesbian Rights Project warned that upholding Georgia's law would elevate "governmental power over the conscience and moral judgment of the individual" concerning "what types of non-harmful sex are appropriate."[31] The Presbyterian Church brief contended that criminal laws "usurp" a "matter fundamentally committed to personal moral choice."[32] Another amicus argued that the intimate associations formed by same-sex couples resembled those of straight couples and reflected the "precious values" the right of privacy protects. As Kennedy would later do, it drew on the Court's language about the centrality of choice concerning "certain intimate human relationships" to defining one's identity.[33]

It's not morality, it's animus and bigotry. Hardwick and his amici argued both that moral disapproval was not a sufficient basis for Georgia's law and that the law embodied animus or "the bare desire to harm an unpopular group." They took this language from *United States Department of Agriculture v. Moreno*, in which the Court found that restrictive rules about which households could receive food stamps stemmed from hostility to "hippies."[34] The purpose of Georgia's law, amici argued, was "public intolerance" and "pure prejudicial discrimination."[35] Amici also drew on *Palmore v. Sidoti*, in which the Court reversed a custody ruling based on racial prejudice, stating that "private biases may be outside the reach of the law, but the law cannot, directly or indirectly, give them effect."[36]

While these amici used synonyms for bigotry, others explicitly connected Georgia's law to bigotry. The Lesbian Rights Project argued: "Homophobia is a burdensome form of bigotry that has been in search of justification for centuries." It defined homophobia as "an irrational fear and hatred of homosexuals and of their sexuality"; for example, "the conviction that homosexual men and women—by reason of sin, sociopathology, or sickness—are not entitled to the full benefits of citizenship."[37] "Anti-gay violence and anti-gay bigotry," together with "pervasive civil discrimination," pose "real and ongoing problems." Lending the Court's "imprimatur" to treating "all sexually active gay, lesbian, and bisexual persons as criminals" would give "permission to discriminate, to malign, [and] to stigmatize."[38] The brief urged the Court to learn from times when it had upheld legal discrimination based on race, sex, and nationality, only to face the "agonizing and delicate" task of undoing such discrimination later: "Blessedly, in this case, this Court has ample information by which to be guided away from the course of ratification of ignorant bigotry" taken in such cases.[39]

The failure to see: the dissents. The maxim that today's dissents become tomorrow's majority opinions would prove true for *Bowers*. The four dissenting justices charged the majority with a *failure to see*. In language quoted by Justice Kennedy's majority opinion seventeen years later in *Lawrence*, Justice Stevens argued that Justice White's majority opinion missed the "clear" implications of the Court's precedents: "The fact that the governing majority in a State has traditionally viewed a particular practice as immoral is not a sufficient reason for upholding a law prohibiting the practice." For example, *Loving* illustrated that "neither history nor tradition could save a law prohibiting miscegenation from constitutional attack." Stevens also argued that the "liberty" married persons enjoy concerning their intimate relationship extends to intimate choices by "unmarried persons," including, by implication, unmarried gays and lesbians. "The essential 'liberty' " animating such prior cases "surely embraces the right to engage in nonreproductive, sexual conduct that others may consider offensive or immoral."[40]

Justice Blackmun's dissent contended: "Only the most willful blindness" could "obscure" the connection between prior privacy cases and what was at stake for Hardwick.[41] He found the parallel between *Bowers* and *Loving* "uncanny." In both, "the State relied on a religious justification" for its criminal law and appealed to "history" and "tradition."[42] "Far from buttressing his case," the attorney general's citation to scripture undermines his argument that Georgia's law is a "legitimate use of secular coercive power." For "[a] State can no more punish private behavior because of religious intolerance than it can punish such behavior because of racial animus." Moreover, Blackmun drew on *Palmore* to argue that "mere public intolerance or animosity" would not justify Georgia's law.[43]

Lawrence v. Texas: Preserving Traditional Morality or Demeaning the Lives of Gays and Lesbians?

It took the Court seventeen years to overturn *Bowers*. In 2003, Justice Kennedy, writing for the majority in *Lawrence*, struck down Texas's sodomy statute, which criminalized *only* same-sex sodomy: "*Bowers* was not correct when it was decided, and it is not correct today. . . . [It] should be and now is overruled."[44] The Court should have been able to see then that the "liberty" at stake in intimate sexual conduct by persons of the same sex has an important family resemblance to the liberty at stake in cases about opposite-sex intimate association and marriage. Furthermore, the criminal law imposes "stigma" and is an invitation to "subject homosexual persons to discrimination in public and private life."[45] I trace the "morality versus animus" arguments in the briefs and then look more closely at the majority, concurring, and dissenting opinions.

The Lawrence *briefs: morality versus animus (or bigotry)*. Texas argued that its law was rooted in morality, not animus.[46] Its amici asserted that the state was not "benighted or bigoted" for the belief that same-sex sexual conduct was immoral.[47] By the time of *Lawrence*, only thirteen states still had criminal laws against sodomy and only four enforced them exclusively against "homosexual conduct."[48] As amici, some of those states repeated arguments that succeeded in *Bowers:* states have the authority to "express and preserve moral standards of their communities."[49] Even if decriminalization in other states indicates an emerging national consensus, other amici argued that each state should be free to chart its own course instead of the Court forcing other states' choices on them.[50]

Drawing on *Romer* (to be analyzed fully in the following sections), petitioners and their amici argued that Texas's law rested on animus. "Rank prejudice," amici asserted, "can never be a legitimate governmental interest."[51] That Texas keeps the law on the books, but rarely prosecutes, shows that its real function is "to target" gays and lesbians "as a class," legitimizing "discrimination, hatred, and even violence" against them.[52]

Some amici pointed to positive social change since *Bowers:* "Our Nation has come to acknowledge and respect that American family life includes gay and lesbian relationships."[53] Indeed, while some amici supporting Texas's criminal law argued that it preserved traditional marriage and its many health benefits, amici for Lawrence countered that marriage would benefit same-sex couples as well.[54]

As in *Bowers*, a group of religious bodies filed a brief to challenge any asserted universal religious condemnation of "homosexuality" or support for criminal sodomy laws. The Alliance of Baptists and numerous other religious groups observed that while they disagreed about the morality of private "sexual intimacy between same-sex partners," they strongly condemned such use of criminal law. They also stated that many religious bodies support the civil rights of gays and lesbians.[55]

The Court: why moral disapproval is not enough. In his majority opinion, Justice Kennedy states: "History and tradition are the starting point but not in all cases the ending point of the substantive due process inquiry."[56] This observation is critical to explaining why moral disapproval is not enough to justify criminal laws like Georgia's and Texas's sodomy statutes. Even though the *Bowers* majority's historical premises about sodomy laws were flawed, Kennedy acknowledges that it was "making the broader point that for centuries there have been powerful voices to condemn homosexual conduct as immoral." Kennedy does not question the sincerity of such religious beliefs, disparage the motives of those who hold them, or call them "animus." To the contrary, he states: "For many people these are not trivial concerns but profound and deep convictions accepted as ethical and moral principles to which they aspire and which . . . determine the course of their lives." But "the issue is whether the majority may use the power of the State to enforce these views on the whole society through operation of the criminal law. 'Our obligation is to define the liberty of all, not to mandate our own moral code.' "[57] On the scope of that liberty, Kennedy quotes from *Planned*

Parenthood v. Casey, one of two Supreme Court opinions casting *Bowers'* holding "into even more doubt." The other opinion, he stated, was *Romer*, which features prominently in Justice O'Connor's concurring opinion.

Casey articulated the Constitution's commitment to respect for "autonomy" in making "personal decisions" that "involve the most intimate and personal choices a person may make in a lifetime." *Bowers* had denied any connection between such choices and same-sex sexual conduct; Kennedy counters that "persons in a homosexual relationship may seek autonomy for these purposes, just as heterosexual persons do." He added that "the State cannot demean their existence or control their destiny by making their private sexual conduct a crime." Kennedy gestures toward the then-percolating controversy over same-sex marriage: the case "does not involve whether the government must give formal recognition to any relationship that homosexual persons seek to enter."[58]

Since Texas's law criminalized "sexual intimacy by same-sex couples, but not identical behavior by different-sex couples," an Equal Protection ruling might have seemed appropriate. Kennedy did not go that route. Justice O'Connor's concurring opinion did, centrally relying on *Romer* to signal the limits of moral disapproval as the basis for law. Texas argued that the law "furthers the legitimate governmental interest of the promotion of morality," an interest the Court found sufficient in *Bowers*. But O'Connor argues that Texas may not assert promoting morality as a reason to criminalize same-sex, and not opposite-sex, sodomy:

> Moral disapproval of this group, like the bare desire to harm the group . . . is insufficient to satisfy rational basis review under the Equal Protection Clause. . . . We have never held that moral disapproval, without any other asserted state interest, is a sufficient rationale under the Equal Protection Clause to justify a law that discriminates among groups of persons.

To such laws, O'Connor explains, the Court applies "a more searching form of rational basis review."[59] O'Connor's concurrence answers Kennedy's question about whether a majority may use "the power of the State" to enforce its moral disapproval of homosexuals and "homosexual conduct" with an emphatic "no." Yet marriage, she argues, is different: "other reasons exist to promote" or preserve "the institution of marriage" beyond "mere disapproval of an excluded group."[60]

In a fiery dissent, Justice Scalia vehemently criticized the Court's overruling of *Bowers*: "Countless judicial decisions and legislative enactments have relied on the ancient proposition that a governing majority's belief that certain sexual behavior is 'immoral and unacceptable' constitutes a rational basis for regulation." Overruling *Bowers*, Scalia predicted, will bring a "massive disruption of the current social order" and decree "the end of all morals legislation." "Many

Americans," he observes, view what the Court portrays as "discrimination" against "homosexual persons" as "protecting themselves and their families from a lifestyle that they believe to be immoral and destructive."[61]

Scalia also predicted that the Court's "cooing" over same-sex intimate conduct foreshadows the end of any distinction between "heterosexual and homosexual unions." He argued that O'Connor's Equal Protection analysis left state laws restricting marriage to opposite-sex couples on "shaky grounds": "preserving the traditional institution of marriage" (quoting O'Connor) is—he contends—"just a kinder way of describing the State's moral disapproval of same-sex couples."[62] This issue would return to the Court a decade later, as same-sex couples challenged "defense of marriage laws" premised on such disapproval.

Voter Initiatives v. Anti-discrimination Laws: *Romer v. Evans*

By 1992, fifteen years after Raspberry framed the "bigotry versus prudence" question about Bryant's campaign against a gay rights ordinance, controversy brewed in Colorado. After several Colorado cities adopted ordinances protecting against discrimination on the basis of sexual orientation, the conservative Christian group Colorado for Family Values (CFV) launched a referendum campaign to amend Colorado's constitution to repeal such ordinances and prevent any other civil rights protections for gays and lesbians. Voters approved the initiative (Amendment 2), but a legal challenge brought by several Coloradans ended up before the US Supreme Court.[63] This section considers how the parties, their amici, and the Court addressed the "morality versus animus" question.

Amendment 2

Amendment 2 provided:

> **No Protected Status Based on Homosexual, Lesbian, or Bisexual Orientation.** Neither the State of Colorado, through any of its branches or departments, nor any of its agencies, political subdivisions, municipalities or school districts, shall enact, adopt or enforce any statute, regulation, ordinance or policy whereby homosexual, lesbian or bisexual orientation, conduct, practices or relationships shall constitute or otherwise be the basis of or entitle any person or class of persons to have or claim any minority status quota preferences, protected status or claim of discrimination.[64]

In the ballot information provided to voters, one argument for Amendment 2 was that extending anti-discrimination protection based on "homosexual, lesbian, or bisexual orientation" may "compel some individuals to violate their private consciences or to face legal sanctions for failure to comply" because "homosexuality, or bisexuality conflicts with their religious values and teachings or their private moral values." Arguments against it stressed that "all individuals should be accorded the same basic dignity, right to privacy, privileges, and protections guaranteed to every citizen." Another argument, which proved important in the legal challenge, was that Amendment 2 violates the Equal Protection Clause, which "prohibits any state from adopting a law which singles out a group for unfavorable or discriminatory treatment without a sufficient basis, or due to prejudice or irrational fears."[65]

The Constitutional Challenge

After the legal challenge to Amendment 2 succeeded in state court, Colorado asked the US Supreme Court to reverse.[66] Petitioner Buddy Romer, Governor of Colorado, and amici argued that Amendment 2 expressed legitimate moral disapproval of homosexuality, not animus or bigotry, and protected family, marriage, and religious liberty. Challengers (respondents) and their amici argued that Amendment 2 was rooted in animus and irrational fears and prejudice; further, moral disapproval alone could not justify such a law. Religious organizations weighed in on both sides.

Arguments in Support of Amendment 2

Morality, not animus. Petitioners and their amici drew on *Bowers* to argue that Colorado voters had the authority to promote their moral values through the political process. CFV contended that "states have the power to pass a wide variety of laws to protect the family and community morality."[67] Concerned Women for America (CWA) argued that Amendment 2 protects public morality by prohibiting "special homosexual rights laws." Such a state interest was "compelling," given that (quoting *Bowers*) "the law . . . is constantly based on notions of morality." Amendment 2, CWA argued, could survive an Equal Protection challenge because "much of our most valued legislation" reflects "moral choices" by majorities that are "contrary to the desires of minorities."[68] Other amici warned the Court not to "usurp the legislature as the vehicle for expressing the people's moral consensus" against homosexuality.[69]

The Oregon Citizens Alliance (OCA) argued that ballot initiatives like Amendment 2 prevented "the trampling of the constitutional rights of conservative Christians at the hands of gay activists." OCA named two rights at risk: (1) "parents' rights to control the education of their children" and (2) the right to "free expression of religious speech." Without such initiatives, schools might indoctrinate children into "the viewpoint of gay activists, specifically that homosexual conduct is to be accepted as a normal and acceptable lifestyle choice."[70]

The "morality, not animus" argument distinguished homosexuality from categories traditionally protected by anti-discrimination law, such as race and sex. One amicus contended: "Discriminating against a black person is irrational and therefore most likely based on animus . . . because the fact that a person is black tells us nothing about his character. But given the moral controversy surrounding homosexuality, when a person 'makes a distinction based upon a person's sexuality, he is making a judgment about the content of the individual's character.' "[71] Such arguments, in effect, grant that in 1996, race discrimination is "irrational" and bigoted, but insist that discrimination based on a disfavored form of sexuality *is* rational.

Protecting religious liberty. Some amici emphasized the legitimate state interest of protecting Coloradans' religious liberty when it conflicted with civil rights laws protecting lesbian, gay, and bisexual (LGB) people.[72] The CWA brief, for example, argued that landlords and employers, exercising their economic and religious liberty, should be able to discriminate against homosexuals.[73] The Christian Legal Society (CLS) and several conservative religious denominations asserted: "Amendment 2 resolves these conflicts, simply and unequivocally, in favor of religious liberty."[74] The brief argued that *no* set of exemptions would be adequate to avoid these conflicts. The CLS asserted that "the social agenda of gays, lesbians, and bisexuals is moral legitimacy for their sexual practices," but "religions, at least orthodox and traditional religions, generally deny them moral legitimacy." This "places religion foursquare in their path." Amendment 2 protects the "free exercise" of religion while the "often intransigent" debate about homosexuality continues.[75]

Arguments Against Amendment 2

Animosity and irrational prejudice. Amici challenging Amendment 2 argued that animus, prejudice, and stereotypes drove the campaign for it. For example, the American Psychological Association and other health organizations (APA brief) related Amendment 2 to the "history and prevalence of prejudice and discrimination against gay people" based on "ignorance and stereotypes." The professional organizations joining the APA brief had, since the early 1970s, shifted in their understanding of homosexuality: from pathological to normal and healthy.

They now urged mental health professionals "to help dispel the stigma of mental illness that had long been associated with homosexual orientation."[76]

The campaign for Amendment 2, amici argued, demonstrated why it was unconstitutional under precedents such as *Cleburne v. Cleburne Living Center*. In *Cleburne*, the Court (relying on *Moreno* and *Palmore*) concluded that requiring a special use permit for "homes for the mentally retarded" rested on "irrational prejudice."[77] The National Bar Association (NBA) argued that Amendment 2's "actual purpose—to target for harm a politically unpopular group—is based on irrational fear and hatred of that group." It contended that the irrational fears and hatred "exacerbated" by CFV were even more alarming than those the Court found "constitutionally impermissible" in *Moreno* and *Cleburne*. CFV distributed pamphlets containing false claims that a large majority of homosexuals admitted to having sex with minors, that "gays 'are 12 times as likely' as heterosexuals to molest children," and are "sex-crazed, disease-ridden perverts out to destroy the traditional family." The NBA described a "climate of intolerance" toward homosexual citizens in Colorado, before and after passage of Amendment 2.[78]

In addition, amici argued that Amendment 2 unconstitutionally singled out a class for moral disapproval based on an immutable aspect of their identity.[79] Religious and civil rights amici also rejected the argument that discrimination based on sexual orientation was unlike other forms of discrimination prohibited by civil rights law because of the issue of character.[80]

These briefs do not explicitly refer to bigotry; one reason may be that such explicit rhetoric is absent from the majority opinions in *Palmore, Cleburne*, and *Moreno*. Notably, some of the briefs filed in *Palmore* on behalf of the white mother stripped of custody because of the supposed effects of her interracial marriage on her daughter, freely used such rhetoric: for example, "while the Constitution cannot prevent bigotry, it can prevent an individual from involving the State, through its Courts, in such bigotry."[81] The Court echoed this premise, but referred to "private bias" and "prejudice" rather than to bigotry.[82]

Religious liberty and freedom of association. Tackling the religious liberty argument for Amendment 2, the American Friends Service Committee (AFSC) and other religious groups argued that discrimination against homosexuals was not a universal religious belief; indeed, such discrimination was "contrary to" their own religious beliefs. Thus, Amendment 2 "creates a special right for . . . anyone . . . to discriminate against another targeted group of citizens they do not like." Amendment 2, the brief argued, violated the Establishment Clause of the First Amendment because it "constitutes State endorsement of one set of religious beliefs over all others."[83] A better way to protect "the religious freedom of Amendment 2's sponsors" without restricting the rights of others was through religious exemptions to anti-discrimination laws.[84]

Amici countered the freedom of association arguments by asserting that Amendment 2 "privileges solely those religious views and associational decisions that reflect private bias against lesbians, gay men, and bisexuals," a form of "invidious private discrimination."[85] The American Bar Association (ABA) invoked *Palmore* to argue that protecting "prevailing preferences" of Coloradans to avoid associations with gays, lesbians, and bisexuals is not a permissible governmental objective: while "private biases may be outside the reach of the law . . . the law cannot, directly or indirectly, give them effect."[86] Analogizing to the problematic zoning rule in *Cleburne*, it also argued that the unconstitutional "fencing out" of a group from the protection of anti-discrimination laws based on prevailing preferences may stem not only from "an unthinking groundswell of antipathy," but also from "predominant religious beliefs or moral sentiment."[87] Challenging "special rights" rhetoric, Atlanta and nine other cities argued that Amendment 2 creates special rights for public officials and private individuals to discriminate "solely on the basis of prejudice."[88]

The US Supreme Court Rules

The Supreme Court ruled that Amendment 2 violated the Equal Protection Clause. In the majority opinion, Justice Kennedy explained: "Identif[ying] persons by a single trait and then den[ying] them protection across the board" is "not within our constitutional tradition." Far from simply denying gays and lesbians special rights, Amendment 2 "imposes a special disability upon those persons alone."[89]

Kennedy nowhere uses the rhetoric of bigotry, but he stated that Amendment 2 "seems inexplicable by anything but animus toward the class it affects." He also observed: "laws of the kind now before us raise the inevitable inference that the disadvantage imposed is born of animosity toward the class of persons affected." In support, he quoted *Moreno*: a "bare . . . desire to harm a politically unpopular group cannot constitute a *legitimate* governmental interest."[90] Here, he focuses on motives for Amendment 2—bad emotive states, like a desire to harm. His statements about animus would play an important role in some later gay rights cases.

Given Amendment 2's "breadth," Kennedy found it "impossible to credit" the justifications Colorado offered for it, such as protecting religious liberty and freedom of association and, "in particular, the liberties of landlords or employers who have personal or religious objections to homosexuality":

We cannot say that Amendment 2 is directed to any identifiable legitimate purpose or discrete objective. It is a status-based enactment

divorced from any factual context from which we could discern a relationship to legitimate state interests; it is a classification of persons
undertaken for its own sake, something the Equal Protection clause
does not permit.[91]

Amendment 2, he added, was "class legislation," "obnoxious" to the Fourteenth
Amendment. Kennedy looks at the presence of bad motives, using the very
sweep of the law to highlight the absence of legitimate objectives.

Justice Kennedy did not mention the rationale that Amendment 2 reflects
moral disapproval of homosexuality and protects marriage and the family.
That rationale was central to Justice Scalia's dissent: "The only sort of 'animus' at issue here [is] moral disapproval of homosexual conduct, the same
sort of moral disapproval that produced the centuries-old criminal laws that
we held constitutional in *Bowers*." Scalia accuses the majority of mistaking
a "culture war" (*Kulturkampf*) for "a fit of spite" and disparaging moral disapproval as bigotry. Amendment 2 was a "modest attempt by seemingly tolerant Coloradans to preserve traditional sexual mores against the efforts
of a politically powerful minority to revise those mores through use of the
laws."[92]

Scalia's evident logic is that while (seemingly tolerant) Colorado had
decriminalized sodomy, Amendment 2 allowed it to continue to express "moral
and social disapprobation of homosexuality" and "prevent piecemeal deteriora-
tion of the sexual morality favored by a majority of Coloradans." Scalia painted a
picture of Coloradan voters reacting to "homosexuals' quest for social endorsement" happening not just in New York, Los Angeles, and San Francisco, but also
in the cities of Colorado.[93] The Court wrongly took sides against such voters,
Scalia charged, by "inventing a novel and extravagant constitutional doctrine to
take the victory away from traditional forces" and "verbally disparaging as bigotry adherence to traditional attitudes."[94] Thus, Scalia's dissent meets the Court's
identification of animus toward "homosexuals" with a charge of bigotry (intolerance) against people (Colorado voters) whom he views, instead, as seemingly
tolerant.

Reactions to *Romer*

The Court's decision in *Romer* signaled a new constitutional landscape on which
future battles over civil rights for gays and lesbians would be fought. One immediate effect of *Romer* was to end the use of such ballot initiatives to limit "gay
people's ability to obtain protection against discrimination."[95] Conservative
critics viewed *Romer* as usurping the political process and limiting the use of

law to preserve traditional morality. Echoing Scalia, Charles Colson warned
that *Romer* "effectively branded a bigot any citizen who considers homosexuality immoral." He also predicted that under *Romer*, the Court would "easily
find no compelling state interest in confining marriage to a man and a woman."[96]
Marriage would soon become a new focus for both conservatives and gay rights
activists.

The Federal Defense of Marriage Act:
United States v. Windsor

In 1996, Republicans in the House and Senate introduced the Defense of
Marriage Act (DOMA) after a constitutional challenge brought by same-sex
couples to Hawaii's marriage law seemed to put same-sex marriage on the ho-
rizon. This section discusses DOMA and its eventual fate in the Supreme Court.

Defending Marriage: Promoting Morality or Anti-Gay Animus?

DOMA had "two primary purposes": (1) "to defend the institution of traditional
heterosexual marriage" and (2) "to protect the right of the States" to have their
own public policy about "legal recognition of same-sex unions."[97] Section 2 provided that states would not have to recognize any out-of-state marriages between
two persons of the same sex. Section 3 defined marriage, for purposes of all federal laws, as "only a legal union between one man and one woman as husband and
wife."[98] This federal definition meant that none of the over one thousand federal
laws referring to "marriage" or "spouse" would apply to marriages between two
men or two women, even if such marriages were valid under state law.[99]

DOMA, the House Report explained, defended "the institution of traditional
heterosexual marriage" and expressed "both moral disapproval of homosexuality
and a moral conviction that heterosexuality better comports with traditional
(especially Judeo-Christian) morality."[100] Given the fate of Amendment 2's appeal to traditional morality in *Romer*, some legislators might have wondered if
DOMA was constitutional. The Department of Justice (DOJ) advised Congress
that it was.[101] The House Report agreed, criticizing *Romer* as "difficult to fathom"
in light of *Bowers*.[102] Just as seventeen years passed between *Bowers* and its
overruling in *Lawrence*, seventeen years after *Romer* and DOMA's passage, the
Court would hold Section 3 unconstitutional, once again tackling the "morality
versus animus" question.

Challenging DOMA: *U.S. v. Windsor*

In 1996, when Congress enacted DOMA, no state in the United States allowed same-sex couples to marry. That changed in 2004, several months after the Supreme Judicial Court of Massachusetts, in *Goodridge v. Department of Public Health*, ruled in favor of same-sex couples' challenge to Massachusetts's marriage law.[103] By the end of the decade, several more states allowed same-sex marriages, and still more would recognize such marriages from other states, even if they did not (yet) allow them. Section 3 of DOMA led to practical problems when marriages, valid under state law, were not valid under federal law. Same-sex couples, surviving spouses, and even states filed lawsuits challenging Section 3's constitutionality.[104]

The DOJ initially defended Section 3, but in 2011, changed direction. In light of cases like *Romer* and *Lawrence* (as well as *Cleburne* and *Palmore*), Attorney General Eric Holder reasoned that the "moral disapproval" that DOMA expressed toward "gays and lesbians and their intimate and family relationships" was "precisely the kind of stereotype-based thinking and animus the Equal Protection Clause is designed to guard against."[105]

In 2012, Edith Windsor, the widow of Thea Spyer, challenged Section 3 in federal district court in New York. Under the provision, she did not qualify for the unlimited marital deduction from federal estate tax and had to pay $363,053 when Spyer's estate passed to her. Windsor was an appealing plaintiff: eighty-three years old, vivacious, and feisty, she and Spyer had been in a "committed relationship" since shortly after meeting in 1963. As Spyer's health deteriorated, they married in Canada in 2007, a marriage recognized by New York, but not by the federal government. Windsor prevailed in federal district court, and the federal appellate court affirmed.[106] Since the DOJ agreed with Windsor, it fell to Congress's Bipartisan Legal Advisory Group (BLAG) to petition the Supreme Court to overturn that ruling.

Marriage and the Morality Versus Animus Debate

The parties and the over eighty amici reprised the morality versus animus debate, but this time on a legal landscape that included *Romer* and *Lawrence*.[107] Did DOMA reflect prudence—being cautious about redefining marriage—or bigotry toward same-sex couples? As the sampling of briefs that follows shows, the relevant stakeholders were divided over these questions, presaging arguments that would play out among the justices.

Arguments for DOMA

"It's not animus, bigotry, or moral disapproval, but…" Amici for BLAG recognized that *Romer* and *Lawrence* made reliance solely on moral disapproval risky, so

many quoted Justice O'Connor's *Lawrence* concurrence: "Other reasons exist to promote the institution of marriage beyond mere moral disapproval of an excluded group." For example, the brief filed by United States Senators for BLAG asserted: "It is simply not irrational or bigoted to oppose the redefinition of marriage in a manner 'unknown to history and tradition.' "[108] The brief attempted to defuse charges of "unconstitutional animus" by shifting from inquiries about the "legislative motive" for DOMA to the legitimate interests it served: "Support for traditional marriage cannot be equated to 'animus.' "[109]

BLAG and its amici downplayed the House Report's language about DOMA expressing moral disapproval of homosexuality by focusing on another "purpose" the report mentions: "encouraging responsible procreation and child-rearing."[110] Indiana and sixteen other states argued that "the traditional definition of marriage has always been about the need to encourage potentially procreative couples to stay together for the sake of the children their sexual union may produce, not about animus toward homosexuals."[111] Other amici contended that support for traditional marriage and the "natural family" was not rooted in animus, irrationality, or ignorance "toward gays and lesbians," but in "sincere belief and sound public policy considerations."[112]

Some amici deflected charges of animus by framing the issue as a robust public debate between competing models of marriage: because the Constitution does not require one model or the other, "the people," not the judiciary, should decide.[113] "Whether the Nation should redefine marriage is principally about the People's values, morals, and policy judgments," the National Association of Evangelicals (NAE) argued; Congress may act to protect a "valued moral norm."[114] Conservative legal scholar Robert George, along with Sherif Girgis and Ryan Anderson, framed the debate as between the (1) *"conjugal* view" of marriage as a *"comprehensive* union" of spouses "begun by commitment and sealed by sexual intercourse . . . by which new life is made," and (2) a *"revisionist* view," in which "marriage is essentially an emotional union, accompanied by any consensual activity," and seen "as valuable while the emotion lasts." Although the conjugal view "has long informed the law," the revisionist view "has informed certain marriage policy changes of the last several decades," undermining the institution of marriage. To redefine civil marriage to include same-sex unions would "obscure the true nature of marriage as a conjugal union" uniquely linked to procreation and childrearing, and undermine marriage's "stabilizing norms."[115] Prudence, in other words, counsels against change.

Some amici for BLAG, however, resisted the changed landscape brought about by *Romer* and *Lawrence*, invoking Scalia's dissents in those cases to assert that expressing moral disapproval *was* a sufficient basis for law. The Foundation for Moral Law argued that history, law, and "traditional morality" speak "with a clear voice that homosexuality is to be opposed and any formal government recognition of a homosexual relationship is to be rejected."[116] Other amici cited Chief Justice Burger's *Bowers* concurrence, arguing that "same-sex intimacy is contrary to centuries of religious teaching . . . [and that it] would 'cast aside millennia of moral teaching' to convert it to a fundamental right."[117]

Arguments against DOMA

"It's animus and moral disapproval, not . . ." Both *Romer* and *Lawrence* scaffolded the arguments by Windsor and her amici about why DOMA was unconstitutional. For example, GLAD and Lambda Legal Defense and Education Fund contended: " 'animus' toward gay people is not a legitimate basis for law." Importantly, the brief also shifted attention away from bad motives, arguing that the "category of prohibited rationales extends well beyond overt animosity, bigotry, or hatred" to include "a more subtle yet harmful 'insensitivity caused by simple want of careful, rational reflection or from some instinctive mechanism to guard against people who appear to be different in some respects from ourselves.' "[118] This quoted language about insensitivity, from a Kennedy opinion, provides a less judgmental way to speak about why people might support a law with harmful effects.

To show that DOMA rested on unconstitutional animus, prejudice, and a "bare desire to harm," many amici quoted the House Report's statement about the "collective moral judgment" against homosexuality and in favor of heterosexuality—and traditional marriage—that DOMA sought to "reflect and honor."[119] The report's "moral disapproval," the brief filed by 172 Members of the US House of Representatives and forty Senators argued, showed impermissible animus.[120] Amici cited *Lawrence* to argue that it was constitutionally insufficient to appeal to tradition or "the fact that the governing majority in a State has traditionally viewed a practice as immoral."[121]

Many amici enlisted O'Connor's *Lawrence* concurrence: "The Court had 'never held that moral disapproval, without any other asserted state interest, is a sufficient rationale under the Equal Protection Clause to justify a law that discriminates among groups of persons.' "[122] O'Connor's words, amici argued, applied equally to *religiously motivated* disapproval, even though "religion plays an important role in the lives of many Americans, and many lawmakers are undoubtedly guided in their legislative decision-making by personal religious and moral beliefs."[123] Such religious motivations, however sincere, are still insufficient to support DOMA: excluding gay people from the state-sponsored institution of marriage may not rest on a "moral argument that homosexuals are sinful."[124]

The history of excluding same-sex couples from marriage, the brief filed by Representatives and Senators argued, "cannot itself justify their *continued* exclusion" from "federal responsibilities and rights that hinge on marriage." After *Lawrence*, "DOMA must rationally serve legitimate federal interests independent of consistency with tradition or historical practice. It doesn't."[125] While the interests in promoting "responsible procreation" and optimal parenting were legitimate, excluding same-sex couples from marriage did not further them. The ABA argued that "as a purely logical matter, excluding gay and lesbian couples from federal benefits cannot create an incentive for heterosexual couples to marry or raise children responsibly."[126] So too, another amicus argued, denying same-sex marriage did not further the governmental interest in protecting children.[127] The American Psychological Association brief rebutted BLAG's assertions that heterosexual marriage was the optimal setting for childrearing with numerous social science studies demonstrating the fitness and capability of gay and lesbian parents and same-sex households.[128]

Amici for Windsor made good use of Scalia's *Lawrence* dissent to challenge BLAG's responsible procreation argument: "the encouragement of procreation," Scalia had argued, could "surely" not be a "justification" for "denying the benefits of marriage to homosexual couples," since "the sterile and the elderly are allowed to marry."[129] Instead, Windsor's amici argued, "DOMA 'seems inexplicable by anything other than animus towards the class it affects.' "[130] DOMA also has harmful effects: it "conveys the federal government's judgment that committed intimate relationships between people of the same sex . . . are inferior to hetero-sexual relationships" and "legitimiz[es] prejudicial attitudes and individual acts against the disfavored group, including ostracism, harassment, discrimination, and violence."[131]

Same-Sex Marriage and Religious Liberty: A Clash of Rights?

Neither "conscience" nor "religious liberty" appears in the House Report about DOMA's purposes, but "conscience, not animus" was a theme in briefs filed by religious amici in support of BLAG. "Changing the definition of [civil] marriage," they argued, would trigger "religious liberty concerns" and create "a conflict of conscience," whereas allowing same-sex couples to enter an alternative legal status like a "civil union" or "domestic partnership" would not. That is because major religious groups "center their teachings regarding sexual morality around opposite-sex marriage."[132] Thus, "[a] person's religiously-motivated refusal to recognize [or facilitate] same-sex unions is not tantamount to unlawful discrim-ination, nor is it irrational animosity."[133] Some amici framed the risk as being a new governmental orthodoxy that would restrict "the ability of the Christian faithful to put their beliefs into practice."[134] Religious amici also rejected any analogy between racism and "traditional religious beliefs regarding sexual orien-tation and sexual conduct."[135]

While these amici posited a close connection between civil and reli-gious marriage, religious amici in support of Windsor stressed their distinc-tion: redefining *civil* marriage leaves all religions free "to define *religious* marriage in any way they choose." To credit arguments that DOMA should be upheld because "civil recognition for the marriages of same-sex couples would alter a longstanding 'Christian' definition of 'marriage,'" the Episcopal Bishops argued, would "enshrine a particular religious belief in the law—itself prohibited under the Establishment Clause—and implicitly privilege religious viewpoints that oppose marriage equality over those that favor it."[136] Some amici argued that religious liberty issues could be worked out with appropriate distinctions between the state *recognizing* "someone else's civil marriage" and the state demanding "that religious organizations or believers recognize or facilitate a marriage in ways that violate their religious commitments."[137]

The Supreme Court Strikes Down DOMA

Justice Kennedy, writing for the 5–4 majority, ruled for Edith Windsor and struck down Section 3 of DOMA.[138] How did Kennedy and the dissenting justices address the morality versus animus dynamics in evaluating the purpose and effect of DOMA? What sort of scaffolding did *Romer* and *Lawrence* provide for the opinion?

DOMA and animus: Romer's role. Kennedy's opinion uses the *Romer* framework to assess DOMA's purpose and effect. He repeatedly stresses both Congress's impermissible motives for DOMA and DOMA's demeaning and stigmatizing effects. For example: "DOMA seeks to injure the very class New York seeks to protect"; its principal effect is "to identify a subset of state-sanctioned marriages and make them unequal." In so doing, DOMA "violates basic due process and equal protection principles," since "the Constitution's guarantee of equality 'must at the very least mean that a bare congressional desire to harm a politically unpopular group cannot' justify disparate treatment of that group." Kennedy combines this directive from *Moreno* with *Romer's* instruction that "in determining whether a law is motivated by an improper animus or purpose, 'discriminations of an unusual character' especially require careful consideration."[139]

Under this framework, DOMA's "unusual deviation from the usual tradition of recognizing and accepting state definitions of marriage" is "strong evidence of a law having the purpose and effect of disapproval of that class." Section 3's "avowed purpose and practical effect" are "to impose a disadvantage, a separate status, and so a stigma" on same-sex couples lawfully married under the "unquestioned authority of the States." Kennedy asserts that "interference with the equal dignity of same-sex marriages . . . conferred by the States in the exercise of their sovereign power" was DOMA's "essence." Similar to his conclusion about Amendment 2, Kennedy writes: "No legitimate purpose overcomes [Section

3's] purpose and effect to disparage and to injure those whom the State, by its marriage laws, sought to protect in personhood and dignity."[140] As in *Romer,* Kennedy nowhere refers to bigotry in explicating DOMA's flaws.

DOMA's denial of dignity: Lawrence *and moral disapproval.* Justice Kennedy appeals to "dignity" to explain the injury that DOMA inflicts on lawfully married same-sex couples. He contrasts New York's attempt to confer dignity and respect on a class—by changing its marriage laws to allow same-sex couples to marry—with DOMA's denial of such dignity and respect. He finds powerful evidence of this "interference" with "equal dignity" in the House Report's reference to moral disapproval of homosexuality and its assertion that "moral approval of heterosexuality better comports with traditional (especially Judeo-Christian) morality." DOMA tells couples that "their otherwise valid marriages are unworthy of federal recognition." In an often-quoted passage, Kennedy added that DOMA also "humiliates tens of thousands of children now being raised by same-sex couples."[141] Here, Kennedy stresses DOMA's harmful social meaning.

The dissents: not animus or bigotry, but prudence. The dissenters agreed on two points: (1) the Court should have let the people resolve the debate over marriage; and (2) in striking down Section 3, the majority failed to credence legitimate rationales for DOMA that could survive ordinary rational basis review, thus tarring Congress and persons who adhered to the traditional definition of marriage as bigots or as motivated by animus.

In dissent, Chief Justice Roberts nowhere mentions *Romer, Lawrence,* or the constitutional status of moral disapproval as a rationale for DOMA. He simply indicates that he rejects the majority's conclusion that DOMA's "principal purpose" was "a bare desire to harm." The "snippets of legislative history" cited by the majority do not make such a showing and, "without some more convincing evidence that the Act's principal purpose was to codify malice, and that it furthered *no* legitimate government interests, [he] would not tar the political branches with the brush of bigotry."[142] Bigotry here seems to connote illegitimate emotion—like an unreasoning hostility—or hate.

Justice Alito, joined by Justice Thomas, framed Windsor's challenge to DOMA as asking the Court to "intervene" in a debate between two views of marriage, which he called the "traditional" or "conjugal" view and the "consent-based" view. The Constitution, Alito stated, "does not codify either of these views." Rather than endorse the consent-based view, the Court should leave the matter to the people. One source Alito cites for the conjugal view is work by George, Girgis, and Anderson. Without citation, he characterizes the consent-based view as conceiving marriage as "the solemnization of mutual commitment—marked by strong emotional attachment and sexual attraction—between two persons," where "gender differentiation is not relevant."[143]

Alito nowhere mentions the moral disapproval language in the House Report. Instead, he shares BLAG's and various amici's concern for prudence or caution: because "the family is an ancient and universal human institution," and changes in its structure "can have profound effects," one can expect that there will be long-term consequences "if same-sex marriage becomes widely accepted." Thus, judges "have cause for both caution and humility."[144]

Finally, Alito refers to bigotry in rejecting Windsor's request that the Court apply "heightened scrutiny" because DOMA discriminates on the basis of sexual orientation. Windsor would "ask us to rule that the presence of two members of the opposite sex is as rationally related to marriage as white skin is to voting or a Y-chromosome is to the ability to administer an estate." To accept such an argument, Alito asserts, "would cast all those who cling to traditional beliefs about the nature of marriage in the nature of bigots or superstitious fools."[145] On Alito's reasoning, drawing analogies to now-repudiated forms of race and sex discrimination casts persons with traditional beliefs as bigots.

Justice Scalia counters the majority's conclusion of animus by appealing both to morality and to prudence. He tackles the DOMA report's language about expressing moral disapproval by quoting his *Lawrence* dissent: "The Constitution does not forbid the government to enforce traditional moral and sexual norms." Not only should legislative motive—or what is in "legislators' hearts"—be irrelevant, but the majority "affirmatively conceal[s] from the reader the arguments that exist in justification for DOMA," contributing to "the illusion of the Act's supporters as unhinged members of a wild-eyed lynch mob." He also asserts that because Section 3 of DOMA "ensure[d] that state-level experimentation did not automatically alter the basic operation of federal law," this reflected "not animus—just stabilizing prudence."[146]

While Kennedy's opinion never drew an explicit analogy to racial prejudice, Scalia's inflammatory allusion to racially motivated violence (the lynch mob) is reinforced by his analogy between the majority's treatment of the Congress that passed DOMA and the Court's earlier condemnation of "some once-Confederate Southern state." Scalia also argued that the marriage debate inspires "passion by good people on all sides," but the majority has "formally declar[ed] anyone opposed to same-sex marriage an enemy of human decency."[147]

Perhaps the most scathing part of Scalia's dissent relates to *Lawrence* and *Windsor*'s disclaimers about marriage. Although the *Lawrence* majority said its opinion did not address formal recognition of same-sex relationships, Scalia famously warned: "Do not believe it."[148] The *Windsor* majority, Scalia observes, now appeals to *Lawrence* to say that "DOMA is invalid because it 'demeans the couples, whose moral and sexual choices the Constitution protects.'" The majority's conclusion that DOMA "is motivated by 'bare . . . desire to harm'" can easily be applied to "state laws denying same-sex marital status."[149] Scalia does not explicitly employ the rhetoric of bigotry, but his language suggests that he reads the majority as saying—as Alito and Roberts do more explicitly—that only bigotry could underlie denying same-sex couples access to marriage.

Does animus equal bigotry? Is *Windsor's* conclusion about animus a charge of bigotry? Some critics answer yes: the majority's opinion practiced a "jurisprudence of denigration" becoming more common in public discourse—charging those on the other side of a constitutional debate with animus, hatred, or bigotry.[150] To call the *Windsor* opinion a jurisprudence of denigration seems to imply that to identify a legislative act as demeaning and disparaging to a targeted class is itself to demean and disparage legislators and the views they represent—to be intolerant or bigoted toward them. Religious critics argued that the analysis of DOMA's purpose and effect threatened to treat "states— and religious communities—that reject the redefinition of marriage" as "backward and bigoted, unworthy of respect."[151] Even some supporters of *Windsor's* outcome regretted its rhetoric, which seemed demeaning to people who had "non-bigoted reasons" for adhering to the one man–one woman definition of marriage.[152]

As Dale Carpenter concludes, however, "these criticisms are overwrought": the issue in *Windsor* was not whether a particular person's or religion's belief about marriage was bigoted, but whether *Congress's* decision, in 1996, to "select one class of potential future marriages for second class status" reflected animus toward the people in that class. In concluding that it did, Carpenter stresses the context in which DOMA was adopted. While Kennedy's opinion focused primarily on the House Report, the legislative record, including the debates, offers ample examples of hostility toward gays and lesbians, stereotypes, and "apocalyptic" prediction about the effects of same-sex marriage.[153] Similar to arguments against the Civil Rights Act of 1964 (discussed in chapter 5), some proponents of DOMA appealed to God's principles and warned that no society that "embraced homosexuality" had ever survived.[154] In *Windsor*, BLAG and its amici appealed to prudence and caution—not in and of themselves reasons rooted in animus—but this appeal "sanitized" the legislative record.[155] Kennedy's conclusion about animus was justified and did not brand all who objected to same-sex marriage as bigots.

As chapter 6 explained, the rapid succession of federal courts striking down state DOMAs in the wake of *Windsor* frequently drew on both Kennedy's majority opinion and the template Scalia's dissent provided for how to do so. The stage was set for the Court to address whether states may exclude same-sex couples from marriage.[156]

The Fundamental Right to Marry:
Obergefell v. Hodges

Nearly thirty years after the *Bowers* majority found no resemblance between precedents about marriage and family and "homosexual activity," Justice Kennedy, in *Obergefell*, wrote that the principles and traditions that show why marriage is fundamental for opposite-sex couples apply equally to same-sex couples.[157] Given *Windsor*'s critical treatment of Congress's appeal to morality as evidencing the animosity that underlay DOMA, one might have expected a similar analysis of the state defense of marriage laws that the Court evaluated in *Obergefell*. Kennedy, however, took a different approach. Perhaps one reason was to avoid *Windsor*-type dissents charging him with branding lawmakers and voters as bigots.

In *Obergefell*, Kennedy's discussion of why states enacted defense of marriage laws eschews any reference to animus, prejudice, or a "bare desire to harm." *Romer* appears only once in the opinion, as a critical turning point in the Court's evolving approach to the "legal status of homosexuals." *Lawrence*, by contrast, appears numerous times. It is also striking that Kennedy explicitly refers to morality only once, when he observes that "until the mid-twentieth century, same-sex intimacy long had been condemned as immoral by the state itself in most Western nations, a belief often embodied in the criminal law."[158] The Court grounds its holding primarily in due process liberty, and the fundamental right to marry, rather than in equal protection (as in *Romer* and *Windsor*), even as it stresses the intertwining of liberty and equal protection.[159] As chapter 6 showed, *Loving* also plays a key role in the narrative of constitutional moral progress that stresses the role of new insights about marriage and constitutional guarantees.

In *Obergefell*, Kennedy avoids what critics of *Windsor* called a "jurisprudence of denigration."[160] Instead, he states that "many who deem same-sex marriage to be wrong reach that conclusion based on decent and honorable religious or philosophical premises, and neither they nor their beliefs are disparaged here." His critical point concerns translating those beliefs into law. As Kennedy explains:

> When that sincere, personal opposition becomes enacted law and public policy, the necessary consequence is to put the imprimatur of the State itself on an exclusion that soon demeans or stigmatizes those whose own liberty is then denied. Under the Constitution, same-sex couples seek in marriage the same legal treatment as opposite-sex couples, and it would disparage their choices and diminish their personhood to deny them this right.[161]

This is a far cry from reasoning that state DOMAs are "inexplicable" by anything other than animus, a bare desire to harm, or private bias. Or, for that matter, bigotry. Kennedy focuses not on motives for such laws, but on their practical effects: the state's practice of denying gays and lesbians access to civil marriage denies them equal liberty. It is the social meaning of these exclusionary practices, not motives, that matters. Kennedy emphasizes the "urgency" of this issue for the same-sex couples and bereaved spouses before the Court: he sketches their lives—implicitly showing their moral worthiness—and insists that they do not seek to denigrate or demean the institution of marriage, but to join it.[162] By comparison, state laws excluding them have demeaning, stigmatizing, and humiliating *effects* on them.

Despite this absence of the rhetoric of animus or bigotry, three of the four dissents criticized Kennedy's opinion for disparaging those with traditional beliefs about marriage as bigots. Chief Justice Roberts charges that Kennedy's opinion portrays any who do not share the Court's evolved understanding that the fundamental right to marry extends to same-sex couples as bigoted.[163] He defended the one man–one woman "universal" definition of marriage as resting on society's need to manage heterosexuality and procreation. Justice Scalia's dissent characterizes the majority as contending that the age-old one man–one woman definition of marriage "cannot possibly be supported by anything other than ignorance or bigotry."[164] And, in a frequently quoted passage, Justice Alito warns that despite the majority's "reassurances" about protecting conscience, those who dissent publicly from the new "orthodoxy" may whisper their beliefs in their homes, but if they utter them in public will "risk being labeled" as bigots and "treated as such by governments, employers, and schools." Alito seems to locate this risk in Kennedy's use of analogy: to compare now-repudiated forms of race and sex discrimination in marriage (such as antimiscegenation laws and the laws of coverture) to the exclusion of same-sex couples from marriage is to invite people to "exploit" the analogy to "vilify" those who oppose same-sex marriage as bigots.[165]

But how would Kennedy's opinion, with all its language about sincere believers, be exploited in this way? Some scholars argue that Kennedy's opinion expresses an important idea associated with animus doctrine: governmental bodies may not disadvantage a group "for no public purpose."[166] Even when government acts on private views that are decent and honorable, and not merely private bias or a bare desire to harm, the *effect* of such action (as Kennedy said) is to subordinate and harm members of the group.[167] *Obergefell*, however, seems quite different from *Romer* and *Windsor* in tone, and it seems strained to relate its reasoning to animus. It seems more likely that Kennedy aimed for an opinion that would weave together a narrative of constitutional moral progress and evolving insights—culminating in recognizing the constitutional right of same-sex couples to marry—while also speaking respectfully to people with traditional beliefs about marriage who might disagree with the Court's holding. In all his years on the Court, Kennedy explicitly referred to bigotry (religious or racial) only a few times. Tellingly, in *Pena-Rodriguez v. Colorado* (2017), which allowed impeachment of a jury verdict because of evidence of racial bias, Kennedy's majority opinion makes clear the potency of a charge of bigotry: because of the powerful stigma linked to overt racial bias, a juror might be reluctant to report another juror's biased statements because to do so would "call her a bigot."[168]

In any case, the dissent's charges of bigotry would likely have been even fiercer if Kennedy had taken a different constitutional route in *Obergefell*, as several post-*Windsor* federal courts had done: conclude that classifications based on sexual orientation were "suspect," by analogy to race and sex, and warranted heightened judicial review. Such an opinion would make analogies to race and sex discrimination more direct. Notably, despite numerous references to *Loving*, Kennedy nowhere described belief in the one man–one woman definition of marriage as comparable to endorsing the "doctrine of White Supremacy." Or what about a ruling (as in some other federal opinions) that the one man–one woman definition of marriage was a relic of the now-repudiated system of gender hierarchy in marriage, inconsistent with contemporary views of marriage or of men's and women's roles? While Kennedy referred to the Court's role in dismantling that hierarchy, he nowhere said that belief in the one man–one woman definition was so implausible as to lack any basis other than animus. It is unlikely that a different type of majority opinion would have avoided the dissenters' charges of bigotry.

The *Obergefell* majority and dissenting opinions set the stage for the controversy that played out in *Masterpiece Cakeshop*. Colorado baker Jack Phillips and amici would enlist language from the *Obergefell* majority and the dissents, and defenders of Colorado's public accommodations law would also rely on Kennedy's language. In this new constitutional landscape, the concern about animus would shift from considering the purposes and effects of anti-gay legislation to asking whether a civil rights commission applying laws protective of LGBT people treated the baker's sincere religious beliefs with hostility or animosity.

This Isn't 1964 Anymore—Or Is It?

Competing Appeals to the Civil Rights Past in Present Controversies over Religious Liberty versus LGBT Rights

> This isn't 1964 anymore. We've moved beyond that. If you open up your doors to the general public, you can't pick and choose who you are going to deal with.
>
> —Frank Keating (former Republican governor of Oklahoma)
> (Quoted in Adam Nagourney, "Arizona Bill Allowing Refusal
> of Service to Gays Stirred Alarm in the G.O.P.," N.Y. Times,
> Feb. 28, 2014, at A11)

> It is unexceptional that Colorado law can protect gay persons, just as it can protect other classes of individuals, in acquiring whatever products and services they choose on the same terms and conditions as are offered to other members of the public.
>
> —Justice Kennedy, *Masterpiece Cakeshop,*
> *Ltd v. Colorado Civil Rights Commission* (2018)

On September 7, 2016, the US Commission on Civil Rights released a report, *Peaceful Coexistence: Reconciling Nondiscrimination Principles with Civil Liberties*, which sparked a firestorm of criticism.[1] The controversy concerned both the rhetoric of bigotry that the commissioners used, in cautioning against allowing broad religious exemptions from anti-discrimination laws, and what the commissioners said about how best to resolve the evident conflict between such laws and claims of religious liberty. That controversy sets the stage for evaluating how the Supreme Court addressed such a conflict in the closely watched case, *Masterpiece Cakeshop, Ltd. v. Colorado Civil Rights Commission.*[2]

In a majority opinion released shortly before Justice Kennedy announced his retirement from the Court, Kennedy focused on rhetoric, chastising the Colorado Civil Rights Commission (CCRC) for the way that some of the members talked about religion in general and the religious beliefs of Colorado baker Jack Phillips in particular. He did *not* say that the commissioners had

Who's the Bigot? Linda C. McClain, Oxford University Press (2020). © Oxford University Press.
DOI: 10.1093/oso/9780190877200.001.0001

characterized Phillips's beliefs as bigoted—as some of Phillips's supporters claimed—but he did conclude that their remarks showed animosity and hostility toward those beliefs, violating the constitutional requirement that public officials treat religious beliefs in a neutral and respectful way.[3]

An alternative title for this chapter might be "How *Not* to Talk about Religion," since both of these controversies show that rhetoric matters. Indeed, in *Masterpiece Cakeshop*, the parties and their amici enlisted the majority and dissenting opinions in *Obergefell v. Hodges* to caution the Court about what kind of message it would send by ruling for or against Phillips's constitutional claims. The majority did not rule on the merits of those claims; Kennedy admonished, though, that future cases must be resolved "with tolerance, without undue disrespect to sincere religious beliefs, and without subjecting gay persons to indignities when they seek goods and services in an open market."[4] This final requirement relates to a significant feature of *Masterpiece Cakeshop*: as the language quoted at the beginning of this chapter shows, Kennedy's opinion affirmed the legitimacy of state anti-discrimination laws (such as Colorado's) that protect "gay persons" against such "indignities." And in observing that sincere religious objections to "gay marriage" did not—"as a general rule"—allow business owners to deny service to customers, even though the views themselves were protected under the First Amendment, Kennedy cited to *Newman v. Piggie Park Enterprises* (mentioned in chapter 5). That case upheld Title II of the Civil Rights Act of 1964 (CRA) against a Free Exercise challenge by a white business owner who objected to serving African American customers.[5] In *Masterpiece Cakeshop*, the parties and their amici made numerous references to the CRA, either to reason by analogy between the civil rights past and the present or to deny the analogy.

The *Peaceful Coexistence* report and *Masterpiece Cakeshop* shed light on the puzzles about bigotry studied in earlier chapters. For example, what does it mean to assert that a civil rights commission statement or judicial opinion tars someone with the brush of bigotry? What role do appeals to past civil rights battles play in present-day controversies over the scope of civil rights laws and their asserted clash with conscience? Is a charge of bigotry inferred simply from someone's asserting that society should learn from past appeals to religion to justify now-repudiated forms of discrimination? Does a charge flow from someone's comparing past religious objections to racial integration and interracial marriage with present religious objections to marriage by same-sex couples?

I begin by discussing how the rhetoric of bigotry featured in the controversy over the *Peaceful Coexistence* report. Then, as a dress rehearsal for *Masterpiece Cakeshop*, I discuss *Elane Photography, LLC v. Willock* (2003), in which the Supreme Court of New Mexico ruled that a photographer who, because of her Christian beliefs, declined to photograph a commitment ceremony be-tween two women violated the state's public accommodations law.[6] Although *Elane Photography* predates *Obergefell*, it became a rallying cry for religious conservatives who predicted a coming collision between the right of same-sex couples to marry and the First Amendment rights of those with religious objections to such marriages. *Elane Photography* does not use the rhetoric of big-otry, but the concurring opinion by Justice Bosson speaks instructively about the demands of tolerance in public life and draws analogies between present-day claims of conscience and past assertions of religious beliefs in landmark civil rights cases such as *Loving v. Virginia*.[7] Indeed, I will argue that Bosson's opinion is a valuable model of how Justice Kennedy, in *Masterpiece Cakeshop*, argues fu-ture cases should be resolved.

The third case study is *Masterpiece Cakeshop*. Some briefs on each side ex-plicitly referred to bigotry; many briefs instead used terms such as animus, discrimination, hatred, intolerance, and prejudice. I evaluate the rhetoric of bigotry in these arguments and how the parties and their amici related bigotry to conscience and sincerity. I then study the rhetoric that the Supreme Court used, focusing on Kennedy's majority opinion and some of the concurring and dissenting opinions.

In these case studies, I highlight the way participants (including the courts) related the present battles over the reach of state public accommodations laws to that of the public accommodations provision of the CRA. In the statement quoted at the beginning of this chapter, Frank Keating (former Republican governor of Oklahoma) invoked the CRA—"This isn't 1964 anymore"—in arguing against a proposed Arizona law intended to protect merchants with religious objections from serving gay and lesbian customers.[8] Keating's remark suggests that the CRA is a benchmark that established a rule about serving the general public. *Elane Photography* and *Masterpiece Cakeshop* accepted that benchmark, but also emphasized that state public accommodations laws reach farther than the CRA and that that broader scope is legitimate. Indeed, as Colorado and its amici argued in *Masterpiece Cakeshop*, these more expan-sive state laws reflect evolving understandings of prejudice and discrimina-tion. Colorado itself is a notable protagonist in this story of evolution, given that in 1992, as chapter 7 discussed, Colorado voters passed Amendment 2, prohibiting protection of lesbian, gay, or bisexual (LGB) people from discrim-ination, while in 2008, the legislature added sexual orientation as a protected category under the Colorado Antidiscrimination Act (CADA). I conclude with some observations about the implications of *Masterpiece Cakeshop*, in light of what the Court did and did not decide, and some thoughts about the form a fruitful resolution of these "religious liberty versus LGBT rights" conflicts might take.

Bigots versus Civil Rights Bullies? Controversy over the *Peaceful Coexistence* Report

Peaceful Coexistence: Reconciling Nondiscrimination Principles with Civil Liberties grew out of an inquiry by the US Commission on Civil Rights that brought together legal scholars and civil rights advocates to advise them on a dilemma: If religious liberty and nondiscrimination principles were in conflict, what was the appropriate balance between them? Should a state provide an exemption from its anti-discrimination laws to a for-profit business owner if such laws conflict with that owner's efforts to practice religious faith? Must it do so, under the First Amendment's protection of the free exercise of religion or state and federal "religious freedom restoration acts"?

In the resulting briefing report, sent to President Obama, Vice President Biden, and House Speaker Paul Ryan, the Commission found that the scale weighed in favor of enforcing anti-discrimination laws: "Religious exemptions to the protections of civil rights based upon classifications such as race, color, national origin, sex, disability status, sexual orientation, and gender identity, when they are permissible, significantly infringe upon these civil rights."[9] In support of its findings, the Commission observed that "religious doctrines that were widely accepted at one time came to be deemed highly discriminatory, such as slavery, homosexuality bans, and unequal treatment of women," and that not allowing exemptions would prevent groups from using "the pretext of religious doctrines to discriminate."[10] The report recommended that any "religious exceptions to civil liberties and civil rights" should be narrowly tailored, since "overly-broad religious exemptions unduly burden nondiscrimination laws and policies."[11]

This rhetoric highlights the significance of time in assessing religious defenses of various forms of inequality: previously accepted, such defenses now appear highly discriminatory. That point seems undeniable, given this book's ample illustrations, such as the theology of segregation and religious defenses of antimiscegenation laws. But in referring to present-day religious doctrines as a pretext to discriminate, are the Commissioners questioning the sincerity of religious believers? Are they suggesting that even if sincerely held, such beliefs should not be accepted as a legitimate reason not to comply with the law?

The report drew swift criticism for branding "people of faith" as bigots.[12] Two dissenting commissioners expressed that view; one's rebuttal enlisted Justice Alito's prediction in dissent in *Obergefell* (discussed in chapter 7) of a not-so-distant future in which "those who cling to old beliefs" about same-sex marriage would be "labeled as bigots and treated as such by governments, employers, and schools" if they stated those beliefs in public.[13] But it was the individual statement of the Commission's Chair, Martin R. Castro, that sparked headlines such as "Obama Administration Says You're A Bigot if You Live Your Religion" and criticisms by some religious leaders that the Commission was "painting those who support religious freedom with the broad brush of bigotry."[14] Critics quoted the following passage, in which Castro does not use the term "bigotry," but does use familiar synonyms:

> The phrases "religious liberty" and "religious freedom" will stand for nothing except hypocrisy so long as they remain code words for discrimination, intolerance, racism, sexism, homophobia, Islamophobia, Christian supremacy or any form of intolerance.[15]

Critics also objected to Castro's contention that "today, as in the past, religion is being used as both a weapon and a shield by those seeking to deny others equality." He stated:

> In our nation's past religion has been used to justify slavery and later, Jim Crow laws. We now see "religious liberty" arguments sneaking their way back into our political and constitutional discourses . . . in an effort to undermine the rights of some Americans. This generation of Americans must stand up and speak out to ensure that religion never again be twisted to deny others the full promise of America.[16]

Castro's concern about religion being twisted to deny the rights of others echoes a rebuttal he and several other commissioners issued that *does* refer to bigotry and question religious sincerity. That rebuttal sounds the alarm about a "tsunami of legislative proposals" that use religious liberties as the justification for limiting the civil rights of LGBT people—permitting public and private actors to discriminate against them: "These laws and proposals represent an orchestrated, nationwide effort by extremists to promote bigotry, cloaked in the mantle of 'religious freedom.' "[17] In this passage, promoting bigotry takes the form of enacting intolerance against LGBT people into law. The cloaked and twisted language may imply that the commissioners question the motives and sincerity of those who asserted the beliefs; or it may mean that the commissioners think that such beliefs distort true religion because they deny equality.

Catholic archbishop Lori and sixteen other faith leaders wrote to President Obama, Senator Orrin Hatch, and Representative Ryan demanding that each "renounce publicly" the ideas that religious liberty and religious freedom are code words or a pretext for discrimination. They demanded that "no American citizen or institution be labeled by their government as bigoted because of their [religious] views and dismissed from [the nation's] political life" for them.[18] Furthermore, they argued, people of faith have championed civil rights and justice. Legal scholar Richard Epstein, a prominent critic of anti-discrimination laws, went further, arguing that the commissioners themselves were bigots and "civil rights bullies."[19] He contended that business owners who seek to do business according to their religious beliefs—and are willing generally to serve gay and lesbian customers, but decline to violate their beliefs by helping to celebrate a same-sex marriage—are not bigots. Invoking Wikipedia's definition of "bigot," he continued: they "bear no relationship to a 'prejudiced or closed-minded person, especially one who is intolerant or hostile towards different social groups.'" By comparison:

> The word[] "bigotry" . . . clearly [does] apply to the five commissioners. . . . They show no tolerance, let alone respect, for people with whom they disagree. . . . They show deep prejudice and hostility to all people of faith.[20]

A similar controversy over whether civil rights commissioners had branded religious believers as bigots—and were themselves bigots—played out when the CCRC ruled that baker Jack Phillips, owner of Masterpiece Cakeshop, violated Colorado's public accommodations law when, in 2012, he declined to bake a cake for a celebration of Charlie Craig and David Mullins's wedding because of his sincere religious belief that marriage was a sacred union only between one man and one woman.[21]

Elane Photography: The Price of Citizenship

My second case study, *Elane Photography, LLC v. Willock*, involves a legal controversy that arose because New Mexico, like most states, has a civil rights law that defines establishments (like for-profit businesses) that provide or offer their "services, facilities, accommodations or goods to the public" as public accommodations; such public accommodations must not discriminate against various classes of persons.[22] Like twenty other states and the District of Columbia, the New Mexico Human Rights Act (NMHRA) includes sexual orientation as one of those classes.[23]

In 2006, Vanessa Willock sent an email to Elane Photography asking whether the business would be available "to photograph her commitment ceremony to another woman." (At that time, New Mexico did not permit same-sex couples to marry, although, unlike many states, it did not have a DOMA expressly prohibiting such marriages.) The couple planned to have a wedding-like ceremony with "vows, rings, a minister, flower girls, and a wedding dress."[24] Elane Huguenin, co-owner of the photography shop and "lead photographer," replied by email that Elane Photography photographed only "traditional weddings." She clarified in a subsequent email that "yes, you are correct in saying that we do not photograph same-sex weddings." Huguenin's reason was that she was "personally opposed to same-sex marriage and will not photograph any image or event that violates her religious beliefs." Willock filed a complaint with the New Mexico Human Rights Commission under the NMHRA for discrimination on the basis of sexual orientation. The Commission concluded that Elane Photography "had discriminated against Willock."[25]

Elane Photography appealed, arguing that its refusal did not violate the NMHRA and that requiring it to accept customers against its will violated its First Amendment rights to free speech and free exercise of religion. Both the lower court and the Supreme Court of Mexico—with no dissents—affirmed the Commission.[26] The New Mexico high court's analysis provided a template for subsequent state court opinions considering similar cases (including that in the Masterpiece Cakeshop litigation). With little rhetorical flourish, the Court methodically explained that by declining to photograph the ceremony, Elane Photography discriminated on the basis of sexual orientation. Disagreeing with Elane Photography's reading of various US Supreme Court precedents, the Court rejected its free speech argument that the NMHRA compelled Elane Photography to speak by "requiring it to photograph a same-sex commitment ceremony, even though it is against the owners' personal beliefs."[27]

On the free exercise of religion claim, the Court applied the legal standard the US Supreme Court stated in *Employment Division v. Smith*: "The right of free exercise does not relieve an individual of the obligation to comply with a valid and neutral law of general applicability on the ground that the law proscribes (or prescribes) conduct that his religion prescribes (or proscribes)."[28] Because the Court concluded that the NMHRA was such a law and did not show hostility toward religion, the Court did not subject the law to "strict scrutiny"—the most stringent form of judicial review—or require New Mexico to show a "compelling interest" to justify the law.[29] Finally, the Court concluded that New Mexico's Religious Freedom Restoration Act, which requires a higher level of judicial review when a "government agency" restricts a person's free exercise of religion, did not apply.[30]

Justice Bosson wrote a concurring opinion with arguments—and rhetorical flourishes—about tolerance, intolerance, and the "price of citizenship" that deserve close analysis. In the wake of *Masterpiece Cakeshop*, this concurrence helpfully models a way to speak about the civil rights past without drawing on the rhetoric of bigotry or expressing hostility toward religion. While the majority opinion in *Elane Photography* begins in the present—with the "policy decision" that the New Mexico legislature made, in 2003, to amend its human rights law to prohibit public accommodations from discriminating against people based on their sexual orientation—Bosson begins in 1943, "the darkest days of World War II," when West Virginia's legislature made a different policy decision. It passed a law requiring students to salute the American flag and "decreed that refusal to salute would be 'regarded as an Act of insubordination,'" leading to expelling the students and taking action against the parents.[31] A challenge brought by students—Jehovah's Witnesses, whose religion interpreted Bible verses that forbade "bow[ing] down" to any "graven images" to prohibit saluting the flag—led to a famous Supreme Court decision affirming First Amendment freedom, *West Virginia State Board of Education v. Barnette* (1943). The Court struck down the law, declaring: "If there is any fixed star in our constitutional constellation, it is that no official, high or petty, can prescribe what shall be orthodox in politics, nationalism, religion, or other matters of opinion or force citizens to confess by word or act their faith therein."[32]

Bosson acknowledges that Elaine and Jonathan Huguenin, owners of Elane Photography, view themselves "in much the same position as the students in *Barnette*." They believe that "certain commands of the Bible . . . must be obeyed."[33] One such command is "an injunction against same-sex marriage"; hence, "creating [the requested] photographs . . . would express a message contrary to their sincerely held beliefs, and . . . would disobey God." He observes that "no one has questioned the Huguenin's devoutness or their sincerity" and adds, *"their religious convictions deserve our respect."*[34] If "honoring same-sex marriage" would pose no less a conflict for the Huguenins than the Jehovah's Witnesses faced in *Barnette*, how can "the State of New Mexico compel them to 'disobey God' in this case?"[35]

In answering this question, Justice Bosson moves forward from the World War II-era *Barnette* opinion to *Loving*, during the "zenith of the Civil Rights era." He first quotes the trial court's famous appeal to the Bible—"Almighty God created [and separated] the races"—and observes: "Whatever opinion one might have of the trial judge's religious views, *which mirrored those of millions of Americans at the time*, no one questioned his sincerity."[36] When Virginia's highest court affirmed the trial court, he added, it also "observed the religious, cultural, historical, and moral roots that justified miscegenation laws." The US Supreme Court, however, struck down Virginia's law for restricting the freedom to marry based solely on a racial classification, showing, Bosson concludes, that "state laws, even those religiously inspired, may not discriminate invidiously on the basis of race."[37]

The lesson Justice Bosson draws from *Loving* for the Huguenin's claim is that while "one is free to believe, think, and speak as one's conscience, or God, dictates," there are constitutional limits on the freedom to act upon "personal, religious, and moral beliefs" when doing so is "to the detriment of someone else's rights." There must be "some accommodation" when "actions, even religiously inspired, conflict with other constitutionally protected rights." In this case, the same-sex couple has a legal right under New Mexico's public accommodations law "to engage in the commercial marketplace free from discrimination." The Huguenins' "refusal to do business"—"no matter how religiously inspired"—was "an affront" to that legal right. This, Bosson reasons, distinguishes their case from that of the students in *Barnette*, whose exercise of their First Amendment right by not saluting the flag did not infringe upon the rights of anyone else.[38] Implicitly, he appeals to well-established jurisprudence that in relieving religious persons of burdens imposed by civil law, the state may not impose costs on third parties.[39]

It is striking that Bosson's account of *Loving* nowhere mentions the Court's identification of "the doctrine of White Supremacy" as the obvious rationale for Virginia's law. Instead, he quotes the trial judge's religious defense and mentions the religious and moral roots of antimiscegenation law. To connect *Loving* to the Huguenin's case, Bosson relates "religiously inspired" but discriminatory state laws to "religiously inspired" but discriminatory refusals to serve customers. Even so, Justice Bosson admits, *Loving* does not give the Huguenins a complete answer, since they "are not trying to prohibit anyone from marrying," but simply "to be left alone to conduct their photography business" according to "their moral convictions" without "endors[ing] someone's lifestyle."[40] Thus, Bosson turns to *Heart of Atlanta Motel v. United States*, in which the US Supreme Court upheld Title II of the CRA. The CRA, he writes, "vindicated nearly a century of frustrated effort to fulfill the promise of the Fourteenth Amendment": to end "second-class citizenship, being denied a seat in a restaurant or a room in an inn—purely on the basis of one's race or religion."[41]

When Congress passed the CRA, many states already had public accommodations laws. Those laws facilitated Congress's acceptance of Title II, prohibiting discrimination in public accommodations (hotels, restaurants, gas stations, and entertainment venues) on the basis of race, color, religion, or national origin. Bosson stresses that the NMHRA is broader than Title II (as are many state anti-discrimination laws). New Mexico's law has expanded to "preclude invidious discrimination in most every public business" (including photography businesses). It also has enlarged the number of "prohibited classifications" from "the historical classes"—those in Title II, as well as sex (or gender)—to include classifications such as sexual orientation.[42] Bosson reasons about this expansion:

> The New Mexico Legislature has made it clear that to discriminate in business on the basis of sexual orientation is just as intolerable as dis-crimination directed toward race, color, national origin, or religion. . . .
> The Huguenins today can no more turn away customers on the basis

of sexual orientation . . . than they could refuse to photograph African-Americans or Muslims.[43]

In this passage, Bosson interprets this expansion in terms of evolving understanding of what forms of discrimination are "intolerable." Implicitly, this intolerance of discrimination is grounded in reasons, and so the New Mexico legislature is not enacting bigotry against discriminators by prohibiting discrimination. (Further, by treating racial, religious, and sexual orientation discrimination as equally intolerable, he implicitly rejects that there is a hierarchy among these forms of discrimination that distinguishes race from the other categories.)

Bosson nowhere says the Huguenins are bigots for the sincere beliefs they hold. To the contrary, "their religious convictions deserve our respect."[44] But are they, as conservative critics charge, being unjustly driven from the "public square"? Bosson acknowledges that the Huguenins are "compelled by law to compromise the very religious beliefs that inspire their lives"—a "sobering result." Nonetheless, he would tell the Huguenins, "with the utmost respect," that this is part of the "price of citizenship" that we all have to pay in "our civic life."[45] Civic life in a "multicultural, pluralistic society" requires some "compromise" with and "accommodation" of the "contrasting values of others." The Huguenins retain the constitutional protection "to think, to say, to believe, as they wish," and to "follow [their God's] commandments in their personal lives," but in "the smaller, more focused world of the marketplace of commerce, of public accommodation," they "have to channel their conduct . . . to leave space for other Americans who believe something different." Notably, Bosson returns to the language of tolerance, concluding that such compromise "is part of the glue that holds us together as a nation, the tolerance that lubricates the varied moving parts of us as a people."[46]

Arguably, this opinion models how to speak respectfully—and with "neutrality" (to anticipate *Masterpiece Cakeshop*)—about why there must be some compromise in civic life in a pluralistic society. Bosson's rhetoric, however, did not take away the sting of the case's outcome. Critics charged that the price of citizenship was higher than sincere believers should have to pay.[47] *Elane Photography* became a cautionary tale in conservative warnings of how LGBT rights and expansive anti-discrimination laws threaten religious liberty. In several other states with public accommodations laws covering sexual orientation, civil rights commissions and state courts similarly ruled that businesses violated the law after they denied same-sex couples wedding-related goods and services, such as cakes, flowers, or facilities for the wedding and reception, because of their religious beliefs.[48] The human stories behind some of those cases generated widespread media attention, particularly when those rulings resulted in the businesses paying money damages or experiencing other economic losses. Some advocates of civil marriage equality and LGBT rights, such as Andrew Koppelman, urged that people who, like the Huguenins, had religious objections to "homosexual sex" were "not homophobic bigots who want to hurt gay people" (even though he regards their "religious ideas" as obviously "wrong"). Further, he claimed that business owners had raised religious objections to providing wedding-related goods and services in only a "handful" of cases. The "gay rights movement" had "won," he argued; it will "not be stopped by a few exemptions," and so it should be "magnanimous in victory."[49]

Masterpiece Cakeshop, Ltd v. Colorado Civil Rights Commission: Branding as a Bigot or Learning from the Past?

No case generated more publicity, focused both on the business owner (Phillips) and the couple denied service (Craig and Mullins), than *Masterpiece Cakeshop*. There was no explicit rhetoric of bigotry in any of the administrative rulings against Phillips or the Colorado Court of Appeals' affirming opinion. Even so, conservative critics interpreted the case as another cautionary tale of a sincere Christian being branded as a bigot and "purged" from the public square.[50] To return to Epstein's charges, civil rights commissions and courts were portrayed as intolerant civil rights bullies. Were such charges warranted?

In proceedings before the CCRC, self-described "cake artist" Jack Phillips, owner of Masterpiece Cakeshop, argued unsuccessfully that applying Colorado's anti-discrimination law to his refusal to create a cake to celebrate Craig and Mullin's wedding—and denying him a religious exemption—violated his First Amendment rights to freedom of speech and the free exercise of religion. In affirming prior decisions by an administrative law judge and the CCRC rejecting these First Amendment claims, the Colorado Court of Appeals drew on *Elane Photography* at many points, including in relying on *Smith* for the relevant standard for reviewing Phillips's free exercise claim.[51] After the Colorado Court of Appeals affirmed the CCRC, Phillips asked the US Supreme Court to decide "whether applying Colorado's public accommodations law to compel artists to create expression that violates their sincerely held religious beliefs about marriage violates the Free Speech or Free Exercise Clauses of the First Amendment."[52]

After the Court agreed to hear Phillips's appeal, over ninety amicus briefs were submitted on behalf of either Phillips and Masterpiece Cakeshop (petitioners) or the CCRC and Craig and Mullins (respondents).[53] Both sides enlisted the rhetoric of bigotry and conscience to connect or distinguish past and present civil rights battles. On each side, some of the amicus briefs explicitly referred to bigotry: fourteen of the forty-five briefs filed in support of Phillips and nine of the forty-six briefs filed in support of the CCRC and Craig and Mullins.[54] Many amici used words often associated with bigotry (intolerance, prejudice, hatred, and homophobia). Some discussed animus. I also highlight competing arguments about whether the CCRC or the Colorado appellate court showed hostility toward Phillips's religion, given the significance of this issue in Kennedy's eventual majority opinion. I then analyze the Supreme Court's opinion.

The Rhetoric of the Briefs: Contrasting Views of Anti-discrimination Law and History's Lessons

A close examination of the rhetoric and arguments in these briefs reveals a set of contrasting positions on basic issues. One contrast concerns the role of analogy between landmark federal civil rights law, such as Title II of the CRA, and state civil rights laws, and, relatedly, the relevance of past religious objections to civil rights laws to present ones. Phillips's supporters argued that relating present-day religious objections to anti-discrimination laws forbidding sexual orientation discrimination—and claims for exemption—to past religious objections to civil rights laws prohibiting race discrimination slanders Phillips and other believers as bigots. Not only is today's sincere religious believer declining to create a wedding cake or otherwise affirm same-sex marriage nothing like the racist (past or present) refusing to serve all black customers; he or she also is nothing like the homophobe refusing to serve any gay or lesbian customers.

Those supporting Colorado's law (CADA) countered that history teaches lessons about past assertions of conscience and religious liberty to justify discrimination and exclusion. While courts themselves, for a time, accepted and even voiced such religious justifications, they have, for many decades, upheld anti-discrimination laws against such challenges.[55] This past counsels caution about arguments that free exercise entails living out one's faith in the marketplace or public square even when doing so includes denying customers goods and services. Furthermore, the framing of "religious liberty v. LGBT rights" obscures the fact that religious traditions differ in their views and also evolve, sometimes spurred by legal change.

Second, the briefs reveal competing views of the legitimate scope of public accommodations laws. Invoking Chief Justice Rehnquist's opinion in *Boy Scouts of America v. Dale*, some of Phillips's supporters contend that the clash between religious liberty and LGBT rights stems from the unwarranted expansion of public accommodations laws to cover more places and more categories, such as sexual orientation and gender identity.[56] Title II of the CRA, on this view, is the paradigm of a justified civil rights law. Some of Phillips's amici, however, grant the legitimacy of states protecting against sexual orientation discrimination, but argue that his conscience-based objection should be accommodated. A number of amici stress the ready availability of good and services from other business owners without such objections.

Supporters of the CCRC and Craig and Mullins defend the scope of state public accommodations laws, arguing that they reflect evolving understanding of prejudice and discrimination. Such laws, indeed, go beyond the scope of Title II of the CRA.[57] Apt here is Justice Stevens's statement, in dissent in *Dale*, that "every state law prohibiting discrimination is designed to replace prejudice with principle."[58] Colorado's expansion of CADA illustrates that dynamic. In *Romer v. Evans*, one rationale for Colorado's Amendment 2, which prohibited protection of LGB people from discrimination, was protecting the religious liberty of landlords and others. In 1996 (as chapter 7 explained), the Supreme Court struck down that amendment as evidently motivated by animus.[59] In 2008, after a hard-fought effort, Colorado affirmatively *required* such protection against discrimination by adding sexual orientation to its anti-discrimination law.[60]

This evolution, in turn, shaped arguments about who should be protected in civic space, as the *Masterpiece Cakeshop* briefs make clear. After this amendment to CADA, conservative groups who, in *Romer*, defended Amendment 2 by asserting the right of a *majority* to enact their view that homosexuality was immoral—now, in *Masterpiece Cakeshop*, argued for the right of a conscientious, dissenting *minority* to protection of those same views against the majority's new orthodoxy about marriage and sexuality.[61] They now argued that *they* were the victims of animus and "invidious discrimination." Such amici stressed the "harm inflicted on vulnerable creative professionals" forced to become "an unwilling mouthpiece of the State."[62] By contrast, amici supporting the CCRC and Craig and Mullins emphasized the vulnerability to discrimination, stigma, and "minority stress" experienced by the LGBT population in Colorado (and elsewhere) and the harms posed by broad exemptions for conscience or "creative expression."[63]

Third, both sides agree on the importance of civility, tolerance, and pluralism, but disagree about what those commitments require. Supporters of people "of conscience" trying to "live out their faith" in the marketplace argue that robust protection of First Amendment freedoms everywhere—including the public square—is the only path to civility, tolerance, and coexisting "peacefully" in a pluralistic society.[64] Resisting efforts to cabin religion, they insist that Phillips's operation of his bakery is as much an act of worship or religious "exercise" as is what goes on in a church or religious service organization.

Defenders of full enforcement of modern civil rights laws argue that civility and tolerance require that there be limits to acting on beliefs—however sincere and religiously motivated—in businesses open to the public. As Justice Bosson explained in *Elane Photography*, that is the price of citizenship that we pay in our civic life.[65] In a religiously diverse nation, unless certain lines are drawn, every conscience (as *Smith* cautioned) would become "a law unto itself," raising "the prospect of constitutionally required religious exemptions . . . of almost every conceivable kind."[66]

Arguments by Phillips and His Amici

Phillips and his amici contended that compelling him to "design" a "custom" wedding cake for a same-sex couple unconstitutionally forces him to "celebrate same-sex marriage"; he "in good conscience" cannot do that, since he "seeks to live his life, pursue his profession, and craft his art consistently with his religious identity."[67] Phillips argued that Colorado violated the First Amendment by compelling a private citizen "to utter what is not in his mind."[68] In support, Phillips invoked *Barnette*, on which the owners of Elane Photography had also relied.[69]

Hostility toward Phillips's religion: the CCRC and the Colorado appellate court. Phillips argued that the CCRC showed hostility toward his religion, citing a comment by an individual commissioner during a hearing on his case. Like Chairman Castro, this commissioner linked past to present and cautioned:

> Freedom of religion and religion have been used to justify all kinds of discrimination throughout history, whether it be slavery, whether it be the Holocaust. . . . And to me it is one of the most despicable pieces of rhetoric that people . . . use their religion to hurt others.[70]

Phillips and his amici also argued that the CCRC's "disdain" for his religious views was evident from its permitting three other bakers to decline to bake cakes with offensive messages disapproving same-sex marriage, but not permitting him to decline to create a cake with a message—offensive to him—supporting same-sex marriage.[71] Amici William Jack, who requested those three cakes (after the CCRC had begun proceedings in Phillips's case), contended that the CCRC "expressed hostility towards [his] traditional religious views" as "odious."[72]

Like the critics of the *Peaceful Coexistence* report, some supporters of Phillips argued that Colorado had been *intolerant* toward him and his sincere religious beliefs, forgetting that "tolerance is a two-way street."[73] Justice Kennedy echoed that idea at oral argument, telling counsel for the CCRC that "tolerance is essential in a free society" and is "most meaningful when it's mutual," but stating that Colorado had "been neither tolerant nor respectful of Mr. Phillips's religious beliefs." In particular, the commissioner's comment quoted earlier troubled

Justice Kennedy, who asked about it at the oral argument; it would prove crucial in the Court's resolution of the case.[74]

To appreciate this hostility argument, it is useful to look at the Colorado Court of Appeals opinion, which affirmed the CCRC. The Court mentioned hostility only in concluding that CADA is a neutral law and that the exemptions it provides to religious institutions undermines the assertion that it is hostile to religion.[75] The Court did not embrace or even refer to the civil rights commissioner's statement about religion being used to hurt people. In a footnote, the Court concluded that Phillips's case was distinguishable from those of the three bakers who refused Jack: they refused not because of Jack's religion (a protected category under CADA), but because of the "offensive nature" of the requested message. By contrast, Phillips's refusal was "discrimination on the basis of sexual orientation," prohibited by CADA.[76]

The Court did not question the sincerity of Phillips's religious beliefs or call him a bigot. It did, however, draw on a civil rights-era precedent rejecting a religious objection to Title II to explain that the freedom to act on religious beliefs has limits. The Court observed that in *Piggie Park*, a federal district court in South Carolina refused "to lend credence or support to [the restaurant owner's] position that he has a constitutional right to refuse to serve members of the Negro race in his business establishment upon the ground that to do so would violate his sacred religious beliefs."[77] Quoting the district court, the Colorado court explained that while free exercise includes a "right to espouse beliefs of [one's] own choosing," it does not include "the absolute right to exercise and practice such beliefs in utter disregard of the clear constitutional rights of other citizens." So, too, the Court reasoned, if Masterpiece Cakeshop wishes to operate as a public accommodation in Colorado, CADA "prohibits it from picking and choosing customers based on their sexual orientation."[78] *Piggie Park* featured in many of the briefs filed in support of the CCRC and Craig and Mullins, as well as in the Supreme Court's opinion in *Masterpiece Cakeshop*.

In upholding CADA, the Colorado court also related the Supreme Court's recognition of states' compelling interest in eliminating discrimination on the basis of race and sex in places of public accommodation to Colorado's interest in eliminating discrimination in such places on the basis of sexual orientation. The Court concluded that CADA "creates a hospitable environment for all consumers," which "prevents the economic and social balkanization . . . when businesses decide to serve only their own 'kind.'"[79]

Sincere merchants of good conscience are not bigots. Only a minority of briefs filed on behalf of Phillips use the explicit rhetoric of bigotry. The majority refer to his conscience and religious sincerity. This is unsurprising: Phillips asserted that CADA violated his free exercise of religion. Having a sincerely held religious belief that is burdened by a law is one requirement for asserting such a claim, whether under the First Amendment or a state religious freedom restoration act.[80] A court does not inquire into whether such sincere beliefs are reasonable or mistaken.

Amici also asserted Phillips's sincerity and his "decent and honorable" beliefs to contrast him with the bigot, racist, or homophobe. Unless the Supreme Court reversed, they argued, it would send a message that Phillips is a bigot, a pariah properly excluded from the public square—contrary to *Obergefell*'s "promise" to conscientious dissenters about their First Amendment rights. In claiming that Phillips has been branded a bigot by the CCRC and the Colorado court, some amici quoted the prediction in Justice Alito's *Obergefell* dissent: "Colorado has unquestionably labeled and treated [Phillips] as a bigot."[81] Unless the Court reversed the Colorado court, it too would "tell him—and all traditional Muslims, Orthodox Jews, and Christians—that acting on beliefs central to his identity is wrong, benighted, even bigoted."[82] But amici also invoked Justice Kennedy's majority opinion in *Obergefell*: "Many who deem same-sex marriage to be wrong reach that conclusion based on decent and honorable religious or philosophical conclusions."[83]

In his brief, Phillips describes himself as "a conscientious man of faith," who "gladly serves people from all walks of life, including individuals of all races, faiths, and sexual orientations," but simply "declines all requests . . . to create custom artistic expression that conflicts with his faith."[84] His amici argue that this conscience-driven refusal to express a message—"celebrating same-sex marriage"—is not like the "invidious discrimination" at the core of laws banning discrimination in public accommodations. In those instances, "a merchant objects to serving some people just because and on the ground that they are black, or female . . . or gay."[85] Amici also draw on the connotation of the bigot as a now-reviled and anachronistic figure whose views are not publicly acceptable. Asserting that Craig and Mullins "suffered no material harm" from Phillips's refusal, they contrasted the serious harms suffered by Phillips: "The State has effectively branded him a bigot and rendered him something of an outcast, seriously harming his reputation in the community."[86]

Downplaying the role of religion in past defenses of racism and discrimination. Some amici draw on the idea of the bigot as a reviled figure to reject any analogies to past uses of religion to defend forms of now-repudiated discrimination, such as racial segregation and antimiscegenation laws. In a brief filled with references to bigotry, Ryan T. Anderson of the Heritage Foundation contrasts opposition to interracial marriage, rooted in "racist bigotry," with support for marriage as a "conjugal union of husband and wife," rooted in "decent and honorable premises." To rule for Phillips would send "no message about the supposed inferiority of people who identify as gay," but instead would say "that citizens who support the historic understanding of marriage are not bigots and that the state may not drive them out of business and civic life."[87]

The "wicked system of white supremacy," Anderson argues, was rooted in bigotry, animus, and convictions about racial hierarchy. That political leaders appealed to theology to justify racial "subordination" showed how religion "was perverted to justify racism and slavery."[88] Here, Anderson is like Castro and the commissioner in *Masterpiece Cakeshop* who condemn twisting or using religion to justify racial discrimination, but he, unlike them, draws a sharp line between past and present.

In setting up this contrast, Anderson downplays both the pervasiveness and evident sincerity of religious rationales marshaled in the past for racial segregation and antimiscegenation laws. Missing from Anderson's account is the history revisited in chapters 4, 5, and 6: white segregationists opposed to *Brown v. Board of Education* and to any form of race mixing vehemently denied charges of bigotry and insisted that they were "waging a fight of morality and conscience." The "theology of segregation" sounded in pulpits and pages of the Congressional Record. Again, in debates over the CRA, some opponents defended segregation as scriptural, rejected the proposed law as violating religious and constitutional principles, and even reversed the charges of bigotry to apply to supporters of the CRA. Furthermore, while Anderson invokes Koppelman's statement (quoted earlier) that merchants like Phillips are not homophobic bigots, he ignores that Koppelman has argued repeatedly that there is an instructive analogy between bans on interracial marriage and those on same-sex marriage.[89]

Even some political leaders who supported ending racial segregation believed that there were (to use *Obergefell's* language) decent and honorable religious grounds for opposing interracial marriage. In 1963, when asked whether intermarriage was the next step in racial integration, President Harry Truman, who had issued an executive order desegregating the military and created the President's Commission on Civil Rights (discussed in chapter 5), answered: "I hope not. I don't believe in it. The Lord created it that way. You read your Bible and you'll find out."[90] By minimizing the role of appeals to scripture and religious belief in defending racism, Anderson attempts to render the civil rights past irrelevant to the present battles over religious exemptions. He also adopts the tactic of presenting past beliefs justifying racial discrimination as so obviously evil, immoral, and "wicked" that they cannot possibly be compared to present-day beliefs that justify sexual-orientation discrimination.[91]

Rejecting analogies to struggles over past civil rights laws. Amici for Phillips also argue that the concerns that led to landmark civil rights laws, such as Title II, are not relevant to Phillips's refusal of service to Craig and Mullins. Particularly notable is that the states making this argument include those whose representatives fervently *opposed* the public accommodations provision of Title II in the 1960s (as chapter 5 detailed). For example, Texas, Alabama, and a number of other states asserted: "Public-accommodations concerns of past eras are not present here."[92] One reason is that "the artist plainly did not act out of invidious discrimination," but to protect his conscience. Another is the distinction between genuine public accommodations, "like restaurants and hotels," and "customized pieces of art," like wedding cakes. A third reason is that Craig and Mullins "had immediate access to other artists," unlike discriminated-against minorities under the Jim Crow practices that Title II sought to end.[93] Thus, Phillips's dignitary and other interests are harmed far more than those of a would-be customer denied service in the current, supposedly gay-friendly marketplace. Given Texas's description of such a marketplace, it is important to note that Phillips would have been free to refuse service in Texas and the other states joining the brief, since Texas and Alabama do not have public accommodations laws and the other states have not expanded their public accommodations laws to prohibit either sexual orientation or gender identity discrimination.[94]

Treating Title II as the paradigm of a narrowly tailored public accommodations law allows amici to contrast CADA as an inappropriate expansion of anti-discrimination law. Like Chief Justice Rehnquist in *Dale*, they argue that such expansion has led to clashes with First Amendment rights. Instead of remedying discrimination, Colorado's law is a "source" of it.[95] Other amici admit that it is legitimate for states to add sexual orientation protections to their public accommodations laws, but insist that goods and services related to same-sex weddings are a special case warranting a conscience-based exemption.[96]

Some amici argue that red states have not extended their public accommodations laws to include sexual orientation out of concern—based on what they see in blue states with such expanded laws—that such laws might not adequately protect the First Amendment rights of "conscientious objectors" like Phillips. For example, the Utah Republican State Senators brief notes that Utah passed "compromise" legislation "add[ing] sexual orientation to the state's housing and employment discrimination laws," but could not reach agreement on a similar expansion of its public accommodations law precisely because of this concern.[97]

The Christian Legal Society's (CLS) brief argued that in the current culture war impasse, "same-sex couples and religious dissenters" have unrecognized common ground: both "face the problem that what they experience as among the highest virtues is condemned by others as a grave evil." Where religious believers see "obedience to a loving God," many supporters of gay rights see "intolerance, bigotry and hate," and where same-sex couples perceive "loving commitments," many religious believers see sinful, "disordered conduct." This "mutual suspicion and hostility" leads blue states to refuse to protect religious liberty—as the CLS argues CADA fails to do—and red states to refuse to "enact gay-rights laws."[98]

The demands of tolerance. Phillips and his amici argue that a ruling against him would fail to realize *Obergefell's* "laudable effort to promote tolerance and mutual respect in a pluralistic national community."[99] The path to peaceful coexistence lies in exemptions in cases of decent and honorable beliefs, so that people of faith are not driven from the marketplace. Some amici contend that tolerance is a two-way street, but Colorado has "employ[ed] the strong arm of the state" to further its "secular ideologies"—"promoting tolerance and respect for some while ruthlessly suppressing others."[100]

Arguments by Respondents and their Amici

Only nine of the forty-six amicus briefs filed on behalf of respondents CCRC and Craig and Mullins explicitly used the terms "bigot," "bigoted," or "bigotry" and just six did so in their arguments.[101] Many more briefs use related terms, speaking of problems of prejudice, hate, and discrimination that anti-discrimination laws address. At the same time, many briefs stressed that anti-discrimination laws aim at conduct, so that motive is not relevant. Quoting *Obergefell*, they contended: allowing "sincere, personal opposition" to same-sex marriage to become "enacted law and policy" would put the state's "imprimatur on an exclusion"—religiously motivated discrimination.[102] A number of amici make an argument that some commentators view as labeling religious persons as bigots (without using that term): that we have heard these religious arguments against civil rights laws before and should learn the lessons of history.

Do respondents and their amici brand Phillips as a bigot? Neither the parties nor most of their amici called Phillips a bigot or motivated by "animosity," instead stressing that CADA focuses on *conduct.* For example, in rejecting Phillips's argument that by contrast to off-the-shelf-goods, customized orders would compel his artistic expression, CCRC cautioned that such a rule would defeat CADA's purposes by allowing a wide range of businesses to discriminate, "whether driven by religious beliefs or merely bigotry, racism, or sexism."[103] Similarly, a brief filed by a group of church-state scholars distinguishes Phillips's religious beliefs from bigotry, but also argues: "CADA forbids discrimination on the basis of sexual orientation—whether motivated by pure bigotry, secular morality, or religious belief." The brief presents Phillips's free exercise claim as a "sympathetic case," posing a dilemma of conscience. Nonetheless, invoking *Smith*, it warns that there is no principled limit to the conscience exemption Phillips seeks, anticipating numerous clashes between "commands of conscience" and laws "that protect fundamental rights, equal protection, health and safety, free markets, or other social goods."[104]

In its amicus brief, Lambda Legal Defense and Education Fund refers to the problem of bigotry toward LGBT persons in the larger society: LGBT people experience "pervasive" discrimination in "nearly every aspect of public life," including the marketplace. The brief refers to bigotry in the context of anti-gay violence: "Tragically, as the violent Pulse nightclub massacre in Florida last year shows, even in such safe spaces members of the LGBT community may be targets of life-shattering, even life-ending bigotry."[105] Putting the stamp of governmental approval on discrimination, the brief argues, has "dangerous repercussions," including more discrimination and an increased risk of anti-LGBT violence.

Lambda does not question Phillips's sincerity, but explains the "dangerous ripple effects" of recognizing religious or creative expression exemptions to anti-discrimination laws. Quoting *Obergefell*, the brief cautions: "When even 'sincere, personal opposition' to treating LGBT people equally 'becomes enacted law and public policy, the necessary consequence is to put the imprimatur of the State itself on exclusion that soon demeans or stigmatizes.' "[106]

A few briefs, however, argue that religiously motivated denials of service can be a form of bigotry, using analogies implying that Phillips's denial is an instance of bigotry. The Center for Inquiry observes that civil rights cases such as *Loving* and *Bob Jones University v. United States* (in which the Court upheld denying a university's tax-exempt status because of its racially discriminatory policies) illustrate that "much prejudice against people of different races in the United States was justified on religious grounds, and racists often still base their bigotry on their religious faith."[107] Bob Jones University, for example, based its prohibition of interracial dating and marriage on the Bible—a prohibition it retained until 2000. The brief warns that precedents like *Bob Jones University* might be at risk if the Court allows religious preferences and beliefs to be sufficient to exempt Phillips from CADA.

Countering Phillips's theory that Craig and Mullins suffered minimal harm in being denied service at a *particular* business, the Center argues: "The true harm comes from being the victim of bigotry." The brief illustrates with hypotheticals involving religiously motivated discrimination based on a potential customer's religion or race: "A Sikh American refused service in a particular restaurant because of his turban and beard, who then is served at a restaurant a block down the street," or "an African American refused a room at an airport hotel who is compelled to cross the parking lot and stay at a less racist hotel."[108] In linking these "victims of bigotry" to Craig and Mullins, the Center is suggesting that religiously motivated denials of service are a form of bigotry.

A brief filed by the Central Conference of Rabbis and other religious organizations also links religion to bigotry in recounting why some religious leaders opposed Mississippi's "conscience protection" bill: "Rabbi Jeffrey Simons perceived [HB 1523] as being 'not about religion . . . [but] about bigotry.'" This type of argument suggests that invocations of religion to justify laws limiting LGBT people's civil rights are, to echo the US Civil Rights Commissioners' formulation, a distortion or misuse of religion. Notably, the brief also rejects the oppositional framing of "religious liberty versus LGBT rights," pointing to "broad religious support for LGBT nondiscrimination" and against "allowing small business owners to deny service to gay or lesbian customers on religious grounds."[109] But the brief also distinguishes religious and civil marriage law, observing that certain religious norms about marriage, such as the prohibition of interfaith marriage or of remarriage after divorce, would be "unenforceable under civil law." CADA, however, does not reach those norms and practices, but focuses on persons not discriminating among customers when selling products offered in the "stream of commerce."[110]

Another brief takes on the claim by Phillips and his supporters that people of faith are being branded as bigots when public accommodations laws are applied to them. The brief criticizes Phillips's attempt to distinguish being willing to serve gay customers generally from being unwilling to bake a cake celebrating a same-sex marriage:

> Opponents contend that they are the victims of secularism—positioned as bigots and pariahs—then leverage that narrative to assert that they are not bigots at all because they are not discriminating based on sexual orientation. Instead, they are making a choice to reject *conduct*—marriage.[111]

The brief positions this attempt to distinguish between identity (status) and conduct (marriage) in a longer history of opposing "civil rights gains for the LGBT community." Notably, this brief does not draw analogies to racial discrimination, but charts the shifting rationales offered to oppose civil rights for LGBT people, relating it to the Court's own trajectory from *Bowers* to *Obergefell* and rejection of the status-conduct distinction.[112]

Learning from the past—with and without referring to bigotry. One of the handful of briefs that expressly uses the rhetoric of bigotry was filed by Massachusetts, along with eighteen other states (and the District of Columbia) that have amended their public accommodations laws to add sexual orientation and/or gender identity.[113] This brief provides a window into an argument that many other amici made, but without using such rhetoric: "We have heard this kind of claim before" and must learn from the past when considering religious objections to civil rights laws.[114] The argument is that the long history of individuals and businesses asserting a variety of First Amendment justifications for race and sex discrimination—and of courts eventually rejecting such justifications—affords reasons for courts to reject present-day religious arguments for exemptions from state laws protecting LGBT persons against discrimination. Anderson argued that those past assertions were an obvious pretext or distortion of religion, but these amici counter that such religious beliefs were genuinely and widely held. They also contend that the same principles that underlie landmark federal public accommodations laws apply to the expansion of state laws to include sexual orientation (and, some amici add, gender identity). They warn that recognizing exemptions based on conscience or religious beliefs threatens to reverse hard-won progress in protecting civil rights and may (quoting *Obergefell*) put the state's imprimatur on discrimination.

The Massachusetts brief argues: "History has taught us to be wary" of the assertion of free exercise claims to justify "refus[ing] equal service to certain members of the public." Public accommodations laws are "a centerpiece of state efforts to combat the economic, personal, and social harms caused by invidious discrimination," including that experienced by LGBTQ people.[115] The brief draws direct analogies between the uses of religious beliefs to justify racial and sexual orientation discrimination. In *Piggie Park*, the brief observes, the Supreme Court characterized as "patently frivolous" the business owner's assertion of a constitutional right not to violate his "sacred religious beliefs" about segregation as the reason for his "refusal to serve members of the Negro race." The brief then contends: "Businesses today have no more of a right to justify their discrimination against LGBTQ individuals on religious grounds."[116] Thus, to Phillips's question as to "whether the States' compelling interest in combatting discrimination extends to discrimination motivated by 'sincerely held religious beliefs,'" the brief insists "the answer is a resounding 'yes.'"[117]

The brief's single reference to bigotry appears in mentioning the violence in Charlottesville, Virginia (in August, 2017) and the sizable minority of the public who still disapprove of interracial marriage as evidence of the persistence of bigoted beliefs. The brief then offers hypotheticals of how those beliefs could translate into discriminatory practices if Phillips's claim for a religious-based exemption from public accommodations laws were successful:

> It remains a sad fact of American society that bigoted beliefs are disturbingly prevalent. Under Petitioners' theory, an anti-Semitic baker could refuse to sell a wedding cake to a Jewish couple because he does not wish "to create expression that he considers objectionable." . . . And a racist architect could refuse to design a family home for an interracial couple.

While the First Amendment "tolerates all manner of odious speech in the public square," it does not insulate businesses from liability for refusing goods and services.[118]

The NAACP Legal Defense and Educational Fund brief also sounds the theme of learning from history, but without using the rhetoric of bigotry. The brief begins by connecting two narratives—separated in time by nearly fifty years—about business owners denying service to three would-be customers because of religious beliefs: the denial of service at a barbeque to three African American customers in 1964—leading to *Piggie Park*—and the denial of service to Mr. Mullins, Mr. Craig, and Mr. Craig's mother in 2012—leading to *Masterpiece Cakeshop*. The brief observes that in 1964, the religious beliefs of Mr. Bessinger, owner of Piggie Park, "were relatively mainstream" and he was not viewed as "fringe or disingenuous." Indeed, that these religious beliefs were not marginal, but sincerely and widely held, made the Court's ruling all the more significant. (Consider, for example, that in 1964, South Carolina still banned interracial marriage, and so Mr. Bessinger could view secular marriage law as mirroring his religious beliefs prohibiting race mixing.) The brief concludes: "The overarching lesson of *Piggie Park, Bob Jones [University]*, and *Loving* is that this Court has repeatedly and unambiguously rejected religious-based justifications for differential treatment . . . for good reasons: the government has a compelling interest in combating discrimination in its various forms."[119]

The Fund brief effectively points out how social judgments about discrimination change over time as a result of new legal rules and judicial enforcement of such rules. For example, Piggie Park remained in business under the new anti-discrimination rules, and the current owner (Mr. Bessinger's son) "speaks openly about rising above his father's legacy on race" (and offers customized barbeque for weddings).[120] The American Bar Association argued that decisions like *Piggie Park* and *Bob Jones University* contributed to the emergence of a "settled social consensus" despite the many sincere moral and religious objections to Title II: "Business owners who offer their goods and services to the public cannot claim constitutional sanctuary from public accommodations laws."[121] Racial segregation in the marketplace and elsewhere likely would have persisted had legislatures and courts allowed broad religious exemptions.

In sum, few of the briefs filed on behalf of respondents characterized Phillips's beliefs as bigotry. Some shifted the inquiry away from animus or motive to putting the state's imprimatur on discrimination. Amici insisted on learning from the past, emphasizing how religious justifications for discrimination become less acceptable over time and also how law helps anti-discrimination norms to take hold. If it isn't 1964 anymore, that is due in part to not having robust religious exemptions to Title II.

The Supreme Court Weighs In

From the moment the Court decided to hear Phillips's appeal, speculation began on how Justice Kennedy would rule: whether he would make his quartet of landmark gay rights opinions (which began, after all, in Colorado with *Romer*) a quintet or whether he would accept Phillips's First Amendment claims. Was the price of citizenship Colorado exacted from Phillips and others trying to live out their faith in the marketplace too high? At the oral argument, Kennedy appeared troubled *both* by Phillips's difficulty in drawing lines carving out an exception from state anti-discrimination laws for "compelled expression" *and* by the lack of tolerance and respect (or the hostility) shown by the Commission toward Phillips's religion. Kennedy also seemed sympathetic to the argument that public accommodations laws like CADA could exempt merchants like Phillips, so long as a gay couple could readily find the same good or service elsewhere. Even so, he expressed concern that a ruling for Phillips could allow a "boycott" of gay marriage and be "an affront to the gay community."[122]

At the oral argument, the liberal justices brought up *Piggie Park*, along with other civil rights era cases, in questioning Phillips's First Amendment claims.[123] They expressed great concern that an exemption could undermine the entire structure of anti-discrimination laws.[124] After observing that "the racial analogy obviously is very compelling," however, Chief Justice Roberts pointed out that *Obergefell* "went out of its way to talk about the decent and honorable people who may have opposing views."[125] Phillips, on this reading of *Obergefell*, is morally distinct from a racist; for Roberts, Phillips presented a meritorious First Amendment claim whereas the *Piggie Park* owner did not.

Some court-watchers speculated that the Court might make a narrow ruling, given the many quagmires in finding a line that would not undermine anti-discrimination laws, not to mention its own precedents (including *Obergefell*).[126] These predictions proved accurate. On June 4, 2018, the Supreme Court released what would be Kennedy's fifth and final gay rights opinion (since he announced his retirement at age eighty-one later that month).[127] The Court reversed the Colorado Court of Appeals on the ground that the CCRC's hostility toward Phillips's religious beliefs "was inconsistent with the First Amendment's guarantee that our laws be applied in a manner that is neutral toward religion."[128] The Court set aside the Commission's order against Phillips, postponing to "later cases" how best to resolve the many "difficult" and "delicate" questions the case raised. Echoing Kennedy's statements at oral argument, his majority opinion stated that "the Commission's consideration of Phillips's case was neither tolerant nor respectful of Phillips's religious beliefs."[129]

In an unusual lineup, the Court's four conservative justices and two of the four liberal justices, Justices Breyer and Kagan, joined Kennedy's narrowly written majority opinion.[130] Indicating that they would have gone farther than the majority did in ruling for Phillips, two of the conservative justices (Gorsuch and Thomas) wrote concurring opinions. By contrast, Justice Ginsburg's dissent (joined by Justice Sotomayor) argued that much of the majority's opinion pointed in the direction of ruling *against* Phillips and challenged the Court's hostility ruling.[131] Providing a blueprint to guide civil rights commissioners in future controversies, Justice Kagan (joined by Breyer) wrote a concurring opinion showing how it could have been possible to apply Colorado's law against Phillips "untainted by any bias against a religious belief."[132] Gorsuch wrote a concurring opinion, strongly disagreeing with Kagan and Ginsburg.[133]

It is illuminating to look at whether and how the rhetoric of bigotry and conscience features in the opinions. First, Kennedy nowhere refers to bigotry. He uses rhetoric about hostility and animosity to condemn governmental actions enforcing laws *protecting* gay persons rather than, as in his previous gay rights opinions, laws *excluding or harming* them. He draws not on the *Moreno/Romer* framework about animus against gays and lesbians, but instead on cases interpreting the Free Exercise Clause to prohibit animosity toward religion. The Constitution, Kennedy writes, "commits government itself to religious tolerance, and upon even slight suspicion that proposals for state intervention stem from animosity to religion or distrust of its practices, all officials must pause to remember their own high duty to the Constitution and to the rights it secures."[134] In this passage, Kennedy quotes *Church of Lukumi Babalu Aye, Inc. v. Hialeah*, in which the Court (in an opinion by Kennedy) ruled that a local ordinance in Hialeah, Florida prohibiting only religiously motivated killing of animals violated the Free Exercise Clause: it was not neutral, but targeted the Santeria Church.[135] Unlike the ordinance in Hialeah, the problem in *Masterpiece Cakeshop* is not the CADA statute itself, but in how the commissioners applied it.

Why Kennedy concluded that the Commission showed hostility warrants a close look. For one thing, his analysis suggests that rhetoric matters. The individual commissioner's comment about using religion to harm others as a "despicable piece of rhetoric" "disparaged" Phillips's religion, Kennedy finds, in "at least two distinct ways": (1) by calling the appeal to religious beliefs "despicable" and (2) by "characterizing it as merely rhetorical—something insubstantial and even insincere." To compare Phillips's religious beliefs about marriage to religious defenses of slavery and the Holocaust, moreover, was a "sentiment . . . inappropriate" for someone charged with "neutral enforcement" of CADA, which protects "on *the basis of religion* as well as sexual orientation."[136] Because no other commissioners objected to the comments and the CCRC did not disavow them, this "cast doubt on the fairness and impartiality" of the Commission's handling of Phillips's case. Another factor showing hostility, Kennedy says, is the disparity in how the Commission treated the "conscience-based objections" by the three bakers who declined to bake the cakes requested by William Jack and how they treated Phillips's religious beliefs—as "illegitimate."[137]

Kennedy's analysis poses a challenging question: How should public officials talk about religion when they consider whether a religiously motivated refusal of service violated civil rights law? What if the Commissioner in question simply observed, as a factual matter, that people have asserted religious beliefs as a reason to discriminate on various bases, including race and sexual orientation, and that there is no absolute protection to act on religious beliefs in the marketplace? Indeed, what if the Commissioner cited, as an example, the theology of segregation revisited in chapter 4? Would even that remark signal a lack of impartiality toward religion? Or what if the Commissioner simply made the following observation:

> The religious and philosophical objections to gay marriage are protected views and in some instances protected forms of expression. Nevertheless, while those religious and philosophical objections are protected, it is a general rule that such objections do not allow business owners and other actors in the economy and in society to deny protected persons equal access to goods and services under a neutral and generally applicable public accommodations law.

This observation is exactly what Kennedy wrote in *Masterpiece Cakeshop*.[138] And it is one reason why Justices Kagan and Breyer concurred with his majority opinion and some LGBT rights groups found a silver lining in it. Perhaps, then, Kennedy's opinion is about "etiquette"—how public officials should talk (and not talk) about religion.[139]

But one curious fact about Kennedy's statement is that one of the sources for this general rule to provide goods and services, despite religious objections, is none other than *Piggie Park*, a centerpiece in the arguments filed on behalf of Craig and Mullins and CADA's constitutionality. In *Piggie Park*, the Court characterized Bessinger's Free Exercise objection to Title II as "patently frivolous" and said nothing "respectful" about his beliefs. In doing so, did the Court "disparage" his religious beliefs about segregation?[140] While Kennedy's citation is without elaboration, Kagan explains that in *Piggie Park*, the Court held that "a barbeque vendor must serve black customers even if he perceives such service as vindicating racial equality, in violation of his religious beliefs." *Piggie Park* illustrates the Court's longstanding holding that "a vendor cannot escape a public accommodations law because his religion disapproves selling a product to a group of customers, whether defined by sexual orientation, race, sex, or other protected trait." Kagan invokes *Piggie Park* to argue that if Phillips sells wedding cakes, he may not discriminate between customers.[141]

A second notable feature of *Masterpiece Cakeshop* is the role of time: the political and constitutional landscape, Kennedy observes, is markedly more respectful toward gay persons than in 2012, when the encounter between Phillips and his would-be customers, Craig and Mullins, occurred. In 2012, Colorado did not permit same-sex couples to marry and, Kennedy writes, it was "not unreasonable" for Phillips to think it lawful to decline to "take an action that he understood to be an expression of support for [such a marriage's] validity." But the world has changed, in part due to the Court's gay rights jurisprudence, including *Windsor* (2013) and *Obergefell* (2015). Kennedy observes: "Our society has come to the recognition that gay persons and gay couples cannot be treated as social outcasts or as inferior in dignity and worth. For that reason the laws and the Constitution can, and in some instances must, protect them in the exercise of their civil rights."[142]

Indeed, Kennedy writes that "it is unexceptional" that laws like CADA "can protect gay persons," as they can protect other classes of individuals, when they seek to acquire "whatever products and services they choose on the same terms and conditions as are offered to other members of the public." This matter-of-fact statement is an important implicit rejection of both the argument that laws like CADA reach too far and the argument that the state's interest in prohibiting race discrimination is far more compelling than addressing other forms of discrimination.[143] Kennedy's opinion also expresses concern about any broad religious exemption to CADA. While gay persons could accept an exception for clergy (from being compelled to perform a ceremony) as not seriously diminishing their "own dignity and worth," he writes:

> If that exception were not confined, then a long list of persons who provide goods and services for marriages and weddings might refuse to do so for gay persons, thus resulting in a community-wide stigma inconsistent with the history and dynamics of civil rights laws that ensure equal access to goods, services, and public accommodations.[144]

In this passage, Kennedy situates CADA in the broader framework of civil rights laws. In another passage, he repeats a concern about the "serious stigma" that would be imposed on "gay persons" if a decision in favor of Phillips, in a hostility-free proceeding, were not "sufficiently constrained": otherwise, "all purveyors of goods and services who object to gay marriage for moral and religious reasons in effect [could] be allowed to put up signs saying 'no goods or services will be sold if they will be used for gay marriages.'"[145] These references to stigma seem to reject arguments that an exemption for religious-based refusals would not impose serious dignitary harm on gays and lesbians.

By contrast, Justice Thomas's concurring opinion fully embraces Phillips's freedom of speech argument, contending that states "cannot punish protected speech because some group finds it offensive, hurtful, stigmatic, unreasonable, or undignified." He rejects, as "foreign" to free speech jurisprudence, Craig and Mullins's appeal to *Heart of Atlanta* on the role of public accommodations laws in protecting would-be customers from denigration of their "dignity."[146] In the only reference to bigotry in any of the opinions, he quotes Justice Alito's *Obergefell* dissent to argue that Phillips may continue to adhere to and express "the traditional understanding" of marriage without being portrayed as bigoted.[147]

In closing, Kennedy offers the following guidance to courts considering future cases: "These disputes must be resolved with tolerance, without undue disrespect to sincere religious beliefs, and without subjecting gay persons to indignities when they seek goods and services in an open market."[148] With Kennedy's retirement, it is difficult to predict how the Court would resolve a future dispute or assess how well a civil rights commission or reviewing court has followed the directive or the guidance offered by Kagan and Breyer.

Masterpiece Cakeshop's hostility holding avoided many complicated issues. When a state law protects LGBT persons from discrimination—so that doing so is the new majority position—to what extent may people with dissenting religious beliefs opt out of the new legal regime? On the one hand, moral or religious disapproval of persons in a protected class is not enough to justify a refusal to obey a public accommodations law. On the other hand, the opinion hints that there may—or should—be some space for people like Phillips to dissent, provided that allowing that space doesn't inflict indignities on gays and lesbians. And in figuring out whether such space is possible, public officials may not show moral disapproval—a "negative normative judgment"—of the religious objections themselves. The focus on how to talk about the problem seems to counsel that public officials addressing these conflicts should avoid polarizing rhetoric at a time when society is undergoing rapid transition. Given that using the rhetoric of animus in gay rights cases lent itself (fairly or unfairly) to charges of branding opponents as bigots, there is a risk that inviting a focus on the hostility or animosity by public officials toward religion could spur charges of anti-religious bigotry and increase polarization.[149]

One early indication of *Masterpiece Cakeshop*'s impact is an opinion issued just a few days after it was decided. An Arizona appellate court cited Kagan's concurring opinion to emphasize that there was no indication that the City of Phoenix had been "anything other than neutral toward and respectful of [the] sincerely-held religious beliefs" of the owners of Brush & Nib Studio when it adopted a new public accommodations ordinance and considered its application to Brush & Nib. The business owners challenged the law before it went into effect, asserting that they were "devout Christians" who could not separate their faith from their work and would be forced to violate their beliefs if they had to "create customer-specific merchandise for same-sex weddings." The Court quoted at length from the majority opinion in *Masterpiece Cakeshop* about society's evolved understanding of the status of gay persons, the basic legitimacy of anti-discrimination laws, and the stigma from broad religious-based refusals. Finally, it quoted Kagan on the general rule that religious disapproval does not allow "escape" from a public accommodations law.[150]

The Supreme Court of Arizona, however, vacated the appellate court opinion (with three of the seven justices dissenting). The court observed that *Masterpiece Cakeshop* "did not hold that public accommodation laws were *immune* from free exercise exemptions" and contemplated that "*some* exemptions, if narrowly confined, were permissible." The court did not challenge the appellate court's finding of no hostility toward the business owners' religion, and it granted that Phoenix's ordinance served the compelling purpose of eradicating discrimination. It concluded, however, that such purpose could not justify forcing the business owners to violate their sincerely held religious beliefs or to compel their speech. On the latter conclusion, the court cited Justice Thomas's *Masterpiece Cakeshop* dissent. In an opening passage evocative of Justice Alito's *Obergefell* dissent, the Arizona Supreme Court declared that free speech and free exercise rights "are not limited to soft murmurings behind the doors of a person's home or church," but include a right to "express" those beliefs in public by creating and selling—and (in this case) by *not* creating and selling. "Tolerance" in a pluralistic society, it concludes, requires protecting such rights.[151]

Conclusion

Charges of being branded as a bigot often relate to the use of analogies between past and present forms of discrimination and exclusion. These charges are often needlessly provocative and groundless. The mere step of drawing analogies between past and present forms of discrimination to point out how, over time, new insights and evolving understandings have led to recognition that such treatment is unjustified is not a charge of bigotry. Nor should a charge be inferred simply from arguments about the constitutional limits of using religious and moral beliefs as a basis for (1) excluding others from a constitutional right or (2) denying them the protection of civil rights laws.[152] As *Masterpiece Cakeshop* illustrated, the respondents and their amici made such arguments while sparingly using the rhetoric of bigotry.

On the other hand, it is also needlessly provocative to portray religious beliefs as a pretext or code word for discrimination in arguing that there must be limits to acting on such beliefs in the marketplace. As *Masterpiece Cakeshop* demonstrated, one can concede religious sincerity while upholding the legitimacy of state anti-discrimination laws. Speaking of pretext focuses too much on bad motive rather than harmful effects and social meaning. The better path, exemplified by Justice Bosson's concurring opinion in *Elane Photography*, is to speak in terms of the requirements of civility and tolerance, or the price of citizenship in a pluralistic society.[153] This concurrence provides a valuable model of respectful rhetoric and of resolving with tolerance, since it explicitly says the Huguenins' beliefs deserve our respect even as it says they must follow New Mexico's law.

Bosson attempted to address the business owners "with utmost respect," while explaining that their freedom to live out their religious beliefs "wherever they lead" in their personal lives must have some limits in "our civic life," including public accommodations. He focuses on the strength of the state's interest in the terms of that civic life to show the force of analogy between forms of discrimination: "The [state] legislature has made it clear that to discriminate in business on the basis of sexual orientation is just as intolerable as discrimination directed toward race, color, national origin, or religion."[154] That intolerance of discrimination is not unreasonable and unwarranted. It is not bigotry or "bullying."

Conclusion

Learning Bigotry's Lessons

Concerns over calling out bigotry in all its forms remain a visible feature of daily public life. People use ecological images to express the harm that bigotry and a "climate of hate" inflict on the "atmosphere of public life" and "the protective layer of civility, which makes political discourse possible."[1] Commentators speak of "rhetorical poison" to describe the bubbling up of expressions of bigotry and hatred, including by elected officials, and the challenge of "quarantining" them.[2] In the United States and abroad, shocking incidents of extremist violence motivated by hatred of religious and racial groups make condemning— and preventing—bigotry urgent. Further, the role of the Internet in fostering hate that erupts into such violence has spurred demands to make social media platforms more accountable.[3]

In the United States, there is both strong agreement over condemning bigotry as inconsistent with American values and sharp partisan disagreement over bigotry's forms and who has the moral authority to call it out. The "who's the bigot?" question with which this book opened is prominent in these conflicts: charges of bigotry are answered with charges of political correctness and countercharges of bigotry. Some speak of political bigotry to warn of a growing intolerance and contempt toward people with different political opinions.[4] As the gears begin to turn for the 2020 election, these conflicts over bigotry are already marked.

In this concluding chapter, I draw some lessons about the rhetoric of bigotry and its puzzles based on this book's examination of past and present controversies over marriage and civil rights. I apply those lessons to some recent battles over calling out bigotry as well as to ongoing conflicts over the legal rights of transgender persons. I ask why the rhetoric of bigotry is not more common in discussion of sexism and misogyny. Finally, I consider whether it is useful— even imperative—to use terms like "bigot" and "bigotry" or whether we should

Who's the Bigot? Linda C. McClain, Oxford University Press (2020). © Oxford University Press.
DOI: 10.1093/oso/9780190877200.001.0001

avoid them or at least be very sparing in using them. What is the way forward to rejecting and preventing the prejudice, intolerance, and discrimination that are given the label of bigotry?

Bigotry's Puzzles, Revisited

In this part, I offer some answers to the four puzzles about bigotry posed in chapter 1.

Bigotry and Motive

The first puzzle was whether bigotry is about the *motivation* for a belief or act. We have seen examples of the argument that a belief or action that is motivated by conscience or a sincere religious belief, rather than by hate, cannot possibly be bigoted. On this logic, if the law prevents people from acting on their conscience, it treats sincere religious believers like bigots. I have argued that equating bigotry only with hateful motives or actions misses the historical prominence of religious bigotry as a form of bigotry. President George Washington's often-quoted reassurance to the Hebrew Congregation of Newport, Rhode Island that "happily, the Government of the United States . . . gives to bigotry no sanction, to persecution no assistance" was that the United States would practice tolerance, not intolerance (religious bigotry).[5]

Religious arguments defending racial segregation and antimiscegenation laws also illustrate the problem with assuming that a belief rooted in conscience or sincere religious belief cannot possibly be bigoted. Such arguments met charges of bigotry with appeals to morality, conscience, scripture, and science. When people read these speeches and sermons today, they may conclude that such appeals were simply a pretext: those clergy and politicians used or twisted religion to justify their prejudice. In *Masterpiece Cakeshop*, discussed in chapter 8, some amici for Jack Phillips distanced sincere believers like Phillips from racist bigots, arguing that the latter used or perverted religion to justify white supremacy. What does "using" mean here? It could mean that they *knew* that they were making pretextual arguments to justify their self-interest. Or it could mean that they read the Bible sincerely and confidently, but wrongly. Recall the segregationist minister in Little Rock who declared, "as sure as I know my name, I know that segregation is pleasing to the Lord." A "creed of segregation" that shaped such ministers' views of the "American creed" helped them oppose integration with a clear conscience.

Religious leaders who condemned racial bigotry and segregation also appealed to conscience and criticized religious defenses of them as twisting or perverting religion and scripture. They cautioned that deeply entrenched prejudice could lead to such distortions. A sobering lesson from the theological defense of racism is that conscience may be mistaken. When the Southern Baptist Convention apologized in 1995 for its failure to condemn slavery and segregation, it stated that the "profoundly distort[ing]" effect of racism on understanding the demands of Christian morality led "some Southern Baptists to believe that racial prejudice and discrimination are compatible with the Gospel."[6] Another lesson is that there is not one religious voice on what conscience demands. Competing appeals to religion have featured in battles over the Civil Rights Act of 1964 (CRA) and in the Supreme Court cases involving race and gay rights.

In sum, the "bigotry versus conscience" framing obscures that a sincere belief or one appealing to conscience may be bigoted, and the recent battles over same-sex marriage and the reach of public accommodations laws suggest that this framing can also be a distraction. In *Masterpiece Cakeshop*, many briefs filed on behalf of the Colorado Civil Rights Commission and Craig and Mullins argued that Colorado's law prohibited merchants like Phillips from discriminating among customers, whatever their motivation. "The question in a discrimination case is not whether any particular person should face moral condemnation as a bigot," but whether there is discrimination that has caused harm to a person.[7] Thus, it is not necessary to label a religious belief bigoted or the moral equivalent of racism to affirm that government has authority to limit one's ability to act on that belief in civic life when doing so harms the rights of others.

Bigotry and Reasonableness

The second puzzle was whether bigotry refers more to the *content* of a belief or attitude than to the motive behind it. On common definitions, bigoted beliefs are strongly held *unreasonable beliefs*. Is it a defense to a charge of bigotry that a belief is *reasonable*? The answer is a qualified "yes," because ideas about what is reasonable and unreasonable change over time in light of moral learning and new insights, typically sparked by social movements seeking justice. As the various struggles over civil rights and marriage presented in this book suggest, the element of time is often critical to contests over what is or is not bigoted.

In struggles over racial segregation in the 1950s and 1960s, opponents of desegregation insisted that what was reasonable and moral in one era must remain so. In the words of Dr. Garner, who testified against the CRA, "moral principles never change": to declare, in 1964, that racial segregation was immoral was to say that "our Founding Fathers" were "immoral men and blasphemers against God."[8] Against this view is the idea of generational moral progress: over time, people come to understand that practices once defended as natural, necessary, or just are subordinating and unjust and lack a reasonable basis. In interpreting the Constitution, new generations realize the Constitution's commitments to liberty and equality. New insights about these commitments lead to repudiating subordinating practices, like antimiscegenation laws and marriage laws based on sex inequality. Justice Kennedy speaks of the Framers understanding that "times can blind us." In 2015, in *Obergefell*, he observed that the Court (a product of its time) failed to see—in 1972—that the fundamental right to marry should extend to same-sex couples. The dissenters, however, rejected this new insights or evolving understanding approach to defining marriage; the universal, unchanging definition of marriage as one man–one woman dated back millennia, was not questioned by those who drafted the Constitution, and, in their view, still had a reasonable basis.

When society has not yet reached a consensus about whether a treatment of a group is unjust or unreasonable, people reach for analogies to the past both to seek such a consensus and to resist it. *Obergefell* and *Masterpiece Cakeshop* suggest that society is at different points in terms of evaluating the reasonableness of moral or religious opposition to interracial marriage and to same-sex marriage. Otherwise, in *Obergefell*, Justice Kennedy would not have referred to the "decent and honorable religious or philosophical premises" that underlie the views of many opponents of same-sex marriage. Nor, in *Masterpiece Cakeshop*, would he have chastised a commissioner for comparing Phillips's "sincerely held religious beliefs" to religious defenses of slavery. Kennedy's opinion implicitly argues that "we need to recognize the virtue of civility as being especially important in . . . transitional moments."[9]

Nonetheless, in *Obergefell*, Justice Kennedy insisted that "sincere, personal opposition" to same-sex marriage could not be enacted into law and policy to exclude same-sex couples from marriage. *Masterpiece Cakeshop* carried that premise forward into the realm of anti-discrimination law: it affirmed protection of "religious and philosophical objections to gay marriage," but also affirmed the general rule that business owners in the marketplace may not act on such objections by denying goods and services. Again, it is not necessary to label a belief as bigoted to justify the limits to acting on religious objections. Charges that someone is being branded as a bigot by being required to comply with a civil rights law can be a distraction.

Bigotry, Time, and Learning from History

The third puzzle is related to bigotry's backward-looking dimension: Is the turn to the term "bigot" or "bigotry" a way of signaling an anachronistic and now-reviled view? The answer is yes, but judgments about bigotry also have a forward-looking dimension. Clearly repudiating beliefs or practices as bigotry may be possible only when a society has already moved significantly away from them. To draw an analogy to economics, bigotry is like a "lagging indicator." A lagging indicator is an economic factor that can be measured only *after* the market moves significantly and the economy begins to follow a specific pattern or trend.[10] As long as such beliefs and practices are contested, people strongly resist charges of bigotry. They may reverse the charges, as did senators who called supporters of the CRA "anti-bigot bigots." Once there is a consensus about beliefs or practices as bigotry, later generations may question how anyone could have defended them since they now seem so clearly immoral, unreasonable, and contrary to core American values.

The forward-looking dimension of bigotry comes into play both when people warn about the flaring up of old forms of bigotry (such as anti-Semitism and white supremacy), and when they draw analogies from these old forms to identify new forms. Learning from the past features in both of these processes, but people do not always agree on the lessons. In the constitutional battle over same-sex marriage, participants vigorously disagreed over the analogy between legal restrictions on interracial marriage and laws defending traditional marriage as between one man and one woman.

The backward-looking dimension of bigotry teaches another lesson: while condemning bigotry seems to be a shared value, the United States has not always lived up to that value. People continue to quote the words of Washington both to affirm that condemning bigotry is a national commitment and to argue that public officials are failing to honor it, in contexts ranging from presidential leadership to immigration policy to LGBTQ rights.[11]

Social scientists Gordon Allport and Gunnar Myrdal spoke of the gap between the American creed and the practice of race discrimination. They urged (as chapter 2 explained) that law could enlist conscience and help to close that gap. In the 1950s and 1960s, as chapters 4 and 5 revealed, religious and political leaders fighting segregation invoked conscience and urged people to live up to America's values. Supporters of the CRA argued that "our spirit is not narrow bigotry" and that all citizens had a stake in renouncing it: the nation must fulfill long-overdue promises of equal citizenship for black citizens. In the battle over the liberty and equality of LGBT persons, reviewed in chapters 6, 7, and 8,

Justice Kennedy's majority opinions appeal to evolving understandings of constitutional guarantees of liberty and equality and new insights about injustice
requiring remedy. In all of these contexts, a shared conviction is that law has a
role to play in closing the gap between professed values and practice.

The role of time in making judgments about bigotry carries risks. One is that
if there is not a consensus today that a discriminatory practice is as evil as a prior
practice, people may conclude that it is not a form of discrimination that the law
should address at all. For example, if people associate racial discrimination only
with the "time-frozen" images of the "blatant white bigotry" of historical figures
like Sheriff Bull Connor, Governor Faubus, and other segregationists, they may
assume that because that era of overt public racism is over, racism itself is a thing
of the past. These "racial ghosts" (as anthropologist John Jackson calls them)
may give a false sense of progress and may distract from present-day problems
like institutional racism and implicit bias.[12]

Anti-racist educator Robin Diangelo suggests that because racism falls on the
"bad" side of the good/bad binary, "to suggest that I am racist is to deliver a deep
moral blow—a kind of character assassination." One reason that white people
may have difficulty perceiving present-day racism is their view that the racist is
"ignorant, bigoted, prejudiced, mean-spirited, old, and Southern" and acts inten-
tionally. To be sure, white supremacists and members of hate groups are potent
present-day symbols of the bad racist, and the persistence of overt racism and
extremist hate should not be denied. But, Diangelo argues, this good/bad binary
misses that "all people hold prejudices, especially across racial lines in a society
deeply divided by race."[13] A focus on bad apples with bad motives, evocative of
famous bigots of the past, distracts from attention to the meaning and effect of
present-day social practices that embody institutional racism and implicit bias.

The Bigot as a Distinct Type versus the Bigot in All Our Brains

The concern about a good/bad binary relates to the fourth puzzle about bigotry
this book has addressed: Is the bigot a distinct type with weak personality or bad
character? Or does singling out "the bigot in our midst" (to quote Allport) miss
"the bigot in our brains": that prejudice is the outgrowth of normal cognitive
processes, like thinking in categories? Is it more accurate to say that we all are
somewhat bigoted?

To speak of the bigot in your brain (discussed in chapter 2) may be a helpful
reminder about how easy it is to get "stuck" in prejudgments about others, which
take place in the "blink of an eye." This image may weaken the strong negative
moral judgment associated with being a bigot. While leading social psychologists

recognize the persistence of overt bigotry, they argue that hidden or implicit bias is the more pervasive form of prejudice despite people's expressed egalitarian beliefs. But they offer a positive, hopeful message, speaking of "good people" with hidden biases: with commitment and effort, it may be possible to recognize and to work to overcome one's biases. However, in a climate of polarization, people sometimes hear even a discussion of implicit bias as a charge of bigotry.

Conflicts over Calling Out Bigotry and Bigotry's Lessons

When people call out bigotry, they urge that we must learn from the past. People do so in the hope that individuals and society can engage in moral learning. Some recent controversies, however, suggest how fraught the rhetoric of bigotry remains. I begin with a recent resolution condemning bigotry adopted by the US House of Representatives. This example shows both that renouncing bigotry is a national commitment, imperfectly realized, and that bigotry has backward- and forward-looking dimensions. Just as Allport warned, in the midst of World War II, that the rise in bigotry threatened democratic values, this resolution shows that people perceive battles over bigotry today as battles over such values. But the controversy over the resolution also highlights disagreement over what the forms of bigotry include and how the "bigotry versus political correctness" dynamic continues to shape battles over bigotry.

The American Creed and Condemning Bigotry

On March 7, 2019, by a bipartisan vote of 407–23, the House of Representatives passed House Resolution 183 (H. Res. 183), which affirms the United States' constitutional commitment to "the principles of tolerance and religious freedom" and to "equal protection of the laws" and declares that "whether from the political right, center, or left, bigotry, discrimination, oppression, racism, and imputations of dual loyalty threaten American democracy and have no place in American political discourse."[14] The resolution gives an expansive list of "traditionally persecuted peoples" who have been targets of bigotry and "weaponiz[ed] hate" in the form of "verbal attacks, incitement, and violence": "African Americans, Latinos, Native Americans, Asian Americans and Pacific Islanders and other people of color, Jews, Muslims, Hindus, Sikhs, the LGBTQ community, immigrants, and others." Most of the resolution, however, focuses on anti-Semitism and anti-Muslim bigotry. The resolution did not specifically name newly elected Representative Ilhan Omar (D-Minnesota), but her tweet that the US government's support of Israel is "all about the Benjamins baby" (referring to the supposed influence on US policy of the lobbying group AIPAC) and her suggestion that Jews who supported Israel had dual loyalty were one reason the resolution emphasized anti-Semitism.[15]

The resolution identifies bigotry, in the form of religious intolerance and racism, as both very old and dangerously present. For example, anti-Semitism is a "centuries-old bigotry and form of racism" that is manifest today in "scapegoating and targeting of Jews," such as the murder of Jews at the Tree of Life Synagogue in October 2018. Similarly, bigotry in the form of "accusations of dual loyalty" against Jews and other religious, ethnic, or racial groups has an "insidious and pernicious history," including dual loyalty accusations directed at Americans of Japanese descent during World War II and at President Kennedy (because of his "Catholic faith"). It is also a present threat, evident in post-9/11 "anti-Muslim bigotry" that includes the "irrational belief that Muslims are inherently violent, disloyal, and foreign."[16]

Bigotry, in the resolution, includes these irrational beliefs about groups and dangerous actions taken against their members, such as a rise in hate crimes against Jews and Muslims and their institutions. In elaborating on white supremacists' bigotry, the resolution lists Charlottesville and the murder by a white nationalist of African American church members at Emmanuel African Methodist Episcopal Church in Charleston, South Carolina, "in the hopes of igniting a race war."[17]

H. Res. 183 treats condemning all forms of bigotry as a national imperative. It invokes Dr. King for the proposition that "persecution of any American is an assault on the rights and freedoms of all Americans." It further asserts:

> All Americans, including Jews, Muslims, and Christians, and people of all faiths and no faith, have a stake in fighting anti-Semitism, as all Americans have a stake in fighting every form of bigotry and hatred against people based on religion, race, or place of birth and origin.

The resolution urges public officials to act so that "the United States will live up to the transcendent principles of tolerance, religious freedom, and equal protection as embodied in the Declaration of Independence and the First and 14th amendments to the Constitution."

It condemns bigotry as contrary to "the values that define the people of the United States." By encouraging "all public officials to confront the reality of anti-Semitism, Islamophobia, racism, and other forms of bigotry, as well as historical struggles against them," it urges that people learn from the past.[18]

Members of Congress who spoke in support of H. Res. 183 also appealed to "our constitutional creed" of tolerance and pluralism.[19] They stressed learning from past failures to call out bigotry. For example, Representative Jerry Nadler (D-New York) described the resolution's unambiguous condemnation of anti-Semitism, anti-Muslim bigotry, and "all forms of prejudice against minorities" as a "statement of our values as a Nation," but added: "Often, our Nation has fallen short of its ideals when they succumbed to the demagoguery of bigots." In that shortfall, he included his colleagues, who, "on both sides of the aisle," had perpetrated "religious and other forms of bigotry."[20]

Representative Steny Hoyer (D-Maryland) observed that "none of us ought to . . . think that we have not fallen short of the principles enunciated in our Declaration [of Independence]"; "if we are to be better than our past, we must reject all forms of bigotry and prejudice directed at any of our fellow human beings and fellow Americans."[21]

But even a resolution condemning bigotry proved controversial. Some of the twenty-three Republicans who voted against it objected that the resolution was "watered down" and "spineless"; by expanding beyond anti-Semitism to include so many other forms of bigotry, it became "so generic that it lost its meaning or significance."[22] (Some Democrats voiced a similar criticism, but in the end, all of them voted for the resolution.) Trump called the resolution "disgraceful" for not expressly criticizing Representative Omar's remarks and labeled Democrats as the "anti-Jewish party." Other Republicans complained that the resolution was underinclusive. Representative Brooks (R-Alabama) criticized its "intentional" and "insulting" omission of discrimination against "Caucasian-Americans and Christians."[23] Representative Collins (R-Georgia) noted the omission of the Church of Jesus Christ of Latter-day Saints, Jehovah's Witnesses, Wiccans, and "disabled people," while insisting: "We don't need a manual to tell us who we can't hate."[24] These negative votes on a resolution condemning bigotry led Republican commentator Jennifer Rubin to marvel that "Republicans have learned nothing" in the last few years: they "remain frightened if not in agreement with the xenophobic, white-grievance crowd, which equates condemning bigotry with 'political correctness.' "[25]

Problems of Moral Authority and Selectivity

As the battle over H. Res. 183 suggests, efforts to condemn bigotry may become mired in questions over which bigotry to call out, or the problem of moral selectivity. Other conflicts concern who has moral authority to call out bigotry and whether people weaponize charges of bigotry for political purposes. On moral selectivity, consider the aftermath of Representative Steve King (R-Iowa) asking aloud: "White nationalist, white supremacist, Western civilization—how did that language become offensive?"[26] His Republican colleagues called him out, took away his committee assignments, and suggested that he resign. Senator Ted Cruz stated that Americans "ought to be united, regardless of party in saying 'white supremacism,' 'white nationalism,' is hatred, it is bigotry, it is evil, it is wrong.' "[27] Critics, however, asked why it took Republicans so long to condemn King, given his fifteen-year record of racially provocative statements. Some contended that King provided Republicans a "safer" and more convenient target than President Trump—"the sacrifice of one wretched bigot to atone for the indulgence of another."[28] Back in Iowa, some of King's supporters insisted he was not a bigot, but just "one of us . . . a pro-life, pro-gun, pro-conservative person."[29]

An incident illustrating disputes about moral authority and weaponizing bigotry concerns President Trump denouncing Representative Omar for the anti-Semitic comments mentioned earlier. After Democratic House leadership issued a joint statement demanding an apology, saying that "Omar's use of anti-Semitic tropes and prejudicial accusations about Israel's supporters is deeply offensive," Omar issued an "unequivocal" apology. She added: "Anti-Semitism is real and I am grateful for Jewish allies and colleagues who are educating me on the painful history of anti-Semitic tropes."[30] President Trump, however, stated that Omar's "lame" apology was not enough since "what she said is so deep-seated in her heart"; he suggested that she resign. Omar retorted: "You have trafficked in hate your whole life—against Jews, Muslims, Indigenous, immigrants, black people, and more. I learned from people impacted by my words. When will you?"[31]

This exchange prompted public discussion about who has moral authority to call out bigotry. Some journalists insisted: "If we're going to demand that politicians apologize for any hint of association with bigotry," we should hold all of Omar's critics "to the same standard"—including Trump.[32] Journalists recapped Trump's numerous bigoted statements for which he neither apologized nor resigned.[33] MSNBC's anchor Chris Hayes argued that "the president has no moral standing whatsoever" and that his Republican party was "fine with all kinds of bigotry." Hayes asked Rabbi Jill Jacobs (Executive Director for T'ruah: the Rabbinic Call for Human Rights) for a "clear standard" about "bigotry, its place, [and] what is worth apologizing for or resigning over?" Jacobs answered that "it's very clear that bigotry is not OK in our public discourse"; because "it's also clear" that racism, sexism, anti-Semitism, homophobia, and xenophobia are "deeply rooted in our society," we "have a responsibility" to call out bigotry "whenever we see it," whether "on the left or the right." She did not believe that there was "one standard that says once somebody crosses this line, then they have to re-sign," but she expressed concern about weaponizing bigotry—using calls only for "our own political means."[34] Jacobs described Trump's calling for Omar's resignation as weaponizing, given his own statements after Charlottesville. She also questioned his moral authority, asserting that he had "made common cause with White nationalists and spurred the kind of hatred that ultimately led a terrorist to walk into [the Tree of Life] synagogue in Pittsburgh and murder 11 Jews while they were praying."[35]

These highly publicized incidents show some of the difficulties with calling out bigotry. Omar's remarks also spurred attention to the need to distinguish carefully between (1) voicing criticism of Israel's policies and (2) resorting to prejudicial, bigoted anti-Semitic images or tropes to do so.[36] So, too, the flurry of anti-Muslim imagery in postings targeting Omar triggered discussion of the distinction between legitimate criticism and anti-Muslim bigotry.

Learning Bigotry's Lessons: The Example of Transgender Rights

What lessons does this book's study of the rhetoric of bigotry offer concerning controversies over the status and rights of transgender persons? These controversies show the inevitable look to past civil rights struggles when a society is wrestling with whether treatment of a particular group is unjust discrimination. Some arguments for transgender rights enlist the language of bigotry to condemn such discrimination, but other arguments connect past and present without such language. Opponents of transgender rights deny that their positions are bigoted, and also claim that they are being wrongly branded as bigots for their beliefs about sex and gender.

"Bathroom Bigotry"?

In recent years, the Equal Employment Opportunity Commission has interpreted the CRA's protection of workers against employment discrimination (in Title VII) based on sex to include discrimination based on sexual orientation and gender identity. Some federal courts have agreed, but others have not. In early 2019, the Supreme Court announced that it would review three cases concerning whether such federal protection extends to transgender and gay workers.[37] Soon after, the House of Representatives passed a law expressly amending the CRA to include protection against discrimination based on sexual orientation and gender identity; the Senate and White House oppose such an amendment, appealing to conscience and concerns for "the safety of women and girls in intimate spaces."[38] Reversing the Obama administration's approach, the Trump administration has proposed that the legal definition of sex in federal civil rights laws should be "a person's status as male or female based on immutable biological traits identifiable by or before birth"; the sex on one's birth certificate would be "definitive proof" of sex unless *genetic* evidence rebutted it.[39]

One eye-catching poster at a protest against the Trump administration's announced approach to defining sex and gender read: "To bigotry no sanction. To persecution no assistance. George Washington, 1790."[40] The bigotry under attack was this proposed narrowing of sex, reversing Obama Administrative guidelines that transgender persons should be protected against discrimination in employment and education (under Title IX of the CRA). Trump's head of the Office of Civil Rights, Roger Severino (formerly of the Heritage Foundation) had criticized the Obama administration for using "government power to coerce everyone, including children, into pledging allegiance to a radical new gender ideology over and above their right to privacy, safety, and religious freedom."[41] That ideology would "impose a new definition of what it means to be a man or a woman on the entire nation."[42]

Within the United States, twenty states and the District of Columbia have embraced this supposedly radical ideology: they expressly include gender identity in their anti-discrimination laws. Many cities do as well, including in states without such laws. By contrast, twenty-eight states do not have such protections.[43] In that group, some states also have laws expressly prohibiting such protection, including conscience protection laws and bathroom bills that require persons to use the bathroom that corresponds with their assigned sex at birth (male or female) rather than the gender with which they identify. Several US Civil Rights Commissioners (in the *Peaceful Coexistence* report discussed in chapter 8) referred to such laws as "an orchestrated, nationwide effort by extremists to promote bigotry, cloaked in the mantle of 'religious freedom.'"[44] Those statements drew sharp criticism from religious leaders for branding religious beliefs as bigotry.

Why label these bills "bathroom bigotry"?[45] Some do so to refer to the "ignorance" and "fact-free fear mongering" that supporters of such laws display—for example, arguing that men will claim to be women in order to harass, prey upon, and assault girls and women in women's restrooms.[46] Robin Fretwell Wilson aptly describes these supposed safety concerns that lack any factual basis as "the nonsense about bathrooms."[47]

One op-ed, "America's Bathroom Bigotry, Then and Now," reminds readers of past times when "bigotry was so ordinary that it was not even recognized as bigotry—except by the victims," as in workplaces that routinely excluded racial and religious minorities.[48] The author recalled how, in 1960, a Japanese woman sent by a temp agency to work in an insurance company (that had no employees of color) was let go after one day because of complaints by female employees after she used the ladies' room. The author draws parallels between the lingering of World War II-era slurs and "idiotic notions" about the Japanese—even into the early 1960s—and current anxieties and fears about transgender persons.[49]

The label "bathroom bigotry" also signals that there are important lessons to be learned from past forms of now-repudiated discrimination, such as racially segregated restrooms. Powerful appeals to that history, however, can be made even without using the rhetoric of bigotry. One example is former Attorney General Loretta Lynch's explanation of why the Department of Justice was going to sue North Carolina over its law, House Bill 2. That law required transgender persons in public agencies to use bathrooms consistent with their sex as noted at birth, rather than bathrooms that fit their gender identity. In arguing that H.B. 2 violated federal civil rights laws, Lynch invoked a progress narrative about the nation learning from past experiences about discrimination. "This action is about a great deal more than bathrooms," she urged. It concerns the "the dignity and respect we accord our fellow citizens" and "the founding ideals that have led this country—haltingly but inexorably—in the direction of fairness, inclusion and equality for all Americans." Lynch connected the current struggle over the rights of transgender persons to prior struggles over the civil rights of African Americans and same-sex couples:

> This is not the first time that we have seen discriminatory responses to historic moments of progress for our nation. We saw it in the Jim Crow laws that followed the Emancipation Proclamation. We saw it in the fierce and widespread resistance to *Brown v. Board of Education*. And we saw it in the proliferation of state bans on same-sex unions intended to stifle any hope that gay and lesbian Americans might one day be afforded the right to marry.[50]

Lynch noted the flurry of bills like H.B. 2 "taking aim at the LGBT community" in the wake of *Obergefell*'s recognition of same-sex couples' right to marry. Noting that some responses reflect "a recognizably human fear of the unknown, and a discomfort with the uncertainty of change," she urged: "This is not a time to act out of fear," but instead "to summon our national virtues of inclusivity, diversity, compassion, and open-mindedness."

Speaking to her fellow North Carolinians, Lynch reminded them of the not-so-distant past, when "states, including North Carolina, had signs above restrooms, water fountains and on public accommodations keeping people out based upon a distinction without a difference." She urged that we "learn from history and avoid repeating the mistakes of the past": "State-sanctioned discrimination never looks good in hindsight." Instead, she implored, "Let us write a different story this time." History also offered lessons to the transgender community, she counseled: "Please know that history is on your side."[51]

In these remarks, Lynch draws on a narrative of the United States making continuing moral progress toward realizing the "promise of equal rights for all."[52] Her speech powerfully connected past and present forms of discrimination without labeling anyone a bigot.

North Carolina, however, resisted this history lesson and joined with other states to sue the DOJ. After the 2016 presidential election, the DOJ, headed by Jefferson Beauregard Sessions, swiftly withdrew the Obama-era guidance documents (such as "Dear Colleague Letters" about the civil rights of transgender students) that had interpreted federal civil rights laws prohibiting sex discrimination to require "access to sex-segregated facilities," such as bathrooms and locker rooms, "based on gender identity."[53] The new "Dear Colleague" letter called for further consideration of the legal issues and also for "due regard" to the primary role of states and local school districts in establishing educational policy. The letter also cited a ruling by a federal district court in Texas that sex, in the federal regulations implementing Title IX, "unambiguously refers to biological sex" (i.e., as determined at birth).[54]

But the court of public opinion led, in 2017, to a partial repeal of North Carolina's law (H.B. 2), which newly elected Governor Roy Cooper, a Democrat, called "an important step to restore our reputation and remove discrimination from our law."[55] A similar concern over reputational harm has played a powerful role in other states that have considered but not passed bathroom laws. In 2016, Texas Governor Greg Abbott and Lieutenant Governor Dan Patrick supported a bill that would require transgender persons to use public restrooms in schools, government buildings, and public universities that corresponded with their biological sex, and would invalidate local ordinances protecting against discrimination on the basis of sexual orientation and gender identity. The Texas business community and LGBTQ advocates fought the bill, leading to such local headlines as "Business Leaders to Battle Bigots in Austin" and "Battle of the Bathroom Bigots."[56] The Texas Association of Business prepared a report, *Keep Texas Open For Business: The Economic Impact of Discriminatory Law on Texas*, which nowhere expressly referred to bigotry, but detailed how "discriminatory legislation," like the proposed Texas law, ran counter to public opinion and corporate policies prioritizing "diversity and inclusion." Cautioning against efforts to strengthen Texas's Religious Freedom Restoration Act by overriding local nondiscrimination laws, the report observed that a high percentage of millennials favor comprehensive nondiscrimination laws and believe that "religion should focus on promoting tolerance and peace rather than on opposing gay rights."[57]

The Texas bill was defeated in 2017. Despite the absence of the language of bigotry in the *Keep Texas Open for Business* report, news stories referred to business leaders joining with LGBT advocates to defeat "bigoted laws" that would tarnish Texas's image and cost billions of dollars.[58] The report offered concrete evidence of those costs, as in states like North Carolina, which experienced boycotts by athletic organizations and large businesses. In running for reelection in 2018, Governor Abbott, facing an openly lesbian Democratic opponent who fought against bathroom bills, indicated that a bathroom bill was no longer on his agenda.[59]

This example suggests how competing appeals to values play out in conflicts over the marketplace, moralizing it in different ways. In *Masterpiece Cakeshop*, many religious and conservative groups urged that business owners had a right to live out their faith and deepest moral convictions in the marketplace, and that expansive anti-discrimination laws threatened that freedom. In Texas, opponents of bathroom bills argued that potential employers, employees, and tourists would affirm values of diversity and nondiscrimination in the marketplace by using the power of boycott and voting with their feet.

The Retort That Biology Isn't Bigotry

In response to the rhetoric of bathroom bigotry, some retort that "biology isn't bigotry."[60] Such appeals are not explicitly religious; they invoke science, as I will discuss. But that does not mean that religious beliefs are irrelevant to objections to transgender rights. Consider Mississippi's H.B. 1523, called the Protection of Conscience from Discrimination Act. H.B. 1523 protects from any form of governmental "discrimination" a cluster of "sincerely held religious beliefs or moral convictions," including that being male or female is immutably fixed at birth by one's biological sex, and that "sexual relations are properly reserved" to marriage, which is "the union of one man and one woman."[61] Someone with such beliefs might argue that bathroom bills are a common sense recognition of natural, God-given, immutable sex differences, not bigotry. Similarly, in one of the three Title VII cases the Supreme Court will decide this term (mentioned in a prior section), *R.G. & G.R. Harris Funeral Homes v. EEOC*, a funeral home owner who fired a transgender female employee, Aimee Stephens, because she planned to live and work as a woman and wear a skirt-suit to work. The owner, Thomas Rost, argued that because he "interprets the Bible as teaching that sex is immutable, he believed that he 'would be violating God's commands' if a male representative of Harris Homes presented himself as a woman [by wearing a skirt-suit] while representing the company."[62]

The "biology, not bigotry" refrain also appeals to science. After the news media leaked the Trump administration's plans to reverse the Obama administration's approach to gender identity, an op-ed published in the *Christian Post* invited people to sign a petition applauding the Trump administration's intention to "uphold the scientific definition of sex in federal law and policy, such that girls and women will regain their sex-based legal protections, and the human rights of all will be preserved." The petition's author, Michael Brown, an evangelical author and host of the radio show *Line of Fire*, protests that the "thesis" that "biological sex should be determined biologically" is now considered bigoted. The petition invokes science to state that human sex "is a binary, biologically determined, and immutable trait from conception forward" and that "sex differences are real and consequential." People who "do not feel at their home [*sic*] with their biological sex (i.e., transgenders) [*sic*] should be treated with dignity and respect under the law," but their "optimal medical treatment" should be "influenced by biological sex."[63]

The petition employs the tactic of charging that one is being branded as a bigot—despite no express mention of bigotry. It asserts that the American Association of University Professors (AAUP), critics of the Trump administration's announced position, would view the petition's signers as "obviously bigots."[64] While the AAUP statement criticizes the Trump administration for insisting upon a "biological basis for gender that has been thoroughly discredited" by research and "lived experience," it nowhere labels the administration bigoted. It flips Severino's charge of "gender ideology" to argue that it is politicians and "religious fundamentalists" who offer gender ideology to "override the insights of serious scholars" at the expense of transgender and gender nonconforming people.[65]

These competing views about defining sex and gender show how battles over civil rights often implicate science and whether positions have a reasonable basis or rest on prejudice, fears, and stereotypes. Religious leaders, politicians, and lawyers invoked science both to defend and attack racial segregation and antimiscegenation laws. Recall *Loving v. Virginia*, when Virginia's attorney attempted to counter the UNESCO report's rejection of any scientific basis for antimiscegenation laws with sociologist Rabbi Gordon's book against intermarriage. Changing scientific understandings of sexuality and sexual orientation—such as the American Psychiatric Association's (APA) shift away from considering homosexuality a disorder—featured in the Court's evolving protection of rights. Scientific understandings of the relationship between biological sex and gender identity are also evolving. In 2013, the APA replaced the term "gender identity disorder" with "gender dysphoria," evidently a shift away from framing transgender identity as pathological and a mental illness to "a rare but normal variation of the human experience."[66]

Generational Change and Fear

As with earlier civil rights battles, both generational change and fear of such change feature in the transgender rights struggle. Just as I opened this book with two advice columns using the language of bigotry, so I offer another advice column to illustrate these dynamics. In December 2018, "Mother of a Free Spirit" wrote to *The Sweet Spot* columnists, Steve Almond and Cheryl Strayed (the "Dear Sugars"), asking whether her reaction to her fifteen-year-old daughter's announcement that she "wants to date a transgender boy" was "shallow and judgmental." The mother's "older Latina mother, who lives with us, disapproves"; the mother herself feels "uncomfortable." The mother also expresses discomfort that some of the kids her daughter hangs out with are "really odd in appearance" and "very narrowly" focused on "gender issues." In the past, the mother has been proud of the daughter's compassion in befriending and helping transgender children, but now she is concerned about her daughter being "labeled" by her peers at school.[67]

The mother's emotions recall the discomfort of the white liberal father as he told Dr. Karpf (in chapter 3) about the family crisis created when his daughter, who previously socialized with black friends, announced that she had a black fiancé. In effect, this column suggests a new variation on the question: "Would you want your child to date/marry a ____?" Answers to that question, we have seen, have served as a measure of prejudices and shifting attitudes toward certain religious, ethnic, and racial groups in the United States.

The mother, who wants to "do what's best" and support her "free spirit" daughter (who identifies as "pansexual"), seeks advice on how to distinguish between "experimental teenage stuff" and "who [her daughter] is." She does not ask, "Am I a bigot?," and neither columnist calls her one. However, one (Steve Almond) connects two kinds of bigotry—ethnic and anti-LBGTQ—in a way that connects fears and generational change. He expresses sympathy for the mother's evident anxiety that her daughter's "sexual identity and desires" aren't "heteronormative": "It's hard enough to move through a world fraught with bigotry as a Latino woman. It becomes that much harder when you identify as pansexual and have a transgender partner." But he also refers to "systems of bigotry" that have shaped the mother's generation's attitudes about gender identity and sexuality, including discomfort about her daughter's friends:

> We're living in a cultural moment in which kids like your daughter are free to think more openly about who they are and whom they might choose to love. That can be unsettling for those of us who grew up without those freedoms, and within systems of bigotry that assailed those freedoms as unnatural or sinful.

Almond praises the mother for being "willing to bear the risks of self-examination" and the daughter for offering the mother the opportunity to "reckon" with the younger generation's freer and more fluid approach to gender identity and sexuality.[68] This advice, referring to "systems of bigotry" and generational change, seems more likely to persuade than dismissing the mother as a bigot.

Are Sexism and Misogyny Bigotry?

Along with ungrounded fears and ignorance about transgender people, deep beliefs about sex and gender also shape the controversies over transgender rights. These beliefs invite a puzzling question: Are sexism and misogyny aptly called bigotry? To be sure, sexism and misogyny do sometimes appear in long lists of all the ways in which President Trump and his administration are bigoted.[69] But the language of bigotry features more often in condemning racism, anti-Semitism, and hostility toward immigrants. In fact, people seem to turn more often to the language of bigotry to criticize transphobia (as just discussed) and homophobia than sexism and misogyny. The 2019 House resolution condemning bigotry, for example, included "the LGBTQ community" among "traditionally persecuted peoples," but did not include women.

If this observation about sexism and the rhetoric of bigotry is true, what might explain it?[70] One answer might center on the belief that there are fundamental differences between men and women. After all, the Supreme Court has recognized that "inherent differences" between men and women "remain cause for celebration," while explaining that such differences may not be the cause for "denigration" and that gender stereotyping may not limit women's and men's opportunities to contribute to the life of the nation.[71] As chapter 6 discussed, defenders of Virginia's DOMA laws unsuccessfully appealed to this language to portray the one man–one woman definition of marriage as celebrating and preserving sex difference and gender complementarity.

Another reason may be the association of bigotry with hate and antipathy toward a religious, racial, or ethnic minority: in constitutional law parlance, a "discrete and insular minority." Not only are women not a minority, they are not "insular" in the sense of being socially isolated from or having limited social contact with men.[72] Sexism as a form of prejudice was scarcely mentioned in Allport's foundational work, *The Nature of Prejudice*, perhaps because of the association of prejudice with an irrational antipathy—or because the book predated the second wave feminist movement. In the decades since, social psychologists have identified sexism as a form of prejudice, taking two forms: "hostile" sexism, such as misogynistic and hateful views of women as a group, and "benevolent" sexism, such as stereotypes about women's supposed positive traits that serve as a reason for them occupying different roles in society.[73] If people associate bigotry with hostility and bad motives, it may seem inapt to call benevolent sexism bigoted.

Hostile sexism, or misogyny, would seem to fit definitions of bigotry that concern irrational hatred or contempt toward a group. Some feminists do speak of misogyny as bigotry.[74] Yet at least until recently, studies of hate groups have overlooked the intersection of misogyny with, for example, white supremacy and that misogyny is "a dangerous and underestimated component of extremism."[75] In the United Kingdom, for example, protests about the absence of misogyny (and misandry) from the hate crimes law spurred the Law Commission to look at whether there were any "gaps" in the law, which included newer protected characteristics, such as sexual orientation and transgender identity, along with more traditional ones, like race and religion.[76]

I am not proposing to expand the usage of the term "bigotry" to encompass sexism, but simply noting the relative absence of a discourse surrounding sexism, misogyny, and bigotry. It may be that the terms "sexism" and "misogyny" are more effective than "bigotry." That said, as "misogyny" seems to be eclipsing "sexism" (or "chauvinism") in popular use—both as a synonym for sexism and to describe institutional structures creating inequalities—there is a concern over moral inflation. When so many things fit under the same umbrella, the term may lose its power.[77] It may be more accurate and clear-headed to call sexism and misogyny by those names rather than to conflate them with bigotry.

Whether and When to Call Out Bigotry

A similar concern over moral inflation attends the use of the rhetoric of bigotry generally: Is one term doing too much work, so that it lacks a clear meaning? Or does the word carry such a heavy moral charge that people believe it should apply only in extreme situations? In highly publicized examples of activists and politicians on the left and right being called bigots for racist or anti-Semitic remarks, some respond, "That's not who I am."[78] They may be urging critics not to dismiss them as morally flawed or beyond redemption based on a single remark. This raises some practical questions about calling out bigotry: When is the language of bigotry imperative, and when should we be sparing in using such language?

In writing this book I have done unscientific polling of family, friends, colleagues, and students on what they think the terms "bigot" and "bigotry" mean and whether they personally find them imperative or even useful. About half insist that it is very important to call out bigotry. The other half avoids the term. Some say it is needlessly polarizing and shuts down conversation; an

additional reason is that they believe more precise terms that name the particular problem are available and more effective. (Such an intuition may underlie
the relative absence of bigotry in discussions of sexism and misogyny.)

Can calling out bigotry be a constructive step in persons freeing themselves
from bigoted beliefs or conduct? During the civil rights movement (as discussed
in chapter 4), ministers who preached against segregation spoke of the need to
reach and free prejudiced persons from the prison of their prejudices. Some
spoke of redeeming the bigot. What can those sermons teach us today?

Some critics of call-out culture worry that it offers no chance for redemption
and no role for empathy: those who call out insist that bigots should be held
accountable and the consequences should be swift and certain. David Brooks,
for example, warns about "binary thinking in which people are categorized as
good or evil."[79] His primary call out examples concern sexual harassment. As
the #MeToo movement gained heightened visibility, and more women spoke
out about sexual harassment and sexual assault, high-level executives no longer
seemed immune from consequences. A chart published in the New York Times
showed that a large number of men had been fired as a result of such charges and
also that nearly half of their replacements were women.[80] Is this zero-tolerance
model an appropriate one for the consequences of calling out bigotry? The answer may depend on the underlying conduct.

Whether to call out bigotry may depend on whether there is hope of a constructive engagement and change. Within social justice movements, an interesting idea of "calling in," as an alternative to the toxicity of "calling out" and
"cancelling" people, has emerged: if an activist within such a movement engages
in problematic speech or behavior, speak to them respectfully privately or sometimes publicly and look for a constructive solution. As black feminist and activist
Loretta Ross argues, this approach recognizes that people have prejudices, are
imperfect, and will make—and hopefully, learn from—mistakes.[81]

To shift away from a fixed, irredeemable type, "the bigot," to the problem of
bigoted beliefs and conduct, is to shift to how to prevent bigotry and prejudice
and combat the thinking that leads to prejudiced views and actions. In the 1940s
and 1950s, Allport and his colleagues stressed several ways to do so: education
in the home and in the school; moral leadership by political, religious, and cultural figures; social contact between members of groups on terms of equality;
and, last but not least, laws prohibiting discrimination and promoting tolerance.
These ways remain important today in a polarized polity as we seek to foster
civility and to close the gap between professed commitments to equality and
other values and actual practices that fail to live up to those commitments and
values.

NOTES

Chapter 1

1. Abigail Van Buren, *Bigots—They're More to Be Pitied Than Censured*, L.A. Times, Sept. 11, 1966, at D5.
2. *Id.*
3. Abigail Van Buren, *Anti-Semitism Could Be Hazardous to Your Health*, Deseret News (Sept. 23, 1992) (reprinting piece by Sam Levenon about anti-Jewish bigots); *Jews of the Week: Dear Abby & Ann Landers*, Jew of the Week (May 22, 2013), https://perma.cc/ J876-H3KL.
4. Philip Galanes, *Social Q's: Bigotry, Defused*, N.Y. Times, Aug. 6, 2017 (Style, p. 8).
5. *Id.*
6. John Corvino, *Trump, Bigotry, and the Ethics of Stigma*, Kennedy Institute of Ethics Journal (July 20, 2017), https://perma.cc/ZY3V-469W.
7. *Id.* (arguing that the term "bigot" "functions as a conversation stopper").
8. *Compare* Amy McCarthy, *You're Morally Obligated to Call Out Your Racist Relatives at Thanksgiving*, Eater (Nov. 20, 2018, 9:32 AM), https://perma.cc/DEH9-PVG5, *with* Doug Friednash, *Political Civility Needs to Be on the Thanksgiving Menu*, Denver Post (Oct. 28, 2018, 9:42 AM), https://perma.cc/RXR8-U3F7.
9. Reva Siegel makes a similar argument about how people "retrospectively judge" as "evil" what was once justified as reasonable. *See* Reva B. Siegel, *Why Equal Protection No Longer Protects: The Evolving Form of Status-Enforcing State Action*, 49 Stanford Law Review 1111, 1112 (1997). Thanks to Doug NeJaime for suggesting this connection between Siegel's and my work. Douglas NeJaime, *Bigotry in Time: Race, Sexual Orientation, and Gender*, 99 Boston University Law Review 2651, 2652–53 (2019).
10. 110 Cong. Rec. 14480 (June 19, 1964) (statement of Sen. Byrd).
11. William M. Ramsey, *Bigotry and Religious Belief*, 94 Pacific Philosophical Quarterly 125, 126 (2013).
12. Steven Levitsky and Daniel Ziblatt, How Democracies Die 168 (New York: Crown, 2018).
13. Chart, GDELT Television Explorer, https://perma.cc/F5GN-M4DN (searched Bloomberg, CNBC, CNN, FoxNews and MSNBC transcripts from 2009–2019 for the word "bigot").
14. Republican Party Platform 2016, at 9, https://perma.cc/TL2S-A37B; Democratic Platform 2016, at 18, https://perma.cc/3EJF-TUDG.
15. Ali Vitali, *Trump: "Hillary Clinton Is a Bigot,"* Politics (Aug. 24, 2016), https://perma.cc/ Q94T-93PM.
16. Maegan Vazquez, *George W. Bush: Bigotry and White Supremacy Are "Blasphemy" Against the American Creed*, CNN (Oct. 19, 2017), https://perma.cc/SMM5-EWGH ("emboldened");

Sasha Abramsky, *How Trump Has Normalized the Unspeakable*, NATION (Sept. 20, 2017), https://perma.cc/Y3ZS-489U; Michael Gerson, *Trump Deepens the Moral Damage to the GOP*, WASH. POST (Aug. 28, 2017), https://perma.cc/LS8L-GFC8.

17. *CAIR Report Shows 2017 On Track to Becoming One of the Worst Years Ever for Anti-Muslim Hate Crimes*, COUNCIL ON AMERICAN ISLAMIC RELATIONS (July 17, 2017), https://perma.cc/SS6T-RWR5.

18. Mythili Sampathkumar, *Trump Impeachment Vote to Happen Next Week, Congressman Promises*, THE INDEPENDENT (Nov. 30, 2017) (quoting Representative Al Green as calling Trump "a billionaire bigot who tolerates anti-Semitism, racism, sexism, ethnocentrism, xenophobia, and homophobia"), https://perma.cc/YL6S-SAHE; Charles M. Blow, *Trump Is a Racist. Period*, N.Y. TIMES, Jan. 15, 2018, at A19.

19. *See Sean Hannity Show*, FOX NEWS TODAY, Dec. 26, 2017 (guest Todd Starnes calls CNN "a dog whistle for race baiting anti-Trump bigots" and argues that those who oppose Trump are bigoted), Dec. 26, 2017 LEXIS News Transcripts 122601cb.253; Shelby Steele, *The Soft Bigotry of Political Correctness*, HOOVER INSTITUTION (Apr. 24, 2017), https://perma.cc/4X2Q-LM9U.

20. LEVITSKY AND ZIBLATT, 168, 222.

21. Rebecca Nelson, *2019's Barrier-Breaking Politicians Get to Work*, MARIE-CLAIRE (Jan. 3, 2019) (for example, Representative Escobar), https://perma.cc/9YYH-SUQC.

22. Kim Hart, *Exclusive Poll: Most Democrats See Republicans as Racist, Sexist*, AXIOS (Nov. 12, 2018).

23. David Blankenhorn, *The Top 14 Causes of Political Polarization*, THE AMERICAN INTEREST (May 16, 2018) (quoting AMY CHUA, POLITICAL TRIBES (New York: Penguin, 2018)), https://perma.cc/E3ZN-248S.

24. Joey Clark, *The Most Pervasive Bigotry Isn't What You Think*, FOUNDATION FOR ECONOMIC EDUCATION (Aug. 22, 2017), https://perma.cc/GLN6-UGCG.

25. *From George Washington to the Hebrew Congregation in Newport, Rhode Island, August 18, 1790*, FOUNDERS ONLINE (Mar. 9, 2018), https://perma.cc/V24F-XTTH.

26. Brief of Constitutional Law Scholars as Amici Curiae in Support of Respondents at 13, Trump v. Hawaii, 138 S. Ct. 2392 (2018) (No. 17-965) (quoting *Letter from Washington to the Jews (Aug. 18, 1790)*).

27. Executive Order 13769, Protecting the Nation from Foreign Terrorist Entry into the U.S., 82 Fed. Reg. 8977 (Jan. 27, 2017).

28. Trump v. Hawaii, 138 S. Ct. 2392, 2418 (2018).

29. Loving v. Virginia, 388 U.S. 1 (1967).

30. *Civil Rights—Public Accommodations: Hearing on S. 1732 Before the S. Comm. on Commerce*, 88th Cong. 1147–50 (1963) (statement of Dr. Albert Garner, President, Florida Baptist Institute & Seminary).

31. Obergefell v. Hodges, 135 S. Ct. 2584, 2626 (2015) (Roberts, C.J., dissenting).

32. *Id.*, 2602.

33. Brief for Petitioners at 1, 2, 8–9, Masterpiece Cakeshop v. Colorado Civil Rights Commission et al., 138 S. Ct. 1719 (2018) (No. 16-111).

34. Amicus Curiae Brief of Ryan T. Anderson, PhD et al., in Support of Petitioners at 3–4, *Masterpiece Cakeshop* (Anderson Brief).

35. Brief of Amicus Curiae Sherif Girgis Supporting Petitioners at 17, *Masterpiece Cakeshop*.

36. *See* Richard A. Epstein, *The Government's Civil Rights Bullies*, DEFINING IDEAS (Sept. 26, 2016), https://perma.cc/LA86-P3KG.

37. John Corvino, *Puzzles About Bigotry: A Reply to McClain*, 99 BOSTON UNIVERSITY LAW REVIEW 2587, 2590 (2019).

38. Heidi Beirich, *Is Demography Really Destiny?*, INTELLIGENCE REPORT, Issue 166 (Spring 2019) (Southern Poverty Law Center) (introducing special report on "the year in hate and extremism").

39. *See Definition of bigotry by the Free Dictionary*, https://perma.cc/HJ4E-8Q68 (collecting several definitions mentioning "prejudice," "intolerance," and "obtuse or narrow-minded intolerance, especially of other races or religions"). The association with insincerity may have roots in an earlier understanding of bigotry as religious hypocrisy. In *Tartuffe*, by Moliere,

the lead character, Tartuffe, poses as a humble monk and deceives Orgon, a wealthy French gentleman, with his false piety and zeal until Orgon's wife reveals his deception. One character says: "Good God, do you expect me to submit/To the tyranny of that carping hypocrite./Must we forgo all joys and satisfactions/Because that bigot censures all our actions." MOLIERE, TARTUFFE 1.1.18 (Richard Wilbur, trans., New York: Mariner Books, 1968).

40. *From George Washington to the Hebrew Congregation in Newport, Rhode Island.*

41. *Pastor Who Prayed at Embassy Opening Is a "Religious Bigot," says Mitt Romney,* THE GUARDIAN (May 14, 2018), https://perma.cc/4G46-MYCN.

42. Tara Smith, *Religious Liberty or Religious License? Legal Schizophrenia and the Case Against Exemptions,* 32 JOURNAL OF LAW & POLITICS 43, 55 (2016).

43. *See* A TESTAMENT OF HOPE: THE ESSENTIAL WRITINGS AND SPEECHES OF MARTIN LUTHER KING, JR. (James M. Washington, ed., New York: Harper One 1986).

44. A number of legal scholars have offered extensive analyses of conscience, in the context of evaluating individual and corporate claims to conscience-based exemptions from various laws. *See, e.g.,* Douglas NeJaime and Reva B. Siegel, *Conscience Wars: Complicity-Based Conscience Claims in Religion and Politics,* 124 YALE LAW JOURNAL 2516, 2560 (2015) (referring one time to bigotry); THE RISE OF CORPORATE RELIGIOUS LIBERTY (Micah Schwartzman, Chad Flanders, and Zöe Robinson, eds., New York: Oxford University Press, 2016).

45. GORDON W. ALLPORT, THE NATURE OF PREJUDICE 444 (1954; New York: Basic Books, 25th anniversary edition, 1979) (hereinafter TNOP).

46. *Definition of bigotry by The Free Dictionary* (quoting The American Heritage Roget's Thesaurus defining bigotry as "irrational suspicion of a particular group, race, or religion"); Ramsey, 125–26 (on "many conventional accounts, bigotry involves a strong and unreasonable commitment to one's own beliefs, and an intolerance of alternative views").

47. Galanes, 8.

48. *Bigot—Definition in the Cambridge English Dictionary* (Feb. 12, 2017), https://perma.cc/C6GF-NAHL.

49. *Bigotry,* RANDOM HOUSE KERNERMAN WEBSTER'S COLLEGE DICTIONARY (2005), https://perma.cc/HJ4E-8Q68.

50. Anderson Brief, 3, 5, 23 (quoting *Obergefell*, 2602).

51. *Id.,* 9, 15–16.

52. Ramsey, 128.

53. Siegel, 1112.

54. JOHN L. JACKSON, JR., RACIAL PARANOIA: THE UNINTENDED CONSEQUENCES OF POLITICAL CORRECTNESS 67–68 (New York: Basic Civitas Books, 2008).

55. Eric Luis Uhlmann et al., *When Actions Speak Volumes: The Role of Inferences About Moral Character in Outrage Over Racial Bigotry,* 44 EUROPEAN JOURNAL OF SOCIAL PSYCHOLOGY 23–24 (2013).

56. Rod Dreher, *Does Faith = Hate?,* AMERICAN CONSERVATIVE (Oct. 9, 2013), https://perma.cc/58FV-37S9 (quoting Ryan Anderson and Maggie Gallagher).

57. *Obergefell,* 2642 (Alito, J., dissenting).

58. Christian Crandall et al., *Social Norms and The Expression and Suppression of Prejudice: The Struggle for Internalization,* 82 JOURNAL OF PERSONALITY AND SOCIAL PSYCHOLOGY 359, 361 (2002).

59. Uhlmann, 24.

60. A. C. Thompson and Karim Hall, *Documenting Hate: A New Generation of White Supremacists Emerges in Charlottesville,* PROPUBLICA (Aug. 13, 2017, 7:59 PM), https://perma.cc/JF7X-UVXV.

61. Sheryl Gay Stolberg and Brian M. Rosenthal, *White Nationalist Protest Leads to Deadly Violence,* N.Y. TIMES, Aug. 13, 2017, at A1. Governor Northam later faced intense public criticism over the surfacing of a page from his medical school yearbook with a photograph of one person in blackface and another wearing a Klan robe.

62. Carly Sitrin, *Read: President Trump's Remarks Condemning Violence "on Many Sides" at Charlottesville,* VOX (Aug. 12, 2017) (transcript of remarks), https://perma.cc/A5SM-E386. For criticism, see Glenn Thrush and Maggie Haberman, *Trump's Remarks on Charlottesville*

Violence are Criticized as Insufficient, N.Y. Times (Aug. 12, 2017), https://perma.cc/3KBR-F74V. These controversial words were evidently ad-libbed. When Trump, at a political rally in Phoenix a few days later, read his prior statement aloud, claiming he had condemned "hatred, bigotry, and violence" in the strongest possible terms, he omitted "from many sides." *President Trump Ranted for 77 Minutes in Phoenix. Here's What He Said*, Time (Aug. 23, 2018), https://perma.cc/7QT3-DPN4 (transcript of rally speech).

63. Rebecca Savransky, *Merck CEO Resigns From Presidential Council Over Trump Remarks*, The Hill (Aug. 14, 2017), https://perma.cc/5HEC-393D.

64. Emily Badger, *Showdown Over How Fringe Views Are Defined in America*, N.Y. Times, Aug. 22, 2017, at A16; Mike Dyson, *Charlottesville and the Bigotracy*, N.Y. Times, Aug. 14, 2017, at A11. *But see* Eduardo Bonilla-Silva, Racism Without Racists 222 (Lanham, MD: Rowman & Littlefield, 5th ed. 2018) (noting this criticism but arguing that even Trump's "racial rhetoric," while "inflammatory," reflects the "color-blind racial regime," in which he had to declare he was "not racist").

65. Thomas F. Pettigrew, *Social Psychological Perspectives on Trump Supporters*, 5 (1) Journal of Social and Political Psychology 107, 110 (2017).

66. Sabrina Tavernise, *In Trump's Remarks, Black Churches See A Nation Backsliding*, N.Y. Times, Jan. 15, 2018, at 10 (quoting Reverend Thabiti Anyabwile).

67. *Id.*

68. For example, in the special election for the US Senate between Judge Roy Moore and Doug Jones, many critics of Moore condemned his bigotry. After Jones's victory, he declared he was "humbled" by "the support of Alabama voters who stood with us on the 'Right Side of History'" (letter received by author from Doug Jones).

69. Timothy Williams and Trip Gabriel, *Virginia's New Attorney General Opposes Ban on Gay Marriage*, N.Y. Times, Jan. 24, 2014, at A12.

70. Brief of the Commonwealth of Virginia as Amicus Curiae in Support of Petitioners at 2–5, *Obergefell v. Hodges*, 135 S. Ct. 2584 (2015) (Nos. 14-556, 14-562, 14-571, 14-574).

71. *Truth Overruled with Ryan Anderson*, Catholic Information Center (Sept. 29, 2015, 6 PM), https://perma.cc/486F-EDZZ; Ryan Shinkel, *The Courage to Be on the "Wrong Side of History,"* Public Discourse (June 18, 2105), https://perma.cc/7KVQ-5BQ2.

72. Uhlmann, 24, 25 (reporting views of Americans about hypothetical treatment of coworkers).

73. *See Definition of bigotry by the Free Dictionary* ("obtuse or narrow-minded intolerance, especially of other races or religions").

74. *See* Siri Carpenter, *Buried Prejudice: The Bigot in Your Brain*, 19 Scientific American 2 (Apr./May 2008); *see also* Corvino, *Puzzles about Bigotry*.

75. *See, e.g.,* Gordon W. Allport, *The Bigot in Our Midst*, XL The Commonweal 582, 583–84 (Oct. 6, 1944).

76. *See* Stephen Eric Bronner, The Bigot: Why Prejudice Persists 7 (New Haven, CT: Yale University Press, 2014) (the bigot treats his "pre-reflective" prejudices as "fixed" and "irreversible in the face of new knowledge") (citing Allport, The Nature of Prejudice).

77. *See* Molly Worthen, *Is There Such a Thing as an Authoritarian Voter?*, N.Y. Times (Dec. 15, 2018), https://perma.cc/86XX-FT6J; Pettigrew, *Social Psychological Perspectives*, 108–110.

78. Mahzarin R. Banaji and Anthony G. Greenwald, Blindspot: Hidden Biases of Good People xii–xv, 158–63 (New York: Bantam, 2016 pbk.); Carpenter, *Buried Prejudice*, 33.

79. Banaji and Greenwald, xii–xv, 158–67. *But see* Jonathan Kahn, Race on the Brain: What Implicit Bias Gets Wrong About the Struggle for Racial Justice (New York: Columbia University Press, 2017) (arguing that individualist focus on one's implicit bias ignores larger problems of institutional racism).

80. Angie Brobnic Holan, *In Context: Hillary Clinton and the "Basket of Deplorables,"* Politifact (Sept. 11, 2016), https://perma.cc/SJCF-TFH9.

81. *Id.*

82. Aaron Blake, *The Fix: This Trump Response to Clinton's Basket of "Deplorables" Comment Was Quite Good*, Wash. Post (Sept. 12, 2016), https://perma.cc/Q34B-7R8D.

83. Ta-Nehisi Coates, *Hillary Clinton Was Politically Incorrect, but She Wasn't Wrong about Trump Supporters*, ATLANTIC (Sept. 10, 2016) (Clinton was factually correct), https://perma.cc/E8FA-R4NM; Asawin Suebsaeng, *Team Trump Goes Full Attack Mode over Hillary's "Basket of Deplorables,"* DAILY BEAST (Sept. 10, 2016), https://perma.cc/VM5L-UPZK.

84. Jenna Johnson, *Meet Donald Trump's "Basket of Deplorables,"* WASH. POST (Sept. 13, 2016), https://perma.cc/8K9H-MR3T.

85. ARLIE RUSSELL HOCHSCHILD, STRANGERS IN THEIR OWN LAND 227 (New York: The New Press, 2016).

86. George Lakoff, *Understanding Trump* (July 23, 2016), https://perma.cc/BE2G-B3WX.

87. William Saletan, *Implicit Bias is Real. Don't Be So Defensive. Mike Pence Heard an Accusation of Bigotry, Not An Acknowledgment of Human Nature*, SLATE (Oct. 5, 2016), https://perma.cc/2R9V-D84H; John A. Powell, *Implicit Bias in the Presidential Debate*, HAAS INSTITUTE, https://perma.cc/Y953-RVTZ.

88. LAWRENCE BLUM, "I'M NOT A RACIST, BUT . . .": THE MORAL QUANDARY OF RACE 15 (Ithaca, NY: Cornell University Press, 2002).

89. BONILLA-SILVA, 1–11 (describing problem of "color-blind racism"); John F. Dovidio and Samuel L. Gaertner, *Aversive Racism*, 36 ADVANCES IN EXPERIMENTAL SOCIAL PSYCHOLOGY 1 (2004).

90. Corvino, *Trump, Bigotry, and the Ethics of Stigma*, 8.

91. BANAJI AND GREENWALD, 170.

92. ALLPORT, TNOP, 377.

93. ROBERT WUTHNOW, THE RESTRUCTURING OF AMERICAN RELIGION: SOCIETY AND FAITH SINCE WORLD WAR II 71 (Princeton, NJ: Princeton University Press, 1988).

94. *See* Reverend Martin Luther King, Jr., *The Role of the Church in Facing the Nation's Chief Moral Dilemma*, *in* RHETORIC, RELIGION, AND THE CIVIL RIGHTS MOVEMENT, Vol. 1, 217, 220 (Davis W. Houck and David D. Dixon, eds., Waco, TX: Baylor University Press, 2014).

95. Martin Luther King, Jr., *The Ethical Demands for Integration* (1952) (quoted in Danielle Allen, *Integration, Freedom, and the Affirmation of Life*, *in* TO SHAPE A NEW WORLD: ESSAYS ON THE POLITICAL PHILOSOPHY OF MARTIN LUTHER KING, JR. 146 (Tommie Shelby and Brandon M. Terry, eds., Cambridge, MA: Harvard University Press, 2018)).

96. ERNEST Q. CAMPBELL AND THOMAS F. PETTIGREW, CHRISTIANS IN RACIAL CRISIS (Washington, DC: Public Affairs Press, 1959).

97. *Civil Rights—Public Accommodations: Hearing on S. 1732 Before the S. Comm. on Commerce*, 88th Cong. 22 (1963) (statement of Robert F. Kennedy, Att'y Gen. of the U.S.).

98. *See* Laurence H. Eldredge, *The Right to be Nasty*, EVENING BULLETIN, July 24, 1963. Eldredge testified against the CRA. 110 CONG. REC. 13817–18 (1964).

99. 379 U.S. 241 (1964).

100. 390 U.S. 400 (1968).

101. *Loving*, 17.

102. ALBERT I. GORDON, INTERMARRIAGE: INTERFAITH, INTERRACIAL, INTERETHNIC 357 (Boston: Beacon Press, 1964).

103. *Obergefell*, 2598.

104. 517 U.S. 620, 636, 652 (1996) (Scalia, J., dissenting).

105. Newman v. Piggie Park Enterprises, Inc., 390 U.S. 400 (1968) (cited in Brief of Amicus Curiae NAACP Legal Defense & Educational Fund, Inc., in Support of Respondents at 2–3, *Masterpiece Cakeshop*).

106. Employment Division v. Smith, 494 U.S. 872, 879 (1990).

107. Jessica Clarke, *Explicit Bias*, 113 NORTHWESTERN UNIVERSITY LAW REVIEW 505, 539–40 (2018).

108. Tom W. Smith, *Changing Racial Labels: From "Colored" to "Negro" to "Black" to "African American,"* 56 PUBLIC OPINION QUARTERLY 496 (1992).

109. RICHARD ROTHSTEIN, THE COLOR OF LAW: A FORGOTTEN HISTORY OF HOW OUR GOVERNMENT SEGREGATED AMERICA XV–XVII (New York: Liverlight Publishing Corp., 2017).

Chapter 2

1. MAHZARIN R. BANAJI AND ANTHONY G. GREENWALD, BLINDSPOT: HIDDEN BIASES OF GOOD PEOPLE 170 (New York: Bantam, 2016 pbk.) (dating the earliest effort to study prejudice scientifically to the 1920s, when sociologist Emory Bogardus surveyed people using a "social distance scale"). Other pioneering surveys include Daniel Katz and Kenneth Braly, *Racial Stereotypes of One Hundred College Students*, 28 JOURNAL OF ABNORMAL & SOCIAL PSYCHOLOGY 280 (1933); Daniel Katz and Kenneth Braly, *Racial Prejudice and Racial Stereotypes*, 30 JOURNAL OF ABNORMAL & SOCIAL PSYCHOLOGY 175 (1935).

2. Max Horkheimer and Samuel H. Flowerman, "Foreword" to BRUNO BETTELHEIM and MORRIS JANOWITZ, DYNAMICS OF PREJUDICE: A PSYCHOLOGICAL AND SOCIOLOGICAL STUDY OF VETERANS VII (New York: Harper & Brothers, 1950).

3. GORDON W. ALLPORT, THE NATURE OF PREJUDICE (1954; New York: Basic Books, 25th anniversary edition, 1979) (hereinafter TNOP).

4. 347 U.S. 483 (1954).

5. ALLPORT, TNOP, ix ("Introduction," by Kenneth Clark).

6. BANAJI AND GREENWALD, xv; *see also* John F. Dovidio, Peter Glick, and Laurie A. Rudman, *Introduction: Reflecting on The Nature of Prejudice Fifty Years After Allport*, in ON THE NATURE OF PREJUDICE: FIFTY YEARS AFTER ALLPORT XIII (John F. Dovidio, Peter Glick, and Laurie A. Rudman, eds., Malden, MA: Blackwell Publishing, 2005) ("There is no doubt that Gordon W. Allport's . . . *The Nature of Prejudice* is the foundational work for the social psychology of prejudice").

7. Dovidio, Glick, and Budman, *Introduction*, 1–9.

8. BANAJI AND GREENWALD, xiv, 208 (describing results from use of the Implicit Association Test (IAT)). Readers may take the IAT at https:/implicit.harvard.edu.

9. JONATHAN KAHN, RACE ON THE BRAIN: WHAT IMPLICIT BIAS GETS WRONG ABOUT THE STRUGGLE FOR RACIAL JUSTICE 137 (New York: Columbia University Press, 2018) (quoting Curtis D. Hardin and Mahzarin R. Banaji, *The Nature of Implicit Prejudice: Implications for Personal and Public Policy*, in THE BEHAVIORAL FOUNDATIONS OF PUBLIC POLICY 15 (Eldar Shafir, ed., Princeton, NJ: Princeton University Press, 2013)).

10. *Id.*, 153–54.

11. *Compare* Gordon W. Allport and Bernard M. Kramer, *Some Roots of Prejudice*, 22 JOURNAL OF PSYCHOLOGY 9 (1946), *with* BANAJI AND GREENWALD, 58–60, 145–65.

12. ALLPORT, TNOP, 281.

13. *Id.*, xv–xvi (emphasis in original).

14. Ralph Hood, *Allport, Gordon*, in ENCYCLOPEDIA OF PSYCHOLOGY AND RELIGION 38 (D.A. Leeming, ed., Boston: Springer, 2d ed., 2014).

15. Horkheimer and Flowerman, vii–viii. *See* THEODORE ADORNO et al., THE AUTHORITARIAN PERSONALITY (New York: Harper & Brothers, 1950).

16. Horkheimer and Flowerman, vii–ix.

17. BANAJI AND GREENWALD, xv (referring to GUNNAR MYRDAL, AN AMERICAN DILEMMA: THE NEGRO PROBLEM AND MODERN DEMOCRACY (New York: Harper & Brothers, 1944)).

18. TO SECURE THESE RIGHTS: THE REPORT OF HARRY S. TRUMAN'S COMMITTEE ON CIVIL RIGHTS (Steven F. Lawson, ed., Boston: Bedford/St. Martin's, 2004).

19. *Foreword*, in ON THE NATURE OF PREJUDICE, xi–xii (describing Allport as a founding member of the Society for the Psychological Study of Social Issues, for which "the topic of prejudice has historically been and continues to be a major focus").

20. *See, e.g.*, GERHART SAENGER, THE SOCIAL PSYCHOLOGY OF PREJUDICE: ACHIEVING INTERCULTURAL UNDERSTANDING IN A DEMOCRACY 259–67 (New York: Harper & Brothers, 1953); ALLPORT, TNOP, 469–71.

21. Gordon W. Allport, *The Bigot in Our Midst*, XL THE COMMONWEAL 582 (Oct. 6, 1944).

22. Gordon W. Allport, *The Religious Context of Prejudice*, 5 JOURNAL FOR THE SCIENTIFIC STUDY OF RELIGION 447 (1966).

23. Patricia G. Devine, *Breaking the Prejudice Habit: Allport's "Inner Conflict" Revisited*, in ON THE NATURE OF PREJUDICE, 326, 329.

24. BANAJI AND GREENWALD, 158–63.
25. *See* John Duckett, *Personality and Prejudice, in* ON THE NATURE OF PREJUDICE, 395–410.
26. Allport, *The Bigot in Our Midst*, 582–85.
27. *Id.*, 583 (emphasis in original).
28. *Id.*
29. *Id.*, 583–84. It was also in 1944 that Myrdal reported that opponents of racial integration and social equality made the issue personal and familial, asking: "Would you want your daughter to marry a Negro"? MYRDAL, 60, 587.
30. Allport, *The Bigot in Our Midst*, 584.
31. *Id.*, 584–85.
32. *Id.*
33. Allport and Kramer, 9, 19.
34. *Id.*, 15, 18–20.
35. *Id.*, 33.
36. *Id.*, 39.
37. *Id.*, 35–36.
38. *Id.* Allport and Kramer found that students "who regard the world as a jungle are more prejudiced; those who do not, are more free from prejudice." *Id.*, 32 (reporting answers to survey question: "To what extent would you agree with the following question: The World is a hazardous place in which men are basically evil and dangerous?").
39. *Id.*, 36.
40. ALLPORT, TNOP, xiv–xvi.
41. Dovidio, Glick, and Budman, *Introduction*, 1–2.
42. ALLPORT, TNOP, 20.
43. BANAJI AND GREENWALD, 78.
44. ALLPORT, TNOP, 20.
45. *Id.*, 19.
46. *Id.*, 22–23.
47. Susan T. Fiske, *Social Cognition and the Normality of Prejudgment, in* ON THE NATURE OF PREJUDICE, 36.
48. ALLPORT, TNOP, 329, 352; *see* Devine, 326, 329.
49. Dovidio, Glick, and Budman, *Introduction*, 12–13.
50. ALLPORT, TNOP, xvii. *See, e.g.,* GUSTAVUS MYERS, HISTORY OF BIGOTRY IN THE UNITED STATES (New York: Capricorn Books ed., 1960) (including several chapters on religious bigotry).
51. ALLPORT, TNOP, xv.
52. *Id.*, xv–xvi.
53. *Id.*, 4–5, 8–9, 13.
54. *Id.*, 13–14.
55. *Id.*, 48–49.
56. *Id.*, 51–52 (quoting a United Nations definition).
57. *Id.*, 33. On the limits of Allport's idea of "prejudice as antipathy" for understanding sexism, see Peter Glick and Susan T. Fiske, *The Ambivalent Sexism Inventory: Differentiating Hostile and Benevolent Sexism*, 70 JOURNAL OF PERSONALITY & SOCIAL PSYCHOLOGY 491 (1996).
58. ALLPORT, TNOP, 129.
59. *Id.*, 188–91.
60. *Id.*, 191–99 (giving examples from the Katz and Braly studies). Allport cites Walter Lippman's description of stereotypes and Bruno Bettelheim and Morris Janowitz's work on projection.
61. *Id.*, 202–03.
62. John T. Jost and David L. Hamilton, *Stereotypes in Our Culture, in* ON THE NATURE OF PREJUDICE, 208, 215–16.
63. *Id.*, 216.
64. ALLPORT, TNOP, 281.
65. Allport and Kramer, 23–25.

66. Allport, TNOP, 277.
67. Id., 268–76.
68. For a thorough treatment, see Thomas F. Pettigrew and Linda R. Tropp, When Groups Meet: The Dynamics of Intergroup Contact (New York: Psychology Press, 2011).
69. Id., 8.
70. Id., 13.
71. Id., 52–54 (discussing work by Gregory Herek and his colleagues); see also L. Martin Overby and Jay Barth, Contact, Community Context, and Public Attitudes Toward Gay Men and Lesbians, 34 Polity 343 (2002).
72. Allport, TNOP, 272–73.
73. Id., 272–74.
74. Id., 237–38.
75. Id., 375–77.
76. Id.
77. Id., 377.
78. Id., 274, 376–77.
79. Id., 444.
80. Allport, The Religious Context of Prejudice, 447.
81. Id.
82. Id., 448.
83. Kenneth I. Mayor et al., Religion, Prejudice, and Authoritarianism: Is RWA a Boon or Bane to the Psychology of Religion?, 50(1) Journal for the Scientific Study of Religion 22 (2011).
84. Bernard E. Whitley Jr., Religiosity and Attitudes Toward Lesbians and Gay Men: A Meta-analysis, 19 International Journal for the Psychology of Religion 21 (2009).
85. Deborah L. Hall et al., Why Don't We Practice What We Preach? A Meta-Anayltic Review of Religious Racism, 14(1) Personality and Social Psychology Review 126, 126–27, 134–35 (2010).
86. Allport, The Religious Context of Prejudice, 449.
87. Allport, TNOP, 455.
88. Allport, The Religious Context of Prejudice, 447–48. Allport quotes Gandhi on the goal of "equimindedness." Gordon W. Allport, Religion and Prejudice, 2 Crane Review 1 (Fall 1959).
89. Allport, The Religious Context of Prejudice, 448.
90. Id.
91. Allport, TNOP, 447.
92. Id.
93. Id., 449.
94. Allport, The Religious Context of Prejudice, 451.
95. Reinhold Niebuhr, A Theologian's Comments on the Negro in America, The Reporter, Nov. 29, 1956, at 24–25.
96. Allport, The Religious Context of Prejudice, 451.
97. Id., 451–52 (emphasis in original).
98. Allport, TNOP, 451.
99. Id.
100. Id., 453–54.
101. Allport, The Religious Context of Prejudice, 454.
102. Id., 452–53.
103. Id., 456.
104. Allport, TNOP, 452–53.
105. Allport, The Religious Context of Prejudice, 456–57.
106. Bruce Hunsberger and Lynne M. Jackson, Religion, Meaning, and Prejudice, 61 Journal of Social Issues 807 (2005); Megan K. Johnson et al., Facets of Right-wing Authoritarianism Mediate the Relationship Between Religious Fundamentalism and Attitudes Toward Arabs and African Americans, 51 (1) Journal for the Scientific Study of Religion 128 (2012). Research subsequent to Allport's also reveals a third orientation to religion, "religion as

quest." *See* C. Daniel Baston and E.L. Stocks, *Religion and Prejudice,* in ON THE NATURE OF PREJUDICE, 413, 417–18.

107. Whitley, 28–29; *see also* Gregory M. Herek, *Religious Orientation and Prejudice: A Comparison of Racial and Sexual Attitudes,* 13 PERSONALITY AND SOCIAL PSYCHOLOGY BULLETIN 34 (1987).

108. ALLPORT, TNOP, 461–62.

109. *See id.,* 469; SAENGER, 260–63 (challenging Sumner's assertion). For a helpful discussion, see Elliot Aronson, *Stateways Can Change Folkways,* in HATRED, BIGOTRY, AND PREJUDICE 227 (Robert M. Baird & Stuart E. Rosenblum, eds., NY: Prometheus Books, 1999).

110. ALLORT, TNOP, 469. *See* Plessy v. Ferguson, 163 U.S. 537, 551 (1896). *Plessy* was overruled in *Brown,* 494–95.

111. ALLPORT, TNOP, 466, 469, 471.

112. *Id.* Allport reports the results of an experiment in a large New York City department store in which a "Negro and white clerk worked side by side"; customers served by the former were interviewed outside the store and, although they "expressed the sentiment that 'they were against being served by Negro clerks,'" one fourth said "no" when asked "if they had ever seen any Negro clerks in department stores," suggesting "apparently they had either failed to perceive (or to recall) the color of the salesperson who had just served them." Allport observes: "Such curious disconnection between verbally expressed prejudice and conduct . . . indicates that in the ordinary stream of living equality will be taken for granted provided only that the issue is not brought into consciousness and verbally articulated." *Id.,* 467.

113. *Id.,* 469–71.

114. *Id.,* 472.

115. MYRDAL, xlix.

116. ALLPORT, TNOP, 471.

117. *Id.,* 470

118. Hall et al., 127.

119. ALLPORT, TNOP, 470–71, 473.

120. *Id.,* 473.

121. *Id.,* 473–74.

122. "The Effects of Segregation and the Consequences of Desegregation: A Social Science Statement," Appendix to Appellants' Brief, Brown v. Board of Education, 347 U.S. 483 (1954), Nos. 8, 101, 191, reprinted in LANDMARK BRIEFS AND ARGUMENTS OF THE SUPREME COURT OF THE UNITED STATES, Vol. 49, 43–61 (Phillip B. Kurland and Gerhard Casper, eds., Arlington, VA: University Publications of America, 1975).

123. ALLPORT, TNOP, xxi (preface to the 1958 edition). Allport is criticizing the 1955 decision implementing *Brown* "with all deliberate speed," Brown v. Board of Education, 349 U.S. 294 (1955).

124. *See* ALLPORT, TNOP, x ("Introduction," by Clark).

125. BANAJI AND GREENWALD, 32–33. Banaji and Greenwald observe that social scientists continued to refine the tool of survey research and "focused increasingly on Black–White relations, which became [and remain] the most intensely studied form of prejudice." *Id.,* 175.

126. *Id.,* 170. Allport, for example, reported on survey results using the Bogardus Social Distance Scale. ALLPORT, TNOP, 450.

127. BANAJI AND GREENWALD, 170 (Fig. 1 reproduces the measure for three groups).

128. *Id.,* 172–73.

129. *Id.*

130. PEGGY PASCOE, WHAT COMES NATURALLY: MISCEGENATION LAW AND THE MAKING OF RACE IN AMERICA 116–18 (New York: Oxford University Press, 2009).

131. Perez v. Sharp, 32 Cal. 2d 711, 728–32 (1948).

132. Allport and Kramer, 12 (Table 1, part II).

133. Bernard M. Kramer, *Dimensions of Prejudice,* 27 JOURNAL OF PSYCHOLOGY 389 (1949).

134. *Id.,* 401.

135. *Id.,* 428.

136. *Id.*

137. *Id.,* 428–29.

138. *Id.*, 428.
139. *Id.*, 443.
140. *Id.*
141. *Id.*, 436.
142. BANAJI AND GREENWALD, 29, 180–81.
143. *Id.*
144. G. M. Gilbert, *Stereotype Persistence and Change Among College Students*, 46 JOURNAL OF ABNORMAL PSYCHOLOGY 245, 251 (1951) (reporting generational change since "pioneer" 1933 study by Katz and Braly, *Racial Stereotypes*).
145. EDUARDO BONILLA-SILVA, RACISM WITHOUT RACISTS: COLOR-BLIND RACISM AND THE PERSISTENCE OF RACIAL INEQUALITY IN AMERICA (Lanham, MD: Rowman & Littlefield, 5th ed. 2018).
146. Siri Carpenter, *Buried Prejudice*, 19 SCIENTIFIC AMERICAN 32, 33 (Apr./May 2008). The online title of the article is "Buried Prejudice: The Bigot in Your Brain."
147. *Id.*, 33–37.
148. They present their work in *Blindspot: The Hidden Biases of Good People*, as will be discussed in a later section of this chapter.
149. Carpenter, 38.
150. Susan T. Fiske, *How Prejudiced Are You?*, GREATER GOOD MAGAZINE (June 1, 2008), https://perma.cc/8D6E-RSJ5.
151. *Id.*, 2.
152. *Id.*, 2.
153. *Id.*, 6.
154. *Id.*, 9.
155. Aaron Blake, *The Fix: The First Trump-Presidential Debate Transcript, Annotated*, WASH. POST (Sept. 26, 2016), https://perma.cc/KYV9-YRPC.
156. *Full Transcript: 2016 Vice Presidential Debate*, POLITICO (Oct. 5, 2016), https://perma.cc/3KSB-NAYS.
157. William Saletan, *Implicit Bias is Real. Don't Be So Defensive. Mike Pence Heard an Accusation of Bigotry, Not an Acknowledgment of Human Nature*, SLATE (Oct. 5, 2016), https://perma.cc/2R9V-D84H.
158. *Id.*
159. BANAJI AND GREENWALD, 41–46 (showing pages from the Race IAT).
160. John F. Dovidio and Samuel L. Gaertner, *Aversive Racism*, 36 ADVANCES IN EXPERIMENTAL SOCIAL PSYCHOLOGY 1, 3–4 (2004).
161. *Id.*, 4–5.
162. BANAJI AND GREENWALD, 159–62.
163. *Id.*, 52.
164. *Id.*, 163–64.
165. *See* JONATHAN HAIDT, THE RIGHTEOUS MIND: WHY GOOD PEOPLE ARE DIVIDED BY POLITICS AND RELIGION 55–71 (New York: Pantheon Books, 2012) (positing "dual process" model of human mind with the primacy of "affective priming" and intuitions before strategic reasoning/thinking); MALCOLM GLADWELL, BLINK: THE POWER OF THINKING WITHOUT THINKING (Boston: Little, Brown, 2005); Fiske, *How Prejudiced Are You?*, 5 (discussing role of snap judgments due to "millennia of tribal warfare and fierce competition for limited resources").
166. BANAJI AND GREENWALD, 13–18, 145–67 (discussing "social mindbugs" and how to "outsmart" them).
167. *Id.*, 57 (quoting Gladwell's remarks in an interview with Oprah Winfrey).
168. *Id.*, 56–57.
169. *Id.*, 70.
170. KAHN, 154–64.
171. DOLLY CHUGH, THE PERSON YOU MEAN TO BE: HOW GOOD PEOPLE FIGHT BIAS xxiii–xxiv, 17–19 (New York: Harper Business, 2018).
172. GLADWELL, 97–98.

173. Carpenter, 37.

174. Bruce Drake, *How LGBT Adults See Society and How the Public Sees Them*, PEW RESEARCH CENTER FACT TANK (June 25, 2013), https://perma.cc/WQ5A-Q8LT; Conor Friedersdorf, *The Key to Same-Sex Marriage's Fast Acceptance: The Courage to Come Out*, ATLANTIC (Mar. 28, 2013), https://perma.cc/DB33-2PYR.

175. Aaron Williams and Armand Emamdjomeh, *America is More Diverse Than Ever, But Still Segregated*, WASH. POST (May 10, 2018), https://perma.cc/GR7K-XUBK (including "segregation map"); David Brooks, *The Quiet Death of Racial Progress: How Can We Stop Backsliding Toward Inequality?*, N.Y. TIMES, July 13, 2018, at A21; Khiara M. Bridges, *Excavating Race-Based Disadvantage Among Class-Privileged People of Color*, 53 HARVARD CIVIL RIGHTS-CIVIL LIBERTIES LAW REVIEW 65 (2018).

176. Joey Clark, *The Most Pervasive Bigotry Isn't What You Think*, FOUNDATION FOR ECONOMIC EDUCATION (Aug. 22, 2017), https://perma.cc/GLN6-UGCG.

177. ROBIN DIANGELO, WHITE FRAGILITY: WHY IT'S SO HARD FOR WHITE PEOPLE TO TALK ABOUT RACISM 72–73 (Boston: Beacon Press, 2018).

Chapter 3

1. *"Bigot, n. & a.,"* OXFORD ENGLISH DICTIONARY (2nd ed. 1989), https://perma.cc/9HEB-ZS7Z.

2. Phyllis Ehrlich, *When the Marriage is Interfaith*, N.Y. TIMES, July 24, 1960, at SM52.

3. *See Gallup Finds Greater Tolerance of Mixed Marriage*, N.Y. TIMES, Nov. 19, 1972, at 57.

4. ROBERT D. PUTNAM AND DAVID E. CAMPBELL, AMERICAN GRACE: HOW RELIGION DIVIDES AND UNITES US 151 (New York: Simon & Schuster, 2010) (reporting poll data).

5. *Gallup Finds Greater Tolerance.*

6. JAMES H. S. BOSSARD AND ELEANOR STOKER BOLL, ONE MARRIAGE, TWO FAITHS: GUIDANCE ON INTERFAITH MARRIAGE (New York: Ronald Press Co., 1957).

7. *Id.*, 39.

8. REBECCA L. DAVIS, MORE PERFECT UNIONS: THE AMERICAN SEARCH FOR MARITAL BLISS 102 (Cambridge, MA: Harvard University Press, 2010).

9. Russell O. Berg, *The Minister and Mixed Marriages*, 12 PASTORAL PSYCHOLOGY 33, 34 (Feb. 1962).

10. *See* ALBERT I. GORDON, INTERMARRIAGE: INTERFAITH, INTERRACIAL, INTERETHNIC (Boston: Beacon Press, 1964).

11. ROBERT WUTHNOW, THE RESTRUCTURING OF AMERICAN RELIGION: SOCIETY AND FAITH SINCE WORLD WAR II 71 (Princeton, NJ: Princeton University Press, 1988).

12. Despite the absence of laws prohibiting interfaith marriage, historically, religious matching of children in adoption and foster case was required or strongly favored by state laws. *See* ELLEN HERMAN, KINSHIP BY DESIGN: A HISTORY OF ADOPTION IN THE MODERN UNITED STATES 125–28, 204–09 (Chicago: University of Chicago Press, 2008).

13. *See* JEROME KARABEL, THE CHOSEN: THE HIDDEN HISTORY OF ADMISSION AND EXCLUSION AT HARVARD, YALE, AND PRINCETON (New York: Houghton Mifflin Harcourt, 2005); NANCY MALKIEL, "KEEP THE DAMNED WOMEN OUT!" (Princeton, NJ: Princeton University Press, 2017).

14. Maurice J. Karpf, *Premarital Counseling and Psychotherapy: Two Cases*, 14 MARRIAGE AND FAMILY LIVING 56 (Feb. 1952) (*Two Cases*); Maurice J. Karpf, *Marriage Counseling and Psychotherapy*, 13 MARRIAGE AND FAMILY LIVING 169 (Nov. 1951).

15. *See* DAVIS, 21.

16. Karpf, *Marriage Counseling*, 170.

17. *Id.*

18. *Id.*, 170–71.

19. *Id.*, 172.

20. *Id.*, 173–74. One discussant of the case questions this decision. *Id.*, 174 (commentary by Rex A. Skidmore).

21. *Id.*, 173.

22. *Id.*, 174.

23. Ernest Porterfield, *Black-American Intermarriage in the United States*, 5:1 MARRIAGE & FAMILY REVIEW 17, 22 (1982) (quoting John A. Osmundsen, *Doctor Discusses Mixed Marriages*, N.Y. TIMES, Nov. 7, 1965, at 73); Hugo G. Beigel, *Problems and Motives in Interracial Relationships*, 2 JOURNAL OF SEX RESEARCH 185, 203–05 (1966).

24. Karpf, *Marriage Counseling*, 174.

25. *Id.*

26. *Id.* (commentary by John F. Cuber).

27. *Id.* (commentary by Rex A. Skidmore).

28. DAVIS, 104–07 (discussing scale developed by sociologist Ernest Burgess).

29. A white father's narrative published the same year as Karpf's case confirms the need for "courage" and a "pioneer spirit" in light of the obstacles interracial couples would encounter. Anonymous, *My Daughter Married a Negro*, HARPER'S, July 1951, at 40.

30. RENEE C. ROMANO, RACE MIXING: BLACK–WHITE MARRIAGE IN POSTWAR AMERICA 133–34 (Gainesville: University Press of Florida, 2006 pbk.).

31. Karpf, *Two Cases*, 56.

32. *Id.* On Karpf as Jewish, see DAVIS, 115.

33. Karpf, *Two Cases*, 56–57.

34. *Id.*

35. *Id.*, 57–58.

36. *Id.*, 58–59.

37. *Id.*, 59–60.

38. *Id.*, 61.

39. *Id. See* DAVIS, 115 (observing that Karpf was "steeped in psychoanalytic theory" and viewed the daughter's "democratic ideals of interfaith toleration" as indicating neurosis).

40. GORDON, 51, 57.

41. Berg, 34–36.

42. *Id.*, 35.

43. *Id.*, 40.

44. *Id.*, 37.

45. JAMES A. PIKE, IF YOU MARRY OUTSIDE YOUR FAITH: COUNSEL ON MIXED MARRIAGES (New York: Harper & Brothers, 1954). For favorable reviews, *see, e.g.*, Ehrlich, *When the Marriage Is "Interfaith"* (discussing Bossard and Boll and mentioning Pike); Edward T. Sandrow, *Book Review*, 18 JEWISH SOCIAL STUDIES 159 (Apr. 1956) (reviewing Pike); KIRKUS REVIEWS, https://perma.cc/M323-XUMY (praising Pike's book); Ruby Jo Reeves Kennedy, *Book Department*, 313 ANNALS OF THE ACADEMY OF POLITICAL AND SOCIAL SCIENCE 192 (Sept. 1957) (reviewing Bossard and Boll as a "significant" contribution). For criticisms of Pike's discussion of Catholicism, see note 83 and accompanying text.

46. BOSSARD AND BOLL, 35.

47. PIKE, 15.

48. BOSSARD AND BOLL, 4.

49. PIKE, 16–17.

50. *Id.*, 17.

51. *Id.*, 17–18.

52. BOSSARD AND BOLL, 6.

53. *Id.*, 6–7.

54. PIKE, 63.

55. BOSSARD AND BOLL, 8.

56. PIKE, 28.

57. DAVIS, 118 (discussing use of chart in 1938 "Maryland Study," *Youth Tell Their Story*).

58. PIKE, 27–28.

59. *Id.*, 39.

60. BOSSARD AND BOLL, 41–42.

61. Berg, 38.

62. BOSSARD AND BOLL, 80 (quoting resolution of the general conference on "the Christian Family," Apr. 1956).

63. *Id.*, 89–90, 91–92.

64. *Id.*, 88–89; *see* PIKE, 43 (religious groups emphasize home as a site for children's religious education).

65. BOSSARD AND BOLL, 124.

66. *Id.*

67. PIKE, 41, 45.

68. BOSSARD AND BOLL, 126–27.

69. *Id.*

70. *Id.*, 126–28.

71. *Id.*, 128.

72. PIKE, 77–78 (including wording of a "typical agreement").

73. *Id.*, 52–53, 61–62.

74. *Id.*, 71, 80.

75. *Id.*, 88 (citation omitted).

76. *Id.*, 89–90.

77. *Id.*, 86–87, 91–92; BOSSARD AND BOLL, 79–85 ("Selected Protestant Attitudes and Policies").

78. PIKE, 93–94.

79. *Id.*, 96.

80. *Id.*, 98–100 (quoting Southern Presbyterian Pastoral Letter, 1948).

81. *Id.*, 19–21.

82. *Id.*, 19–20, 40.

83. Gerald J. Schnepp, S. M., *Review*, 15 AMERICAN CATHOLIC SOCIOLOGICAL REVIEW 349 (1954) (reviewing Pike).

84. WUTHNOW, 72, 74–76. On Protestants as bigoted, Wuthnow quotes a speech by Francis Cardinal Spellman over public funding for buses for parochial school. *Id.*, 75.

85. *Id.*, 76.

86. *Id.*, 76–77.

87. PIKE, 142, 154.

88. *Id.*, 142.

89. *Id.*, 143–44.

90. BOSSARD AND BOLL, 108, 154, 159.

91. PIKE, 146.

92. *Id.*, 105, 108–09, 128.

93. BOSSARD AND BOLL, 151–58.

94. *Id.*, 170.

95. *Matrimonia Mixta* (On Mixed Marriages), Oct. 1, 1970.

96. Leonard D. Pivonka, *Ecumenical or Mixed Marriages in the New Code of Canon Law*, 43 THE JURIST 103, 107 (1983).

97. Ladislus Orsy, *Mixed Marriages: The New Instruction*, 16 QUIS. CUSTODIET 90 (1967). *See also* James I. O'Connor, S. J., J. C. D., *Cases and Studies: Should the Present Canonical Form be Retained for the Validity of Marriage?*, THE JURIST 66, 73 (1965) (observing that the law "seems to foster intolerance").

98. Orsy, 84, 87 (discussing *Declaration on Religious Freedom* (Dignitatis Humanae) (1965) and *Decree on Ecumenism* (Unitatis Redintegratio) (Nov. 21, 1964)). *See* Edward B. Fiske, *Religion: Catholics on Mixed Marriage*, N.Y. TIMES, 1966, at 8E ("younger Catholics have appeared inclined in many instances to leave the church rather than compel their mates to make the pledge").

99. Pivonka, 123.

100. George Collins, *Mixed Marriage Held Force for Broader Christian Unity*, BOSTON GLOBE, Nov. 4, 1967, at 12 (quoting Right Reverend G. J. Beck).

101. *Id.* (emphasis added). *See also* John H. Fenton, *Interfaith-Marriage Guidelines Issued*, N.Y. TIMES, Jan. 24, 1970, at 34.

102. *Matrimonia Mixta*, 1.

103. Pivonka, 124.

104. Only the state of Iowa asked marriage applicants their religious affiliations, but estimates for the 1950s and 1960s are included in: Joseph Maier, *Intermarriage: A Survey of Unresearched*

Problems, in Intermarriage and Jewish Life: A Symposium 92 (Werner J. Cahnman, ed., New York: Herzl Press and the Jewish Reconstructionist Press, 1963) (citing a national intermarriage rate of 7.2% and local estimates ranging from 17% to 37%).

105. Gordon's book included interviews with intermarried couples and the results of a survey of student opinions and attitudes toward intermarriage. Gordon, xi–xiii. One reviewer began her review by quipping: "A rabbi and a social scientist wrestled mightily with one another for control of the hand that penned this book. The rabbi wanted passionately to make the best possible case against intermarriage; the social scientist warned against polemics." Jessie Bernard, *Book Review*, 27 Journal of Marriage & Family 117, 117 (1965).

106. Brief and Appendix on Behalf of Appellee at 47, Loving v. Virginia, 388 U.S. 1 (1967) (No. 395).

107. *See* Erich Rosenthal, *Studies of Jewish Intermarriage in the United States*, American Jewish Year Book (1963); Werner J. Cahnman, *Intermarriage against the Background of American Democracy, in* Intermarriage and Jewish Life, 174–75, 177–78.

108. Rosenthal, 8–9 (on the "race relations cycle," citing Robert E. Park and Ernest W. Burgess, Introduction to the Science of Society (Chicago, 1924)).

109. *Id.*, 9, 25–26; Cahnman, 178.

110. Maier, *Intermarriage: A Survey of Unresearched Problems*, 107.

111. *Intermarriage in the United States*, 71 American Jewish Yearbook 101, 101 (1970) (quoting Judah Cahn, *The Rabbi, Mixed Marriages and Jewish Education*, Reconstructionist, Feb. 19, 1965).

112. *Id.* On Rabbi Cahn's life, see *Judah Cahn, Founding Rabbi of Metropolitan Synagogue*, N.Y. Times, Mar. 26, 1984, at B6 (obituary).

113. *Intermarriage in the United States*, 101 (quoting Rabbi Ralph Simon, Rabbinical Assembly of America); *id.* (quoting Rabbi Robert Gordis, Judaism in a Christian World 186 (1966), on "price" paid for freedom and equality in open society).

114. Marshall Sklare, *Intermarriage & the Jewish Future*, Commentary, Apr. 1, 1964, at 52; *see also* Gordon, 350 (referring to "responsibilities" and "risks" of living in an "open society," including "risk" of intermarriage).

115. Sklare, 52.

116. *Id.*

117. *Intermarriage in the United States*, 117.

118. Sklare, 52.

119. *Intermarriage in the United States*, 117.

120. Gordon, 355, 369.

121. *Id.*, 354.

122. *Id.*, 369–70.

123. *Id.*, 323.

124. *Id.*, 357–58.

125. *See* Sklare, 51.

126. Gordon, 6, 51, 57 (surveying students at forty colleges and universities).

127. *Id.*, 40–41; *see also Interreligious Marriages Increasing, Rabbi Says*, Boston Globe, Feb. 26, 1963, at 9 (quoting Gordon that "religious indifference among college students" is a major cause of intermarriage).

128. Gordon, 43.

129. *Id.*, 44.

130. *Id.*, 36.

131. *Id.*, 72.

132. *Id.*, 52–54.

133. Sklare, 51 (quoting Rabbi Rubenstein).

134. *Intermarriage in the United States*, 116.

135. Cahnman, 183, 190.

136. *Id.*, 188–89 (quoting Mordecai Kaplan, Judaism as a Civilization: Toward a Reconstruction of American Jewish Life 418–19 (New York: MacMillan Co., 1934)).

137. Gordon, 367, 368–69.

138. *Id.*, 358–59.

139. *Id.*, 350.
140. *Id.*, 350–51. *See* Berg, 5 (emphasizing a "vital Protestant home" as deterring Protestant-Catholic marriage).
141. Cahnman, 188 (quoting KAPLAN, 418–19).
142. *Id.*, 187.
143. *Id.*, 189 (quoting KAPLAN, 418–19).
144. *Id.*, 191–92.
145. NAOMI SCHAEFER RILEY, 'TIL FAITH DO US PART: HOW INTERFAITH MARRIAGE IS TRANSFORMING AMERICA 35–38 (New York: Oxford University Press, 2013).
146. PUTNAM AND CAMPBELL, 148–52.
147. *Id.*, 158, 160. They also find, however, that "ethnic minorities have a stronger preference for in-group marriage . . . because they have more religiously homogeneous social networks [and] because ethnic identification itself discourages religious intermarriage."
148. ROBERT WUTHNOW, AMERICA AND THE CHALLENGES OF RELIGIOUS DIVERSITY 259–84 (Princeton, NJ: Princeton University Press, 2005).
149. *Id.*, 279–81.
150. Michael Lipka, *A Closer Look at America's Rapidly Growing Religious Nones*, PEW RESEARCH CENTER, (May 13, 2015), https://perma.cc/KH94-ZAER.
151. ROBERTA ROSENTHAL KWALL, REMIX JUDAISM: PRESERVING TRADITION IN A DIVERSE WORLD (Lanham, MD: Rowman & Littlefield, 2020).
152. Mark Oppenheimer, *Same-Sex Interfaith Couples Face Roadblock to Marriage in Judaism*, N.Y. TIMES (Jan. 20, 2015).
153. *See* RILEY, 54–55 (finding that more than half of interfaith couples did not discuss religion of any future children before marrying); WUTHNOW, AMERICA AND THE CHALLENGES OF RELIGIOUS DIVERSITY, 259–61 (referring to guidebooks).
154. RILEY, 16–22.
155. *See* Sandra Dutky, *Mixed Marriage and Roots of Religious Continuity*, L.A. TIMES, June 15, 1974, at B4 (responding to letter calling rabbis who opposed mixed marriage bigots and defending rabbis who do not perform marriages that strike "at the root of religious continuity—the practice of religion in the home").

Chapter 4

1. Extension of Remarks of Hon. John Bell Williams (Miss.), 103 CONG. REC. A6511, A6513 (Aug. 9, 1957) (85th Cong., 1st Sess) (putting in the Appendix of the Congressional Record the article, Rev. G. T. Gillespie, *A Southern Christian Looks at the Race Problem*, SOUTHERN PRESBYTERIAN JOURNAL (June 5, 1957)).
2. Dr. Martin Luther King, Jr., *The Role of the Church in Facing the Nation's Chief Moral Dilemma*, *in* RHETORIC, RELIGION, AND THE CIVIL RIGHTS MOVEMENT, VOL. 1, 217, 218–20 (Davis W. Houck and David E. Dixon, eds., Waco, TX: Baylor University Press, 2006) (RRCRM, Vol. 1) (speech delivered at the Conference on Christian Faith and Human Relations, Vanderbilt University, Nashville, Tennessee, Apr. 25, 1957).
3. *Id.*, 219.
4. For an argument that sermons and political pamphlets are overlooked sources of American political thought, see BARRY SHAIN, THE MYTH OF AMERICAN INDIVIDUALISM: THE PROTESTANT ORIGINS OF AMERICAN POLITICAL THOUGHT (Princeton, NJ: Princeton University Press, 1996).
5. *See* ANDREW M. MANIS, SOUTHERN CIVIL RELIGIONS IN CONFLICT: CIVIL RIGHTS AND THE CULTURE WARS (Macon, GA: Mercer University Press, 2002).
6. *Acts* 17:26.
7. Jane Dailey, *Sex, Segregation, and the Sacred After Brown*, 91 JOURNAL OF AMERICAN HISTORY 119 (2004).
8. *Id.*, 120 (contrasting, in the first category, Paul Harvey and Andrew Manis with, in the second, David Chappell).
9. *See*, e.g., RYAN ANDERSON, TRUTH OVERRULED: THE FUTURE OF MARRIAGE AND RELIGIOUS FREEDOM 233 n. 44 (Washington, DC: Regnery, 2015).

10. *See* Bob Jones University v. United States, 461 U.S. 574 (1983) (upholding IRS's denial of tax exemption to Bob Jones University because its religiously based policies banning interracial marriage and dating were at odds with the "common community conscience" and "the declared position of the whole government").

11. Dailey, 122.

12. Address by Hon. John Bell Williams (Miss.), Before the Defenders of State Sovereignty and Individual Liberties, Extension of Remarks of Hon. William M. Tuck (Va.), CONG. REC. 4339 (85th Cong., 1st Sess) (Mar. 25, 1957).

13. *Id.*, 4341.

14. Gillespie, *A Southern Christian*, A6511, A6513.

15. Brown v. Board of Education, 347 U.S. 483 (1954); Brown v. Board of Education, 349 U.S. 249 (1955).

16. *See* Merrimon Cuninggim, *To Fashion as We Feel*, *in* RHETORIC, RELIGION, AND THE CIVIL RIGHTS MOVEMENT, VOL. 2, 95 (Davis W. Houck and David E. Dixon, eds., Waco, TX: Baylor University Press, 2014) (RRCRM, Vol. 2) (address delivered Apr. 25, 1957, in Nashville, Tennessee).

17. King, *Role of the Church*, 219.

18. *Id.*, 220–21.

19. ERNEST Q. CAMPBELL AND THOMAS F. PETTIGREW, CHRISTIANS IN RACIAL CRISIS: A STUDY OF LITTLE ROCK'S MINISTRY 132–33 (Washington, DC: Public Affairs Press, 1959) (quoting MARTIN L. KING, JR., STRIDE TOWARD FREEDOM 205–11 (1958)).

20. Cuninggim, 95.

21. I sample sermons and speeches in the two volume collection, RRCRM, Vol. 1 and RRCRM, Vol. 2.

22. *See* MANIS, 145–48.

23. CAMPBELL AND PETTIGREW.

24. Thomas Buford Maston, *I Have Not A Demon*, *in* RRCRM, Vol. 2, 34.

25. *See* W. STUART TOWNS, PUBLIC ADDRESS IN THE TWENTIETH-CENTURY SOUTH: THE EVOLUTION OF A REGION 193 (Westport, CT: Praeger Publishers, 1999) (referring to the "conscience of the South" as "mobilized by a long string of events," including *Brown* and key civil rights movement events, so that "things changed—seemingly overnight—when the nation heard Jimmy Carter tell Georgians at his inaugural, 'the time for racial discrimination is over.'").

26. *See* Paul Harvey, *Religion, Race, and the Right in the South, 1945–1990*, *in* POLITICS AND RELIGION IN THE WHITE SOUTH 116–17 (Glenn Feldman, ed., Lexington, KY: University Press of Kentucky, 2005).

27. *Id.* (quoting the remarks of a Baptist layperson in 1974).

28. On "massive resistance," see, for example, RICHARD KLUGER, SIMPLE JUSTICE (New York: Vintage Books, 1977); MICHAEL KLARMAN, FROM JIM CROW TO CIVIL RIGHTS: THE SUPREME COURT AND THE STRUGGLE FOR RACIAL EQUALITY (New York: Oxford University Press, 2006).

29. *See* Anders Walker, *The Ghost of Jim Crow: Law, Culture, and the Subversion of Civil Rights, 1954–1965* (PhD diss.), at 15–18. Walker's subsequent book is THE GHOST OF JIM CROW: HOW SOUTHERN MODERATES USED *BROWN V. BOARD OF EDUCATION* TO STALL CIVIL RIGHTS (New York: Oxford University Press, 2009).

30. *The Decision of the Supreme Court in the School Cases—Declaration of Constitutional Principles*, 102 CONG. REC. 4459 (1956).

31. Address by Hon. John Bell Williams, 4339–40.

32. *Id.*, 4341. Disraeli was born Jewish.

33. *Id.*

34. *Id.*, 4342.

35. Gillespie, *A Southern Christian*, A6511. In her elaboration of the "southern white Protestant theology of separate races," Fay Botham summarizes a 1954 address by Reverend Gillespie. FAY BOTHAM, ALMIGHTY GOD CREATED THE RACES 109 (Chapel Hill: University of North Carolina Press, 2009).

36. Gillespie, *A Southern Christian*, A6512.

37. *Id.*
38. *Id.*
39. *Id.*, A6512–13.
40. *Id. See* CHARLES WILLIAM ELIOT, SOME ROADS TOWARD PEACE: A REPORT TO THE TRUSTEES OF THE ENDOWMENT ON OBSERVATIONS MADE IN CHINA AND JAPAN IN 1912 (1913).
41. Gillespie, A6513.
42. *Genesis* 11:1–8.
43. Gillespie, A6513.
44. *Id.*
45. BOTHAM, 109.
46. *Id.*, 94–101.
47. Gillespie, A6513.
48. *Id.*
49. *Id.*
50. Dailey, 125 (quoting Dr. W. M. Caskey at Mississippi College, a "leading Baptist institution," indicating agreement with Governor Ross Barnett).
51. *Id.*
52. Harvey, 107.
53. *Id.*
54. *See* RRCRM, Vol. 2, 21. This is the King James Version, quoted in Harvey, 107. Some other translations do not use the word "blood," as discussed in note 93.
55. Harvey, 107; *see also* Dailey, 137–38 (quoting church resolutions citing Acts 17:26 to oppose integration and reject their national bodies' stance).
56. MANIS, 99–100.
57. *Id.*, 99 (quoting "Foreword" to Tom P. Brady, *Black Monday* (Association of Citizens' Councils, 1955).
58. *Id.*, 135–36 (quoting *Black Monday*, 89).
59. *Id.*, 98–99.
60. *Id.*, 12.
61. Walker, 36–37.
62. Steven G. Calabresi and Gary Lawson, *The Depravity of the 1930s and the Modern Administrative State*, 94 NOTRE DAME LAW REVIEW 821, 833 (2018).
63. Judge Tom P. Brady, *A Review of Black Monday* 16 (address made to Indianola Citizens' Council, Oct. 28, 1954), http://diglic.usm.edu/printview/collection/manu/id/1778/compoundobject/show/1762.
64. *Governor Ross Robert Barnett, Mississippi Still Says "Never!," in* TOWNS, 144.
65. Kenneth Kersch, "Civil Rights," 1–3 (unpublished book chapter, dated Nov. 13, 2017, on file with author) (quoting William F. Buckley Jr., *Why The South Must Prevail*, 4 NATIONAL REVIEW 148–49 (Aug. 1957)).
66. Walker, 135.
67. 100 CONG REC. 7251, 7253 (1954) (statement of Sen. Eastland).
68. W. E. B. DUBOIS, THE SOULS OF BLACK FOLK 81 (1901; New Haven, CT: Yale University Press, 2015).
69. Williams, 4341.
70. Harvey, 102.
71. MANIS, 134 (quoting W. A. Criswell, *Segregation in Society*, in JAMES E. TOWNS, SOCIAL CONSCIENCE OF W. A. CRISWELL 228–30 (1977)). On the role of antimiscegenation laws in maintaining a white supremacist state, see JULIE NOVKOV, RACIAL UNION: LAW, INTIMACY, AND THE WHITE STATE IN ALABAMA, 1865–1954 (Ann Arbor: University of Michigan Press, 2008).
72. Harvey, 106.
73. Brady, *Black Monday*, 106 (quoted in MANIS, 122); *see also* RRCRM, Vol. 2, 14–15 (quoting Brady as illustrating "dread specter" of "black-male-on-white-female sex").
74. CAMPBELL AND PETTIGREW, 137 (introducing Appendix: Statements of the Churches on Desegregation and Race Relations).
75. *Id.*

76. *Id.*, 144 ("Congregational Churches, General Council").
77. The Reformed Church of America declares that "the Church misconceives its function when it actively hinders, forestalls, or denies, the marriage of any two people who, loving Christ, love each other." *Id.*, 164 (Credo on Race Relations, June 7, 1957). The Catholic Bishops' 1958 pastoral letter, *Discrimination and Christian Conscience*, is quoted later in this chapter; see notes 84–87 and accompanying text.
78. *Id.*, 160–61 ("The Presbyterian Bodies").
79. *Id.*, 160.
80. *Id.*, 162 (General Assembly, The Presbyterian Church in the U.S. [Southern], 1957).
81. *Id.*, 137 (Resolution of the Southern Baptist Convention, June 2–5, 1954, St. Louis, Missouri).
82. *See* WAYNE FLINT, ALABAMA BAPTISTS: SOUTHERN BAPTISTS IN THE HEART OF DIXIE (Tuscaloosa: University of Alabama Press, 1998).
83. CAMPBELL AND PETTIGREW, 141 (National Baptists Convention, U.S.A., Inc.).
84. *Id.*, 167 (Statement of the Roman Catholic Bishops of the U.S., Nov. 13, 1958). Since Campbell and Pettigrew include only an excerpt, I quote from the full pastoral letter, *Discrimination and Christian Conscience*, reproduced in PASTORAL LETTERS OF THE UNITED STATES CATHOLIC BISHOPS, VOL. II, 1941–1961, at 201–06 (Hugh J. Nolan, ed., U.S. Catholic Conference, 1984).
85. *Discrimination and Christian Conscience*, 202.
86. *Id.*, 204.
87. *Id.*, 204–05.
88. *See* MANIS, 151–52 (reporting view of Fred Shuttlesworth).
89. These and many other sermons and speeches from 1954–1965 appear in RRCRM, Vol. 1 and Vol. 2.
90. Maston, *I Have Not A Demon*, 34.
91. *Id.*, 34–37.
92. *Id.*, 38.
93. *Id.* Maston quotes a translation of this verse that does not say "from one blood," as some others do.
94. *Id.*
95. *Id.*, 39, 42–43.
96. *Id.*, 44–45.
97. *Id.*, 45–47.
98. *Id.*
99. *Id.*, 48 (emphasis added).
100. PAUL HARVEY, CHRISTIANITY AND RACE IN THE AMERICAN SOUTH 151 (Chicago: University of Chicago Press, 2016).
101. Dr. Benjamin E. Mays, *The Church Amidst Ethnic and Racial Tensions* (Second Assembly, World Council of Churches, Evanston, Illinois, Aug. 21, 1954), in RRCRM, Vol. 1, 56–64.
102. *Id.*
103. *Id.*, 57.
104. *Id.*, 59.
105. *Id.*
106. *Id.*, 60–61.
107. *Id.*, 61. The language that Mays quotes is from UNESCO's STATEMENT ON THE NATURE OF RACE AND RACE DIFFERENCES 3 (1952). As discussed in chapter 6, the Lovings and their amici cited this report to refute any scientific basis for Virginia's antimiscegenation law.
108. Mays, 61.
109. *Id.*, 63.
110. Charles P. Bowles, *A Cool Head and A Warm Heart*, Dilworth Methodist Church, Charlotte, North Carolina, May 23, 1954, in RRCRM, Vol. 1, 31, 34.
111. *Id.*, 33, 34.
112. Dr. Haywood N. Hill, *This I Believe*, Trinity Presbyterian Church, Atlanta, Georgia, Jan. 1961, in RRCRM, Vol. 1, 405.
113. *Id.*, 406.

114. *Id.*, 406–07.
115. *Id.*
116. Martin Luther King, Jr., *Stride Toward Freedom*, excerpted in A TESTAMENT OF HOPE: THE ESSENTIAL WRITINGS AND SPEECHES OF MARTIN LUTHER KING, JR. 478 (James M. Washington, ed., New York: Harper One, 1986); Mays, 62 (segregation "scars not only the soul of the segregated but the soul of the segregator as well").
117. *See* A TESTAMENT OF HOPE (for example, King, *The Power of Nonviolence*, 12; *Kenneth B. Clark Interview*, 334–35).
118. Charles Kenzie Steele, *The Tallahassee Bus Protest Story* (1956), in RRCRM, Vol. 2, 71, 77.
119. Rabbi Herbert Baumgard, *Those Who Have Felt the Lash of the Taskmaster*, Union of American Hebrew Congregations and Temple Beth Ann, Miami, Florida (1956), in RRCRM, Vol. 2, 65.
120. Cuninggim, 95, 99.
121. Reverend William B. Selah, *Brotherhood*, in RRCRM, Vol. 2, 241 (address given on Nov. 11, 1961 in Jackson, Mississippi).
122. *Id.*, 238.
123. *Id.*, 240.
124. Lillian Smith, *Are We Still Buying a New World with Old Confederate Bills?*, in RRCRM, Vol. 2, 217, 219–21 (address given on Oct. 16, 1960, in Atlanta, Georgia).
125. *See, e.g.*, Baumgard, 65 (describing actual experience of white man from Alabama in an integrated army school); Thurgood Marshall, *The Good People Sat Down*, in RRCRM, Vol. 2, 104, 116 (predicting that social contact in schools, colleges, and military will lead children to learn that "a man is measured by his worth and not his race").
126. Baumgard, 66.
127. Jacob Rothschild, *And None Shall Make Them Afraid* (Oct. 17, 1958), in RRCRM, Vol. 2, 178 (speaking after bombing of Hebrew Benevolent Synagogue).
128. CAMPBELL AND PETTIGREW, viii.
129. *Southern Ministers Speak Their Minds*, PULPIT DIGEST 13 (Dec. 1958).
130. CAMPBELL AND PETTIGREW, v–viii.
131. *Id.*, 129.
132. *Id.*, vii (recounting facts).
133. Reprinted in TOWNS, PUBLIC ADDRESS, 134–37.
134. Carolyn Gray LeMaster, *Civil and Social Rights Efforts of Arkansas Jewry*, in THE QUIET VOICES: SOUTHERN RABBIS AND BLACK CIVIL RIGHTS, 1880s TO 1990s 105–08 (Mark K. Bauman and Berkley Kalin, eds., Tuscaloosa: University of Alabama Press, 1997).
135. CAMPBELL AND PETTIGREW, 140.
136. MARY L. DUDZIAK, COLD WAR CIVIL RIGHTS 132–33 (Princeton, NJ: Princeton University Press, 2001).
137. CAMPBELL AND PETTIGREW, vii.
138. *Id.*, 17–18.
139. *Id.* They do not give the name of the minister, but from their description of the sermon, it is Boggs, *The Crucial Test of Christian Citizenship*, which appears in RRCRM, Vol. 1, 272. Campbell and Pettigrew summarize the sermon but I quote directly from the reproduced text.
140. Boggs, 271.
141. CAMPBELL AND PETTIGREW, 19–20.
142. *Id.*, 25.
143. *Id.*, 26–28.
144. *Id.*, 29.
145. *Id.*, 30, 32.
146. *Id.*, 33–34.
147. *Id.*, 31.
148. *Id.*, 37.
149. Campbell and Pettigrew use this characterization. *See id.*, 41.
150. *Id.*, 38–39.
151. *Id.*

152. *Id.*, 59, 60 (emphasis added).
153. *Id.*, 52–53.
154. *Id.*, 51. To the question, "Do you think the Bible gives clear guidance on the integration-segregation issue?," a higher percentage of segregationist ministers than integrationist ministers answered "yes."
155. *Id.*, 38–39, 50 (giving example of Acts 17:26).
156. *Id.*, 53–54.
157. *Id.*, 61.
158. *Id.*
159. Reinhold Niebuhr, *A Theologian's Comments on the Negro in America*, THE REPORTER, Nov. 29, 1956, at 24–25.
160. CAMPBELL AND PETTIGREW, 92.
161. *Id.*, 129.
162. Niebuhr, 25. Botham, however, suggests that the official Roman Catholic position met with resistance from "the American hierarchy as well as the laity, and in all regions of the United States." BOTHAM, 122.
163. CAMPBELL AND PETTIGREW, 129.
164. Thomas Pettigrew, *Religious Leadership and the Desegregation Process* (delivered at Race Relations Institute, Fisk University, Nashville, Tennessee, June 27, 1960) in RRCRM, Vol. 2, 192.
165. *Id.*, 197–98, 202.
166. *Id.* For a similar criticism, see Rothschild, 178.
167. *Martin Luther King's "Letter from Birmingham Jail,"* ATLANTIC (Apr. 16, 2013, 11:00 AM), archived at http://perma.cc/783D-89E8 (reprinting letter on fiftieth anniversary, Apr. 16, 2013).
168. Pettigrew, 203.
169. *Southern Ministers Speak Their Minds*, 15. The *Pulpit Digest* study found that "91% of the ministers in areas where integration is fully or partially in effect are in favor of integration of schools, whereas the ratio is only 73% in places where integration has not yet started."
170. Pettigrew, 205.
171. Maston, 48.
172. Southern Baptist Convention, *Resolution on Racial Reconciliation on the 150th Anniversary of the Southern Baptist Convention* (Atlanta, Georgia 1995).
173. *Id.*
174. Lawrence Ware, *I'm Done Being a Southern Baptist*, N.Y. TIMES, July 17, 2017, at A19.

Chapter 5

1. TO SECURE THESE RIGHTS: THE REPORT OF PRESIDENT HARRY S. TRUMAN'S COMMITTEE ON CIVIL RIGHTS iv, 59 (Steven F. Lawson ed., Boston: Bedford/St. Martin's, 2004). Lawson argues: "Although the committee cited Myrdal only once in its final report, the document [it] produced . . . was infused with his central assumptions." *Id.*, 22.
2. RICHARD GERGEL, UNEXAMPLED COURAGE: THE BLINDING OF SGT. ISAAC WOODARD AND THE AWAKENING OF PRESIDENT HARRY S. TRUMAN AND JUDGE J. WATIES WARING 137 (New York: Sarah Crichton Books, 2019).
3. TO SECURE THESE RIGHTS, 158. On the foreign policy reason, see MARY DUDZIAK, COLD WAR CIVIL RIGHTS 80–81 (Princeton, NJ: Princeton University Press, 2000).
4. TO SECURE THESE RIGHTS, 117.
5. *Id.*, 183.
6. *Id.*, 33.
7. REBECCA ZIETLOW, ENFORCING EQUALITY: CONGRESS, THE CONSTITUTION, AND THE PROTECTION OF INDIVIDUAL RIGHTS 103–04 (New York: NYU Press, 2006).
8. For example, Shelley v. Kraemer, 334 U.S. 1 (1948) (holding that judicial enforcement of a private covenant to discriminate racially in housing violated the Fourteenth Amendment). On the mixed impact of *Brown v. Board of Education*, 347 U.S. 483 (1954), see MICHAEL J.

KLARMAN, FROM JIM CROW TO CIVIL RIGHTS: THE SUPREME COURT AND THE STRUGGLE FOR RACIAL EQUALITY (New York: Oxford University Press, 2004).

9. DUDZIAK, 204.
10. ZIETLOW, 104–05.
11. KLARMAN, 435; *see also* DUDZIAK, 169–79.
12. President John F. Kennedy, Radio and Television Report to the American People on Civil Rights (June 11, 1963) (transcript available at https://perma.cc/TEE6-PZSZ) (quoted in DUDZIAK, 179).
13. *Civil Rights—Public Accommodations: Hearing on S. 1732 Before the S. Comm. on Commerce,* 88th Cong. 811–40 (1963) (statement of Father John F. Cronin, Associate Director, Social Action Department, National Catholic Welfare Conference; accompanied by Rabbi Irwin Blank, Chairman, Social Action Commission, Synagogue Council of America; and Dr. Eugene Carson Blake, Stated Clerk of the United Presbyterian Church in the U.S.A.) ("Statement of Father John F. Cronin").
14. 42 USCA § 2000a.
15. *See* BRUCE ACKERMAN, WE THE PEOPLE, VOL. 3: THE CIVIL RIGHTS REVOLUTION 136 (Cambridge, MA: Harvard University Press, 2014) (arguing that key speeches by civil rights leaders and lawmakers about landmark civil rights law like the CRA deserve "a central place in our understanding of the Second Reconstruction").
16. Lyndon B. Johnson, *Remarks to Members of the Southern Baptist Christian Leadership Seminar,* THE AMERICAN PRESIDENCY PROJECT (Mar. 25, 1964), https://perma.cc/T62F-C74J.
17. 110 CONG. REC. 6557 (Mar. 30, 1964) (statement of Sen. Kuchel).
18. 110 CONG. REC. 7387 (Apr. 9, 1964) (statement of Sen. Young).
19. Martin Luther King, Jr., *Why We Can't Wait,* in A TESTAMENT OF HOPE: THE ESSENTIAL WRITINGS AND SPEECHES OF MARTIN LUTHER KING, JR. 540 (James M. Washington, ed., New York: Harper One, 1986).
20. 110 CONG. REC. 12315 (June 1, 1964) (statement of Sen. Long).
21. *Civil Rights—Public Accommodations: Hearing on S. 1732 Before the S. Comm. on Commerce,* 88th Cong. 1147–50 (1963) (statement of Dr. Albert Garner, President, Florida Baptist Institute & Seminary) (Statement of Dr. Garner).
22. *See* Laurence H. Eldredge, *The Right to Be Nasty,* EVENING BULLETIN (July 24, 1963) (communication entered into the record *Civil Rights—Public Accommodations: Hearing on S. 1732 Before the S. Comm. on Commerce* Part 2, 88th Cong. 1283–84 (1963)).
23. 110 CONG. REC. 10519 (May 11, 1964) (statement of Sen. Carlson).
24. *See* Eldredge, *The Right to be Nasty,* 1283–84.
25. For example, Brief for the State of Texas, Alabama et al. as Amici Curiae in Support of Petitioners at 3, Masterpiece Cakeshop, Ltd. v. Colorado Civil Rights Commission, 138 S. Ct. 1719 (2018) (No. 16-111).
26. For example, Brief of Amicus Curiae NAACP Legal Defense & Educational Fund, Inc. in Support of Respondents at 2–3, *Masterpiece Cakeshop.*
27. *See* GORDON W. ALLPORT, THE NATURE OF PREJUDICE 469 (1954; New York: Basic Books, 1979) (discussing William Graham Sumner's assertion and its modern counterpart).
28. *Id.,* 472.
29. *Id.,* 463–64.
30. *See, e.g., Equality Now: The President Has the Power,* in A TESTAMENT OF HOPE, 152.
31. *Civil Rights—Public Accommodations: Hearing on S. 1732 Before the S. Comm. on Commerce,* 88th Cong. 619-20 (1963) (statement of Sen. Case).
32. Statement of Sen. Kuchel, 6557.
33. *Civil Rights—Public Accommodations: Hearing on S. 1732 Before the S. Comm. on Commerce,* 88th Cong. 22 (1963) (statement of Robert F. Kennedy, Att'y Gen. of the United States).
34. *Id.*
35. *Civil Rights: Hearings on H.R. 7152 as amended by Subcomm. No. 5 Before the H. Comm. on the Judiciary,* 88th Cong. 22 (1963) (statement of Robert F. Kennedy, Att'y Gen. of the United States).

36. ACKERMAN, 136 (quoting speeches by Hubert Humphrey; arguing that supporters of the CRA identified *"institutionalized humiliation"* as "the heart of the problem of racism in America").

37. *Martin Luther King's "Letter from Birmingham Jail,"* ATLANTIC (Apr. 16, 2013, 11:00 AM), *archived at* http://perma.cc/783D-89E8 (reprinting letter on fiftieth anniversary, Apr. 16, 2013).

38. *Civil Rights—Public Accommodations: Hearings on S. 1732 Before S. Comm. on Commerce,* A1564 (1963) (statement by Council for Christian Social Action, United Church of Christ, entered into record by Sen. Magnuson).

39. *Id.,* A1565-66 (Statement on Public Accommodations by Constituent Organizations of the National Community Relations Advisory Council) (entered into record by Sen. Magnuson) (Statement by Constituent Organizations).

40. 110 CONG. REC. 1625 (Feb. 1, 1964) (statement of Rep. Rooney).

41. 110 CONG. REC. 2803 (Feb. 10, 1964) (statement of Rep. Giaimo).

42. 110 CONG. REC. 6574 (Mar. 30, 1964) (statement of Sen. Morse).

43. 110 CONG. REC. 2789 (Feb. 10, 1964) (statement of Rep. Anderson).

44. 110 CONG. REC. 7387 (Apr. 9, 1964) (statement of Sen. Young).

45. 110 CONG. REC. 2773 (Feb. 10, 1964) (statement of Rep. Hawkins).

46. 119 CONG. REC. 7408 (Apr. 9, 1964) (statement of Sen. Magnuson).

47. 110 CONG. REC. 6574 (Mar. 30, 1964) (statement of Sen. Morse).

48. Statement of Father John F. Cronin, 811.

49. *Id.,* 829 (An Appeal to the Conscience of the American People).

50. *Id.,* 814–15.

51. Statement by Council for Christian Social Action, A1538.

52. 110 CONG. REC. 10,416 (1964) (quoting a letter from the Presbyterian organization, "A Fellowship of Concern," submitted by Sen. Humphrey).

53. ROBERT WUTHNOW, THE RESTRUCTURING OF AMERICAN RELIGION: SOCIETY AND FAITH SINCE WORLD WAR II 146–47 (Princeton, NJ: Princeton University Press, 1988).

54. *Civil Rights: Hearings on Miscellaneous Proposals Regarding the Civil Rights of Persons Within the Jurisdiction of the United States Before Subcomm. N. 5 of the H. Comm. on the Judiciary,* 88th Cong. 1939 (1963) (written testimony of Walter P. Reuther, President, UAW) (Reuther Testimony).

55. *Id.,* 2193 (statement of Gus Tyler, Assistant President, International Ladies' Garment Workers' Union).

56. *Civil Rights–The President's Program, 1963: Hearing on S. 1731 and S. 1750 Before the S. Comm. on the Judiciary,* 88th Cong. 20–21 (1963) (statement of Sen. Edward V. Long).

57. *Id.,* 21. *See also* Additional Views on H.R. 7152 of Hon. William M. McCulloch, H.R. REP. No. 88-914, pt. 2, at 8 (1963).

58. *Equal Employment Opportunity: Hearings on H.R. 405, 2999, 4031 and Similar Bills Before the H. General Subcomm. on Labor of the H. Comm. on Educ. and Labor,* 88th Cong. 124 (1963) (statement of Murray A. Gordon, the American Jewish Congress).

59. They sought to avoid the law meeting the same fate as the nineteenth-century, post-Civil War federal public accommodations law struck down by the Supreme Court in *Civil Rights Cases,* 109. U.S. 3 (1883). *See generally* RICHARD C. CORTNER, CIVIL RIGHTS AND PUBLIC ACCOMMODATIONS: THE HEART OF ATLANTA MOTEL AND MCCLUNG CASES (Lawrence: University Press of Kansas, 2001).

60. 379 U.S. 241 (1964).

61. *Excerpts from Rights Cases Argument,* N.Y. TIMES (Oct. 6, 1964), *archived at* http://perma.cc/ HND5-XZ3J.

62. *Heart of Atlanta,* 257.

63. *Civil Rights: Hearing on H.R. 7152 Before the H. Comm. On Rules,* 88th Cong. 184 (statement of Rep. Celler).

64. *Civil Rights—Public Accommodations: Hearing on S. 1732 Before the S. Comm. on Commerce,* 88th Cong. 652 (1963) (statement of Sen. Williams).

65. *See Equal Employment Opportunity: Hearings on H.R. 405, 2999, 4031 and Similar Bills Before the H. Gen. Subcomm. on Labor of the H. Comm. on Educ. and Labor,* 88th Cong. 31 (1963) (statement of Rev. Richard Allen Hilderbrand, President, New York City Branch, NAACP).

66. *Id.*
67. *See Equal Employment Opportunity: Hearing on S. 773, S. 1210, S. 1211, and S. 1937 Before the S. Subcomm. on Emp't and Manpower of the Comm. on Labor and Public Welfare,* 88th Cong. 219–20 (1963) (statement of James Farmer, National Director, Congress of Racial Equality).
68. *Civil Rights: Hearing on 7152 Before the H. Comm. on Rules,* 88th Cong. 207–08, 246 (1964) (statement of Rep. William M. McCulloch). President Kennedy said of McCulloch's support for the CRA, "Without him it can't be done." *See* JONATHAN ROSENBERG AND ZACHARY KARABELL, KENNEDY, JOHNSON, AND THE QUEST FOR JUSTICE: THE CIVIL RIGHTS TAPES 177 (NY: W.W. Norton & Co., 2003).
69. *Civil Rights: Hearing on H.R. 7152 Before the H. Comm. On Rules,* 88th Cong. 184 (statement of Rep. Celler).
70. *Civil Rights—Public Accommodations: Hearings on S. 1732 Before the S. Comm. on Commerce,* 88th Cong. 183 (1963) (statement of Sen. Hart).
71. Reuther Testimony, 88th Cong. 1940 (1963).
72. *Civil Rights—Public Accommodations: Hearings on S. 1732 Before S. Comm. on Commerce,* 88th Cong., 1548 (1963) (statement of the Council for Christian Social Action, entered into the record by Sen. Magnuson).
73. *See Civil Rights: Hearings on Miscellaneous Proposals Regarding the Civil Rights of Persons Within the Jurisdiction of the United States Before Subcomm. No. 5 of the H. Comm. on the Judiciary,* 88th Cong. 1148 (1963) (statement of Edmond F. Rovner, Civic Affairs Director, International Union of Electrical Workers, AFL-CIO).
74. ALLPORT, 466–67.
75. Statement by Constituent Organizations, A1566.
76. *Civil Rights: Hearings on Miscellaneous Proposals Regarding the Civil Rights of Persons Within the Jurisdiction of the United States Before Subcomm. No. 5 of the H. Comm. on the Judiciary,* 88th Cong. 1985–86 (1963) (statement of Richard Bennett, Chairman, Community Relations Division, American Friends Service Committee, Philadelphia, PA).
77. S. REP. No. 88-872, at 21–22 (1964).
78. *See* GAVIN WRIGHT, SHARING THE PRIZE: THE ECONOMICS OF THE CIVIL RIGHTS REVOLUTION IN THE AMERICAN SOUTH 76–77, 101 (Cambridge, MA: Harvard University Press, 2013).
79. *See Civil Rights—Public Accommodations: Hearings on S. 1732 Before the S. Comm. on Commerce,* 88th Cong. 1117–18 (1963) (statement of Hon. Karl F. Rolvaag, Governor of Minnesota).
80. *See Civil Rights—Public Accommodations: Hearings on S. 1732 Before the S. Comm. on Commerce,* 88th Cong. 1179 (1963) (statement of Gov. George Romney, Michigan).
81. *Civil Rights: Hearings on Miscellaneous Proposals Regarding the Civil Rights of Persons Within the Jurisdiction of the United States Before Subcomm. No. 5 of the H. Comm. on the Judiciary,* 88th Cong. 2529 (1963) (statement of the Japanese-American Citizens League).
82. Robin Fretwell Wilson, *Bargaining for Civil Rights: Lessons from Mrs. Murphy for Same-Sex Marriage and LGBT Rights,* 95 BOSTON UNIVERSITY LAW REVIEW 951, 973 (2015).
83. *See Civil Rights: Hearings on H.R. 7152 as Amended by Subcomm. No. 5 Before the H. Comm. on the Judiciary,* 88th Cong. 2700 (1963) (question by Mr. Poff).
84. Wilson, 974–75 (quoting 110 CONG. REC. 2466 (1964) (statement of Rep. Carl Elliott)).
85. *Id.,* 975 (sources omitted).
86. Statement by Constituent Organizations, A1569.
87. Statement of Father John F. Cronin, 832.
88. *Id.* (answer by Rabbi Blank).
89. Statement of Dr. Garner, 1148.
90. Brian K. Landsberg, *Public Accommodations and the Civil Rights Act of 1964: A Surprising Success?,* 36 HAMLINE JOURNAL OF PUBLIC LAW & POLICY 1, 5–6 (2015) (quoting Rev. Albert Gorner [sic], Transcript of Meeting of the President with Religious Leaders (June 17, 1963), *in* CIVIL RIGHTS, THE WHITE HOUSE, AND THE JUSTICE DEPARTMENT, vol. 9, 106, 115 (Michael R. Belknap ed., 1991)).
91. Statement of Dr. Garner, 1147. Garner was "a particularly notable graduate" of Missionary Baptist Seminary, in Arkansas. *See Missionary Baptist Seminary,* THE ENCYCLOPEDIA OF ARKANSAS HISTORY & CULTURE, https://perma.cc/6MVW-UBE3.

92. Statement of Dr. Garner, 1147 (quoting Resolution No. 2, Florida State Baptist Association, Jacksonville, Fla., July 17, 1963).

93. *Id.*, 1148–49.

94. *Id.*, 1149.

95. Joseph T. Leonard, *Morality in Race Relations*, 11 CATHOLIC LAWYER 202, 202–03 (1965) (reporting quotation in *Washington Post*, June 11, 1964).

96. 110 CONG. REC. 12967 (1964) (testimony of Sen. Thurmond, submitting a letter by Rev. Niederhuth); *see also* 110 CONG. REC. 13670 (1964) (testimony of Sen. Thurmond, submitting a resolution by Pastor Johnson). *See* WUTHNOW, 146 (observing that "loud cries of 'foul play'" from clergy and "many in the pews" stemmed from disagreement about the proper ways to engage "the public conscience" and "lingering ambivalences toward racial equality").

97. 110 CONG. REC. 13309 (daily ed. June 9, 1964) (statement of Sen. Byrd).

98. Byrd might have added that President Johnson did not receive the support he requested from Southern Baptist leaders, despite his admonition of their great responsibility to support the bill.

99. *See Civil Rights—Public Accommodations: Hearings on S. 1732 Before the S. Comm. on Commerce*, 88th Congress 589–90 (1963) (statement of J. Setta, Chairman, Referendum Committee of Easton, Maryland).

100. *Id.*

101. Steven G. Calabresi and Gary Lawson, *The Depravity of the 1930s and the Modern Administrative State*, 94 NOTRE DAME LAW REVIEW 821, 833 (2018).

102. *See Civil Rights Commission: Hearings on S. 1117 and S. 1219 Before the Subcomm. on Constitutional Rights of the Comm. on the Judiciary*, 88th Cong. 41–43 (1963) (statement of Sen. Ervin).

103. *See Civil Rights—Public Accommodations: Hearings on S. 1732 Before the S. Comm. on Commerce*, 88th Congress 893–911 (1963) (statement of R. Carter Pittman, Attorney, Dalton, Ga.).

104. 110 CONG. REC. 14498–500 (daily ed. June 19, 1964) (sermon of Dr. Walter R. Courtney, First Presbyterian Church, Nashville, Tennessee, "The Problem of Equality," offered by Sen. Tower); *see* 110 CONG. REC. 5248 (daily ed. Mar. 13, 1964) (statement of Sen. Talmadge praising sermon as "splendid").

105. Courtney, "The Problem of Equality," 110 CONG. REC. 14499–500.

106. *See Civil Rights—Public Accommodations, Part I: Hearings on S. 1732 Before the S. Comm. on Commerce*, 88th Cong. 394–96 (1963) (statement of Gov. Ross Barnett).

107. *See Civil Rights—Public Accommodations: Hearings on S. 1732 Before the S. Comm. on Commerce*, 88th Cong. 584 (1963) (statement of C. Maurice Weidemeyer, Delegate to the Maryland General Assembly).

108. *Civil Rights: Hearings on Miscellaneous Proposals Regarding the Civil Rights of Persons Within the Jurisdiction of the United States before the H. Comm. on the Judiciary*, 88th Cong. 1705, 1713–14 (1963) (statement of Rep. Watson).

109. Statement of Sen. Ervin.

110. Statement of C. Maurice Weidemeyer, 563.

111. *Civil Rights—Public Accommodations: Hearings on S. 1732 Before the S. Comm. on Commerce*, 88th Cong. 498 (1963) (statement of Gov. Wallace).

112. *Civil Rights—The President's Program, 1963: Hearings on S. 1731 and S. 1750 Before the S. Comm. on the Judiciary*, 88th Cong. 40 (1963) (statement of Sen. Ervin); *Civil Rights: Hearings on Miscellaneous Proposals Regarding the Civil Rights of Persons Within the Jurisdiction of the United States Before the H. Comm. on the Judiciary*, 88th Cong. 1714 (1963) (statement of Rep. Watson); *Civil Rights: Hearing on H.R. 7152 Before the H. Comm. on Rules*, 88th Cong. 563 (1964) (statement of Rep. Gillis W. Long).

113. 110 CONG. REC. 1913–14 (Feb. 4, 1964) (statement of Rep. Jones).

114. 110 CONG. REC. 14502–03 (June 19, 1964) (statement of Sen. Tower).

115. 110 CONG. REC. 8175 (Apr. 16, 1964) (statement of Sen. Tower).

116. 110 CONG. REC. 10519 (daily ed. May 11, 1964) (statement of Sen. Carlson).

117. *Civil Rights: Hearings on Miscellaneous Proposals Regarding the Civil Rights of Persons Within the Jurisdiction of the United States Before Subcomm. No. 5 of the H. Comm. on the Judiciary*, 88th Cong. 2382–83 (1963) (statement of Jack Lowery, Esq.).

NOTES 255

118. 110 CONG. REC. 7022 (1964) (statement of Sen. Holland).
119. 110 CONG. REC. 5990 (daily ed. Mar. 23, 1964) (statement of Sen. Smathers).
120. 109 CONG. REC. 401, 405 (July 12, 1963) (testimony of James J. Kilpatrick quoting pamphlet published by Commission, "Civil Rights and Legal Wrongs"). *See also* James J. Kilpatrick, *Civil Rights and Legal Wrongs*, NATIONAL REVIEW, Sept. 24, 1963, at 231, 234.
121. *See* Kenneth I. Kersch, "Civil Rights," 56 (unpublished book chapter, dated Nov. 13, 2017, on file with author).
122. Eldredge, *The Right to Be Nasty*. Eldredge's testimony appears at 110 CONG. REC. 13817–18 (1964) (statement of Lawrence H. Eldredge, lawyer). For entries of the article into the record, see *Civil Rights—Public Accommodations: Hearing on S. 1732 Before the S. Comm. on* Commerce, 88th Cong. 1283 (1963) (testimony of Sen. Erwin, submitting statement by Laurence H. Eldredge); *Civil Rights—Public Accommodations: Hearing on S. 1732 Before the S. Comm. on* Commerce (1963) (entering article by Eldredge); *Civil Rights—The President's Program, 1963: Hearing on S. 1731 and S. 1750 Before the S. Comm. on the Judiciary*, 88th Cong. 235 (1963) (entering article by Eldredge).
123. Eldredge, *The Right to be Nasty*, 1283–84 (emphasis added).
124. *Id.*
125. Robert Bork, *Civil Rights—A Challenge*, NEW REPUBLIC, Aug. 31, 1963, at 21, https://perma.cc/AB38-HWD2.
126. *Civil Rights—A Challenge: Extension of Remarks of Hon. Olin D. Johnston, South Carolina*, 109 Cong. Rec. A5609-A5610 (Sept. 4, 1963). Representative Waggoner (Louisiana) entered into the record Bork's editorial, "Against the Bill," published in an exchange with Phillip B. Kurland in the *Chicago Tribune*. CONG. REC. 5181 (Mar. 12, 1964).
127. Bork, 22.
128. *Id.*, 24.
129. 110 CONG. REC. 14457 (June 19, 1964) (statement of Sen. Johnston).
130. 110 CONG. REC. 7876 (Apr. 14, 1964) (statement of Sen. McClellan); 110 CONG. REC. 13325 (June 10, 1964) (statement of Sen. Tower).
131. *Civil Rights—Public Accommodations: Hearings on S. 1732 Before the S. Comm. on Commerce*, 88th Cong. 428 (1963) (statement of James J. Kilpatrick, Editor of the *Richmond News Leader*). *See* Garrett Epps, *The Littlest Rebel: James J. Kilpatrick and the Second Civil War*, 10 CONSTITUTIONAL COMMENTARY 10 (1993).
132. *See Civil Rights: Hearing on H.R. 7152 Before the H. Comm. on Rules*, 88th Cong. 602 (1964) (statement of Rep. Fountain).
133. *Civil Rights: Hearing on H.R. 7152 Before the H. Comm. on Rules*, 88th Cong. 444, 459 (1964) (statement of Rep. Whitener).
134. *Civil Rights: Hearings on Miscellaneous Proposals Regarding the Civil Rights of Persons Within the Jurisdiction of the United States Before the H. Comm. on the Judiciary*, 88th Cong. 1596 (1963) (statement of Rep. Dorn). Dorn compared unsuccessful federal efforts to pass an anti-lynching law with state successes.
135. *Civil Rights: Hearing on H.R. 7152 Before the H. Comm. on Rules*, 88th Cong. 170 (1964) (statement of Rep. Colmer).
136. *Civil Rights: Hearings on Miscellaneous Proposals Regarding the Civil Rights of Persons within the Jurisdiction of the United States Before Subcomm. No. 5 of the H. Comm. on the Judiciary*, 88th Cong. 1573–74 (1963) (statement of Rep. Dorn).
137. *See Civil Rights: Hearing on H.R. 7152 Before the H. Comm. on Rules*, 88th Cong. 170 (1964) (statement of Rep. Colmer).
138. 110 CONG. REC. 12315 (June 1, 1964) (statement of Sen. Long).
139. 110 CONG. REC. 14480 (June 19, 1964) (statement of Sen. Byrd).
140. 110 CONG. REC. 1972 (Feb. 5, 1964) (statement of Rep. Colmer).
141. *Heart of Atlanta*, 261–62; 379 U.S. 294 (1964).
142. *LBJ Hails Acceptance—Praises Southern Reaction to Law*, BIRMINGHAM POST-HERALD, Dec. 15, 1964, at 9.
143. ACKERMAN, 134–53.
144. DUDZIAK, 234.
145. ACKERMAN, 96 (quoting Lyndon B. Johnson, "Special Message to Congress: The American Promise," LBJ PRESIDENTIAL LIBRARY (Mar. 15, 1965), https://perma.cc/89SF-XZX7).

146. *Id.*, 97.
147. Brief of Amicus Curiae Legal Defense & Educational Fund, Inc. in Support of Respondents at 13–14, *Masterpiece Cakeshop.*
148. Newman v. Piggie Park Enterprises, 256 F. Supp. 941 (D. S. Car. 1966), *aff'd,* 377 F. 2d 433 (4th Cir. 1967), *aff'd,* 390 U.S. 400 (1968) (per curiam).

Chapter 6

1. 388 U.S. 1 (1967).
2. *See* R.A. Lenhardt, Tanya K. Hernandez, and Kimani Paul-Emile, *Foreword: Fifty Years of* Loving v. Virginia *and the Continued Pursuit of Racial Equality,* 86 FORDHAM LAW REVIEW 2625 (2018); *see also* Dorothy E. Roberts, Loving v. Virginia *as a Civil Rights Decision,* 59 NEW YORK LAW SCHOOL LAW REVIEW 175 (2015); Melissa Murray, *Strange Bedfellows: Criminal Law, Family Law, and the Legal Construction of Intimate Life,* 94 IOWA LAW REVIEW 1253, 1272 (2009) (arguing that *Loving* is also a significant criminal law case because it concerns decriminalizing rules around sexuality and marriage).
3. *Loving,* 17. In addition to the cinematic story told in *Loving* (2016), and the HBO documentary, *The Loving Story* (2012), a careful and engaging account is given in PETER WALLENSTEIN, TELL THE COURT I LOVE MY WIFE: RACE, MARRIAGE, AND LAW—AN AMERICAN HISTORY (New York: Palgrave Macmillan, 2002) and WALLENSTEIN, RACE, SEX, AND THE FREEDOM TO MARRY: *LOVING V. VIRGINIA* (Lawrence: University Press of Kansas, 2014). *See also* SHERYLL CASHIN, LOVING: INTERRACIAL INTIMACY IN AMERICA AND THE THREAT TO WHITE SUPREMACY 100–118 (Boston: Beacon Press, 2017).
4. 135 S. Ct. 2584 (2015).
5. *Compare* Amicus Brief of Ryan D. Anderson, PhD et al. in Support of Petitioners at 11, Masterpiece Cakeshop, Ltd. v. Colorado Civil Rights Commission, 138 S. Ct. 1719 (2018) (No. 16-111) (quoting *Obergefell*), *with* Brief of Amicus Curiae NAACP Legal Defense & Educational Fund, Inc., in Support of Respondents at 8–10, 12–13, *Masterpiece Cakeshop.*
6. Mildred Loving, "Loving for All" (public statement on 40th anniversary of *Loving v. Virginia*) (quoted in Bostic v. Rainey, 970 F. Supp. 2d 456, 460 (E.D. Va. 2014)).
7. *Obergefell,* 2598.
8. Lawrence v. Texas, 539 U.S. 558, 578–79 (2003).
9. United States v. Virginia, 518 U.S. 515, 557 (1996) (*VMI*).
10. *See generally* JAMES E. FLEMING, FIDELITY TO OUR IMPERFECT CONSTITUTION: FOR MORAL READINGS AND AGAINST ORIGINALISMS (New York: Oxford University Press, 2015).
11. *See generally* JACK BALKIN, CONSTITUTIONAL REDEMPTION: POLITICAL FAITH IN AN UNJUST WORLD (Cambridge, MA: Harvard University Press, 2011).
12. Brenner v. Scott, 999 F. Supp. 2d 1278, 1281 (N.D. Fla. 2014) (granting a preliminary injunction against Florida's ban on same-sex marriage).
13. Adam Liptak, *A Steady Path to Supreme Court as Gay Marriage Gains Momentum in States,* N.Y. TIMES, Feb. 14, 2014, at A1 (quoting Koppelman after federal district court struck down Virginia's ban on same-sex marriage).
14. Timothy Williams and Trib Gabriel, *Virginia's New Attorney General Opposes Ban on Gay Marriage,* N.Y. TIMES (Jan. 23, 2014).
15. Ryan T. Anderson, *7 Reasons Why the Current Marriage Debate is Nothing Like the Debate on Interracial Marriage,* DAILY SIGNAL, Aug. 27, 2014, http://dailysignal.com.
16. *Loving,* 3 (quoting trial court).
17. 87 S.E.2d 749, 753, 756 (Va. 1955).
18. 32 Cal.2d 711 (1948).
19. Loving v. Virginia, 147 S.E.2d 78, 80 (Va. 1966).
20. *Naim,* 751, 755 (quoting Maynard v. Hill, 125 U.S. 190, 205 (1888)).
21. *Loving,* 11.
22. *Id.,* 12.
23. Brief and Appendix on Behalf of Appellee at 6, Loving v. Virginia, 388 U.S. 1 (1967) (No. 395) (Brief of Appellee). All the briefs and oral argument in *Loving* are available in the database, United States Supreme Court Records and Briefs 1832–1978, Gale, Cengage Learning.

See also LANDMARK BRIEFS AND ARGUMENTS OF THE SUPREME COURT OF THE UNITED STATES, Vol. 64 (Phillip B. Kurland and Gerhard Casper, eds., Arlington, VA: University Publications of America, 1975). I use original page numbers.

24. Brief of Appellee, 38, 41. For such "scientific authorities," the brief (at 41–47) quotes those cited in the dissent in *Perez*, 33–45. In the only amicus brief filed in support of Virginia, North Carolina asserted that appeals to science—with its competing "experts"—will never "settle the question." Brief of the State of North Carolina as Amicus Curiae at 5, *Loving*.

25. Brief of Appellee, 47 (citing ALBERT I. GORDON, INTERMARRIAGE: INTERFAITH, INTERRACIAL, INTERETHNIC (Boston: Beacon Press, 1964)).

26. Transcript of Oral Argument, 20, *Loving*.

27. *Id.*, 32.

28. *Id.*, 27–28, 33–34.

29. *Id.*, 28.

30. Brief of Appellee, 27–28.

31. Transcript of Oral Argument, 44.

32. *Id.*, 28. Gordon disavowed any reliance on a biological argument in his tallying of the costs of intermarriage. GORDON, 220–21.

33. Brief of Appellee, 48 (quoting GORDON, 357–58) (emphasis supplied).

34. Transcript of Oral Argument, 29.

35. *Id.*, 30, 44.

36. *Id.*, 28. Notably, in *Perez*, the majority opinion observed: "If miscegenous marriages can be prohibited because of tensions suffered by the progeny, mixed religious unions could be prohibited on the same ground." *Perez*, 727.

37. Brief of Appellee, 28.

38. For example, four chapters (pages 87–209) of Gordon's *Intermarriage* address interfaith marriage: chapter 4, Interfaith Marriages; chapter 5, The Protestant Positions; chapter 6, The Catholic Point of View; and chapter 7, The Jew and Intermarriage. Gordon addresses interracial marriage in two chapters (pages 263–94): chapter 8, Interracial Marriages; and chapter 9, Negroes and Whites. There is one short chapter on "Interethnic Marriages" (chapter 10, pages 295–309). His chapter, "What of the Children?" (chapter 11, pages 310–47) contains more narratives about interfaith marriages than interracial ones.

39. Brief of Appellee, Appendix B (App.) 9, 10–11 (quoting GORDON, 367, 368–70).

40. *Id.*, App. 9 (quoting GORDON, 368–69).

41. *Id.*, App. 7 (citing GORDON, 359).

42. *Id.*, App. 6 (quoting GORDON, 358–59) (emphasis in Appendix); see also App. 8 (quoting GORDON, 367–69) (criticizing "mistaken premise" that intermarriage assures "universalism and human brotherhood").

43. *See* GORDON, 220–21.

44. *Id.*, 66.

45. *Id.*, 333.

46. *Id.*, 333–34.

47. *Id.*, 334.

48. Brief of Appellee, App. 11 (quoting GORDON, 369–70).

49. GORDON, 334.

50. Brief of Appellee, App. 4 (quoting GORDON, 348–49).

51. GORDON, 348–49.

52. *Id.*, 349 (emphasis added).

53. *Id.* In *Prince v. Massachusetts*, 321 U.S. 158, 170 (1944), the Court stated: "Parents may be free to become martyrs themselves. But it does not follow that they are free . . . to make martyrs of their children."

54. Brief of Appellee, 47. I have not been able to find this statement by Allport.

55. GORDON, viii. In doing his questionnaires, Gordon evidently used the computers at MIT and at Harvard's Laboratory of Social Relations, with which Allport was associated. *Id.*, vii.

56. GORDON W. ALLPORT, THE NATURE OF PREJUDICE 377 (1954; New York: Basic Books, 25th anniversary edition, 1979)).

57. Transcript of Oral Argument, 46.

58. Brief for Appellants, 1, 8, *Loving*.

59. *Id.*, 9, 15, 20–24.

60. Brief of NAACP Legal Defense and Educational Fund, Inc., as Amicus Curiae at 6, 9–10, 14, *Loving* (Fund brief).

61. Brief for Appellants, 24, 27 (quoting GUNNAR MYRDAL, AN AMERICAN DILEMMA: THE NEGRO PROBLEM AND AMERICAN DEMOCRACY 591 (1944)).

62. *Id.*, 27–28 (quoting MYRDAL, 66, 590–91).

63. *Id. See also* Brief of the National Association for the Advancement of Colored People as Amicus Curiae at 1, 6, *Loving* (NAACP brief) (arguing that the Court should strike down such laws as "relics of the system of human slavery").

64. *Maynard*, 205, quoted in *Naim*, 751, and Brief of Appellee, 51–52.

65. Brief of Amici Curiae Japanese American Citizens League at 6, *Loving* (JACL brief).

66. *Id.*, 4, 10.

67. *Id.*, 30.

68. Brief for Appellants, 12.

69. Fund brief, 11 (quoting PHYSICAL ANTHROPOLOGISTS & GENETICISTS, UNESCO, STATEMENT ON THE NATURE OF RACE AND RACE DIFFERENCES art 7 (1952)); NAACP brief, 9 (same).

70. Fund brief, 5.

71. Brief for Appellants, 37.

72. Transcript of Oral Argument, 30.

73. *Id.*, 30–32, 40.

74. Brief Amicus Curiae, Urging Reversal, On Behalf of John J. Russell, Bishop of Richmond et al., *Loving* (NCCIJ brief).

75. *Id.*, 6, 7–10, 20.

76. *Id.*, 13 (quoting West Virginia Bd. of Ed. v. Barnette, 319 U.S. 624, 639 (1943)).

77. *Id.*, 14–16 (emphasis in original).

78. *Id.*

79. *Id.*, 17 (quoting *Perez*, 25).

80. 466 U.S. 429 (1984).

81. RENEE C. ROMANO, RACE MIXING: BLACK–WHITE MARRIAGE IN POST-WAR AMERICA 190 (Gainesville: University Press of Florida, 2006 pbk.). James Oleske also observes that despite the pervasiveness of religious objections to interracial marriage, academics did not write articles calling for accommodation of such objections through religious exemptions. James Oleske, *The Evolution of Accommodation*, 50 HARVARD CIVIL RIGHTS-CIVIL LIBERTIES LAW REVIEW 99 (2015).

82. ROMANO, 186.

83. *Id.*, 186–87.

84. *Id.*, 190.

85. PASCOE, 289.

86. *Id.* (giving examples of federal cases).

87. *Id.*, 290.

88. *Id.*, 292.

89. *Id.*, 291, 293.

90. *Id.*, 294. *See Loving*, 11 (quoting Hirabayashi v. U.S., 320 U.S. 81, 100 (1943)).

91. PASCOE, 294 (citing *Hirabayashi*, 100).

92. *Loving*, 11 (quoting Korematsu v. U.S. 323 U.S. 214 (1944)). Trump v. Hawaii, 138 S. Ct. 2392, 2423 (2018) officially overruled *Korematsu*, yet upheld what President Trump had called his "Muslim ban," which he had analogized to President Roosevelt's exclusion order upheld in *Korematsu*.

93. PASCOE, 293.

94. ROMANO, 191 n.34 (quoting N.Y. TIMES, June 20, 1967, at p. 39).

95. *Mixed Marriage Pleases Secretary Rusk*, CHICAGO DEFENDER, Sept. 30, 1967, at 31; *Secretary Rusk's Daughter is Married*, BOSTON GLOBE, Sept. 22, 1967, at 1; Bosley Crowther, *Screen: 'Guess Who's Coming To Dinner' Arrives*, N.Y. TIMES, Dec. 12, 1967, at 56; *Council of Churches Honors Kramer for Interracial Film*, L.A. TIMES, Mar. 14, 1968, at B1. On both

the Rusk wedding and the movie, see ROMANO, 201–08. Romano observes that, by this time, black nationalists, emphasizing black pride and Black Power, were critical of interracial marriage and of viewing it as a "courageous and symbolic act of racial brotherhood." ROMANO, 217–18.

96. PASCOE, 296.

97. Pew Research Center, *Intermarriage in the U.S. 50 Years After Loving v. Virginia*, 7–8 (May 16, 2017). The persistence of "popular images and stereotypes of biracial children" as "confused" and the "innocent victims" of their parents also raises questions about progress on "race, family, and intimacy." *See* ANGELA ONWUACHI-WILLIG, ACCORDING TO OUR HEARTS 270–74 (New Haven, CT: Yale University Press, 2013).

98. *A love letter to supporters of #RepresentLove*, N.Y. TIMES, Mar. 5, 2019, at A7 (placed by tinder).

99. *See* SONU BEDI, PRIVATE RACISM 132–33 (New York: Cambridge University Press 2020).

100. PASCOE, 296.

101. John Eligon, *Virginia Suit Asks, Why Should Couples Have to List Their Race to Marry?*, N.Y. TIMES, Sept. 9, 2019, at A14; Rogers v. Virginia State Registrar, Civil Action No 1:19-cv-01149-RDA-IDD at 3–6, 17–18 (E.D. Va. Oct. 11, 2019).

102. Baker v. Nelson, 191 N.W.2d 185 (Minn. 1971).

103. For this history, see WALLENSTEIN, RACE, SEX, AND THE FREEDOM TO MARRY, 176–209.

104. *Id.*, 178 (quoting oral argument by Michael Wetherbee).

105. *Id.*, 179; *Baker*, 186.

106. *Baker*, 186.

107. 410 U.S. 810 (1972).

108. Transcript of Oral Argument at 12, Hollingsworth v. Perry, 133 S. Ct. 2652 (2013) (No. 12-144) (responding to Charles J. Cooper's reliance on *Baker*).

109. 798 N.E.2d 941, 958 (Mass. 2003).

110. *Id.*, 966.

111. For elaboration, see Linda C. McClain, *Reading DeBoer and Obergefell Through the "Moral Readings Versus Originalisms" Debate: From Constitutional "Empty Cupboards" to Evolving Understandings*, 31 CONSTITUTIONAL COMMENTARY 441, 457–59, 466–74 (2016).

112. *Goodridge*, 970–74 (Greaney, J., concurring). *See also* Latta v. Otter, 771 F. 3d 456 (9th Cir. 2014) (Berzon, J., concurring) (making sex discrimination argument).

113. United States v. Windsor, 133 S. Ct. 2675, 2691 (2013).

114. Bostic v. Rainey, 970 F. Supp. 2d 456, 461 (E.D. Va. 2014).

115. *Id.*

116. *Id.*, 464 (citing Va. Code § 20.45.2).

117. *Id.*, 465 (citing Article I, Section 15-A of the Virginia Constitution).

118. *Virginia's New Attorney General Will Not Defend Gay Marriage Ban*, MORNING EDITION (Jan. 23, 2014), https://perma.cc/646C-H7RX.

119. Transcript of Proceedings at 17, Bostic v. Rainey, 970 F. Supp. 2d 460 (E.D. Va. 2014) (No. 13-CV-00395), ECF 132.

120. *Id.*, 19–20 (citing Romer v. Evans, 517 U.S. 620 (1996), *Lawrence*, and *Windsor*).

121. *Id.*, 21–22.

122. *Id.*

123. *Id.*, 31.

124. *Id.*, 39. Oakley asserted that the Supreme Court's summary affirmance in *Baker* was highly significant.

125. *Id.*, 48–49.

126. *Id.*, 52–53. In support, Nimocks cites Justice Ginsburg. In *VMI*, she wrote: "'Inherent differences' between men and women, we have come to appreciate, remain cause for celebration, but not for denigration of the members of either sex or for artificial constraints on an individual's opportunity." *VMI*, 533.

127. Transcript of Proceedings, 48–51 (endorsing reasoning of Hernandez v. Robles, 855 N.E. 2d 1 (N.Y. 2006)).

128. *Naim*, 756.

129. Transcript of Proceedings, 16.

130. *Id.*, 73.

131. *Id.*, 72–73.
132. *Id.*, 4–5.
133. *Id.*, 11.
134. *Id.*, 80.
135. Robert Barnes and David Farentold, *Who's the Judge in Virginia Gay Marriage Ban Case? A Seeker of a "More Perfect Freedom,"* WASH. POST (Feb. 14, 2014).
136. *Bostic*, 460 (quoting Mildred Loving's statement, "Loving for All, Public Statement on the 40th Anniversary of Loving v. Virginia"). The Fourth Circuit (with one judge dissenting) affirmed the federal district court. Bostic v. Schaefer, 760 F.3d 352 (4th Cir. 2014). *Bostic v. Rainey* was republished with slight revision at 2014 WL 10022686 with no effect on the quoted language.
137. *Bostic*, 460.
138. *Id.*, 464 n.5, 471–73, 473.
139. *Id.*, 472 n.8 (citing *Loving*, 7 (quoting *Naim*, 756)).
140. *Id.*, 474 n.9 (quoting Nimocks).
141. *Id.*, 474 (citing Heller v. Doe, 509 U.S. 312 (1993)).
142. *Id.*, 474 n.9.
143. *Id.*, 474–75.
144. *Id.*, 476 (citing *Windsor*, 133 S. Ct. at 2709 (Scalia, J., dissenting)), 481.
145. *Id.*, 483 n.18 (citing numerous cases from 1932 to 1996, including *Loving*).
146. *Rogers*, 18.
147. Brenner v. Scott, 999 F. Supp.2d 1278, 1281 (N.D. Fla. 2014).
148. *Id.*
149. *Id.*
150. *Id.*, 1289–90.
151. *Id.*, 1292.
152. Brief Amicus Curiae of the U.S. Conference of Catholic Bishops in Support of Respondents and Affirmance at 2, Obergefell v. Hodges, 135 S. Ct. 2584 (2015) (Nos. 14-556, 14-571, 14-574).
153. Brief of Louisiana et al as Amici Curiae Supporting Respondents at 24–25, *Obergefell*. The states are: Utah, Texas, Alaska, Arizona, Arkansas, Georgia, Idaho, Kansas, Montana, Nebraska, North Dakota, Oklahoma, South Dakota, and West Virginia.
154. *Id.*, 25–26 (quoting *Hernandez*, 8).
155. *Id.*, 24–25.
156. Those other states are: Arkansas, Georgia, Oklahoma, Texas, and West Virginia. *See* Appendix II to Fund brief (filed in *Loving*), 19–20 (listing states still prohibiting interracial marriage as including, among others, Arkansas, Georgia, Louisiana, Oklahoma, Texas, and West Virginia).
157. Brief of Louisiana, 25 (quoting *Baker* and noting Supreme Court's summary dismissal).
158. Brief of Amicus Curiae State of South Carolina in Support of Respondents at 30–31, *Obergefell*.
159. Brief of Robert J. Bentley, Governor of Alabama, as Amicus Curiae in Support of Respondents at 22, *Obergefell*.
160. *Id.*, 22–23.
161. *See* JULIE NOVKOV, RACIAL UNION: LAW, INTIMACY, AND THE WHITE STATE IN ALABAMA, 1865–1954 (Ann Arbor: University of Michigan Press, 2008).
162. Brief of the Commonwealth of Virginia as Amicus Curiae in Support of Petitioners, *Obergefell*.
163. *Id.*, 2–5.
164. Brief for the NAACP Legal Defense & Educational Fund, Inc., and the National Association for the Advancement of Colored People as Amici Curiae Supporting Petitioners at 25, *Obergefell*.
165. *Id.*, 32–33.
166. *Compare* Brief of Amici Curiae Carlos A. Ball et al. in Support of Petitioners at 4, 13, *Obergefell* (arguing that "the empirical-sounding, pseudoscientific assertions of jurists and counsel in defending marital bans in one era often are *revealed* as invidious and indefensible

discrimination over time"). *See also* CARLOS A. BALL, SAME-SEX MARRIAGE AND CHILDREN (New York: Oxford University Press, 2014).

167. *Obergefell*, 2603–04.
168. *Id.*, 2598.
169. *Id.*
170. *Id.*, 2603.
171. *Id.* Bruce Ackerman criticizes *Loving* for not "vindicating *Brown*'s enduring insights" and stressing the "humiliation" inflicted by antimiscegenation laws. BRUCE ACKERMAN, WE THE PEOPLE, VOL. 3: THE CIVIL RIGHTS REVOLUTION 302–03 (Cambridge, MA: Harvard University Press, 2014).
172. *Obergefell*, 2604.
173. *Id.*, 2598–99.
174. *Id.*, 2605.
175. *Id.*, 2599.
176. *Id.*, 2601.
177. *Id.*, 2602 (citing *Loving* and *Lawrence*).
178. *Id.*, 2599–601.
179. *Id.*, 2602. The second and third principles are that "the right to marry is fundamental because it supports a two-person union unlike any other in its importance to the committed individuals" and that "marriage safeguards children and families." *Id.*, 2599–601.
180. *Id.*, 2619 (Roberts, C.J., dissenting).
181. *Id.*, 2642–43 (Alito, J., dissenting).
182. *Id.*, 2602 (majority opinion).
183. In the words of concurring Justice Carter, California's laws "are the product of ignorance, prejudice and intolerance." *Perez*, 732.

Chapter 7

1. William Raspberry, *Anita Bryant and Gay Rights: Bigotry or Prudence?*, WASH. POST, May 2, 1977, at A23.
2. MARK D. JORDAN, RECRUITING YOUNG LOVE: HOW CHRISTIANS TALK ABOUT HOMOSEXUALITY 129–36 (Chicago: University of Chicago Press, 2011).
3. Raspberry, A23 (emphasis in original). Raspberry, who later won a Pulitzer Prize, was "one of the most widely read black journalists of his generation." *William Raspberry Dies at 76; Prize-Winning Columnist*, L.A. TIMES (July 18, 2012), https://perma.cc/G473-HSZ7.
4. JORDAN, 135 (70% voted yes on the referendum).
5. Jon Nordheimer, *Miami Homosexuals See a Victory Despite Defeat of Antibias Law*, N.Y. TIMES, Dec. 28, 1977, at 14.
6. JORDAN, 129, 148–49.
7. *See* CARLOS A. BALL, FROM THE CLOSET TO THE COURTROOM: FIVE LGBT RIGHTS LAWSUITS THAT HAVE CHANGED OUR NATION 99–105 (Boston: Beacon Press, 2010).
8. Romer v. Evans, 517 U.S. 620, 632 (1996).
9. *Id.*, 652 (Scalia, J., dissenting) (citing Bowers v. Hardwick, 478 U.S. 186 (1986)).
10. *Compare* United States v. Windsor, 133 S. Ct. 2675, 2693 (2013), *with* Obergefell v. Hodges, 135 S. Ct. 2584, 2595, 2602 (2015).
11. See WILLIAM D. ARAIZA, ANIMUS: A SHORT INTRODUCTION TO BIAS IN THE LAW (New York: New York University Press, 2017). For other helpful accounts, see Dale Carpenter, *Windsor Products: Equal Protection from Animus*, 2013 SUPREME COURT REVIEW 183 (2014); Susan Pollvogt, *Unconstitutional Animus*, 81 FORDHAM LAW REVIEW 87 (2012).
12. *Obergefell*, 2602.
13. *Id.*, 2626 (Roberts, C.J., dissenting); 2630 (Scalia, J., dissenting); 2642–43 (Alito, J., dissenting).
14. H.R. Rep. No. 104-664 (1996).
15. Bowers v. Hardwick, 478 U.S. 186, 190–91 (1986), *reversing* Hardwick v. Bowers, 760 F.2d 1202 (11th Cir. 1985).

16. *Bowers*, 193–94.

17. *Id.*, 196–97 (Burger, C.J., concurring).

18. *Id.* (citing Bailey); Brief of Petitioner Michael J. Bowers, Attorney General of Georgia at 21, Bowers v. Hardwick, 478 U.S. 1039 (1986) (No. 85-140), 1985 WL 667939 (citing Bailey). All "WL" citations given for the party and amicus briefs are to the Westlaw data base.

19. HEATHER R. WHITE, REFORMING SODOM: PROTESTANTS AND THE RISE OF GAY RIGHTS 173 (Chapel Hill: University of North Carolina Press, 2015).

20. Brief of Amici Curiae the Presbyterian Church (U.S.A.) et al. at *12–15, *Bowers*, 1986 WL 720447. *See also* Brief of the American Jewish Congress, Amici Curiae, in Support of Respondents at *v, *Bowers*, 1985 WL 667945 (AJC brief) (although Jewish law unambiguously forbids same-sex sexual acts, the "moral beliefs" of a majority of voters are not sufficient to "regulate intimate sexual association . . . within the privacy of the home").

21. Brief of Presbyterian Church, Appendix A at *1A–14A.

22. *Id.*, *11A.

23. *Id.*, *6 (citing Loving v. Virginia, 388 U.S. 1, 3 (1967)).

24. *Id.*, *14–15.

25. Brief for Respondent at *26, *Bowers*, 1986 WL 720442.

26. Brief of Petitioner, *27.

27. Brief of the Rutherford Institute et al. in Support of the Petitioner at *3, *23, *26, *Bowers*, 1985 WL 667943.

28. Brief for the Catholic League for Religious and Civil Rights, Amicus Curiae, in Support of Petitioner at *4, *Bowers*, 1985 WL 667940.

29. Brief of Petitioner, *24–25.

30. *Id.*, *32–34; Brief of the Rutherford Institute, *27 (including bestiality and necrophilia).

31. Brief Amicus Curiae for Lesbian Rights Project et al at *20, *Bowers*, 1985 WL 667944.

32. Brief of Presbyterian Church, *5, *7–8.

33. Amici Curiae Brief on Behalf of the Respondents by Lambda Legal Defense and Education Fund, Inc. et al at *7, *12, *Bowers*, 1986 WL 720449.

34. Brief of National Gay Rights Advocates et al at *16, *Bowers*, 1985 WL 667946 (citing U.S. Dep't of Agriculture v. Moreno, 413 U.S. 528, 534 (1973)).

35. *Id.*, *17; Brief for the National Organization for Women as Amicus Curiae in Support of Petitioners at *26–27, *Bowers*, 1986 WL 720446.

36. National Gay Rights Advocates Brief, *17 (citing Palmore v. Sidoti, 466 U.S. 429 (1984)).

37. Brief for Lesbian Rights Project, *12 n.14 (attributing coinage of "homophobia" to George Weinberg, author of SOCIETY AND THE HEALTHY HOMOSEXUAL (New York: St. Martin's Press, 1972)).

38. *Id.*, *22–23.

39. *Id.*, *28–30 (citing Bradwell v. State, 83 U.S. 130 (1873), Plessy v. Ferguson, 163 U.S. 537 (1896), and Korematsu v. U.S., 323 U.S. 214 (1944)).

40. *Bowers*, 216–18 (Stevens, J., dissenting).

41. *Id.*, 205 (Blackmun, J., dissenting).

42. *Id.*, 210 n.5.

43. *Id.*, 212.

44. Lawrence v. Texas, 539 U.S. 558, 578 (2003).

45. *Id.*, 575.

46. Respondent's Brief at 41, Lawrence v. Texas, 123 S. Ct. 2472 (2003), (No. 02-102), 2003 WL 470184.

47. Brief Amicus Curiae of United Families International in Support of Respondent at *29, *Lawrence*, 2003 WL 345829.

48. *Lawrence*, 573.

49. Brief for the States of Alabama, Utah, and South Carolina as Amici Curiae in Support of Respondent at *1, *Lawrence*, 2003 WL 470172.

50. Brief Amicus Curiae for the Center for Law and Justice International Supporting Respondent at *3, *Lawrence*, 2003 WL 469830.

51. Brief Amici Curiae of Mary Robinson et al in Support of Petitioners at *18, *Lawrence*, 2003 WL 164151.

52. Brief of the American Bar Association as Amicus Curiae in Support of Petitioners at *12, *Lawrence*, 2003 WL 164108 (ABA brief); Brief of the Republican Unity Coalition and Hon. Alan K. Simpson in Support of Petitioners at 21, *Lawrence*, 2003 WL 152351.

53. Brief of the CATO Institute as Amicus Curiae in Support of Petitioners at *24, *Lawrence*, 2003 WL 152342; Amicus Curiae Brief of the Log Cabin Republicans and Liberty Education Forum in Support of Petitioners at *16, *Lawrence*, 2003 WL 164149.

54. *Compare* Brief of Texas Legislators et al. as Amicus Curiae Supporting Respondents at *18, *Lawrence*, 2003 WL 470181, *with* ABA brief, *19–20.

55. Brief of the Alliance of Baptists et al as Amici Curiae Supporting Petitioners at *4–16, *Lawrence*, 2003 WL 152331.

56. *Lawrence*, 572.

57. *Id.*, 571 (quoting Planned Parenthood v. Casey, 505 U.S. 833, 850 (1992)).

58. *Id.*, 574, 578.

59. *Id.*, 580, 582 (O'Connor, J., concurring).

60. *Id.*, 582, 585.

61. *Id.*, 589 (Scalia, J., dissenting).

62. *Id.*, 600–02, 605.

63. BALL, 99–105. *See also* LISA KEEN AND SUZANNE B. GOLDBERG, STRANGERS TO THE LAW: GAY PEOPLE ON TRIAL (Ann Arbor: University of Michigan Press, 1998).

64. LEGIS. COUNSEL OF THE COLO. GEN. ASSEMB., AN ANALYSIS OF 1992 BALLOT PROPOSALS, GEN. ASSEMB. 58–369, 9–10 (1992).

65. *Id.*, 11–12 (emphasis added).

66. Evans v. Romer, 854 P.2d 1270, 1272 (Colo. 1993).

67. Brief for Colorado for Family Values as Amicus Curiae Supporting Petitioners at *1, Romer v. Evans, 517 U.S. 620 (1996) (No. 94-1039), 1995 WL 17008427.

68. Brief for Concerned Women for America, Inc. as Amicus Curiae Supporting Petitioners at *14, *15–16, *Romer*, 1995 WL 17008430 (Westlaw) (CWA brief).

69. Brief for Family Research Council as Amicus Curiae Supporting Petitioners at *9 (quoting *Bowers*, 194–95), *Romer*, 1995 WL 17008422.

70. Brief for Oregon Citizens Alliance et al. as Amici Curiae Supporting Petitioners at *10–11, *Romer*, 1995 WL 17008451.

71. *Id.*, *12, *15–16.

72. *Id.*

73. CWA brief, *20.

74. Brief for Christian Legal Society et al. as Amici Curiae Supporting Petitioners at *8, *10, *11–14, *Romer*, 1995 WL 17008428.

75. *Id.*, *25, *26.

76. Brief of the American Psychological Ass'n et al. as Amici Curiae in Support of Respondents at *17–19, *27, *Romer*, 1995 WL 17008445 (APA brief).

77. Cleburne v. Cleburne Living Center, 473 U.S. 432 (1985).

78. Brief for National Bar Ass'n as Amicus Curiae Supporting Respondents at *5, *7, 1995 WL 17008431; Brief of the American Bar Ass'n as Amicus Curiae in Support of Respondents at *3, *Romer*, 1995 WL 17008433 (ABA brief).

79. ABA brief, 16–17, *21, *Romer*; Brief of the Human Rights Campaign Fund (HRCF) et al as Amici Curiae in Support of Respondents at *8, *21, *28–30, *Romer*, 1995 WL 17008436.

80. *See* Brief for Amici Curiae of Affirmation: United Methodists for Gay, Lesbian, and Bisexual Concerns et al as Amici Curiae in Support of Respondents at *2, *Romer*, 1995 WL 17008438; Brief for the NAACP Legal Defense & Educational Fund, Inc. et al. as Amici Curiae in Support of Respondents at *15, *Romer*, 1995 WL 17008435; Brief for Amici Curiae Asian American Legal Defense & Education Fund et al. in Support of Respondents at *10, *Romer*, 1995 WL 17008434.

81. Brief Amici Curiae of Leigh Earls et al in Support of Petitioner at 2, Palmore v. Sidoti, 466 U.S. 429 (1984), No. 82-1734 (available on Proquest Supreme Court Insight).

82. Palmore v. Sidoti, 466 U.S. 429, 433 (1984).

83. Brief of Amicus Curiae of the American Friends Service Committee et al. in Support of Respondents (AFSC brief) at *1, *Romer*, 1995 WL 17008442; *see also* Brief of Amicus

Curiae of James E. Andrews as Stated Clerk of the General Assembly of the Presbyterian Church (U.S.A.) in Support of Respondents at *1, *2, *4, *Romer*, 1995 WL 17008443 (Establishment Clause violation).

84. AFSC brief, *2, *10.

85. ABA brief, *22, *23, *Romer*.

86. *Id.*, *18, *19 (citing *Palmore*, 433).

87. *Id.*, *19 (internal citations omitted).

88. Brief of the Cities of Atlanta, Baltimore et al. as Amici Curiae in Support of Respondents at *4, *Romer*, 1995 WL 17008444.

89. Romer v. Evans, 517 U.S. 620, 631, 633 (1996).

90. *Id.*, 632, 634 (citing *Moreno*, 534).

91. *Id.*, 636 (citing *Civil Rights Cases*, 109 U.S. 3, 24 (1883)).

92. *Id.*, 641, 644 (Scalia, J., dissenting).

93. *Id.*, 645–47, 653.

94. *Id.*, 652.

95. KEEN AND GOLDBERG, 226–27, 235, 238.

96. Charles W. Colson, *The End of Democracy?: Kingdoms in Conflict*, FIRST THINGS (Nov. 1996), https://perma.cc/MS68-MG4F.

97. H.R. Rep. No. 104–664, at 2.

98. Defense of Marriage Act of 1996, §§ 2–3, 28 U.S.C. § 1738C (2006).

99. U.S. Gov't Accountability Office, GAO-04-353R, DEFENSE OF MARRIAGE ACT: UPDATE TO PRIOR REPORT 1 (2004), https://perma.cc/ZG85-HJ23; H.R. Rep. No. 104-664, at 10 ("The word 'marriage' appears in more than 800 sections of federal statutes and regulations, and the word 'spouse' appears more than 3,100 times.").

100. H.R. Rep. No. 104-664, at 16.

101. *See id.*, 34 (DOJ letter advising Rep. Canady: "*Romer v. Evans* does not affect the Department's analysis (that H.R. 3396 is constitutionally sustainable)").

102. *Id.*, 32–33 (A Short Note on *Romer v. Evans*) (citing *Bowers*, 196).

103. 798 N.E.2d 941 (Mass. 2003).

104. *See* Massachusetts v. U.S. Dept. of Health and Human Servs., 682 F.3d 1 (1st Cir. 2012).

105. Letter from Attorney General Eric Holder to Hon. John A. Boehner, Speaker, U.S. House of Representatives, 4 (Feb. 23, 2011).

106. Windsor v. United States, 833 F. Supp.2d 394, 398–400 (S.D.N.Y. 2012), *aff'd*, 699 F.3d 169 (2d Cir. 2012) (concluding that New York uniformly recognized Windsor's marriage by 2009). In 1993, they had registered as domestic partners in New York City.

107. For a list, see Supreme Court Information, United States v. Windsor, https://perma.cc/6G68-G4KP. (I joined an amicus brief filed in support of Windsor, Brief of Amici Curiae Family and Child Welfare Law Professors and in Support of Respondents.) All briefs filed in *Windsor* may be found at the following case file on SCOTUSblog: https://perma.cc/7FK4-CCN5. Unless otherwise indicated, all briefs mentioned are on the merits, not on whether to grant certiorari.

108. Brief of United States Senators Orrin G. Hatch et al. as Amici Curiae Supporting Respondent BLAG at 28, United States v. Windsor, 133 S. Ct. 2675 (2013) (No. 12-307).

109. *Id.*, 26 (citing *Romer*, 635).

110. H.R. Rep. No. 104-664, at 13. For example, Brief for Liberty Counsel as Amicus Curiae Supporting Respondent BLAG at 36, *Windsor*; Amicus Curiae Brief of Manhattan Declaration in Support of Respondent BLAG at 3 n.15, *Windsor*.

111. Brief Addressing the Merits of the State of Indiana and 16 Other States as Amici Curiae in Support of Respondent BLAG at 2–3, *Windsor*.

112. Brief of Manhattan Declaration, 3, n.15; *see also* Amicus Curiae Brief for Coalition for the Protection of Marriage in Support of Hollingsworth and BLAG at 35, *Windsor*.

113. *Amicus Curiae* Brief of Concerned Women for America, Addressing the Merits and Supporting Respondent BLAG and Reversal at 33, *Windsor*.

114. *See* Brief Amici Curiae of National Ass'n of Evangelicals et al. in Support of BLAG at 1, 2, 11–13, *Windsor*.

115. Amici Curiae Brief of Robert P. George et al. in Support of Hollingsworth and BLAG at 5–6, 15, *Windsor*.

116. Brief for Foundation for Moral Law as Amicus Curiae Supporting Respondent BLAG at 3, 26, *Windsor.*
117. Brief for Liberty, Life, and Law Foundation and North Carolina Values Coalition as Amici Curiae Supporting Hollingsworth and Respondent BLAG at 3–4, *Windsor* (quoting *Bowers*, 197).
118. Brief for Gay & Lesbian Advocates & Defenders and Lambda Legal Defense and Education Fund, Inc., as Amici Curiae Supporting Respondent Edith Windsor and the United States at 17, *Windsor* (citing Bd. of Trs. of the Univ. of Ala. v. Garrett, 531 U.S. 356, 374 (2001) (Kennedy, J., concurring)).
119. *See id.,* 22–25 (quoting H.R. Rep. No. 104–664, at 15–16).
120. Brief of 172 Members of the U.S. House of Representatives and 40 U.S. Senators as Amici Curiae in Support of Respondent Edith Schlain Windsor at 20, *Windsor.*
121. *See, e.g.,* Brief for the Anti-Defamation League et al. as Amici Curiae in Support of Respondent Edith Windsor at 20, *Windsor* (quoting *Lawrence,* 577).
122. *Id.*
123. *Id.,* 19.
124. Brief Amicus Curiae of the American Humanist Ass'n et al. in Support of Respondents, at 20, *Windsor.*
125. Brief of 172 Members, 22 (quoting *Lawrence,* 560; Heller v. Doe, 509 U.S. 312, 327 (1993)).
126. Brief of *Amicus Curiae* The American Bar Association in Support of Respondent Edith Schlain Windsor at 33, *Windsor* (ABA brief).
127. Brief for the American Jewish Committee as Amicus Curiae Supporting Individual Respondents at 8–9, *Windsor* (AJC brief).
128. Brief of the American Psychological Association et al. as Amici Curiae at 14–26, *Windsor.*
129. Brief Amici Curiae Family & Child Welfare Law Professors in Support of Respondents at 5, *Windsor* (quoting *Lawrence,* 604).
130. *Id.,* 36 (quoting *Romer,* 632).
131. APA brief, 34–35.
132. Brief *Amicus Curiae* of the Becket Fund for Religious Liberty in Support of Hollingsworth and BLAG at 29, *Windsor.*
133. Brief for Liberty, Life, and Law Foundation, 16–17.
134. Manhattan Declaration Brief, 15–19.
135. Brief for Catholic Answers, Christian Legal Society, and Catholic Vote Education as Amici Curiae Supporting Respondent BLAG at 11, *Windsor.*
136. Brief of Amici Curiae Bishops of the Episcopal Church in the States of California et al., in Support of Respondent Edith Schlain Windsor at 3, 5, *Windsor.*
137. AJC brief, 3–4.
138. United States v. Windsor, 133 S. Ct. 2675, 2694 (2013).
139. *Id.,* 2693 (citing *Romer,* 633; *Moreno,* 534–45).
140. *Id.,* 2693, 2696.
141. *Id.,* 2693–94.
142. *Id.,* 2696 (Roberts, C.J., dissenting) (emphasis in original).
143. *Id.,* 2718–19 (Alito, J., dissenting) (citing SHERIF GIRGIS, RYAN ANDERSON, AND ROBERT GEORGE, WHAT IS MARRIAGE? MAN AND WOMAN: A DEFENSE (New York: Encounter Books, 2012) as offering a "philosophical" account of the "conjugal" view). The authors discussed these models in their amicus brief, mentioned earlier.
144. *Windsor,* 2716.
145. *Id.,* 2718.
146. *Id.,* 2707–09 (Scalia, J., dissenting).
147. *Id.,* 2710–11.
148. *Lawrence,* 604 (Scalia, J., dissenting).
149. *Windsor,* 2708–10.
150. *See* Stephen D. Smith, *The Jurisprudence of Denigration,* 48 UNIVERSITY OF CALIFORNIA-DAVIS LAW REVIEW 675 (2014).
151. Richard W. Garnett, *Worth Worrying About? Same-Sex Marriage & Religious Freedom,* COMMONWEAL (Aug. 5, 2013).

152. Michael J. Perry, *Right Result, Wrong Reason: Same-Sex Marriage & the Supreme Court*, COMMONWEAL (Aug. 5, 2013).

153. Carpenter, 263–70 (giving examples from DOMA debates).

154. *Id.*, 270 (giving examples).

155. *Id.*, 263.

156. Kennedy's majority opinion indicated: "This opinion and its holding are confined to those lawful marriages," that is, marriages permitted or recognized under state law, but denied recognition by DOMA. *Windsor*, 2694.

157. Obergefell v. Hodges, 135 S. Ct. 2584, 2599 (2015).

158. *Id.*, 2596, 2598–2604, 2606.

159. *Id.*, 2604–05.

160. *See* Smith, 677–78.

161. *Obergefell*, 2602.

162. *Id.*, 2594–95. *See* Carlos A. Ball, *Bigotry and Same-Sex Marriage*, 84 UNIVERSITY OF MISSOURI KANSAS CITY LAW REVIEW 639 (2016) (criticizing dissenters' rhetoric of bigotry).

163. *Obergefell*, 2626 (Roberts, C.J., dissenting).

164. *Id.*, 2630 (Scalia, J., dissenting).

165. *Id.*, 2642–43 (Alito, J., dissenting).

166. ARAIZA, 168.

167. *Id.*, 168–69.

168. Pena-Rodriguez v. Colorado, 137 S. Ct. 855, 869 (2017). In another rare example, in City of Boerne v. Flores, 521 U.S. 507, 530 (1997), Kennedy's majority opinion observed that the record for the federal Religious Freedom Restoration Act lacked examples of "modern instances of generally applicable [state] laws passed because of religious bigotry."

Chapter 8

1. U.S. COMMISSION ON CIVIL RIGHTS, PEACEFUL COEXISTENCE: RECONCILING NONDISCRIMINATION PRINCIPLES WITH CIVIL LIBERTIES (2016) (PEACEFUL COEXISTENCE).

2. Masterpiece Cakeshop, Ltd. v. Colorado Civil Rights Commission, 138 S. Ct. 1719 (2018).

3. *Id.*, 1721, 1731.

4. *Id.*, 1732.

5. *Id.*, 1727.

6. Elane Photography, LLC v. Willock, 309 P.3d 53 (N.M. 2013).

7. 388 U.S. 1 (1967).

8. Frank Keating, former Republican governor of Oklahoma (criticizing a proposed Arizona law allowing businesses to deny service to gays and lesbians, based on religious objections). *See* Adam Nagourney, *Arizona Bill Allowing Refusal of Service to Gays Stirred Alarm in the G.O.P.*, N.Y. TIMES, Feb. 28, 2014, at A11.

9. PEACEFUL COEXISTENCE, 25 (Finding 3). The transmittal letter is included in the report.

10. *Id.*, 26 (Finding 7).

11. *Id.*, 26 (Recommendation 1).

12. *See* Joan Frawley Desmond, *Are Religious Freedom Advocates "Christian Supremacists"?*, NATIONAL CATHOLIC REGISTER (Sept. 14, 2016, 8:44 AM), https://perma.cc/R6VM-6WR6.

13. Commissioner Peter Kirsanow Statement, *in* PEACEFUL COEXISTENCE, 105 (quoting Obergefell v. Hodges, 135 S. Ct. 2584, 2642–43 (2015) (Alito, J., dissenting)). *See also* Commissioner Gail Heriot Statement and Rebuttal, *in* PEACEFUL COEXISTENCE, 151 n.52 (quoting similar prediction of labeling as bigots made by Harvard Law School professor Mary Ann Glendon, in 2004, after Massachusetts began allowing same-sex couples to marry) (citation omitted).

14. Nicholas Senz, *Obama Administration Says You're A Bigot If You Live Your Religion*, FEDERALIST (Sept. 19, 2016), https://perma.cc/AP7T-K8CE; *USCCB Religious Liberty Chairman Responds to Statement of Chairman of U.S. Commission on Civil Rights*, (Sept. 13, 2016), https://perma.cc/4G3F-AC37 (quoting Archbishop Lori).

15. Chairman Martin R. Castro Statement, *in* PEACEFUL COEXISTENCE, 29.
16. *Id.*
17. Commissioners Achtenberg, Castro, Kladney, Narasaki, and Yaki Rebuttal, *in* PEACEFUL COEXISTENCE, 155, 160 (giving as examples Mississippi's "Protection of Conscience from Discrimination Act" (House Bill 1523) and North Carolina's House Bill 2, requiring transgender persons to use public facilities corresponding to their sex at birth).
18. Letter from Most Reverend William E. Lori and others to President Obama, Hon. Orrin G. Hatch, and Congressman Paul Ryan (Oct. 7, 2016), https://perma.cc/K3HU-S58V.
19. Richard A. Epstein, *The Government's Civil Rights Bullies,* DEFINING IDEAS (Sept. 26, 2016), https://perma.cc/45N6-F78D; *see* Richard A. Epstein, *Public Accommodations Under the Civil Rights Act of 1964: Why Freedom of Association Counts as a Human Right,* 66 STANFORD LAW REVIEW 1241 (2014).
20. Epstein, *The Government's Civil Rights Bullies,* 2.
21. Craig v. Masterpiece Cakeshop, 370 P.3d 272 (Col. Ct. App. 2015). The Supreme Court granted Phillips's petition for certiorari on June 26, 2017 and subsequently reversed.
22. *Elane Photography,* 59; *see* Elizabeth Sepper, *The Role of Religion in Public Accommodation Law,* 60 SAINT LOUIS UNIVERSITY LAW JOURNAL 631 (2016) (providing overview of development of state public accommodations laws and listing such laws in 46 states). Alabama, Georgia, Mississippi, and Texas do not have such laws. *Id.* North Carolina added one in 2016. *Id.*
23. *Elane Photography,* 59; *see* State Public Accommodation Laws, NATIONAL CONFERENCE OF STATE LEGISLATURES (Apr. 8, 2019), https://perma.cc/B9LY-F9VA.
24. *Elane Photography,* 59–60 n. 1.
25. *Id.,* 59–60.
26. *Id.,* 79. The U.S. Supreme Court denied Elane Photography's petition seeking review of the New Mexico Supreme Court's ruling. Elane Photography, LLC v. Willock, 134 S. Ct. 1787 (2014) (mem.).
27. *Elane Photography,* 309 P.3d at 61–76.
28. *Id.,* 73 (quoting Employment Division of Human Resources of Oregon v. Smith, 494 U.S. 872, 879 (1990)). In *Smith,* the Court sustained, against a Free Exercise challenge, denial of unemployment compensation when dismissal of employees for peyote ingestion was pursuant to a neutral, generally applicable criminal law.
29. *Elane Photography,* 73.
30. *Id.,* 76 (because it involved a lawsuit between "private parties").
31. *Id.,* 77 (Bosson, J., concurring) (discussing West Virginia State Board of Education v. Barnette, 319 U.S. 624, 626–29 (1943)).
32. *Id.* (quoting *Barnette,* 642).
33. *Id.,* 78.
34. *Id.* (emphasis added).
35. *Id.*
36. *Id.* (emphasis added).
37. *Id.* (citing *Loving,* 12).
38. *Id.,* 78–79.
39. *See* Burwell v. Hobby Lobby Stores, Inc., 134 S. Ct. 2751, 2787, 2790 (2014) (Ginsburg, J., dissenting) (discussing precedents that accommodating religious belief "must not significantly impinge on the interests of third parties").
40. *Elane Photography,* 79.
41. *Id.* (citing Heart of Atlanta Motel, Inc. v. U.S., 379 U.S. 241, 244–46 (1964)).
42. *Id.; see also* Sepper, 638–44 (discussing categories covered in state laws).
43. *Elane Photography,* 79.
44. *Id.,* 83.
45. *Id.,* 79–80.
46. *Id.,* 80. For an analysis of the exemption issue that draws on Justice Bosson's reasoning, see George Thomas, *Religious Liberty, Same-Sex Marriage, and Public Accommodations,* 16 PERSPECTIVES ON POLITICS 58, 67–68 (2018).

47. *See* Dr. Robert M. Myers, *Disobey God? Sure … It's the Price of Citizenship,* HUFF. POST (Oct. 30, 2013), https://perma.cc/QZA4-DDVG.
48. Examples include: Gifford v. McCarthy, 23 N.Y.S.3d 422, 2016 (N.Y. App. Div. 2016) (farm that hosts religious and secular weddings); Klein v. Oregon Bureau of Labor and Industries, 289 Or. App. 507 (Or. Ct. App. 2017) (wedding cake); State v. Arlene's Flowers, Inc., 389 P.3d 543 (Wash. 2017), *vacated and remanded,* 138 S. Ct. 2671 (2018) (flowers). In 2018, a lower court in California reached a contrary ruling, concluding that "the right to freedom of speech under the First Amendment outweighs the State's interest in ensuring a freely accessible marketplace." The Court did not reach the free exercise of religion claim. Dep't of Fair Employment and Housing v. Cathy's Creations, Inc., BCV-17-102855 (Cal. Super. Ct, County of Kern, Feb. 5, 2018).
49. Andrew Koppelman, *Gay Rights, Religious Accommodation, and the Purposes of Antidiscrimination Law,* 88 SOUTHERN CALIFORNIA LAW REVIEW 619, 628 (2015); Andrew Koppelman, *A Zombie in the Supreme Court: The* Elane Photography *Cert Denial,* 7 ALABAMA CIVIL RIGHTS & CIVIL LIBERTIES LAW REVIEW 77, 92–93 (2016).
50. *See* Ryan Anderson and Leslie Ford, *Bake Us A Cake, or Else!,* NATIONAL REVIEW (Feb. 8, 2014), https://perma.cc/ZV9M-5P2L.
51. *Craig,* 272.
52. Brief for Petitioners, Masterpiece Cakeshop v. Colorado Civil Rights Commission at 19, 138 S. Ct. 1719 (2018) (No. 16-111). This brief and all other party and amicus briefs from *Masterpiece Cakeshop* are available at SCOTUSblog: https://www.scotusblog.com/case-files/cases/masterpiece-cakeshop-ltd-v-colorado-civil-rights-commn/.
53. There were four additional briefs submitted in support of neither party. *See Docket for 16-111,* https://perma.cc/8NBW-EWVF.
54. This count reflects electronic searches (of all the amicus briefs posted on SCOTUSblog) for "bigot," "bigoted," and "bigotry." I also searched "conscience," variants of "sincere," and a series of other terms. I focus primarily on Phillips's free exercise argument, rather than his free speech argument, which the Court did not address.
55. *See* Brief of Amicus Curiae NAACP Legal Defense & Educational Fund, Inc. in Support of Respondents at 11–12, *Masterpiece Cakeshop* (Fund brief) (citing William N. Eskridge Jr., *Noah's Curse: How Religion Often Conflates Status, Belief, and Conduct to Resist Antidiscrimination Norms,* 45 GEORGIA LAW REVIEW 657 (2011)).
56. Boy Scouts of America v. Dale, 530 U.S. 640, 664 (2000).
57. On this expansion, see Robin Fretwell Wilson, *Bathrooms and Bakers: How Sharing the Public Square is the Key to a Truce in the Culture Wars,* in RELIGIOUS FREEDOM, LBGT RIGHTS, AND THE PROSPECTS FOR COMMON GROUND 402 (William N. Eskridge Jr. and Robin Fretwell Wilson, eds., New York: Cambridge University Press, 2019).
58. *Dale,* 664 (Stevens, J., dissenting).
59. Romer v. Evans, 517 U.S. 620, 631 (1996).
60. Brief for Colorado Organizations and Individuals as Amici Curiae Supporting Respondents at 2, *Masterpiece Cakeshop.*
61. *Compare* Brief for Concerned Women for America, Inc., as Amicus Curiae Supporting Petitioners at 15–16, Romer v. Evans, 517 U.S. 620 (1996) (No. 94-1039), *with* Brief Amicus Curiae of Concerned Women for America in Support of Petitioners and Urging Reversal at 1–2, 21, *Masterpiece Cakeshop* (CWA brief).
62. Brief for 479 Creative Professionals as Amici Curiae Supporting Petitioner at 27, *Masterpiece Cakeshop;* Brief for International Christian Photographers et al as Amici Curiae Supporting Petitioners at 4–5, *Masterpiece Cakeshop.*
63. *See, e.g.,* Brief of Amici Curiae Ilan H. Meyer, PhD et al., as Amici Curiae in Support of Respondents at 9, 26, *Masterpiece Cakeshop;* Brief of Amici Curiae Colorado Organizations and Individuals in Support of Respondents at 2, *Masterpiece Cakeshop.*
64. Brief of Amici Curiae United States Conference of Catholic Bishops et al. in Support of Reversal at 4–6, 28–32, *Masterpiece Cakeshop.*
65. *See Elane Photography,* 79–80 (Bosson, J., concurring).
66. *Smith,* 879.
67. Brief for Petitioners, 14–17.
68. *Id.,* 2.

69. *Id.*, 3, 15 (citing *Barnette*, 624).

70. *See id.*, 42–43 (quoting remark); Brief of Amicus Curiae Liberty Counsel in Support of Petitioner Seeking Reversal at 40, *Masterpiece Cakeshop.*

71. Brief for Petitioners, 40–43.

72. Brief of Amici Curiae William Jack and the National Center for Law and Policy in Support of Petitioners at 2, 16, *Masterpiece Cakeshop.*

73. Brief of North Carolina Family Values Coalition and the Family Research Council as Amici Curiae in Support of Petitioners at 3–4, *Masterpiece Cakeshop.*

74. Transcript of Oral Argument at 62, *Masterpiece Cakeshop; Masterpiece Cakeshop*, 1729–30.

75. *Craig*, 291.

76. *Id.*, 281 n.8.

77. *Id.*, 280.

78. *Id.*, 291–92 (quoting Newman v. Piggie Park Enterprises, 256 F. Supp. 941, 945 (D.S.C. 1966), *aff'd*, 377 F.2d 433 (4th Cir. 1967), *aff'd*, 390 U.S. 400 (1968) (per curiam)).

79. *Id.*, 293–94.

80. Marc O. DeGirolami, *Religious Accommodation, Religious Tradition, and Political Polarization*, 20 LEWIS & CLARK LAW REVIEW 1127, 1139 (2017) (discussing cases).

81. Brief of North Carolina Family Values Coalition et al at 22, *Masterpiece Cakeshop.*

82. Brief of Amicus Curiae Sherif Girgis Supporting Petitioners at 17, *Masterpiece Cakeshop.* Robert George appears as counsel of record.

83. *Id.* (quoting *Obergefell*, 2602).

84. Brief for Petitioners, 8–9, 52.

85. Brief of Amici Curiae 34 Legal Scholars in Support of Petitioners at 13, *Masterpiece Cakeshop.*

86. Brief of the Ethics & Religious Liberty Commission of the Southern Baptist Convention et al. in Support of Petitioners at 30, *Masterpiece Cakeshop.*

87. Amicus Curiae Brief of Ryan T. Anderson, PhD and African-American and Civil Rights Leaders in Support of Petitioners at 3–4, Masterpiece Cakeshop (Anderson brief). Anderson also quotes Andrew Koppelman that such merchants are not "homophobic bigots who want to hurt gay people." *Id.*, 29 (citing Koppelman, *A Zombie in the Supreme Court*, 13).

88. *Id.*, 15–16.

89. See Andrew Koppelman, *Beyond Levels of Scrutiny: Windsor and "Bare Desire to Harm,"* 64 CASE WESTERN RESERVE LAW REVIEW 1045 (2014). More recently, Koppleman argues that "religious heterosexism" (including objections to same-sex marriage) is the moral equivalent of racism, but should be accommodated. One reason is that while allowing religious objections to the CRA, in 1964, would have defeated that law's aims, accommodating religious conservatives is possible without defeating modern anti-discrimination law's purposes. *See* Andrew Koppelman, The Unnecessary Conflict Between Gay Rights and Religious Liberty (draft book manuscript, Feb. 2019).

90. *Truman's Sympathy with Dixie, also against Mixed Marriage*, BOSTON GLOBE, Sept. 12, 1963, at 10.

91. On this dynamic, see Douglas NeJaime, *Bigotry in Time: Race, Sexual Orientation, and Gender*, 99 BOSTON UNIVERSITY LAW REVIEW 2651, 2652 (2019) (citing Reva Siegel, *Why Equal Protection No Longer Protects*, 49 STANFORD LAW REVIEW 1111 (1997)).

92. Brief for the States of Texas, Alabama et al. as Amici Curiae in Support of Petitioners at 3, *Masterpiece Cakeshop.*

93. *Id.*

94. *See State Public Accommodation Laws; Sepper*, 638 n.19. In some of these states, however, local ordinances prohibit such discrimination in the marketplace.

95. Brief of Liberty Counsel, 18.

96. Brief of Amici Curiae 34 Legal Scholars, 26.

97. Brief of Amici Curiae Utah Republican State Senators in Support of Petitioners and Reversal at 3, 4–11, 24–25, *Masterpiece Cakeshop.*

98. Brief of Christian Legal Society et al as Amici Curiae in Support of Petitioners at 11–12, *Masterpiece Cakeshop. See also* CWA Brief, 23 (reporting online comments that shop owners who declined to provide flowers for same-sex marriage were bigots who "use religion to

hide their hate"). The authors of the Christian Legal Society brief, by contrast to many of the groups on the brief, support same-sex marriage. *See* Douglas Laycock and Thomas Berg, *We're Lawyers Who Support Same-Sex Marriage. We Also Support the Masterpiece Cakeshop Baker*, Vox (Dec. 6, 2017), https://perma.cc/9L63-YLBN.

99. Brief of Amici Curiae 34 Legal Scholars, 27.

100. Brief of North Carolina Values Association, 3–4.

101. Three amicus briefs refer to bigotry only in the statements of interest explaining that an organization joining the brief is dedicated to fighting bigotry. *See* Brief of Americans United for Separation of Church and State et al as Amici Curiae in Support of Respondents at 1a, *Masterpiece Cakeshop* (interest of Anti-Defamation League); Brief of the National Women's Law Center and Other Groups as Amici Curiae in Support of Respondents at 3a, *Masterpiece Cakeshop* (interest of Hadassah); Brief for Lawyers' Committee for Civil Rights Under Law et al as Amici Curiae Supporting Respondents at 5a, *Masterpiece Cakeshop* (interest of Southern Poverty Law Center).

102. *See* Brief of Amici Curiae Public Accommodation Law Scholars in Support of Respondents at 30–31, *Masterpiece Cakeshop* (quoting *Obergefell*, 2602).

103. Brief for Respondent Colorado Civil Rights Commission, 61, *Masterpiece Cakeshop*.

104. Brief of Church-State Scholars as Amici Curiae in Support of Respondents at 4, 12, *Masterpiece Cakeshop* (quoting *Smith*, 890).

105. Brief of Amici Curiae Lambda Legal Defense and Education Fund, Inc. et al. in Support of Respondents at 37–38, *Masterpiece Cakeshop*.

106. *Id.*, 39–40 (quoting *Obergefell*, 2602).

107. Brief of Amici Curiae the Center for Inquiry et al. in Support of Respondents at 25, *Masterpiece Cakeshop*.

108. *Id.*, 26, 27.

109. Brief for Amici Curiae the Central Conference of Rabbis in Support of Respondents at 18–19, 20, *Masterpiece Cakeshop* (citation omitted).

110. *Id.*, 23–24.

111. Brief of Amici Curiae Legal Scholars in Support of Equality in Support of Respondents at 10, *Masterpiece Cakeshop* (citing "preservation through transformation" dynamic described in Reva Siegel, *"The Rule of Love": Wife Beating as Prerogative and Privacy*, 105 YALE LAW JOURNAL 2117 (1996)).

112. *Id.*, 4–19.

113. Brief of Massachusetts et al. as Amici Curiae in Support of Respondents at 2, *Masterpiece Cakeshop*.

114. *Id.*, 2.

115. *Id.*, 2, 4–10.

116. *Id.*, 26 (citing *Piggie Park*, 402 n.5).

117. *Id.*, 21.

118. *Id.*, 32.

119. Fund brief, 2–3, 14–15. The brief cites media coverage of Mr. Bessinger. *Id.*, 14. It also points out that barbeque was and is regarded as an art form, a point relevant to the compelled artistic expression claim.

120. *Id.*, 5.

121. Brief of the American Bar Association as Amici Curiae in Support of Respondents at 5, 21, *Masterpiece Cakeshop*.

122. *Id.*, 27.

123. Transcript of Oral Argument, 20–21 (Justice Sotomayor).

124. *Id.*, 43–44 (Justice Breyer).

125. *Id.*, 73.

126. Adam Liptak, *Justices Sharply Divided in Gay Rights Case*, N.Y. TIMES (Dec. 5, 2017), https://perma.cc/WS3P-EBXP.

127. Michael D. Shear, *Supreme Court Justice Anthony Kennedy Will Retire*, N.Y. TIMES (June 27, 2018), https://perma.cc/FUE8-LEBG.

128. *Masterpiece Cakeshop*, 1723.

129. *Id.*, 1731–32.

130. To be precise: Justice Thomas concurred in part of the opinion and concurred in the judgment.

131. *Masterpiece Cakeshop,* 1748 (Ginsburg, J., dissenting).

132. *Id.,* 1732–34 (Kagan, J., concurring).

133. *Id.,* 1734–35 (Gorsuch, J., concurring).

134. *Id.,* 1731.

135. *Id.,* 1731–32 (quoting Church of Lukumi Babalu Aye, Inc. v. Hialeah, 508 U.S. 520, 547 (1993)).

136. *Id.,* 1729–30 (emphasis added).

137. *Id.,* 1730.

138. *Id.,* 1727.

139. *See* Leslie Kendrick and Micah Schwartzman, *The Etiquette of Animus,* 137 HARVARD LAW REVIEW 133 (2018).

140. Mark Storslee, Commentary on McClain, *Who's the Bigot?,* Book Symposium, 5th Annual Shawnee Trail Conference, University of Missouri, March 2019 (on file with author). Storslee argues that holding the objection "frivolous" was unsurprising, given free exercise doctrine at that time, which denied an exemption if enforcing the law was the "least restrictive means" of furthering government's compelling interest in ending discrimination.

141. *Masterpiece,* 1733 (footnote *) (Kagan, J., concurring).

142. *Id.,* 1728.

143. *See* Douglas NeJaime and Reva Siegel, *Religious Exemptions and Antidiscrimination Law in Masterpiece Cakeshop,* YALE LAW JOURNAL FORUM 201 (Sept. 14, 2018).

144. *Masterpiece Cakeshop,* 1727.

145. *Id.,* 1729.

146. *Id.,* 1746 (Thomas, J., concurring in part) (quoting Brief for Respondents, quoting *Heart of Atlanta,* 292 (Goldberg, J., concurring)).

147. *Id.,* 1747.

148. *Id.,* 1732.

149. Thomas C. Berg, *Masterpiece Cakeshop: A Romer for Religious Objectors?,* 2017 CATO SUPREME COURT REVIEW 139, 170 (2018).

150. Brush & Nib Studio, LC, et al. v. City of Phoenix, 418 P.3d 426, 431–32, 434–39, 443 n.13 (Ariz. Ct. App. 2018), *vacated in part,* No. CV-18-0176-PR (Ariz. Sept. 16, 2019).

151. Brush & Nib Studio, LC v. City of Phoenix, No. CV-18-0176, slip op at 3–4, 15, 31, 48–51 (Ariz. Sept. 16, 2019) (emphasis in original).

152. For a critique of the rhetoric of the *Obergefell* dissents along similar lines, see Carlos A. Ball, *Bigotry and Same-Sex Marriage,* 84 UNIVERSITY OF MISSOURI-KANSAS CITY LAW REVIEW 639 (2016).

153. *See Elane Photography,* 79–80 (Bosson, J., concurring).

154. *Id.*

Chapter 9

1. Robert Darnton, *Voltaire Versus Trump,* N.Y. TIMES, Jan. 2, 2019, at A19.

2. Ross Douthat, *Racists to the Right, Anti-Semites to the Left: In a Populist Age, Can Party Establishments Sideline Bigots?,* N.Y. TIMES (Jan. 16, 2019), https://perma.cc/L6WS-WRD4.

3. Damien Cave, *The Global Push to Make Social Media Accountable for Its Content,* N.Y. TIMES, Apr. 1, 2019, at A5.

4. Joey Clark, *The Most Pervasive Bigotry Isn't What You Think,* FOUNDATION FOR ECONOMIC EDUCATION (Aug. 22, 2017), https://perma.cc/GLN6-UGCG.

5. *From George Washington to the Hebrew Congregation in Newport, Rhode Island, August 18, 1790,* FOUNDERS ONLINE, https://perma.cc/V24F-XTTH.

6. *Resolution on Racial Reconciliation on the 150th Anniversary of the Southern Baptist Convention,* SOUTHERN BAPTIST CONVENTION (1995), https://perma.cc/NAC5-HB4R.

7. Jessica Clarke, *Explicit Bias,* 113 NORTHWESTERN UNIVERSITY LAW REVIEW 505, 539–40 (2018).

8. *Civil Rights—Public Accommodations: Hearing on S. 1732 Before the S. Comm. on Commerce,* 88th Cong. 1147–50 (1963) (statement of Dr. Albert Garner, President, Florida Baptist Institute & Seminary).

9. Stephen Macedo, Draft Comment on Linda McClain's, *Who's the Bigot?,* 2, presented at book conference, Universidad Nacional Autónoma de México, Oct. 5, 2018 (on file with author) .

10. *See* James Chen, *"Lagging Indicator,"* INVESTOPEDIA (Aug. 6, 2018), https://perma.cc/S4PX-G2CB. Thanks to Daniel Kanstroom for suggesting this comparison.

11. *See* Thomas L. Friedman, *George Washington for President,* N.Y. TIMES, Oct. 31, 2018, at A27 (reprinting Washington's letter to the Hebrew Congregation to remind us of a president who focused more "on loving our country" than on "hating others").

12. JOHN L. JACKSON, JR., RACIAL PARANOIA: THE UNINTENDED CONSEQUENCES OF POLITICAL CORRECTNESS 66–67 (New York: Basic Civitas Books, 2008).

13. ROBIN DIANGELO, WHITE FRAGILITY: WHY IT'S SO HARD FOR WHITE PEOPLE TO TALK ABOUT RACISM 72–73 (Boston: Beacon Press, 2018).

14. H. Res. 183, 116th Cong. (2019), at 1.

15. Sheryl Gay Stolberg, *House Measure Condemns Hate In All Its Forms,* N.Y. TIMES, Mar. 8, 2019, at A1.

16. H. Res. 183, at 2–4.

17. *Id.* at 2.

18. *Id.* at 5–7.

19. CONG. REC. H2548 (Mar. 7, 2019) (statement by Rep. Raskin).

20. CONG. REC. H2547, H2548 (Mar. 7, 2019) (statement by Rep. Nadler).

21. CONG. REC. H2547, H2550-H2551 (Mar. 7, 2019) (statement by Rep. Hoyer).

22. *See Rep. Zeldin Explains "No" Vote on "Watered Down," "Spineless" Anti-Hate Resolution,* AMERICA'S NEWSROOM (Mar. 8, 2019), https://perma.cc/Z6XY-UC66; *Press Release: Gohmert on the Watered Down H. Res. 183 Which Did Not Condemn Very Anti-Semitic Remarks* (Mar. 7, 2019), https://perma.cc/833K-59SR.

23. *The Latest: Trump Calls House Resolution "Disgraceful,"* U.S. NEWS (Mar. 8, 2019), https://perma.cc/GAV2-FALF; *Press Release: Brooks Votes Against Resolution that Condemns Discrimination Against Virtually Everyone ... Except Caucasians and Christians!* (Mar. 7, 2019), https://perma.cc/U88G-DMC5.

24. CONG. REC. H. 2547, H2551, H2553 (Mar. 19, 2019) (statement by Rep. Collins).

25. Jennifer Rubin, *Republicans Manage to Get Democrats Out of A Jam—By Showing the GOP's True Colors,* WASH. POST (Mar. 7, 2019), https://perma.cc/7DSG-NQ4W.

26. *See* Jonathan Martin, *Republican's Racism Is Punished. Some Ask Why It Took So Long,* N.Y. TIMES, Jan. 16, 2019, at A1.

27. Frank Bruni, *Republicans, Racism, and Steve King,* N.Y. TIMES, Jan. 16, 2019, at A25 (quoting remark by Sen. Cruz on Chuck Todd's *Meet the Press,* NBC, Jan. 13, 2019).

28. *Id. See also* Martin, *Republican's Racism Is Punished.*

29. Trip Gabriel, *They Believe King's No Bigot. But They Agree He's Finished,* N.Y. TIMES, Jan. 18, 2019, at A10.

30. Dana Milbank, *Unite Against the Real Haters,* WASH. POST (Feb. 12, 2019), https://perma.cc/2KX2-J8WK.

31. Phillip Bump, *How Offensive Have Trump's Past Comments on Race and Religion Been? You Tell Us,* WASH. POST (Feb. 15, 2019), https://perma.cc/KV9G-397T.

32. Peter Beinart, *The Sick Double Standard in the Ilhan Omar Controversy,* THE FORWARD (Feb. 12, 2019), https://perma.cc/5EVP-RUFF.

33. *See* Bump, *How Offensive;* Chris Hayes, *All In With Chris Hayes,* MSNBC (Feb. 12, 2019), https://perma.cc/7T7J-36UT.

34. *All In With Chris Hayes.*

35. *Id.*

36. Some journalists argued that Israel's treatment of the Palestinians in the West Bank *was* bigotry. Beinart, *Sick Double Standard.*

37. Adam Liptak, *Justices to Weigh Wider View of Sex Bias Law,* N.Y. TIMES, Apr. 23, 2019, at A1. On October 8, 2019, the Court heard oral argument in the three cases: Bostock v. Clayton

County, Georgia, No. 17-1618; Altitude Express Inc. v. Zarda, No. 17-1623; and R.G. & G.R. Harris Funeral Homes v. EEOC, No. 18-107.

38. Catie Edmonsdon, *Civil Rights Bill Advances But Is Unlikely to Get Far*, N.Y. TIMES, May 18, 2019, at A15.

39. *Id.*

40. Erica L. Green, Katie Benner, and Robert Pear, *'Transgender' Could Be Defined Out of Existence Under Trump Administration*, N.Y. TIMES (Oct. 21, 2018), https://perma.cc/3AY2-6TYM (showing poster at event in New York in 2017 "protesting the tightening of gender policy in federal programs").

41. Roger Severino, *DOJ's Lawsuit Against North Carolina is Abuse of Power*, DAILY SIGNAL (May 9, 2016), https://perma.cc/3D77-9Y7F.

42. *See* Green et al., *'Transgender Could Be Defined Out of Existence* (quoting Severino commentary).

43. *LGBTQ Americans Aren't Fully Protected in 30 States*, FREEDOM FOR ALL AMERICANS (2018), https://perma.cc/3VZ8-BLXP.

44. U.S. COMMISSION ON CIVIL RIGHTS, PEACEFUL COEXISTENCE: RECONCILING NONDISCRIMINATION PRINCIPLES WITH CIVIL LIBERTIES 155, 160 (2016) (statement of Commissioners Achtenberg, Castro, Kladney, Naraski, and Yaki Rebuttal).

45. *See, e.g.*, Richard Cohen, *America's Bathroom Bigotry: Then and Now*, WASH. POST (May 23, 2016), https://perma.cc/HR9U-JJHK.

46. Dr. Joe Wenke, *Bathroom Bigotry and the Battle for Transgender Rights*, HUFF. POST (Dec. 6, 2017), https://perma.cc/ZE9A-4GET.

47. Robin Fretwell Wilson, *The Nonsense About Bathrooms: How Purported Concerns Over Safety Block LGBT Nondiscrimination Laws and Obscure Real Religious Liberty Concerns*, 20 LEWIS & CLARK LAW REVIEW 1373 (2017).

48. Cohen, *America's Bathroom Bigotry.*

49. *Id.*

50. Attorney General Loretta E. Lynch Delivers Remarks at Press Conference Announcing Complaint Against the State of North Carolina to Stop Discrimination Against Transgender Individuals, DEPARTMENT OF JUSTICE (May 9, 2016), https://perma.cc/Z6BJ-N9V9.

51. *Id.*

52. *Id.*

53. Dear Colleague Letter (from DOJ Civil Rights Division and Department of Education Office for Civil Rights) (Feb. 22, 2017), https://perma.cc/9SZD-RC3S.

54. *Id.* The case was *Texas v. United States*, 201 F. Supp. 3d 810, 832–23 (N.D. Tex. 2016), *order clarified*, No. 7:16-CV-00054-O, 2016 WL 7852331 (N.D. Tex. Oct. 18, 2106).

55. Office of Governor Roy Cooper, House Bill 2 Repeal Fact Sheet, https://perma.cc/NT9P-6Q8R.

56. Chris Tomlinson, *Business Leaders to Battle Bigots in Austin*, HOUSTON CHRONICLE (Dec. 6, 2016), https://perma.cc/2R5J-QK8T; Mary Tuma, *Battle of the Bathroom Bigots*, AUSTIN CHRONICLE (May 27, 2016), https://perma.cc/Z7Z5-T7SG; *see also Editorial: Texas' Transgender Bill Idiocy*, N.Y. TIMES (Jan. 7, 2017) (referring to Lt. Governor Dan Patrick's "ignorance and bigotry"), https://perma.cc/X2T7-69QM.

57. Texas Association of Business, *Keep Texas Open for Business: The Economic Impact of Discriminatory Legislation on the State of Texas* 14 (2016), https://perma.cc/UT8Q-BSLM.

58. *See* Chris Tomlinson, *Texas Businesses Rallying Against Bathroom Bill*, HOUSTON CHRONICLE (July 18, 2017), https://perma.cc/U2QY-KA83 ("Hundreds of groups and businesses have promised to boycott Texas if the bill becomes law, and recruiters warn that people don't want to live in places with bigoted laws.")

59. *Texas Governor Says 'Bathroom Bill' Is No Longer a Priority*, NBC NEWS (Oct. 1, 2018).

60. Ryan Anderson, *Biology Isn't Bigotry: Why Sex Matters in the Age of Gender Identity*, THE HERITAGE FOUNDATION (Feb. 16, 2017), https://perma.cc/SHZ9-PSGF.

61. H.B. 1523, 2016 Miss. Laws 427.

62. Petition for Writ of Certiorari, R.G. & G.R. Harris Funeral Homes v. EEOC, at 5 (No. 18-107).

63. Michael Brown, *Sign This Petition and Proclaim that Biology is Not Bigotry*, CHRISTIAN POST, (Dec. 17, 2018), https://perma.cc/XY6L-YV5A.

64. *Id.*

65. American Association of University Professors, *The Assault on Gender and Gender Studies* (Nov. 2018), https://perma.cc/3TMR-CBQC.

66. JAMI K. TAYLOR ET AL., THE REMARKABLE RISE OF TRANSGENDER RIGHTS 246–48 (Ann Arbor: University of Michigan Press, 2018) (describing terminology change in the American Psychiatric Association, Diagnostic and Statistical Manual of Mental Disorders (DSM 5)).

67. Steve Almond and Cheryl Strayed, *The Sweet Spot: Supporting a Free-Spirited Child*, N.Y. TIMES, Dec. 6, 2018, at D2.

68. *Id.*

69. For example, Jessica Chasmar, *Bernie Sanders: Trump "Most Racist, Sexist, Homophobic, Bigoted President in History,"* WASH. TIMES (Nov. 2, 2018), https://perma.cc/TUF8-93ZY.

70. I thank Douglas NeJaime for raising the question about the relationship between gender and bigotry. Douglas NeJaime, *Bigotry in Time: Race, Sexual Orientation, and Gender*, 99 BOSTON UNIVERSITY LAW REVIEW 2651, 2668–69 (2019).

71. United States v. Virginia, 518 U.S. 515, 533–35 (1996).

72. *See* JOHN HART ELY, DEMOCRACY AND DISTRUST 146 (Cambridge, MA: Harvard University Press, 1980).

73. Peter Glick and Susan Fiske, *The Ambivalent Sexism Inventory: Differentiating Hostile and Benevolent Sexism*, 70 JOURNAL OF PERSONALITY AND SOCIAL PSYCHOLOGY 491 (1996).

74. *See, e.g.,* Catharine A. MacKinnon, *#MeToo Has Done What the Law Has Not*, N.Y. TIMES (Feb. 4, 2018) (referring to "sex bigotry"), https://perma.cc/RS6K-XX3E.

75. Anti-Defamation League, *When Women are the Enemy: The Intersection of Misogyny and White Supremacy* 6 (2018), https://perma.cc/H7WE-FGK4.

76. *Review of UK Hate Crime Law to Consider Misogyny and Ageism*, THE GUARDIAN (Oct. 15, 2018), https://perma.cc/UT6Y-L96Z.

77. Nina Renata Aron, *What Does Misogyny Look Like?: A Brief History of the #MeToo Moment's Touchstone Term*, N.Y. TIMES (Mar. 8, 2019), https://perma.cc/5DQJ-G9TY.

78. Theodore Kupfer, *What Tamika Mallory Could Learn from Being Called a Bigot*, NATIONAL REVIEW (Mar. 14, 2018), https://perma.cc/G767-UNG8.

79. David Brooks, *The Cruelty of Call-Out Culture*, N.Y. TIMES, Jan. 15, 2019, at A23.

80. Audrey Carlsen et al., *#MeToo Brought Down 201 Powerful Men. Nearly Half of Their Replacements Are Women*, N.Y. TIMES (Oct. 29, 2018).

81. Kyli Rodriguez-Cayro, *What Does Call-In Mean? When Call-Out Culture Feels Toxic, This Method Can Be Used Instead*, BUSTLE (May 15, 2018), https://perma.cc/98WW-B25B; Loretta Ross, *Call-Out Culture is Toxic*, N.Y. TIMES, Aug. 17, 2019, at SR 11.

INDEX

For the benefit of digital users, indexed terms that span two pages (e.g., 52–53) may, on occasion, appear on only one of those pages.